Ireland's House Party

What the Estate Agents don't want you to know

Derek Brawn

Gill & Macmillan

Gill & Macmillan Ltd
Hume Avenue, Park West, Dublin 12
with associated companies throughout the world
www.gillmacmillan.ie

© Derek Brawn 2009
978 07171 4617 8

Type design by Make Communication
Print origination by Carole Lynch
Printed by ColourBooks Ltd, Dublin

This book is typeset in Linotype Minion and Neue Helvetica.

The paper used in this book comes from the wood pulp of
managed forests. For every tree felled, at least one tree is
planted, there

Contents

PROLOGUE   VII

1.   The main stages of a property bubble   I
2.   The property cycle: A four-part correction
     process   II
3.   The engine of Irish growth no longer firing
     on all cylinders   20
4.   The growth forecast: A consensus approach   31
5.   The Hibernian Bear   40
6.   The wealth forecast: A barometer of success
     or misguided view of wellbeing?   45
7.   The new misery index   55
8.   The stamp duty debacle   61
9.   The creeping construction conundrum   67
10. Housing stock uncovered   76
11. New-homes supply lookout   91
12. Land values determine house prices, not
     the other way around   107
13. Residential bail-out and buy-back   126
14. House-price bonanza (or should that be
     'bananas'?)   132
15. The negative-feedback price loop   141
16. Top of the Drops   151
17. Money supply and the end of the
     consumer boom   180
18. 'Help! I'm a debt addict. Get me out of here!'   184
19. Rate expectations: Follow the money trail   190
20. The interest-rate fallacy unravelled   201

21. 'Please mind the gap': The negative-equity
    trap   208
22. Similarities between the American and Irish
    property markets   221
23. When have you heard an Irish estate agent
    tell the truth?   230
24. Tall tales; but where's the density?   240
25. Rising rumours, falling rents   250
26. Rates v. rents, and the importance of yield   267
27. The art of spin   271
28. The global credit crisis: Ramifications for
    Irish home prices   278
29. Ireland's next top MODEL   292
30. The Gazunderer's apprentice   311
31. The 2008 Paddy Power Hibernian Bear
    House-Price Championship Hurdle   322

EPILOGUE: The party's over   326
APPENDIX A: The interest-rate crystal ball
               explained   330
APPENDIX B: Empirical research on the demand
               for housing   334
APPENDIX C: Historical first-time buyer
               experience   338
APPENDIX D: Making sense of rents and yields,
               as well as Daft indices   340
APPENDIX E: A real-life worked rent v. cash
               example   344

Prologue

At the end of May 2007 a relatively small but hardly innocuous article appeared in the business section of the *Irish Independent*, entitled 'House prices must fall to become affordable again.' The writer was Brendan Keenan, an old hand at the *Indo* and one of the few highly respected journalists with a reputation for writing balanced accounts of what was really going on in the economy.

Brendan was no sensationalist looking for a quick headline: he knew the previous day, while talking on the phone to myself—newly appointed head of research at Ireland's largest estate agents, Savills Hamilton Osborne King—that this was dynamite. It was the first time that a spokesperson employed by the property market's best-known VIPs (vested-interest parties), the estate agents, had admitted that Irish house prices were falling and—more to the point—had further to fall.

Furthermore, the big political hot potato of the day, the whole issue of stamp duty reform, which was due to be announced the following month, had dogged the property market since the autumn of the previous year, according to estate agents; but the sub-heading on that infamous newspaper article was 'Estate agent economist says that cuts in stamp duty will not help.' This was also 'off message' and contrary to what estate agents had been telling everyone. They had put the blame for the demise of the property market squarely on two individuals: Jean-Claude Trichet, president of the European Central Bank, for hiking up interest rates, and Michael McDowell, former Tánaiste, for his comments regarding the need for stamp duty reform.

The blame game was in fact a big ruse to deflect attention from the two real factors that pushed the market into becoming a speculative bubble, namely the enormous increase in property prices coupled with a massive increase in the oversupply of new homes. From their viewpoint this was not good: this was bad, this was somebody from the vested-interest camp telling it like it is—a public relations disaster!

To make matters worse, competitors and clients of Savills HOK had begun to phone in complaints about the article to the senior management. The chairman, Aidan O'Hogan, received a call from Colliers Jackson Stops asking him what they were up to, undermining the market, while upstairs another director took a call from a major property developer, complaining profusely, particularly as he was having little success in shifting two-bedroom apartments in South Dublin for more than half a million a pop in a development for which he owed the banks about €100 million at that time. Needless to say, all this negative feedback was directed quite quickly to me.

What had infuriated the big property developers so much was not just the point that house prices must fall but also the comment that developers had made millions during the boom years and could now afford to try to sit and wait it out. What I actually said was that builders had tried marketing and special offers to sell new houses at existing prices but without much success. 'They have made so much money they can afford to wait, but the penny will drop in the second half of the year and they will realise they are not going to get those prices.'

This was actually a conclusion drawn from the Merrion Stockbroker Irish builders' annual survey, which had been published earlier that month, and I had used those figures during the discussion with Brendan Keenan to make a simple point. That point was one that the dogs in the street already knew: builders would rather sell less at a higher price than cut their margins and precipitate further falls, in effect creating a sort of domino effect. This is what economists often refer to as the negative feedback loop, where price falls lead to further falls, as everyone adjusts their price expectations downwards, leading many buyers to adopt a wait-and-see stance, thus remaining sidelined. This is precisely what has happened to the Irish property market since October 2006.

The other phenomenon accurately predicted in that newspaper article, of builders being forced to capitulate and cut prices, also materialised quite strongly during late 2007 and early 2008, with price discounts on new housing schemes averaging 20 per cent from their original elevated levels. Hindsight, as they say, is 20-20 vision; but it must be stated that I and others knew by then that price drops on new homes were a given, they were inevitable, especially as discussions to that effect were taking place with developers and had occurred as early as March 2007.

In fact during one of those meetings in the early spring attended by a director of a leading Irish home builder as well as two directors of Savills HOK (one from Land, the other from New Homes) and the head of research, the question arose as to how you justify a price drop of €100,000 or more on a two-bedroom apartment in South Dublin. It was suggested by one of the Savills HOK directors that the builders could reduce the specification on the interior of the apartments quite substantially. When asked how, he merely replied, 'Just go to Woodie's and buy the doors.'

A thought flashed through my mind back then: 'Prime Time', with a picture of Miriam O'Callaghan or Mark Little sitting opposite some developers, asking them how they could justify a price drop of 20 per cent and still make money. Or worse, what about the poor unfortunates who had already paid the higher price, having borrowed the lion's share of the purchase price, but were now left with negative equity, effactually in an instant. I knew that it was only a matter of time before the media latched on to this one. However, that programme took place not in the RTE studios but in the Gravity Bar in the Guinness Storehouse on May Day, 2008. It was listed as a 'Prime Time' economy special, the subject of which is explored in greater detail later in this book.

The 450-word article that appeared in the *Independent* contained almost 300 words of direct quotation. Normally articles contain some quotations, but the journalists usually make their own point and tell the story as they see it. Not in this case. Keenan knew that he didn't have to say very much at all. These comments included:

'We are just telling the facts as we see them. There is no point in talking things up for the sake of it. The rapid rise in interest rates has put a huge dent in affordability and everyone has to adjust to that reality.'

'Most first-time buyers don't pay stamp duty. Cuts for people are not materially significant compared with rising rates. They might even put more pressure on the price of new houses.'

'Interest rates have gone up seven times, and are expected to go up once more by the end of the year. They are likely to stay at those levels for a couple of years and that is the reality everyone must face.'

'It would not really matter if prices fell by 10pc over the next two years, so as to let middle-income buyers back into the market. When inflation is added, such a fall might amount to a 20pc drop in real terms. But they went up so much over the last decade, does it really matter?'

As far as the chairman of Savills HOK was concerned, these comments did really matter. The day after the article appeared, Thursday 24 May 2007, we went into the MD's office, which was vacant at the time, and closed the door but left the lights off. Aidan O'Hogan was unhappy, as was apparent by his demeanour. The conversation didn't last long. He wanted an immediate response; he wanted a note to go out listing the ten reasons why people should be buying Irish property now; he also instructed me to put my phone on divert for the rest of the day. It didn't help that the *Evening Herald* had published the story with the tag line 'Buyers find homes too pricey' on the evening of the same day as the original *Irish Independent* article, or that the next morning the *Star* had an article under the headline 'Interest rates hit house prices. Market drop is welcomed.' To cap it all, on the Wednesday morning Ronan O'Driscoll, a director in the firm's New Homes Division, sent me an e-mail message with the subject line HOK *versus Hooke & MacDonald—DANGER*.

Derek,

The thrust of our research on the housing is probably correct, but I am very worried about the PUBLIC direction it is taking.

In my opinion, it is absolutely crazy for us to consider participating in a printed debate on the housing market with Hooke & MacDonald with us predicting that prices will fall and them saying the exact opposite. This will result in us being seen by our clients as extremely negative. Today's article in the business section of the Indo (whilst I agree with the points made) does nothing to help us or our clients. It makes our job much harder and more importantly puts us in a very bad light with our clients.

By pursuing an argument which is seen as very negative in the eyes of developers, we are associating ourselves with the doomsday economists. We have a vested interest in ensuring that we do not hinder our clients in their business. Many of our clients are trying to complete sales in large housing developments. We cannot be publicly stating that the market needs to drop by 10% or more. This will encourage people to walk away from property and not complete sales. The potential is disastrous.

In the strongest possible terms, can I urge caution or silence? Let us not be the ones who are seen to be killing the market. We need to support our clients. We are far better off saying NOTHING rather than entering into this debate. We are playing into the hands of our competitors Hooke & MacDonald who will have a field day saying to the builders that HOK are hindering the housing market.

The consequences of us continuing with this negative publicity on the housing market will be the loss of significant clients and fees. When things eventually turn positive, we will be remembered as the doomsday merchants. Irrespective of our views, we need now to say nothing or to say something positive.

(I stress, the quality of the research is good. I privately agree with the views, but for goodness sake, the bigger picture is far more important.)

This message was circulated to the chairman, the managing director, and five other directors of the firm. It resulted in the dressing-down in the MD's office on the Thursday morning and in another prescriptive e-mail message being sent to me, telling me to remedy the situation but also creating a bigger problem for me. I attempted to articulate this to the chairman the next day when once again I was called into the darkened empty office, to be told that I had not done what I had been asked to do. I tried to explain that it was not about being right or wrong, or preserving integrity, but about credibility.

'It's all about credibility. You can put a spin on things—fine; but at least be believable,' I protested; but my protestations fell on deaf ears. 'Look at last Friday's *Indo* article,' I said, 'Hooke and MacDonald's view that you had to get in quick following the election, since the stamp duty issue would be resolved and property prices would race up 3 per cent before year end. Nobody believes that: it's just not credible.'

But I might as well have been talking to myself. 'I'm not interested,' the chairman interrupted. 'I don't care. You didn't do what I asked you to.' He had been sent a draft copy of a note with ten positive points, but he was still not happy and he wanted it redone 'in the context of the zero price growth forecast for the market,' as it had subsequently become known. His reply went like this:

From: Aidan O'Hogan
Sent: 24 May 2007 13:56
To: Derek Brawn
Subject: RE: Draft copy of 10 reasons etc.

Derek

I don't think this is what I asked you for. I asked you to re approach the zero growth and other issues you have publicised and to put them in bullet point in a positive format e.g.

Buying opportunity—better access to the quality product and to select the primest—not queuing for choice

Rents are rising—investors know this—that is why we have seen them as the most active buyers in the last few weeks

Following the clarity on the Stamp duty situation two weeks ago there was a very significant increase in the number of viewers—probably doubled

Planning permissions are slowing down dramatically—your own statistics—so limiting supply

Builders are adjusting their build rate to reflect slower speed of sales—easy and quick to turn off the tap—very slow to start it. Thus supply is going to be limited

Temporary hike in interest rates creates affordability delays for some—but not all—but doesn't abolish demand—just defers it

With deferred demand and slowing supply—stage is set for surge as soon as people feel interest rates have peaked

Second hand market "gap" factor but buoyancy continues especially at the upper end where sensitivity to interest rates far less

Previous hesitancy in market in early 2001 demonstrated that those who got in there whilst market was sluggish got great deals, best of choice etc.—because fundamental demographic demand (as now) is so strong so when confidence returns everybody scrambles at the same time to get in and it's not that easy to restore supply

Fixed term mortgage rates—still attractive—it's about cash flow (if this is true etc.)

Do you get the drift and can you re-address this please.

Aidan

Note that the supportive 'deferred' demand, coupled with reduced supply, sounds plausible. Well, not to the trained eye. These are all relative terms, keywords designed to hit the right buttons with Joe Public, especially the 'surge' word. Imagine all that deferred demand overflowing like a frothy pint! Pity it would be a long time before the financial markets allow rates to fall and credit availability to rise to facilitate this 'surge'. It's not simply a case any more of portraying the market as a glass half full rather than half empty: the glass has been turned on its side and is draining. You simply can't put a positive spin on the fact that the average middle-income couple, having bought a home in the commuter belt a couple of years ago, had seen their monthly mortgage increase by half, while their equity has been quietly evaporating.

The chairman of Savills HOK is skilled at putting a positive spin on the market. Citing the top end of the market—where addresses are highly desirable but availability limited—as a segment of the market that is not rate-sensitive, implying in effect that the high end is recession-proof because demand is always there, is crazy. The same economics that drives wealth and conspicuous consumption is also going to affect the privileged few who can afford homes at the top end. The property ladder is a ladder of sorts, after all: if you take away the bottom rungs it's only a matter of time before the ripple effects reach the top.

Fear is one of the most powerful human emotions (alongside greed), and property purchase is a very emotive situation. All estate agents revert to type when they feel that their back is to the wall. They raise the spectre of scarcity and the impending lack of supply, as the tap is rapidly turned off, the ensuing race back to the top as prices naturally rebound (like a coiled spring), compounded further by the ever-faithful enormous demand driven by demographic change. Estate agents know that home purchase involves an emotional element, and they play on that, using reverse psychology. Think about all those first-time buyers in recent years who were afraid of missing the property boat, taking on forty-year loans of eight to ten times their annual salaries (four to five times the combined salary of a couple), just to get onto the property ladder.

Estate agents treat their fellow-countrymen like sheep, to be sheared for all the money they can possibly extract from them, just so they can claim to be a home-owner. The prices of apartments and houses in

Ireland are so high that it's no longer about buying a property to get onto the property ladder, it's now about 'living the dream' or 'living the life-style,' and this is how those new homes are marketed today.

The fundamental problem between the former head of research at Savills HOK and the old guard was a philosophical difference of opinion. They believed in the separation between public and private views, whereas I believed that there was only one view: reality. As I didn't have a real estate background but an investment banking background, my view was more binary: everything in the markets was either a 'buy' or a 'sell', it was 'true' or 'false', 'black' or 'white'. Sure, I believe in compromise and consensus, but believability is vital. I knew that at some point it would become foolhardy to tell people the opposite to what was happening on the ground. They could see that for themselves.

By the middle of 2007 it was apparent that Irish property prices would end the year lower then where they began. The industry insiders knew this because of the four to five-month delay in the way property prices and, in particular, the way the benchmark PTSB-ESRI house-price index is reported two months in arrears, with figures for national average prices that are based on completed purchases using mortgage draw-downs, in effect relating to 'sale agreed' property that had occurred some two to three months previously. So by the early summer they already knew, based on current sales activity, what the likely outturn for the index would be when reported in the late autumn. From then to the end of the year was just a couple of months' numbers, which would be decided upon during the traditionally quiet summer period.

It's not difficult to predict the direction of the national house-price indices for the coming months if you know exactly what is going on in the property market today. The agents knew this, and they also knew that developers would eventually be forced to lop huge chunks off the price of the growing backlog of unsold new homes. They knew that negative equity would become the harsh reality and a dominant theme for the housing sector in subsequent years, but the last people they wanted this information passed on to were the unsuspecting potential first-time buyers.

A week later I resigned from Savills HOK—not because of these differences of opinion with former colleagues about the presentation of research output or the tone of the message but for a more fundamental reason: its content. It had taken me three to four months there to build up a clear picture of the supply-demand imbalances that existed in the residential property market. I didn't wish to be associated with inform-ation that I believed to be unsustainable.

Shortly after I had joined Savills HOK in January 2007 I was asked to contribute a piece for their periodic *Irish Property Outlook* supplement, which goes out three times a year with the *Irish Times*. I wrote a general piece on the strength of the economy, taking the forecast for property prices from the draft copy of the head of the residential division. It took time to wade through the data that was coming in for the latter part of 2006.

Even within the firm, information was sketchy. All that people seemed to be interested in was higher interest rates and 'poor sentiment' over stamp duty. Information was gradually coming out about how bad sales activity was in the New Homes Division. It was only in May of that year that it became apparent that business had almost dried up, with fewer than a hundred sales for the first five months of the year, compared with 3,000 units sold during 2006. There was a multiplicity of views internally within the firm, all negative and some extremely 'bearish', with predictions of price falls in 2007 of 15 per cent or more. It seemed there was a universal opinion that the inevitable property crash had begun, but at the same time there existed a vein of hopefulness, or wishful thinking, that confidence would return, interest rates would soon reverse course, and the market could get back to its true path and its rightful, inexorable rise to infinity.

Merely reporting prospective increases in interest rates, using data on investors' bets on short-term three-month interest rate futures, was met with disdain from some quarters, as if it was the research people's fault that the European Central Bank was raising rates. The problem I encountered then, which still holds true today, is that those involved in the property market are backward-looking. Just read any of the research output or marketing documents of any estate agent, commercial or residential: they deal primarily with what has just occurred and never with what is likely to happen. There are never accurate forward-looking statistics, as you can't argue with history, because it has already happened.

During my exit interview in July 2007 the human resources director of Savills HOK, Ann Hinds, asked me if I would reconsider and stay on. I told her what I'm saying now: that the problems with the Irish property market were firmly entrenched and that a multi-year correction was the most likely scenario. For me that meant a 'Catch 22' situation, so I had no choice but to leave.

Chapter 1

The main stages of a property bubble

Ireland is in the midst of its first major property recession since property price records began in the early 1970s. The property bubble was pricked in early 2007, and in every part of the country, including the new-homes market, discounts of 20 per cent or more have become the norm, thus breaching the classic definition of a 'bear' market. The backward-looking home price indices have yet to catch up with this reality. Indeed these very indices failed to measure the true appreciation of the tenfold increase in home prices throughout the Dublin suburbs during the decade 1996–2006. History will show that the 'Celtic Tiger' era was truly a one-horse race for those fortunate enough to have been in on the property lottery.

Before we examine how the property bubble arose in the first place, let's jump forward a couple of years to take a glimpse of one possible (perhaps even probable) future . . .

13 September 2010

'A surplus of unsold homes on the market, combined with continuing concerns about mortgage repossessions and general affordability issues associated with more restrictive lending standards and the high level of interest rates, continue to take a significant toll on builders' confidence,' according to the latest report by the Irish Home Builders' Association, issued today.

'The bottom line is that the Irish housing market is still in a correction process, following the historic and unsustainable highs of the 2003–07 period,' said the IHBA chief economist, Joseph Dismal.

'Builders have trimmed prices and are still offering buyers generous incentives to reduce their stock, but there is still a large supply of vacant existing homes on the market, and affordability problems persist, despite efforts to attract new buyers.

'In spite of these challenges we expect to see home sales get back on an upward path later this year, and we also expect housing starts to begin a gradual recovery process by early next year. At that point this market will be operating well below its long-term potential, providing plenty of room to grow in 2011 and beyond.'

The highlight of this week's economic calendar will be the Central Statistics Office's estimate for June housing starts, due out on Wednesday. Economists expect a further 2 per cent drop to 1,250 new dwellings, taking the annual rate to 22,000 for the twelve-month period to June—the second-lowest annual total in the past seventeen years and the lowest pace of residential construction activity since 1993.

Despite Dismal's hopes for a rebound, builders throughout the country grew more pessimistic in August. The latest Ulster Bank Construction PMI index shows that builders' confidence was the lowest recorded since 2000, when this data was first analysed. The total construction activity index hit a new low of 18, down a further two points on the previous month. Once again it was the housing activity component that dragged the overall index down. The housing PMI dipped further, to just 15 (a reading above 50 equals expansion and a number below means contraction), and was further compounded by matching low levels in the 'new business' and 'employment' sub-components. Only the 'input prices' index rose on the month, from 49.5 to a reading of 51 last month.

The Ulster Bank's chief economist, Simon Hopeful, stated that although the readings were disappointing they were not totally unexpected, and he expects a marked improvement from here. 'With the European Central Bank expected to raise interest rates early next month back above 3 per cent, and with prices starting to show some recovery as unemployment has now stabilised at 12 per cent, economic growth is expected to be largely flat at zero per cent for the full year. The outlook is now improving, and the worst is clearly now behind us,' he said.

'Furthermore, if estate agents' predictions are correct—that property prices will grow by 2 to 3 per cent next year—then the number of homes with negative equity will decline from an estimated 200,000, or one in four of all mortgaged properties, to below 175,000, or 9 per cent of the total housing stock.' He went on to say that 'this will bring confidence back to the property market for the first time in four years and there is already strong anecdotal evidence that consumer sentiment is now on a firm recovery path.'

31 March 2017
Average national house prices rose by a further 0.4 per cent in February, according to the latest edition of the PTSB-ESRI house-price index. This follows a similar rise in January of 0.3 per cent and is the nineteenth consecutive monthly gain.

'Measuring the rate of growth in the twelve months (so year on year) to February, average national house prices were up by 4.8 per cent, compared with a gain of 4.5 per cent recorded in the twelve months to January.

'The average price paid for a house nationally in February 2017 was €311,180, compared with €309,013 in December 2016.'

Commenting on the results, Niall O'Grady, general manager, marketing, Permanent TSB Bank, said: 'The continued rate of price increases over the first two months of the year is higher than many people might have expected. We are finally above the previous peak in the index, achieved in February 2007, at €311,078. It has taken the property market a decade to recover to this level, thanks to the six successive positive growth years that have undone the price losses that occurred during the 2007–11 property recession.'

September 2008; back to reality.

Unlike economics, mathematics is an exact science. Sums do add up— but how many people fail to grasp the importance of sums! A 20 per cent price drop—from, say, 100 to 80—requires a subsequent 25 per cent gain to restore the balance. Using the analogy of 'feast' followed by 'famine', we can see that if the property market was to decline by 10 per cent per year for only three years, to be followed by six long years of good price growth—let's say, for argument's sake, plus 5 per cent growth each year— this would only bring the market level back to where it was before the downturn. In fact in this instance it would take seven years of positive growth of this magnitude for prices to recover completely.

Put it another way. Take a three-bedroom semi-detached family home in the Cork or Dublin suburbs that was valued at half a million in early 2007. Now assume that over a four-year period the price halves, falls by 50 per cent—not unrealistic, given that most suburban homes in Ireland have already witnessed 20 to 25 per cent falls in asking prices over a little more than a year and a half. The 2011 price of that home would then be €250,000. Now assume that house prices recover and begin rising again for a solid six years—let's say by a good 7 per cent per year each and every year from 2012 until 2017, which would be equivalent to a 50 per cent total gain. The 2017 price would now only be €375,000, up a half on the quarter of a million 2011 price. So a 50 per cent decline followed by a 50 per cent rise still leaves prices 25 per cent below their previous peak price! Now ask yourself, Is property a good ten-year bet?

Assume for a moment that this is indeed Ireland's case, then the old adage that property is always a great long-term investment and that over a ten-year period one is likely to do well goes completely out the window. Timing becomes everything. The very fact that property prices have

fallen month on month for more than a year and a half now is proof that
the market had reached an overvaluation state. Just how much it was
overvalued will probably determine the size of the subsequent fall.

Various national and international commentators, such as the
International Monetary Fund, were warning about the impending Irish
property bubble as early as 2000, and they reiterated this stance again in
August 2003, stating that property prices were 20 per cent overvalued back
then. In November 2005 the Central Bank agreed with an OECD report that
property prices were at least 15 per cent above fair value. Not long after
that, in March 2006, the stockbrokers J. and E. Davy published a report
with the dubious title 'Dublin house prices heading for 100 times rent
earned,' and their economist Rossa White wrote: '. . . Yields have been
driven down to unprecedented depths. Something does not feel right. In
the property market, capital appreciation is theoretically a function of
rental return. Houses are habitually selling for 20% more than advised minimum values (AMVs) at present. To us this looks like boundless optimism.'

Even the *Irish Times*, in October 2007, conducted an opinion poll
through its web site Ireland.com, asking the important question, 'Are we
heading for a property crash?' The results were quite revealing: 64 per
cent of respondents said 'Yes,' while only 36 per cent replied 'No.'

At that juncture the national average house price reported for August
(in the September PTSB-ESRI monthly report) was still above €300,000,
and prices were only down 3.3 per cent on the previous year. So even at
that early stage people had become pessimistic about the future direction
of property prices, by a large majority of two to one. Often the people on
the ground are the first to see what is really happening to the market.

The latest IMF report—*World Economic Outlook, 2008*—included a
section on the housing cycle, with special attention devoted to assessing
overvaluation in house prices in seventeen major international markets.
For each country it modelled growth in house prices as a function of
seven fundamental factors, namely affordability, changes in disposable
income, short-term interest rates, long-term interest rates, credit growth,
performance of stock market prices, and finally demographic factors, as
measured by the size of the population of working age. The portion of
the actual house-price increase that could not be explained by these
'fundamentals' was determined to be the 'house-price gap'.

The study looked at the ten-year period 1997–2007, so it was quite
relevant to Ireland from a time viewpoint. Guess which country topped
the poll with the biggest house-price gap? Yes, you got it: Ireland, at a
whopping 33 per cent!

By the law of averages, the IMF will eventually get it right. Perhaps it
has in this instance, because this time its reference period included the
beginning of the Irish property slump. Notwithstanding the fact that

property prices officially fell by almost 7½ per cent in 2007, the IMF still estimates that homes are out of synch with reality by as much as a third. This means that the IMF believed that the Irish housing market was 40 per cent overvalued to begin with at its peak.

The following picture is a perfect illustration of the six principal phases of a classic housing bubble, put in the context of the Irish property market with respect to both price and time dimensions.

Fig. 1: Key stages of the housing bubble, 1976–2016

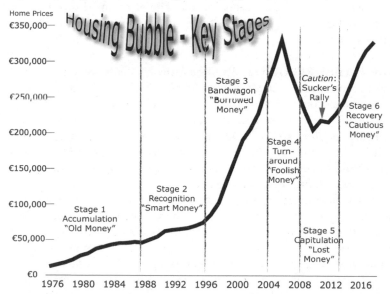

This forward-looking diagram of the housing bubble assumes that property prices will have retrenched by a third by the end of 2010. It further assumes that a recovery then ensues, with an average annual growth in prices of about 5 per cent (a couple of per cent above expected inflation). The logic behind the choice of a market bottom taking place at the end of 2010 is not arbitrary: it's by design, and will be explained in greater detail in the next chapter.

Needless to say, with a turning-point for the market having already been reached, the $64,000 question is, which point are we now at in the post-bubble cycle? To answer this question fully we first need an explanatory synopsis and an understanding of each phase and what it entails.

STAGE 1: THE ACCUMULATION PHASE
This was the period many years ago when really clever money was salted away in 'real assets'. Old money was invested in 'bricks and mortar,' as

property portfolios were assembled by shrewd long-term investors, primarily as a form of supplemental income or a form of saving for retirement, particularly by self-employed people. Often, too, sole traders and self-employed people would hide cash earnings away (mainly undeclared income) by buying cheap properties to let, thereby generating further cash income.

During the 1970s and 80s personal tax rates were punitive, while inflation was rampant, so housing acted as a store of wealth. Rental income provided a cash stream at a time when not many people had much by way of disposable income. Those fortunate enough to be landlords back then became accidental multi-millionaires a quarter of a century later.

STAGE 2: THE RECOGNITION OR AWARENESS PHASE

Not everyone could afford to spend a lot on property during the late 1980s and early 90s, but the advent of bank deregulation and the subsequent liberalisation of credit opened up new avenues of opportunity for those with the foresight to see that the market was about to take off. The writing was on the wall for those investors who realised that the economy was becoming leaner, the demographic tide was about to turn, and Ireland prepared for entry to EMU.

Professional investors always jump into the market 'feet first' when they recognise that capital values are rising. This doubles demand but, adversely, starts to crowd out natural home-buyers. This was why in 1997 the Minister for Finance, Ruairí Quinn, introduced the 9 per cent rate of stamp duty: to deter property speculators. At that time it was estimated that it would generate £16 million in new revenue for the Government. Little did they know back then what was about to happen and that billions would flow into the Government's coffers as a direct result of that 9 per cent property purchase tax. In 1996 receipts from stamp duty on property were €247 million; by 2006 the total was €3,112 million—a twelvefold increase in a decade!

This awareness phase of the housing bubble is best summed up by the new mantra that you have to own your own home, rent is dead money, and anyway renting is for the poor and for immigrant workers.

STAGE 3: THE BANDWAGON (MEDIA MANIA) PHASE

New property speculators are born. Young first-time buyers flock to the market and second-home fever takes hold, whether it's a holiday home or a rental flat bought for the children for when they go to university. The 'If you're not in you can't win' mentality pervades the national psyche. You have to get onto the property ladder at all costs, even if it means extending the term of your home loan to forty years, using interest-only finance for the first couple of years, as well as the 'no savings' (100 per cent loan-to-value) purchase.

This stage in the bubble is characterised by a seismic shift in traditional property-buying metrics, the best example of which is the emergence of the dual-income property-purchasing couple as the new norm.

The media play a huge part in this stage of the process. Newspapers are filled with stories about how well everybody is doing and how much money is being made on property. The results of auction sales read like a litany of lottery-winners. Property fever takes hold; everyone wants a slice of the action. It seems that nobody pays any attention to the academics' and economists' warnings that massive borrowings are what underpin this madness. Huge media attention promotes enthusiasm, enthusiasm propagates greed, and greed spurs delusion. Household debt is mistaken for wealth. The new paradigm has arrived!

A parallel situation occurred in the technology shares boom of the late nineties, particularly in North America, where the 'risk-free' rate became ingrained in the national psyche at somewhere around 20 per cent. Joe and Jane Public suddenly believed that they could double their money every two to three years, and that they didn't have to work any more: they would let their capital do the work for them. Unfortunately, then as now, the market would eventually turn, they would be caught offside, and—using the 'fire in the cinema' analogy—would all head for the exit at the same time, many getting burnt in the process.

STAGE 4: THE TURNAROUND (OR DENIAL) PHASE

Nothing lasts for ever, the great Irish property 'bull' market being no exception. The financial market saying is that markets don't always move in a straight line. Eventually the party ends, the market tops; but participants and vested-interest commentators who have been hooked on the 'one-horse race' scenario are not so easily persuaded. Denial is the order of the day. By this stage in the housing bubble, platitudes, anecdotes and rhetoric have replaced rational thinking. Genuine fundamentals are ignored, and, as prices drop, some home-buyers fall into the 'bear market trap,' when they think there are potential value deals because of these price cuts.

There may even be a short-lived 'suckers' rally' on the way down, or a 'dead cat bounce,' in stock market parlance. With estate agents and construction industry groups constantly talking the market up, the public becomes confused, and some potential home-buyers see it as a second chance to make up for missed opportunities. Others see the glimmer of recovery around every corner. Indeed, just as market prices don't always move in a straight line on the way up, they are just as unlikely to move in a linear fashion on the way down (at least that's the case so far).

Sometimes markets pause and a short-lived technical correction in prices occurs, which is normal once values have dropped by a certain amount—because, after all, a market involves both buyers and sellers, each with varying opinions about value. The mirage of normality may fool many once they see flat or nil price growth reported in the media, possibly followed by a couple of months of very modest price improvement. This is pounced upon by the VIPs, who herald a new dawn for the property market and the beginning of a new one-horse race to property riches.

Beware the suckers' rally! You have been warned: already the lobby groups and spin doctors for the construction industry are calling the market bottom in 2008! No doubt after ECB rates trough at around 2 per cent in mid-2009, the VIPs will herald this as the nadir for the property market and the time to buy again, even though the fundamentals of the housing market will still be awful and the economic backdrop worse.

STAGE 5: THE CAPITULATION (OR THROWING-IN-THE-TOWEL) PHASE

Confidence now shatters, fear takes over, and irrational behaviour leads the way. Sharp drops in price fuel further price reductions through the negative feedback loop. Banks and credit institutions pull back in an attempt to rein in their exposure to the property sector. Developers begin heavy price-discounting of unsold new homes: discounts of 25, 30 or even 40 per cent become commonplace. Indeed estate agents once immovable on the whole issue of possible large price reductions (recall the 'temporary slowdown', the 'cooling market', the much-needed 'soft landing') change tack and now attempt to make a virtue of these enormous price cuts— price cuts, incidentally, that push recent clients of the same self-righteous estate agents into the unenviable position of negative equity.

Meanwhile the estate agents and property lobbyists are still predicting an early recovery, merely deferred until the second part of the year. According to the VIPs, the worst is always over and the next three to six months will inevitably be better. How many times have you heard the VIPs utter the words 'The market will remain weak for the first half of the year, but a recovery is expected in the second half'? That tired phrase has become so commonplace that it is inspissatingly boring. However, when they're proved wrong time and time again, market fear gives way to despair. Shortly after this panic period the market finally hits bottom, thus enabling the move to the final phase.

STAGE 6: THE RECOVERY PHASE

The market having hit bottom—the level at which fundamental factors suggest that prices are at or below what can reasonably be described as 'fair value'—a much-needed confidence can return to the market. Muted or modest positive annual price gains reinforce this process, and the market reverts to mean or long-term trend growth. At this stage, badly bitten and now twice-shy investors are still reeling from their recent losses. It becomes an opportunity for 'real' home-buyers to get back onto the property ladder at much more realistic price levels.

It should be noted that in recent times, particularly during the fourth stage of the housing bubble, as prices began to fall many market commentators spoke incessantly about poor sentiment or a lack of confidence among potential property-buyers, often using 'sentiment' and 'confidence' interchangeably. They're wrong, for the following but crucially important reason: 'sentiment' relates to consumers' attitudes towards purchasing now, today, whereas 'confidence' refers to a fundamental belief in value. This is not just a subtle semantic difference but an important one. 'Sentiment' tells us that potential buyers may simply defer purchasing a property for a year or so; 'confidence' tells us whether or not buyers will buy at all, at a given price level. When *sentiment* is bad, prices drift lower (as they have done now for twenty consecutive months), but when *confidence* turns negative, prices plummet. At the end of 2008 we're moving from late stage 4 to stage 5. This is where the market is now.

The VIPs don't believe in the bubble theory. Pragmatic realism is not for them: they cling to the past and the wishful thinking that the erroneous market dynamics they believed to be sacrosanct during the meteoric rise in property prices still hold true today.

What are these supportive fundamentals that remain unchanged? They are the three general maxims that are repeatedly touted as the factors underpinning growth in house prices: the 'strong' economy, the 'sound' fundamentals, and of course high demand because of 'demographics'. The simple truth is that the economy is heading south rapidly; the fundamentals associated with housing are awful; and demand is changing as population growth slows and fewer foreigners move here, as evidenced by the drop in the number of PPS numbers being issued. Nonetheless the mandarins at the largest representative body for estate agents, the Irish Auctioneers' and Valuers' Institute, refuse to believe so, as shown by their recent comments. 'Overall, I would say to people that the market is beginning to stabilise. The worst is over,' said Robert Ganly, former president of the IAVI (*Irish Times,* 21 January 2008). Ganly was quoted by Dominic Coyle in the same article as saying: 'While prices would continue to fall in 2008, this levelling off should begin to reverse itself in early 2009, and we would hope to see the property market growing again sometime during that year.'

This doesn't exactly tie in with his earlier comment regarding the worst being over: in fact it directly contradicts it and would suggest to all prospective sidelined property-buyers that they should wait for at least another year before considering taking the property plunge.

His successor as president of the IAVI, Edward Carey, when addressing the members during the annual general meeting in April 2008 told them that 'Ireland's housing market has undergone a correction that will prove to be a short-term blip.' He also told them that 'the 10 per cent correction has brought prices back to end-of-2005 levels, and allegations of a property crash should be taken in context against huge cumulative increases since the early 1970s until the market slowdown in March last year.' He cited increases of 3,175 per cent for second-hand homes since 1974 and 4,800 per cent for new homes since 1970.

The fact is that the residential property market has been in a downturn or recession for almost two years now. The rate of new building has fallen by two-fifths over the last two years, and prices have declined for six consecutive quarters. What other definition of a property recession is there? They say a week is a long time in politics; how about two years in property? One could hardly call it a short-term blip.

Finally, not only is Carey's reference to the enormous price gains enjoyed by home-owners over the last three to four decades further testament that the property bubble existed in the first place but his resorting to such historical figures merely serves as an indictment that this bubble has indeed finally popped.

Ireland's decade-long house party is well and truly over. The hangover has begun, in the form of unsold supply but also in a legacy of excessive prices. The partygoers are confined to their old beds, so to speak, but the vested-interest parties are offering them the 'hair of the dog' in the guise of new 'just-reduced' ones. The property media (predominantly financed by advertising) are now playing a different tune.

However, it's not all doom and gloom: it will get better, but it's going to take at least a few years.

Chapter 2

The property cycle:
A four-part correction
process

As was mentioned before, by the end of 2010 home prices will probably have given up two-fifths of the extraordinary gains achieved during the great property 'bull' market of the late 1990s and early 2000s. In real terms (as economists are fond of saying), house prices adjusted for inflation may well have halved, with a good chunk of this improved affordability being due to higher inflation. Property valuations should come back into line not just with our international peers and neighbours but also with regard to domestic measures, such as 'earnings multiples' and the proportion of take-home pay needed to service mortgage debt.

All human beings require three essentials for survival: food, energy, and shelter; and in recent years one could be forgiven for thinking that hidden forces were conspiring to cheat us on all these fronts, particularly as the third (housing cost) had soared to unsustainable levels. Now all of us have faced double-digit increases in food and energy prices, so it's a relief that housing costs (both rents and prices) are falling. Ireland will emerge as a better place following the continuing retrenchment in construction output and the much-needed correction in property prices.

A natural symmetry exists in all markets, both on the way up and then on the decline. It's no different for the property market. No market can sustain high growth rates for ever, and when a turning-point has been reached a shake-out occurs, often following an evolutionary path akin to a journey. Ireland is now on that property journey, and it's important to remember that, like any journey, there's a beginning and an ultimate destination. It's not possible to move from point A to point E without passing through points B, C and D. This is the sin of omission committed by the Construction Industry Federation and the estate agents who see a nascent recovery around every corner, constantly telling us that the property recession is merely a temporary blip or a slowdown in the market. We have passed that point. The classic definition of a recession is six straight months of falls and contraction. Ireland satisfies that criterion both in prices and in supply. In a bubble situation, supply overwhelms demand, yet prices continue to rise. When the bubble bursts, the pendulum is forced to swing the other way before a recovery can occur.

So what are these 'waypoints' to recovery? In short, these milestones are facets of the market in which each requires a turning-point. Firstly, we need to see a bottom in the building of new homes. The Construction Industry Federation is calling for 45,000 new homes to be built this year and only 37,000 for 2009. (We won't know how many new properties are built this year until 2009 at the earliest.) Next we need to witness a recovery in sales activity, with turnover returning to the levels of 2004–05 at the very least. About 6 or 7 per cent of homes change hands each year, but since the middle of 2006 the sales of existing homes have halved and sales of new homes have been non-existent. (Activity has plunged by 75 to 90 per cent in that sector.) The third milestone is by far the most important: the reduction in stock, or, put another way, the elimination of the oversupply. The proportion of housing stock for sale is now well in excess of a good year's turnover. Way back in July 2007 there were 38,000 unsold new apartments in the greater Dublin area alone (some already built, some work in progress), in some 252 development schemes (listed later in chapter 11). That figure has increased substantially since then, as evidenced by the growing vacancy rate (one property in six is now unoccupied), the doubling in the number of new homes for rent, and the 81,600 or more new homes completed between August 2007 and November 2008. Even the most optimistic commentators would admit that it will take at least two years—to 2010 or beyond—to clear this backlog of unsold new homes.

The fourth and final turning-point is of course 'price' itself. To call an end to the property recession we need to see six months of positive price appreciation or, as economists would say, two successive quarters of price gain. The only mix-weighted (two-bedroom apartments, three-bedroom semis etc.) house-price index in Ireland is the PTSB-ESRI index, based on one lender's mortgage draw-downs and so reflecting 'sale agreed' that occurred two to three months previously, then published a full two months after the quoted month, so we have to wait nearly five months to discover where prices are going. This is analogous to a driver looking in their rear-view mirror but only seeing the road five miles back.

Before a recovery in property prices happens, all the other 'waypoints' must be reached first. So it will take another calendar year after those criteria are met before we can categorically state that the property recession is over. What we're talking about in essence is a sequence of events or, to use a fashionable phrase, a 'roadmap to recovery'.

The last Bacon Report, published in June 2000, incorporated a very accurate demand model. This model not only predicted subsequent record supply but showed that the biggest factors influencing demand were the existing housing stock, new supply, and prices. Interest rates came in only at sixth place. The vested-interest parties refer only to higher mortgage rates, taxation and sentiment as the causes of the property slump. Deliberately, they avoid the principal issue facing the property market: oversupply. You don't have to be an economist to understand the basic laws of supply and demand, which reach equilibrium with respect to two factors: price and quantity.

If the construction industry builds too many houses (as it did over the five years 2003–07, when a total of 400,000 new homes were finished) because it has overestimated demand, then a serious oversupply situation will exist. The figures are frightening: a quarter of the 1.92 million homes in the country (in September 2008) were constructed since 2002. That's a very scary number indeed, and what's more worrying is that it's readily apparent to all and sundry that this building boom was driven solely by cheap credit, which in turn spawned speculative property-buying. The builders and property developers responded by ratcheting up the new build rate, which we can see from the following chart, reaching a peak at close to 90,000 new homes in 2006.

Fig. 2: Annual new-home completions, 1978–2010

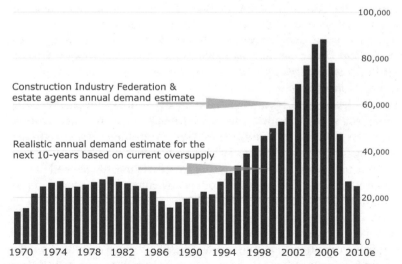

Source: Department of the Environment, Heritage and Local Government, Consensus Forecasts

The difficulty now is weaning the builders off the notion that there's a huge natural demand for new homes. The estate agents and the Construction Industry Federation (including its sister-organisation, the Irish Home Builders' Association) continually make reference to the strong demand for housing, which they place at 60,000 units per year.

THE REALITY GAP

A reality gap now exists between perceived demand and actual demand. The population increased by 8 per cent between 2002 and 2006, according to the census, yet the number of new homes increased by 20 per cent during the same period. Nobody can justify that differential. As we shall see later, the big jump in new construction took place after the end of the 'Celtic Tiger' era (1994–2001) but during the 'consumer boom' era (2002–07), which was characterised by a huge increase in borrowing by businesses and individuals. This so-called *private-sector credit* stood at €127 billion in December 2002 but had increased threefold, to €400 billion, by September 2008. Moreover, total mortgage debt has mushroomed, from €47 billion to almost €148 billion, over the same period.

On 14 June 2007, at a construction conference in Dublin hosted by the American investment bank Merrill Lynch, the chief executive of Bank of Ireland, Brian Goggin, presented a slide as part of his presentation that was very telling. It was a simple pie chart showing the bank's exposure to the residential mortgage market. It was very telling for a simple reason: it showed that the proportion of the bank's total outstanding mortgage lending (then at €25 billion) to 'buy-to-let' investors was 28 per cent— the same as the total amount lent to first-time buyers. In essence, Bank of Ireland Group has lent as much money to speculators as it has to ordinary people seeking to get a roof over their heads and get onto the property ladder.

This factor fundamentally altered the dynamics of the market, especially when one considers that, even though there are fewer property investors than first-time buyers, we know from the quarterly mortgage statistics of the Irish Banking Federation that they typically spend about €100,000 more on property purchase than first-time buyers, and borrow on average about €75,000 more to boot. Therefore they're more important from the viewpoint of a seller of new homes. We also learn from the Irish Banking Federation's figures for the third quarter of 2008 that the number of buy-to-let investors has fallen considerably, from a peak of more than 28,141 in 2006 to 11,206 during the first nine months of 2008— equivalent to an annual rate of 15,000, or slightly more than half the level of previous years.

A smaller number of property investors creates two problems. Firstly, total demand is far less than it was in recent years, especially as the number of first-time buyers has more than halved also. Secondly, it leaves the builders with a terrible dilemma: a reduced number of customers who can't afford their prices. It was considerably easier at the height of the property boom to sell a €500,000 two-bedroom apartment to a wealthy investor who already had equity savings accumulated in existing properties than it was to sell the same property to a poor first-time buyer struggling to scrape together the deposit. The net result was that developers had to cut prices, a process that has already begun but has much further to go.

Hooke and MacDonald, estate agents who specialise in the sale of new homes rather than existing homes, have estimated from their own experience during 2007 that approximately 27 per cent of all new homes sold were sold to buy-to-let investors. This figure tallies with the Irish Banking Federation's mortgage data when re-mortgages and top-up loans are excluded. So a quarter of all new homes sold during the boom years were not for people to live in but to rent out. Essentially, a two-tier market had been created.

The other troubling factor is that the total number of new mortgages being taken out is dropping faster than the number of new home completions, particularly when 'mover' mortgages (taken out by people trading up or down) are excluded. Even assuming that all investors buy only 'new' homes and all first-time buyers also buy only new homes (a ridiculous assumption, given the new stamp duty changes), the number of new mortgages for new home purchase during the first nine months of 2008 was slightly more than 27,000, but 40,000 new homes were completed. That leaves quite a shortfall—or are they all being bought for cash? Very well, so some of those properties would have been bought by existing home-owners trading up or down; but including these still doesn't close the gap. We're left with no 'mover' mortgages for purchasing existing or 'second-hand' homes. Whichever way you look at it, home sales have fallen, both new and existing, and that certainly doesn't bode well for the industry.

'QUADRUPLE-BOTTOMING' REVISITED
Bottom no. 1: Supply
The first market bottom that needs to be observed, as previously mentioned, is the 'turning-off of the supply tap.' Over the first eleven months of 2008 more than 48,000 new homes were completed, equivalent to an annual rate of 52,500—far more than the Construction Industry Federation's prediction of 45,000. In May 2008 Davy's revised downwards their estimate for new housing supply for 2009 to 25,000 units but left their prediction for 2008 at 45,000, the same as that of the Construction Industry Federation.

Davy's chief economist, Rossa White, proclaimed that 'it is vital that new housing sales overtake house completions. That inflection point will probably be reached sometime in the first half of 2009.' He went on to say that 'house prices may fall 10.7 per cent on average in 2008, followed by a further decline of 7.2 per cent in 2009.'

His forecasts are heavily influenced by the relationship between housing 'starts' and 'completions', where he assumes there's a nine-month delay or 'lead time' between them; however, there's an issue of data integrity here.

Completion numbers are published by the Central Statistics Office one to two months in arrears and are compiled by using ESB meter connections, so they're reasonably accurate (though the meter may be connected by the builder during construction if the site needs power). The problem arises with the accuracy of the housing starts data. There are thirty-four local authorities (for planning purposes), and they record commencement notices differently. Some would record a builder building three homes on a plot of land as three commencements, while others would record it as one. So Rossa White uses structural guarantee registrations as a proxy for new home starts, which he then models, making a further assumption about the proportion of one-off houses, which he adds to the total.

Since the annual rate of new home warranty registrations has declined sharply, from a peak of 68,759 in September 2006 to 13,275 for the twelve months to November 2008—a drop of 67 per cent on the previous November—the Davy model predicts a big tailing off in the number of completions for 2008. The same pattern emerges if we use the CSO data for commencement notices, which total slightly more than 22,000 for the first eleven months of 2008, suggesting a build rate of about 27,000 for the calendar year 2009.

This all fits in neatly with what the construction industry groups would like you to believe, but there are just too many embedded assumptions—such as, for instance, the nine-month build period. When you speak to the providers of the structural guarantee products, the insurers who provide these ten-year new home warranties, they tell you that the construction period varies by site, from their initial inspection of the foundations to the final one, which could be twelve to fifteen months later. Secondly, they sell their product to builders of one-off houses too. Thirdly, there's no legal requirement for builders to buy these products anyway, so during a property recession there's less of an incentive for developers and builders to spend additional money on them (though for apartment blocks they can cost as little as a couple of hundred per unit—cheap compared with the sales and marketing value).

Historical figures suggest that during the property boom at least eight out of every ten new homes came with one of these structural warranties (as many as nine out of every ten new homes in Dublin—mainly apartments). But recent numbers imply that this may no longer be so, and the corresponding ratio could be as low as four or five out of every ten. Newspaper advertisements appear to support this hypothesis. On balance it would appear that the jury is still out with regard to whether or not such a large reduction, one that's sorely needed by the market, will actually take place. Housing starts, according to Davy's, were running at an annualised rate of about 30,000, but this level was a bare minimum according to the CSO data on commencement notices at that time, as well as the high rate of planning applications. (The important issue of the supply of new homes is further explored in subsequent chapters.) Suffice it to say here that no improvement will take place and there can be no end in sight for the property recession until the number 1 issue of supply is addressed.

Once again, we won't know what the final outcome will be for 2008 until the spring of 2009 at the earliest. This is the most serious milestone in the critical path of the recovery process. The fact that we're told that supply has been cut doesn't meant that it's been cut enough. A completion rate above 50,000 for the full year 2008 would be disastrous, as it would mean that the supply mountain was growing enormously.

Bottom no. 2: Sales activity
Ireland has no national register of property, nor has it a national body that publishes house sales, either for existing homes or for new homes. We're just told by estate agents and their lobby organisations that supply equals demand. We're given fluffy information periodically to the effect that 'viewings are up,' or 'sales are brisk.'

In the United States the Bureau of the Census publishes new home sales monthly, and the National Association of Realtors publishes existing home sales monthly. It even publishes 'pending' sales, which comprise second-hand home sales where the deposit has been paid and contracts signed but the conveyance has not taken place. All these figures are available both regionally and nationally. Ireland is stuck in the dark ages when it comes to the availability of data and the timeliness of housing statistics. Many property transactions take place by 'private treaty' and are not subsequently disclosed to the public or the media. In the recent past it was discovered that a property in Dublin was sold for €620,000 but the price was reported in the national press as being in the region of €950,000! This prompted the property editor of the *Irish Times* to complain to the National Consumer Agency, which in turn met representatives of the Irish Auctioneers' and Valuers' Institute and the Institute of Professional Auctioneers and Valuers, who promised to ensure that their members would report exact prices in the future.

Once a floor has been put under the market in the form of a definitive bottoming of the supply of new homes, it will be imperative that property sales transactions recover next. We know from the mortgage statistics as well as anecdotally that property sales are still weak and perhaps still falling annually. The market really needs the annual pace of new home sales to increase substantially: there has to be a quantum leap upwards in the volume of these sales, primarily to eliminate the backlog.

In Davy's weekly market commentary on 15 September 2008 Rossa White stated that only approximately 7,000 new housing units had been sold thus far in 2008—a sales level of only 10 to 15 per cent of the 2005 and 2006 levels. Furthermore, he estimated that there were at least 40,000 unsold completed units in the hands of the developers. One week later Dr Colm McCarthy, the 'M' of DKM Consultants and a lecturer in economics at NUI, Dublin, stated in a radio interview that he believed there were another 40,000 completed unsold units in the hands of investors as well, bringing the grand total of the supply backlog to 80,000 new homes! We may never know the true figure.

Bottom no. 3: Stock reduction
Since the middle of 2007 the ratio of the stockpile of unsold new homes to sales has skyrocketed. The American property recession began a full year before the Irish one. Its oversupply began in 2005, when nearly 2.2 million new homes were built against a likely demand of only 1.5 million. In Ireland's case the 88,419 homes constructed in 2006 were probably 20,000 more than was needed. Nobody really knows. (We have no hard, factual sales figures, and stamp duty receipts don't help us, as new homes are largely exempt.) What we do know is that the heady pace of construction continued well into the following year, and the number of vacant new properties on the market waiting for a buyer exceeded 40,000—roughly equivalent to several years' sales at today's lower rate of sales activity. (Remember that turnover has halved but the backlog remains.)

In the United States many property pundits described the situation as drastic when their ratio of stock to sales hit ten to eleven months' supply. Their response in early 2007 was big price discounts—price cuts of 20 to 25 per cent; yet this ratio has remained elevated at or above ten months' supply. On top of that, new home building has been pared back to an annual clip of 1 million units, less than half of what it was two years earlier.

This needs to happen here in Ireland. Estate agents and other property market commentators need to come clean about the size of the backlog, as well as giving a more accurate picture of sales activity. Without both sets of numbers we won't know what the rate of stock reduction is, if any. Just as the supply bottom won't be fully known until 2009, the bottom in sales activity may begin before then, but we will need to witness year-on-year growth before we can categorically state that inroads are being made into the oversupply backlog. At best that takes us into late 2009 or 2010. It could conceivably take two years of good sales turnover to reduce the supply backlog to six months' worth, bringing us possibly into 2011. Then, and only then, will property price pressure be alleviated and price discounting have ended.

Bottom no. 4: Price recovery
The final bottom that's essential for the ultimate turnaround to drag Ireland up from the mire of property recession is of course a reversal of property prices. This is conditional on the three other bottoms occurring first. Because of the time frames of the other prerequisite stages in the recovery, this is unlikely to happen before the end of 2010 at the earliest. It's inconceivable that property prices will rise again while the continuing supply of new homes is too big, while the level of turnover is low, and when there's a large stock of unsold new homes just sitting there on the market. The initial price discounts by developers were merely the starting-gun for the new 'race to the bottom'. Good news for potential first-time buyers, though.

Unfortunately, because of the delays in the way national property price indices are calculated and reported, even when property prices do begin to recover it will be several months before the public receives confirmation through publication of the house-price index. Indeed, true confirmation that Ireland's property recession is officially over would require two consecutive quarters of capital (price) appreciation. This brings the time line well into 2011, so there remains plenty of time for sidelined purchasers to pick their property-purchase moment.

Think of it the way a bookmaker would. If the vested-interest groups are correct and this analysis is flawed, then waiting another year before taking the property plunge could cost the prospective first-time buyer an additional €10,000 to €12,000 if prices rebound by 2 to 3 per cent. However, if they're wrong about the impending recovery and this analysis proves correct, the first-time buyer waiting in the wings could save another 20 to 25 per cent, or €70,000 to €100,000, by waiting another year or so. As a bookie would say, if the latter option was an even-money bet the VIPs' call would be the ten-to-one outsider. These odds are right on the mark, especially in the context of the potential monetary savings.

Chapter 3

The engine of Irish growth no longer firing on all cylinders

Economic growth during the eight-year 'Celtic Tiger' era, 1994–2001, averaged 8 per cent per year in national income (GNP) and almost 9 per cent per year in output (GDP). It was truly a unique period in Ireland's economic history. Éire Teoranta outperformed all the big industrialised countries during that period, with the exception of China, where economic growth averaged almost 9½ per cent. Germany managed only a paltry 2 per cent per year, whereas Britain and the United States managed more respectable average growth rates of 3 per cent and 3½ per cent, respectively.

Before we examine what the immediate future holds in prospect for Éire Teoranta we need to set the scene in terms of what is driving the economy now. We especially need to know from the viewpoint of the housing market what the outlook for economic growth is over the short to medium term. To do this we have to examine the engine of Irish growth in greater detail.

The best way to think of the economy is to think of the sophistication of a car engine in all its complexity. Yet the basic design of the internal-combustion engine has hardly changed over the last century, when Henry Ford first mass-produced the Model T.

For the purpose of illustration we shall use a six-cylinder engine. These cylinders—in no particular order—are (1) the construction and property market, (2) foreign direct investment, (3) foreign trade (exports minus imports), (4) private consumption, (5) productivity and jobs and (6) net inward migration.

Just like a car, it's possible for the economy to move forward and not be firing on all cylinders: as everyone knows, you can drive a car with a cylinder misfiring, but you don't move too quickly. You may even be able to get some way down the road with several cylinders not functioning properly; but how far do you get when half or more cease working or are operating only at half capacity? Let's examine each of these in turn so that we can make some kind of judgement about how each one is functioning right now as well as the immediate outlook for each.

Three of these cylinders are what could be categorised as domestic factors, while the other three are externally driven (just as a V6 engine is split 3 + 3 in a V shape). The three domestic cylinders of growth are the labour market, the construction industry, and consumer spending. On the other side the three external factors are external trade, foreign investment by transnationals, and of course demographic change, as characterised by net inward migration.

Fig. 3: The six-cylinder engine of economic growth

Before we briefly examine each in turn to provide a snapshot of how the economy is faring it's worth remembering that over the last year all these factors have deteriorated—yet the vested-interest parties have continued to bang the drum of denial, proclaiming that 'the economy is strong' and 'the fundamentals are sound.' They particularly like to play the demographic 'wild card' as the reason why economic growth will remain high.

Even as all the economic forecasters have downgraded their estimates for 2008/09 (as we shall see in the next chapter), the Taoiseach and Tánaiste are still proclaiming that the economy is in great shape—as recently as July 2008, when Mary Coughlan proclaimed so in a television interview. But platitudes and banalities don't serve the public well.

It's one thing to talk down a growing economy; it's an entirely different matter to deny the facts that Éire Teoranta is heading south fast and that none of the cylinders of growth will be operating at full capacity again, possibly for years.

CYLINDER NO. 1: BUILDING AND CONSTRUCTION

Much of the economic miracle of the last decade and a half was due to the boom in construction, both residential and commercial. As recently as June 2007 the *Quarterly Economic Commentary* produced by the Economic and Social Research Institute published an article by Professor Morgan Kelly of NUI, Dublin, with the ominous title 'On the likely extent of falls in Irish house prices.' He stated that a mature economy usually gets about 5 per cent of its income from building new houses but that Ireland was deriving nearly three times as much. In 2006, 13 per cent of Irish national income came from construction, and a similar proportion of the total work force was employed in the industry—some 282,000 at the height of the building boom. It was therefore the second-largest employer in the country, after the public sector. This over-dependence on one industry was tantamount to putting all one's eggs in one basket or, to use a horse-racing analogy, putting all one's bets on one horse in the first race.

Fig. 4: **Annual change in construction employment, 1976–2008**

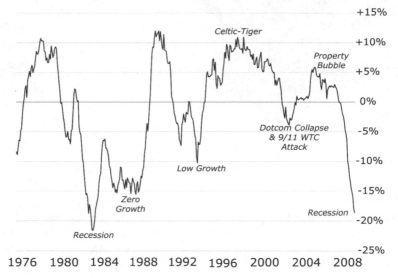

Source: Central Statistics Office

The Central Statistics Office compiles a monthly index of employment in construction, a sort of barometer of how healthy that industry is. The latest figure reveals that the 19 per cent annual drop in numbers employed in September 2008 was worse than the economic slowdown in either 1986 or 1991 and is heading for a recessionary decline like that of 1983. In 2006 the CSO produced a book, *Construction and Housing in Ireland*, which is the most up-to-date source. Included in it is a summary table compiled by the Statistical Office of the European Communities (Eurostat), which shows that the average proportion of workers employed in the building industry for the twenty-seven EU member-countries was 7.9 per cent at the end of 2005; at that time the two highest countries were Ireland (12.6 per cent) and Spain (12.4 per cent). The figure that Eurostat used for building employment in Ireland was 240,000. We know that it peaked at more than that, at 282,000 or 13½ per cent of the work force.

If the numbers employed in building were to return to the EU average of about 8 per cent, about 40 per cent of all construction workers would have to lose their job as the total number employed in the building game fell back to 169,000. Already it seems that about 52,000 construction workers have been let go, and the total number employed could easily fall to about 220,000 by the end of 2008.

Whatever way you look at it, fewer new homes will be needed, as housing sales are down and stocks are rising fast. Shortly after Morgan Kelly warned of this impending fall in July 2007 the then Taoiseach, Bertie Ahern, was prompted to utter the now infamous remark 'Sitting on the sidelines cribbing and moaning is a lost opportunity. I don't know how people who engage in that don't commit suicide . . .' It was because of the media attention surrounding the article written by Kelly that Ahern found it necessary to issue some response. Hindsight is a wonderful thing, as we all know; but so is foresight, when it's listened to.

Suffice it to say that the building and construction cylinder of the Irish engine of growth is cracked, lacking compression (metaphorically), and will probably be malfunctioning for several years to come.

CYLINDER NO. 2: THE LABOUR MARKET: JOBS AND PRODUCTIVITY

The unemployment rate in Ireland increased from less than 4 per cent at the end of the 'Celtic Tiger' era in late 2001 but remained reasonably low, at less than 4½ per cent, until September 2007. Within twelve months it had accelerated to 7 per cent, and most economists are predicting a rate of between 8 and 10 per cent by December 2009. To go from 'full employment'—where those who want a job have one—back to levels not seen since before 1998 is simply awful.

The speed at which this cylinder of growth has begun to misfire is astonishing. However, in the light of the large numbers in construction being let go, it's not surprising. But this will affect the rest of the economy quite seriously. When you have fewer people gainfully employed there's less money in the economy. It's also quite a fiscal drag on the exchequer, as the state has to fork out for all that extra money on unemployment benefits.

What is also worrying is that it now appears that Irish unemployment could exceed that of the euro zone by the end of 2009. The rate in the euro area has fallen to around 7½ per cent. The last time the Irish unemployment rate was above the euro-zone average was December 1996.

Another aspect of the labour-market cylinder of growth that has shown unusual wear and tear is productivity, or total output produced per person employed. Remember that a central feature of the 'Celtic Tiger' era was the 4½ per cent annual gains in productivity that led to rising living standards. Most of that high productivity was as a direct result of the numerous American transnationals operating in Ireland. By 2007 Irish productivity had fallen to a third of that rate, or about 1½ per cent, which is slightly above the EU average. What a turnaround! And growth in productivity has been considerably weaker since 2003. If we were to include productivity from the public sector—the largest employer in the country—things would look even worse. There's a lot of anecdotal evidence that public-sector productivity is static at best and negative at worst. Take the HSE and the health service as a prime example. More than 110,000 people are employed in the health system, yet the service appears to be deteriorating rapidly. Despite the consolidation of the eleven regional health boards into the Health Service Executive, no economies of scale were achieved, and no jobs were shed.

As a side note to this topic, think back to the 2007 general election and the great 'leaders' debate' on television. One of the potential gaffes and a possible knock-out blow for the leader of Fine Gael, Enda Kenny, was when the former Fianna Fáil leader Bertie Ahern bragged about bloating the public sector by a further 40,000 jobs during the previous Government. Unfortunately, Kenny stuck to his script, and the television audience determined that Ahern won that debate by a nose.

More worrying, though, for Éire Teoranta is the fact that it is now spending more on pensions for the said workers than on servicing the national debt. The latest figures from the National Treasury Management Agency at the Central Bank is that Government coffers are being emptied rather more rapidly to fund the National Pensions Reserve Fund than to service the national debt, which has crept up to 27 per cent of GDP. On 24 July 2008 the NPRF reported that its return on investment for the first half of 2008 was −12 per cent, or a loss of €1.7 billion. The Government has in effect borrowed money abroad (higher national debt and increasing budget deficit) to invest in international equities that have subsequently fallen in value!

Who says Éire Teoranta is not returning to the bad old days of the 1980s? At least back then everyone knew that fiscal rectitude was the order of the day, and the so-called Tallaght Strategy was adopted by the major political parties as a policy response to the burgeoning debt problem.

That issue was fixed within a decade. How long will Éire Teoranta have to pay juicy defined-benefit pensions (two-thirds final salary) to the legions of former public-sector workers who were hired during the boom era? A lot longer than a decade, I would imagine, in accordance with increased life expectancy.

CYLINDER NO. 3: CONSUMPTION CRUMBLES

Half the Irish economy, or about €90 billion, is based on private consumption. As the inimitable Michael Caine might say, 'Not a lot of people know that.' It is, though; and a big chunk of that is what you and I spend every day on goods and services or, as it's more commonly called, *consumer demand*. One of the best measures of consumer spending is of course retail sales. In May 2007 the annual growth in the volume of retail sales was almost 10 per cent. One year later, in May 2008, it was close to −5 per cent, and by October of last year the volume was down 7.5 per cent and heading for a 10 per cent overall decline for the year. I won't bore you with another chart at this juncture (it's on my web site for those really interested), but retail sales have fallen off a cliff. Part of the problem was probably the ssia effect last year, when a large chunk of special savings incentive accounts matured. The other part of the problem, though, has been the big drop-off in sales of new cars.

Just like the rapid increase in unemployment, growth in retail sales turned negative only in February 2008. January was still a record month for new private car sales: apparently the lure of the 08 registration was just too strong for some people.

During the 'consumer boom' era, 2002–07, annual growth in retail sales averaged about 5 per cent. The big decliners so far in 2008, as well as the motor trade, which is down 28 per cent in terms of annual new car registrations, were furniture and lighting (down 22 per cent), electrical goods (down 16 per cent) and household equipment (down 14 per cent on the same time last year). The obvious culprit was declining new home sales.

Seeing that consumption by businesses and individuals makes up half the economy, as new home building slows this year and next, and as more workers are laid off, spending is likely to contract a lot further. In addition (as we shall see later in chapter 17), the growth in money supply has also turned negative, just like retail sales. With less money circulating in the economy—and money is the 'oil' that protects the cylinder heads of growth—combined with the fires of inflation that are burning up this oil too quickly, the net result will be an overheated cylinder, which expands and begins to stick and misfire within the engine. This has already begun to occur, and all the indicators for this consumption cylinder are that things will probably get a lot worse before they begin to get better.

CYLINDER NO. 4: THE TRADE SURPLUS

Ireland's economic prowess in the late 1990s could be best summed up by its export performance. Ireland's best year for exports was 2002, at almost €94 billion, or 268 per cent growth from the 1993 level. The *external trade position,* as it's more formally called, is both exports and imports, with the difference between them called the *trade surplus.* As the next illustration graphically shows, this was the defining feature of the 'Celtic Tiger' era.

Fig. 5: External trade balance (exports minus imports), 1970–2009

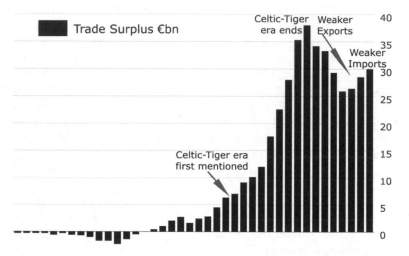

Source: Central Statistics Office

Since the €38 billion surplus recorded in 2002 there has been a steady decline in this rate. Well-known economic commentators, such as the former Taoiseach Dr Garret FitzGerald, have written numerous articles complaining that this was a serious issue that needed to be addressed. Unfortunately, those warnings appear to have fallen on deaf ears. Dr FitzGerald, like many of his peers, repeatedly warned of the dangers of concentrating too much attention on the construction industry. He understood that, as an island nation, Ireland's prosperity very much depends on trade. Part of the problem with a declining trade balance may have to do with the stronger euro; but, as the previous chart shows, the surplus has been in steady decline, and import growth took off.

Obviously, higher prices for crude oil pushed up the amount Éire Teoranta spent on energy. Ireland consumes about 200,000 barrels of oil equivalent each day, or about 72 million barrels per year. With the near-doubling of crude oil prices in only one year (in euro terms, that is, not dollars), Éire Teoranta had to spend an additional €2.8 billion for 2008 for the same 'black gold' that it consumed the previous year.

Even if the euro was to depreciate further against the US dollar—say, back to the $1.15 level (the average exchange rate since the introduction of the euro in 1999)—it would mean, other things being equal, that Ireland's energy costs would soar if the dollar price of oil returned to $100 per barrel or above. So a weaker currency to improve our lost competitiveness would be a double-edged sword if oil prices returned to the comparatively high levels witnessed last year. Indeed, this is precisely what the International Energy Agency is predicting for two years' time, once the global economy comes out of recession and demand increases from India and China.

This cylinder of economic growth is still firing; it's just not operating at full potential. One recent disturbing fact was that services exports, which had been the golden boy within exports, have begun to falter. This is a cause for concern; for if Éire Teoranta loses its comparatively strong external trade sector, and the trade balance continues to decline, the general economy is in for a real shock. For 2009 it looks as if the annual trade surplus will once again hit €30 billion, as exports decline by a percentage point or so (in line with the reduction in world trade), but imports could fall off sharply, by close to 5 per cent, as the recession causes consumption to shrink. Hence, net trade will have a positive contribution to Irish growth, but the danger is that it could be short-lived.

CYLINDER NO. 5: FOREIGN DIRECT INVESTMENT

A big driver of the aforementioned stellar export performance of Éire Teoranta during the high-growth years was, of course, the huge level of direct investment by foreign companies and in particular the American transnationals. Such areas as bio-pharmaceuticals, chemicals and information and communications technology (ICT) were drawn to the Emerald Isle for broadly three reasons: Éire Teoranta was the only English-speaking country within the new euro zone; tax rates were low; and there was an abundance of skilled labour in the form of young educated Irish people.

Foreign direct investment includes not only inward flows but flows going abroad too. What is important, however, is that the gap between them has been narrowing, as the following table for the last decade illustrates.

Table 1: Foreign direct investment, 1998–2008 (€ million)

	Investment abroad	Investment in Ireland	Balance
1998	−3,483	7,905	4,422
1999	−5,734	17,092	11,358
2000	−5,024	27,980	22,956
2001	−4,543	10,785	6,242
2002	−11,715	31,158	19,443
2003	−4,917	20,185	15,268
2004	−14,552	−8,543	−23,095
2005	−11,509	−25,482	−36,991
2006	−12,215	−4,418	−16,633
2007	−15,178	22,351	7,173
2008, q3	−7,110	−3,033	−10,143

Source: Central Statistics Office

The most recent period for which data was available is the first quarter of 2008, which shows that about €10 billion more went out than came in. A lot of the inflows are actually reinvested earnings by foreign companies established in Ireland. Almost €50 billion left the country between the second quarter of 2005 and the same quarter in 2006, which, according to the cso, relates to 'loan outflows by foreign owned enterprises in Ireland to their affiliates abroad.'

The treatment of direct investment flows is complicated and con-voluted, far beyond the scope of this book. Suffice it to say that foreign direct investment is important in terms of the money flows, but to get a clearer picture of what is actually happening one ought to look at the total number of new projects taking place.

This more telling picture is revealed by Ernst and Young in their annual *European Investment Monitor* report for 2007, which showed that Ireland held its position that year by increasing the number of projects received from 74 in 2006 to 80 the following year. The two biggest sources of foreign direct investment are, as one might expect, the United States and Britain. However, during 2007 investment by both countries declined by 9 per cent, to 12 per cent from Britain and 47 per cent from the United States, the latter being the biggest direct investor during the 'go-go' years.

The following table summarises the positions of the countries that were the biggest recipients of foreign direct investment projects during 2007. As one can plainly see, Ireland failed to make it into the top 10 and just about held on to the 2.1 per cent achieved in 2006.

Table 2: Foreign direct investment by country, 2007

Rank	Country	FDI projects	Percentage total
1	United Kingdom	716	19.3%
2	France	541	14.6%
3	Germany	305	8.2%
4	Spain	256	6.9%
5	Belgium	175	4.7%
6	Romania	150	4.0%
7	Poland	146	3.9%
8	Russia	139	3.7%
9	Hungary	135	3.6%
10	Netherlands	124	3.3%
n/r	Ireland	80	2.2%

Source: Ernst and Young, EIM, 2007

In general, then, as a cylinder of growth foreign direct investment is holding up well enough. The trend appears to be slightly down with regard to the negative flows, but a large part of that could be due to significant equity outflows. As long as foreign companies established in Ireland continue to reinvest their earnings, foreign direct investment will probably not become a serious balance-of-payments issue.

CYLINDER NO. 6: NET INWARD MIGRATION
The whole topic of demographic change is covered in great detail in a separate section available as a PDF file from my web site. As most people are aware, Ireland has benefited from a huge demographic dividend, thanks to a net inward migration of 411,000 people between 1997 and 2007. However, a strong word of caution is warranted here. In the summer 2008 *Quarterly Economic Commentary* the prediction of the Economic and Social Research Institute was that net outward migration of the order of 20,000 would occur in 2009. By the end of the year they amended this figure to 50,000. Clearly this would reduce the demographic cylinder of economic growth, though the natural rate of increase has shifted up a gear, to about 40,000 more new Irish people (births minus deaths). We must expect slower population growth in the near future, possibly in the region of half of one per cent, or a quarter of the growth rate that occurred between 2002 and 2006 (based on the census), and we can no longer rely on positive net migration.

The demographic cylinder of growth is one that could move either way. It needs to be given particular attention, especially from the viewpoint of those property investors who invested in buy-to-let homes.

THE MECHANIC'S VERDICT

If Éire Teoranta was a car with the aforementioned six-cylinder engine and a mechanic was to give it a thorough inspection, they would probably advise the owner not to drive it any more, as there was serious risk of the cylinder head cracking or at least a head gasket blowing. They might recommend a replacement engine, possibly a reconditioned one or, if finances permitted, a whole new engine.

Seriously, though, what all this tells us is that Éire Teoranta needs to reinvent itself. There has been much talk and commentary of late, both in the media and within political circles, of Ireland becoming a 'knowledge economy' or 'value economy'—put simply, an economy based on knowledge and experience and centred on fourth-level research and development (i.e. employing graduates with PhDs). In principle this is fine, it even makes perfect sense. Éire Teoranta could use Finland and Sweden as examples of high R&D or value economies. The only problem, though, is that both those countries consistently spend 3½ to 4 per cent of their annual GDP on R&D. Ireland spends roughly 1.2 per cent. That leaves a big gap.

The Irish strategy appears to be based on Enterprise Ireland promoting higher R&D expenditure by approximately two hundred large and medium-sized companies. This will never provide the solution. In every country where R&D investment is a prominent factor in the economy the biggest spender or investor is, of course, the state. In the United States, for example, the biggest investor in R&D is the Department of Defense.

Another problem that Ireland faces is that there are not enough fourth-level graduates, especially in the necessary disciplines or fields of research. Ireland has a serious shortage of engineers, and the trend among new entrants to the universities is worrisome indeed. It's the opposite of what Éire Teoranta needs. Not enough young school-leavers and graduates are choosing the scientific and engineering disciplines. A quick fix would be to import them from overseas; India and China would be a good start. The Government would need to invest heavily in technology parks, probably adjacent to universities and technical colleges.

By the end of 2008 the Irish engine of growth has spluttered to a halt and shifted into reverse gear. In the next chapter we examine where the pundits believe it will be in a year or two.

Chapter 4

The growth forecast: A consensus approach

The majority of people living in Ireland are genuinely concerned about the financial health of the nation and the immediate outlook for growth, as well as the prospects for jobs and investment levels, particularly in such areas as housing.

In this chapter we take a brief look at six pillars of the economy that will affect every citizen in some shape or form over the coming years. The approach used is called a consensus view, which simply means that we take all the major economic items of interest and then see what the individual projections are from the principal economic commentators. These are the main banks, stockbrokers and economic consultancy groups. Finally, we summarise their collective views at the end in the form of a summary matrix. None of this is subjective, as the opinions are all independently taken from other economic forecasters. The beauty of such an approach is that it enables us to see quite quickly which forecasters are above consensus and which are below.

Table 3: Growth forecast consensus, 2007–10

Economic factor	2007	2008E	2009F	2010F
Growth (GDP)	6.0%	−1.9%	−2.5%	0.7%
Unemployment	4.5%	6.2%	8.2%	9.4%
Inflation	4.9%	4.2%	1.3%	1.9%
Consumer spending	5.4%	−0.4%	−1.3%	0.3%
Investment	0.2%	−18.3%	−17.5%	−4.3%
Housing (new homes)	78,027	47,318	27,000	25,000

Source: various

What the consensus forecasts tell us about the economy is that growth is expected to slow sharply, to be negative during 2008 and 2009, and to show only a modest improvement in 2010. The only thing expected to increase is the number on the dole. Everything else is expected to shrink, particularly fixed capital investment, because of a big drop-off in the build rate of new homes.

PILLAR NO. 1: GROWTH AND OUTPUT TO FALL SHARPLY

The consensus has shifted rapidly from the comparatively high rates of growth being predicted only a few months ago. The charge had been led by the Economic and Social Research Institute, which produces quarterly economic commentaries and updated quarterly predictions. Recently it chopped the growth forecast in its June outlook significantly from its previous prediction a few months earlier. That was a common theme among all the forecasters sampled below until October, when major downward revisions were made.

Table 4: Growth and output forecasts, 2008–10

Institution	Forecaster	2008E	2009F	2010F
Davy Stockbrokers	Rossa White	−1.7%	−3.2%	+0% (2010e)
Bank of Ireland	Dr Dan McLaughlin	−1.6%	−1.0%	
AIB Group	John Beggs	−1.5%	−2.5%	+1.5%
Ulster Bank	Pat McArdle	−2.7%	−4.4%	+1.1%
Goodbody Stockbrokers	Dermot O'Leary	−2.2%	−4.0%	
ESRI	Dr Alan Barrett et al.	−2.4%	−3.9%	
Central Bank of Ireland	John Flynn	−0.8%	−0.9%	−0.1%
IBEC	Danny McCoy	−2.0%	−4.0%	
National Irish Bank	Dr Ronnie O'Toole	−1.5%	−2.8%	
Friends First	Jim Power	−2.6%	−2.5%	+2.3%
KBC Ireland	Austin Hughes	−1.5%	+1.5%	
Economist	Economist Intelligence Unit (20 Nov. 2008)	−2.5%	−2.3%	−0.5%
Consensus (average)		−1.9%	−2.5%	+0.7%

The problem with calculating consensus forecasts is twofold. Firstly, very few organisations publish economic predictions: most people, including the estate agents, tend to copy each other or copy the few that do publish. Secondly, even fewer are prepared to offer a more long-term forecast. Typically, you get an estimate for the current year, then a prediction for the following year (2009 in this case).

The consensus was for flat or no growth as recently as the end of July, with only Rossa White at Davy's predicting a negative outturn for 2009. Another issue back in the late summer of 2008 was that two of the predictions—those of the *Economist* and the Central Bank—were approximately one to three months out of date, so excluding these would have taken the average forecast to a slight contraction (−0.2 per cent) instead of a slight rise at that juncture. This is the perennial problem with economic forecasts: not only are the actual figures always several months out of date but often the forecasters' forecasts are too.

The two most pessimistic predictions were from Goodbody Stockbrokers (a subsidiary of AIB Group), which is ironic, because the chief economist of their parent company has one of the most optimistic views. Goodbody's, unlike AIB, has obviously not lent anyone money to buy a house. And, secondly, Davy's (now independent of Bank of Ireland since the management buy-out) were the only forecasters warning of two consecutive years of declining growth at the mid-year stage.

Jim Power of Friends First, despite working for a home-loan company, in early autumn foresaw very poor growth for 2008, modest expansion in 2009, and resumption of a trend towards growth thereafter to +3.5 per cent in 2010 (which he then moderated to +2.3 per cent). John Beggs at AIB was also calling for strong positive growth for 2008, 2009 and 2010 at the half-year stage of +1.3, +2.5 and +4 per cent, respectively. He subsequently downgraded his growth forecasts, around the same time as everyone else (October), to the negative ones that you see above, with the exception that he stills sees a modest pick-up in growth in 2010.

Rossa White at Davy's was the first to predict the economic contraction now being experienced. In mid-October he published quarterly predictions for growth that were very pessimistic, expecting the Irish economy to shrink in volume terms up to the last quarter of 2009. He expects the domestic sector (GNP), excluding output from foreign companies operating in Ireland, to experience a 4.1 per cent fall in 2009 and a 0.5 per cent fall in 2010 (after a 2 per cent drop in 2008). In economic terms that is enormous. To put those figures into historical perspective, GNP fell only 1.3 per cent in 1982 and 1.9 per cent in 1983, during the last major recession.

The consensus growth forecast is for at least two years of deep recession, followed by only a modest improvement in fortunes for 2010. In fact both the *Economist* and the Central Bank are now forecasting that 2010 will be a negative year as well!

PILLAR NO. 2: UNEMPLOYMENT: THE JOBLESS RATE IS TO SOAR

Among our pool of economic pollsters there was considerably more uniformity when it came to foretelling job losses and the inevitable rising unemployment rate.

AIB was the most sanguine about the jobs outlook at mid-year and still was by late autumn. Davy's and Goodbody's were the most pessimistic; and the former is the only one to predict a double-digit unemployment rate in 2010. The Economic and Social Research Institute was one of the

first to predict the unemployment rate rising above 7 per cent after it ratcheted down its growth expectations by two percentage points, from +1.6 to
−0.4 per cent, over the course of three months, between the first-quarter
and second-quarter economic commentaries. In addition, it is now predicting an increase in net emigration of some 50,000. So no surprise then,
really, that everyone is predicting a steep increase in the dole queues.

Table 5: Unemployment estimates, 2008–10

Institution	Forecaster	2008E	2009F	2010F
Davy Stockbrokers	Rossa White	7.4%	10.2%	11.7%
Bank of Ireland	Dr Dan McLaughlin	5.8%	7.4%	
AIB Group	John Beggs	5.5%	7.6%	8.3%
Ulster Bank	Pat McArdle	5.7%	8.5%	9.0%
Goodbody Stockbrokers	Dermot O'Leary	6.5%	7.6%	
ESRI	Dr Alan Barrett et al.	6.1%	9.4%	
Central Bank of Ireland	John Flynn	5.9%	7.5%	
IBEC	Danny McCoy	6.6%	8.0%	
National Irish Bank	Dr Ronnie O'Toole	6.5%	8.0%	
Friends First	Jim Power	5.9%	7.8%	8.5%
Consensus (average)		6.2.%	8.2%	9.4%

Like AIB, the other big Irish bank, Bank of Ireland, doesn't see the unemployment rate running as high as the others. Dr Dan McLaughlin, its
chief economist, changed the bank's forecasts in July 2008 quite significantly in response to the increases in the European Central Bank rate.
(Since then he has raised the 2009 estimate by just under 1 per cent.)
Nonetheless, he foresees a rising unemployment rate of 7.4 per cent in
2009; but by October 2008 the rate had already touched 7.1 per cent. Both
the 'Big 2' mortgage lenders (AIB and Bank of Ireland) remain below
consensus on the jobs front.

Dermot O'Leary of Goodbody's was one of the most negative on this
front, probably because of its gloomy prediction of a sharp contraction
in economic output during 2008 and no real growth recovery envisaged
before 2010. Dermot has been one of the few commentators to spot the
pivotal problem of the growing stock of unsold new homes against the
backdrop of declining sales activity.

Rossa White of Davy's is the most negative on the jobs front. By the
end of December he was forecasting double-digit unemployment in 2009
and almost 12 per cent by the end of 2010.

In general, expectations are for the unemployment rate to hit 6 per
cent by the end of 2008 and at least 8 per cent by December 2009. These

figures appear conservative against the background of a massive reduction in residential building activity.

PILLAR NO. 3: INFLATION: THE MUGGER IN YOUR WALLET
Just as there was a general meeting of minds on the expected increase in unemployment, a similar pattern emerges when our economic pundits were making predictions about the general price level and likely increases in the cost of goods. Consumers are already acutely aware of the price increases that are due to annual inflation, running at 5 per cent on average over the last two years: they have felt it in their pockets. But there is some good news on the horizon.

Table 6: Inflation estimates, 2008–10

Institution	Forecaster	2008E	2009F	2010F
Davy Stockbrokers	Rossa White	+4.2%	+0.0%	+1.8% (2010e)
Bank of Ireland	Dr Dan McLaughlin	+4.5%	+2.2%	
AIB Group	John Beggs	+4.3%	+1.0%	+1.2%
Ulster Bank	Pat McArdle	+4.1%	−0.5%	+1.7%
Goodbody Stockbrokers	Dermot O'Leary	+4.5%	+2.2%	
ESRI	Dr Alan Barrett et al.	+4.5%	−2.0%	
Central Bank of Ireland	John Flynn	+4.4%	+1.9%	
IBEC	David Croughan	+4.6%	+3.2%	
National Irish Bank	Dr Ronnie O'Toole	+3.0%	+1.0%	
Friends First	Jim Power	+4.5%	+2.8%	+2.5%
Economist	Economist Intelligence Unit (16 June 2008)	+3.6%	+2.6%	+2.2%
Consensus (average)		+4.2%	+1.3%	+1.9%

One observation that must be mentioned at this point, though, is that as a rule economists tend to assume that inflation is *mean-reverting*: that is to say, it will return to some long-term average or trend level. None of our pundits has estimated that inflation will continue to rise. A large part of this is due to mortgage interest rates and the fact that the European Central Bank is past the peak in the interest-rate cycle and is well and truly in easing mode. A good chunk of the 2007 inflation was caused by rising mortgage payments.

However, the same economists and their organisations are not predicting a major fall in the euro or, put another way, an increase in the value of the dollar. They're probably correct over the short term. However, we are not yet witnessing deflation, merely disinflation—or a drop in the inflation rate.

A major part of the inflationary problem is the large increases permitted annually (15 to 20 per cent) in the price of gas and electricity by the state-owned monopolies, such as the ESB and An Bord Gáis. The Government is all too ready to blame Ireland's economic woes on external factors or the international economic climate, but it could begin by looking closer to home.

The consensus on the general price level is that *demand destruction* (lower consumer spending), coupled with cheaper food and energy prices, should see the annual rate of inflation dip well below 2 per cent next year.

PILLAR NO. 4: CONSUMER SPENDING: THRIFT TO REPLACE PROFLIGACY

The Irish consumer has long been the stalwart of the economic growth miracle of the 1990s and early 2000s. As our next table shows, virtually all the analysts see moderate growth in the volume of personal consumption this year and next, with the notable exceptions of the two main stockbrokers, Davy's and Goodbody's—although Dr Ronnie O'Toole at NIB and Jim Power at Friends First recently took the knife to their original forecasts, slashing 2009 forecasts by 5 per cent and 3.5 per cent, respectively. Ronnie had been forecasting 3 per cent growth in consumer spending as late as the end of July, but a couple of months later he revised that down to −2 per cent.

Table 7: Spending estimates, 2008–10

Institution	Forecaster	2008E	2009F	2010F
Davy Stockbrokers	Rossa White	−0.8%	−3.8%	−2.5%
Bank of Ireland	Dr Dan McLaughlin	+0.0%	+0.0%	
AIB Group	John Beggs	+0.5%	−1.7%	−0.2%
Ulster Bank	Pat McArdle	−1.0%	−3.0%	+0.5%
Goodbody Stockbrokers	Dermot O'Leary	+0.0%	+0.5%	
ESRI	Dr Alan Barrett et al.	−2.2%	−3.6%	
Central Bank of Ireland	John Flynn	+0.4%	+0.4%	
IBEC	David Croughan	+1.5%	+2.0%	
National Irish Bank	Dr Ronnie O'Toole	−0.7%	−2.0%	
Friends First	Jim Power	−2.0%	−1.5%	+1.0%
Consensus (average)		−0.4%	−1.3%	−0.3%

Consumption, or *private personal consumption,* as economists tend to call it, represents the lion's share of the economy. Almost half the €185-billion-a-year Irish economy is accounted for by private consumer spending. This is one area that really could upset the apple cart. If consumers replace extravagant spending with frugality, begin saving a lot more and spending a lot less, the growth figures really will deteriorate quite quickly.

Rossa White, chief economist at Davy's, wrote in a recent weekly economic comment entitled 'Irish economy set to shrink in 2009' that, because of tighter credit conditions, a 'financial accelerator' may prolong the slump. He concluded by stating that 'precautionary saving will increase from historically low levels both this year and next.'

The consensus is for a modest decline in consumer spending in 2009. Not everyone, though, is predicting falls. The Central Bank recently lopped 3 per cent off its 2008 and 2009 estimates; but that still left both estimates as positive ones. The most aggressive forecasts for the drop in 2009 spending were those of Pat McArdle at Ulster Bank and Rossa White at Davy's.

PILLAR NO. 5: INVESTMENT TO DISAPPEAR

When economists talk about investment they mean *fixed capital investment* or big capital investment in plant and machinery, as well as property (both residential and commercial). The economic panel of forecasters is predicting a seismic shift in the amount of money invested in capital items. The annual growth rate is expected to contract by nearly 18 per cent in both 2008 and 2009. In economic terms this is enormous. The main culprit is, of course, the steep decline in expected home completions.

Table 8: Investment estimates, 2008–10

Institution	Forecaster	2008E	2009F	2010F
Davy Stockbrokers	Rossa White	−18.8%	−25.0%	−13.7%
Bank of Ireland	Dr Dan McLaughlin	−17.5%	−11.9%	
AIB Group	John Beggs	−19.5%	−22.5%	−5.0%
Ulster Bank	Pat McArdle	−19.9%	−21.2%	−1.5%
Goodbody Stockbrokers	Dermot O'Leary	−16.6%	−11.7%	
ESRI	Dr Alan Barrett et al.	−19.8%	−19.3%	
Central Bank of Ireland	John Flynn	−17.3%	−16.8%	
IBEC	David Croughan	−15.3%	−4.8%	
National Irish Bank	Dr Ronnie O'Toole	−18.0%	−22.0%	
Friends First	Jim Power	−20.0%	−20.0%	+3.0%
Consensus (average)		−18.3%	−17.5%	−4.3%

As we shall see in the next chapter, the number of new homes to be built is likely to contract very sharply. Davy's have the most negative outlook as far as investment is concerned; this is because they have ratcheted down their expectations for non-residential property investment, and they already had one of the lowest forecasts for the supply of new homes in 2009 anyway. They have recognised that the commercial property sector is about a year behind the residential segment, and that overbuilding has occurred there too in the not-so-distant past.

Opinions appeared to be more divided about the pattern of investment growth for 2009 before the big sea-change in opinions that occurred in October. Some forecasters were predicting single-digit negative rates, whereas others (such as the stockbroking firms) see a similar pattern to 2008 and more large double-digit falls. Virtually all forecasters are predicting that investment will shrink by almost a fifth.

Suffice it to say that capital investment has been a major pillar of economic growth during the boom periods. Every 10,000 new homes built increases GDP or output growth by between 0.8 and 0.9 per cent. So, if new home building falls from a peak of 90,000 in 2006 to a trough of, say, 25,000 in 2009, that alone wipes 5 per cent off annual economic growth—taking it, in effect, to nil, other things being equal (or negative).

PILLAR NO. 6: HOUSING SUPPLY: THE TAP IS EVENTUALLY TURNED DOWN

A central feature of the consumer boom era was the record number of new homes built in the country. As we shall see throughout this book, it's the biggest problem facing the residential property market. The entire issue of oversupply will be a recurring theme, especially with regard to misconceptions about how many new homes are actually required each year.

Table 9: Housing supply estimates, 2008–10

Institution	Forecaster	2008E	2009F	2010F
Davy Stockbrokers	Rossa White	50,000	25,000	
Bank of Ireland	Dr Dan McLaughlin	50,000		
AIB Group	John Beggs	47,500	25,000	25,000
Ulster Bank	Pat McArdle	48,000	20,000	20,000
Goodbody Stockbrokers	Dermot O'Leary	48,000	30,000	
ESRI	Dr Alan Barrett et al.	45,000	25,000	
Central Bank of Ireland	John Flynn	47,000	25,000	
IBEC	David Croughan	45,000	35,000	
National Irish Bank	Dr Ronnie O'Toole	50,000	30,000	
Friends First	Jim Power	50,000	25,000	30,000
KBC Ireland	Austin Hughes	40,000	30,000	
Consensus (average)		47,318	27,000	25,000

Almost everyone has seriously downgraded their predictions for the number of new homes to be built over the next two years. As recently as the early autumn the consensus for 2009 was 35,000 new homes; two months later that predicted level was slashed to 27,000. The contrast for 2010 was even starker, as the consensus for the number of new residential dwellings has been cut from 41,250 back to 25,000; and some economists, such as Pat McArdle at Ulster Bank, are predicting only 20,000 new homes for that year. That is a big drop, back to the late-1980s build rate, when mass emigration was the biggest problem facing the construction industry.

We cover the issue of new home supply in detail in subsequent chapters. Nevertheless, as fewer homes are likely to be built in 2008 and even fewer during 2009, the consequential effects on employment will be huge. It also negatively affects consumer spending and retail sales, as we discovered in the last chapter, just as we saw that employment in construction is already at recessionary levels.

The outlook for the Irish economy for the next two years at least, possibly longer, is decidedly 'bearish'. That's the consensus.

Chapter 5

The Hibernian Bear

The term 'Celtic Tiger' was first used in 1994 in an economic research report written by a British economist working for an American investment bank in London. It was an apt description at that time of what was about to happen to the economy of Ireland, a Celtic country on the fringe of western Europe. The word 'tiger' was a direct comparison with the 'Asian tiger' economies of south-east Asia, such as those of Taiwan, Malaysia, Singapore, Indonesia, and South Korea, which had enjoyed tremendous economic growth since the 1980s, largely export-driven, reflecting not just their emerging industrial base and manufacturing prowess but also a climb from a position of low or below OECD average standards of living. In effect, part of their high growth stemmed from the fact that they were playing catch-up with the economies of the 'First World'. It was universally accepted that to be a 'tiger' economy you needed high growth of more than 7 per cent per year in real output or GDP.

It's quite common today to hear populist commentators asking who could have predicted the enormous economic growth that occurred in Ireland during the 'Celtic Tiger' era. However, a decade and a half ago it was widely expected by economists and market commentators that this would indeed occur. It was just that it was not being said within Ireland but externally, especially in the City of London. The rapid transformation in the state of the public finances, the demographic turnaround and the preparation for the introduction of the new single currency had all been duly noted. Ireland then not only had the youngest population in the European Union but was the only English-speaking country preparing to go into the euro zone.

The 'Celtic Tiger' era lasted from 1994 to 2001. It was a period when economic growth averaged almost 9 per cent per year. There was a whole host of reasons why this economic transformation occurred when it did: education, demography, reduced taxes and imported productivity growth from American corporations, as well as the improvement in public finances and the decision to join the euro, to name but a few.

Unfortunately the term 'Celtic Tiger' took on a whole new meaning among the general population: it morphed into an idea and became part of the *zeitgeist*. It has seeped deep into the Irish psyche, especially among the younger 'Generation Y', those born since 1980 and who were too young to remember the bad old times. In 21st-century Ireland there are Celtic Tiger people (Celtic Cubs), clothes (Abercrombie and Fitch), television programmes (e.g. 'Xpose'), homes, cars, and so on. Incredibly, it appears to have become fixed in the outlook of many people as a way of life.

What all these people forget, or perhaps never realised, is that the term actually referred to an era. An era has a beginning and an end, like the Great Famine, the Great Depression, the Second World War or the oil crises in the 1970s, all of them distinct eras.

If we examine the economic experience of Ireland over the last forty years we see that there were several boom and bust periods. Since the last recession, which occurred a quarter of a century ago, three distinct phases of economic growth have come and gone.

Fig. 6: Annual economic growth rates, 1970–2010

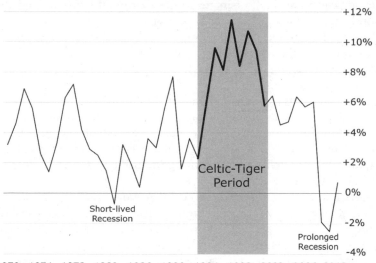

Source: Central Statistics Office, Consensus Forecasts

Firstly, there was the pre-Celtic Tiger period, or what has become more commonly known as the horrible 80s and rotten early 90s. The most notable aspects of that time were rampant inflation and massive unemployment. But despite this, between 1982 and 1993 economic growth averaged a little below 3 per cent, though it fluctuated wildly, as our graphic above shows.

The second phase was the 'Celtic Tiger' era, which began in 1994 and lasted until 2002. Economic growth or national income rose by an average of nearly 9 per cent per year during that period. In the late 1990s Éire Teoranta grew at an even faster pace than the Chinese Dragon economy. China today is still enjoying near-double-digit growth; Éire Teoranta is not but has shifted into reverse gear.

There were two defining characteristics that one could point to as a clear sign that the 'tiger' economy was done. The first was the obvious moderation of growth after 2002 as the global economy wobbled following the abrupt stock market crash in technology shares, as well as the attacks on the World Trade Center in New York in 2001. The second identifiable factor was the peak in exports and the external trade surplus that occurred in 2002, when annual exports hit nearly €94 billion and the surplus (exports minus imports) reached a record of €38 billion. The surplus in 2009 is expected to be €28 billion or ten billion less than what it was seven years earlier.

That should have been a defining moment for the Irish economy; but the subsequent slashing of interest rates by central banks around the world after the New York attacks set the scene for the next phase in Irish economic history, the 'consumer boom' era. This third phase disguised the fact that Ireland was no longer a tiger economy. The consumer boom lasted five years, from 2003 to 2007, and could be summed up in one word: credit. According to the Central Bank, borrowings by individuals and businesses, also known as private-sector credit, expanded rapidly. In January 2003 total private-sector credit was €128 billion, but by September 2008 it had grown to more than €400 billion—an increase of more than €270 billion in 290 weeks. Put another way, this represents an additional €1,000 million of borrowing by Irish people and companies each week for five years!

Let's put these figures into a context that most people would understand more easily. Total private credit in Ireland by mid-2008 equalled more than €90,000 for every man, woman and child in the country. Therefore, one could easily be forgiven for making the assumption that this comparatively high rate of growth was built on a false base, namely other people's money. As with all loans, at some point the lender expects the principal to be repaid.

Then along came the global credit crisis or, what it should really be called, the global liquidity crunch, which erupted on 9 August 2007 and swiftly put an end to the Irish consumer boom. Contrary to popular opinion, the doubling of interest rates by the European Central Bank from December 2005 to June 2007 had very little impact on Irish credit growth, other than moderating the annual rate of credit growth from a huge 30 per cent back to a high 20 per cent rate. The changing availability of credit, and not the cost of credit as measured by interest rates, was the final nail in the coffin for this era.

Nevertheless, Ireland was about to enter a new phase of significantly lower growth, higher inflation and a 'bear' downturn in the property and stock markets. (A 'bear' market is one where prices fall for a sustained period, usually by more than a fifth in terms of magnitude, and that remains in a secular down trend for an extended period, often for a minimum of five to seven years. Bear markets don't last weeks or months.)

Many academics and journalists had known for some time that the 'Celtic Tiger' was dead, and they searched in vain for, or attempted to invent, a more appropriate catchphrase, one that was catchy and that more accurately reflected the changing state of the nation. So far none of these has caught on. It's not difficult to understand why when we consider that all attempts have depended upon retaining the 'Celtic' part while substituting a different animal, and so we were offered the Celtic Hare, the Celtic Tortoise and, more recently from a Sunday newspaper, the Celtic Hyena.

But plugging the name of a different creature into the term without sound logic or rationale is mere folly, as it ignores the entire point of the expression in the first place. Beyond that, it's obvious to all that certain animals don't strike a common chord with the average citizen, largely because of their negative connotations or the disparaging undertones for Irish society. After all, who wants to be likened to a laughing hyena, or to a slow, crawling tortoise or a long-eared, timid rabbit?

The country needs an expression that's in keeping with past economic success and so befits our new largesse while simultaneously reflecting the mood of the people in an accurate representation of how we feel about the state of the economy—not to mention the reversal of fortune in both the stock market and the property sector. Lastly, it needs to be one that people are comfortable with, especially from an international viewpoint, despite the change in economic direction.

Enter the Bear, and the new Hibernian Bear economy.

The first word is very appropriate today, for lots of different reasons, but suffice it to say that contemporary Ireland is indeed a neo-Hibernian society, both socially and economically. The second word is also suited on many different levels. Obviously, it reflects the bear market in property prices and shares as well as the bear economy in the form of reduced or falling economic growth and recession. The bear, like the tiger, is both a noble and a ferocious creature; but, unlike the carnivorous tiger, the bear is an omnivore and will eat anything—perhaps a reflection that Ireland too will have to change and adapt to the new economic circumstances. Unlike tigers, which are active all year round, bears like to hibernate in the winter. This form of stasis may appear quite appealing to many Irish businesses as they face a prolonged period of slower sales, of pursuing creditors and reluctant debtors.

The Hibernian Bear era has already been initiated by the dramatic change in economic forecasts made by the Economic and Social Research Institute in mid-2008. Growth has been revised downwards to a negative number for 2008. Unemployment is projected to increase sharply and inflation expected to remain persistently high.

Plugging these new forecasts into the growth illustration above, even allowing for the modest recovery anticipated by the consensus to a little less than 1 per cent growth in 2010, growth in the medium term will feel very sluggish when compared with the recent 'consumer boom' era, and it will definitely feel like a recession when compared with the heady days of the 'Celtic Tiger'. The Hibernian Bear is here to stay, for several years at least.

Assuming that the ESRI is correct in its medium-term forecasts and that economic growth rebounds to 3½ per cent by 2011 and stays at that level for four to five years, the average economic growth rate during the Hibernian Bear era, say 2008–16, would be only about 1.5 per cent. You see, two negative years plus one more low-growth year dramatically reduces the average. The director of the ESRI, Frances Ruane, said on the TV3 'Nightly News' with Vincent Browne that growth should return to its trend rate of 4 per cent within the medium term (which is economists' jargon for the next five years). However, the standard definition of trend growth is a linear average of annual growth over a long period. Since 1970 the average annual growth in GDP has been nearly 5 per cent. GDP measures the output of the economy in a given year, so it includes foreign companies operating here, such as the American transnationals. Even GNP growth, which measures the change in national income and in Ireland is generally lower than GDP or output growth, has averaged 4¼ per cent over the last forty years.

The basic idea of trend growth is that it should also reflect the natural rate of growth in the economy, when everyone who wants a job is gainfully employed—in other words, when there is 'full employment'. But the ESRI is predicting a 60 per cent increase in unemployment, so the economy won't be operating at capacity and will definitely be below trend. Perhaps this is why they have opted for a lower trend growth rate in the future.

Whichever way one chooses to look at it, it doesn't really matter. Ireland is in an economic downturn, already in recession. The country is in the midst of a bear market—the Hibernian Bear—so people will have to get used to the new reality and just grin and bear it, or take a chill pill and hibernate for a few years.

Chapter 6

The wealth forecast: A barometer of success or misguided view of wellbeing?

W hen one speaks about wealth one needs to define what wealth really means to people. To some, such as accountants and economists, wealth generally refers to assets minus liabilities, whereas financial advisers and banks will talk about investments in property, bonds and shares as well as cash deposits. But there are other forms of wealth too, such as the collective wealth of a nation as measured by health, education and social standards. To others still, wealth may constitute real assets, such as land, livestock, crops or other tangibles, even including collectibles, for instance art or jewellery.

Whichever view one takes it doesn't really matter in the final analysis. What does matter, though, is that the obsession with wealth as an end in itself is a failure in understanding the true benefits to society that gains in wealth may bring. To display wealth garishly is simply vulgar; to brag about the collective wealth of one country above others and to assume false pride in international wealth 'league tables' is the height of arrogance. A good example of this is the annual GDP *per capita* league tables— a sort of economic Premiership, if you will.

The unprecedented growth of the last decade has resulted in a manifold increase in both living standards and income; however, this is a very narrow view of how the country has changed. For instance, it doesn't take account of the infrastructural problems that the country is now experiencing, nor does it take into account the increasing gap between rich and poor. And it's completely at odds with the deficits in the health service and in education. It belies the fact that many state schools are in a shoddy state of repair and that many young pupils have to go to school every day in prefabricated buildings that are more of a throwback to the late twentieth century than an indication of a strong, dynamic economy in the twenty-first century.

On 29 October 2007 on the RTE television programme 'One-to-One' Bryan Dobson interviewed Dr Ken Whitaker (voted the greatest living Irish person in 2002), who voiced his concern about widening income disparities in Irish society. Whitaker was widely viewed as the architect of the reformed Irish economy in the 1960s and 70s.

Dobson asked him what he thought of the economy today and how a rising tide was supposed to lift all boats. (Whitaker said firstly that he didn't like the term 'Celtic Tiger'.) Part of the conversation went as follows:

Dobson: And have we used our wealth wisely?

Whitaker: We could have done more, I think, to improve social equity. There were budget times in reasonably recent years when I would have been happy to be the little boy that Santa Claus forgot! In other words, I didn't think that people who were well off needed as much improvement in taxation relief and so on as they got—that more should have been done to ensure greater social equity; and that is still the position.

Dobson: So you wouldn't be advocating further cuts in tax rates, or income tax rates, for example?

Whitaker: I would regard that as quite unnecessary, and I would rather see the money go to improve health and social welfare.

Dobson: Have we lost some of that social cohesion that might have been more evident in your youth?

Whitaker: I think we may have, because so many people enjoyed the uplift they may have tended to forget those who were being left behind.

Dobson: And yet the arguments are being made that if you incentivise work you reward people for effort, then everybody benefits from that: it raises all boats, to coin a phrase.

Whitaker: No, but there are differences. I think we have big social problems: how to prevent young people from dropping out, dropping out of society, joining methods of achieving honour and parity of esteem and so on which are illegal and very harmful to society.

What Whitaker was referring to there was, of course, the rising drug trade that has accompanied the rising wealth of the nation, through increased drug addiction among the Celtic Cubs. The growing divide between rich and poor has encouraged those in the lower socio-economic strata of society to drop out of school and seek riches by profiting from this buoyant new drug trade.

Earlier comments from Whitaker, to the effect that those who benefited most from the 'Celtic Tiger' era have forgotten (read: don't care any more) about the rest of society is a damning indictment, a poor reflection on Irish society as a whole. During the bad old days of the 1980s people may not have had much by way of material wealth but at least there was a visible community spirit or soul, which is lacking in Ireland today.

LEAGUE TABLES REVISITED

A big problem with using these league tables, which are a narrow, one-dimensional and myopic view of the world, is that many citizens see them as a flag waving exercise. This may actually be damaging to the country's reputation internationally. It's this international reputation that academics such as Professor Morgan Kelly refer to when they talk about how Ireland's reputation around the globe may be adversely affected. To continually wallow in one's self-importance and to persistently draw attention to these very league tables and the country's ranking within them, drawing comparisons with our nearest neighbours, may actually be quite damaging in the long run. Here's why.

It's always a good idea to put oneself in the other person's shoes. For example, how would we feel if our nearest neighbour, Britain, were to draw attention to the growing disparity in income per head between their country and ours, while at the same time thousands of British people were coming here to buy up commercial property as well as residential properties, and bragging about how great things were economically and financially back home? They would be perceived as too big for their boots, big-headed opportunists experiencing temporary success. They would be seen as setting themselves up for a fall.

This is precisely what has gone on, and is still going on today, in Ireland, fuelled incessantly by both television and the print media. Not only that but I have personally witnessed, while living and working abroad, many Irish people, particularly those investing in property over-seas, bragging about the 'Celtic Tiger' or how wealthy a country Ireland has become—as if the 'Celtic Tiger' was an unstoppable locomotive of wealth. True, it has left the country with a legacy of some sizeable material wealth, but it's a legacy that won't last for ever.

On one occasion while in an Irish bar in southern Spain I stood beside an Irish architect, the chairman of a large and well-known Irish company, who remarked to an Englishman present, 'Sure everyone in Dublin is now a property millionaire.' This was from an educated man who was fortunate enough to purchase a property in Sandymount, near Lansdowne Road, long before the 'Celtic Tiger' economy took hold—and, yes, he himself was a property millionaire. To suggest that all Dubliners are millionaires is, of course, not true. The look on the Englishman's face was plain to see: he saw this as *nouveau-riche* trumpet-blowing.

Sadly, this was not so, but the Irishman genuinely believed it to be so. He was in his mid-sixties, and many of his generation who had bought properties in the 1960s and 70s had indeed become accidental property millionaires. But this is the way it was perceived. Nonetheless, as is often quoted in financial markets, 'perception is reality.'

Economic criteria such as income per head don't encapsulate the true position of a properly functioning economy. The whole point is that the 'Celtic Tiger' is no more: it was an eight-year period that ended several years ago. But this is apparently not so according to the great unwashed. Listening to the media one could be forgiven for thinking that the Celtic Tiger is still among us. Right up to the economic slowdown in 2008 the media were still pumping the question 'Is the Celtic Tiger dead?'

They can't shake free of the fact that it's no longer an appropriate description of the modern, mature Irish economy. During the late 1990s it was an apt description of the transformation of a country lagging behind its peers in Europe, with the new Asian-like double-digit growth that was experienced back then. The danger today is that people take higher economic growth for granted. This becomes the new norm. Nowhere is this more prevalent than in the growing sector of the financial industry known as 'wealth management'.

WEALTH OF THE NATION

The recent wealth report by National Irish Bank entitled 'The Emerald Isle: The wealth of modern Ireland', published in February 2008, is a testament to this. This 24-page glossy brochure is embarrassing in its claims. First of all, I would strongly dispute its figures, especially the claim that aggregate household wealth in Ireland will pass €1 trillion for the first time in early 2008. My initial criticism of this report was that the figures were an exaggeration, because they were based on the fact that property has been the primary asset, accounting for almost 70 per cent of total wealth, in particular residential property, which accounts for 48 per cent of all household wealth, with a further 19 per cent accruing from investment property.

The simple fact of the matter is that total residential property wealth in Ireland in the latter part of 2008 was approximately €510 billion, but with an associated €148 billion of debt tied to those homes. Total owner-occupied housing wealth had declined since the spring of 2007 by more than €59 billion as house prices fell and net residential property wealth, excluding residential mortgages, declined to below €365 billion.

Almost €700 billion is the amount that NIB comes up with for privately owned homes in addition to other residential property. Though significant investments of several billion per year are being made in overseas properties, many of those properties don't generate any income. Estimated total investment in overseas property by Irish people from 2000 to 2007 was €61 billion.

The biggest problem, which should be obvious to most people, is that your home is not a financial asset—which is the principal reason why it's exempt from capital gains tax. Indeed, at the top of its section entitled 'The sources of wealth' NIB highlights the page with the following quotation: 'While owner occupied housing is an important form of wealth, it's also highly illiquid as people will always need somewhere to live.' In effect they have answered their own question. You can't monetise the value of your home directly by just selling it for cash. You can, however, sell your home when the market prices are at a record high and choose to rent, trade down to a smaller and cheaper property or move from an expensive area to a more affordable one. An alternative approach favoured by very few people, who would be viewed as too radical by the majority, is the value trade gained by selling your property in Ireland and moving abroad.

One of the more inane comments in the NIB report is the following. 'We now have 20 to 30 of the latest model Porsche 911 models ranging from about €175,000 to €250,000, including several new 911 turbos which retail at around €250,000. All of these have a substantial waiting list.'

What a crass comment to make in a report of this nature! It's indicative of the level of immaturity of Irish society as a whole (as well as the inordinately high taxes imposed on new vehicles). To single out a specific new model is daft; to mention that there are a couple of dozen new ones in the country is worse. This is another example of the ineptitude that pervades Irish society today; and we should ask ourselves, how will this look internationally?

The analogies don't stop there: it gets worse. It's stated that nearly 4 per cent of all passenger vehicles in Ireland now are BMWs, and that there are more Mercedes-Benz cars per capita in Ireland than in Germany, where they're made. But the authors fail to tell us that in Germany the Mercedes is nothing special and is considered just a good-quality saloon car, rather than a prestige marque, as it is in Ireland.

You will never see a financial institution in London bragging about the number of Porsches, Bentleys or Rolls-Royces in that city. Have you ever seen a report from one of the bulge-bracket Wall Street brokers boasting about the number of new Hummers, stretch limousines, Cadillacs or Dodge Vipers that are being sold to New Yorkers?

The NIB wealth report attributes the meteoric growth in Irish wealth during the last ten years to two factors: firstly, the spectacular growth in exports during the 'Celtic Tiger' period, and secondly, the liberalisation of credit in the early 1990s (which we shall explore later in the chapter on debt). Both are indeed very true. However, like much of the debate in Ireland today, both are backward-looking. They have already occurred and are historical facts that few would argue with.

But we need forward-looking indicators today, and what better forward-looking beast than the stock market. It's universally accepted that the stock market digests information rapidly and discounts events by up to eighteen months ahead. What this means in effect is that market prices today are reflecting where investors perceive the economy to be in a year or so, or late 2010 in this case.

Therefore, a confirmed bottom in the ISEQ *Overall Index* would be a barometer of better things to come a couple of years down the road. Since the stock market peak in February 2007 the Irish market has shed more than two-thirds of its value. On 20 February 2007 the ISEQ index peaked at 10,028, breaking the 10,000 barrier, and it closed that day at 9,981. The total combined value of Irish shares multiplied by their respective prices in May 2007 was €130 billion. A little more than one year later, by mid-November 2008, that market value had plummeted to €32 billion. According to the NIB report, nearly a quarter of total wealth is accounted for by stocks and shares; so this is very significant indeed.

The Irish banks have been big losers, shedding €57.3 billion of market value in just twenty-two months. It's fair to say that globally banks have been hit, but Irish banks have underperformed all their European peers, with the notable exception of Northern Rock, which has now been nationalised. The drop in values is roughly 95 per cent for the Big Four domestic players. Irish Life and Permanent, as well as Bank of Ireland—the two most exposed to the residential property sector—have been hit hard, falling close to 95 per cent (Anglo down 99 per cent). It's fair to say that if you want to 'short-sell' the Irish property sector, what better than flogging the banks that lent the money to home-buyers in the first place, who may face serious exposures some time down the road.

If you thought that only the banks have been hit hard, just take a look at the fall in the market value of Grafton and Kingspan, a drop of more than 85 per cent in each instance. Next, both Readymix and Siteserv PLC have lost well in excess of nine-tenths of their respective market valuations. McInerney, the publicly traded home-building stock, has witnessed the collapse of its value, from €637 million to €35 million. Its share price plunged more than 90 per cent, from a peak of €3.40 on 26 February 2007 to a mere €0.17 in the winter of 2008.

All in all, another €20 billion and more of shareholders' holdings has been lost. It was no surprise that, at the time of writing, a report was published by Rubicon Investment Consultancy on the failure of many Irish pension funds in beating inflation over the last decade. The headline read: 'Half of Irish managed pension funds fail to beat inflation over the long term.' The average ten-year return was 4.1 per cent per year, only slightly above the decade's average inflation rate of 3.7 per cent. With the now-aging population there will be a lot of elderly Irish people in the next twenty years or so who may become more dependent on the state for retirement income. It speaks volumes for market timing. This message should not be lost with regard to the property market as an investment. How many people do you know who have bought a property as part of their pension? In real terms, property prices fell 12 per cent in 2007 and are projected to fall another 10.7 per cent in nominal prices in 2008, according to Davy's. Add in money inflation for 2008 and this all comes to a 23 per cent 'real' or inflation-adjusted decline in two years. It takes many years of positive gains to make up for lost values after a few short years of these types of price falls.

HOME EQUITY CUSHION DEFLATES

A topic widely referred to is the 'home equity cushion'—the value of all property minus the amount of debt associated with residential property, namely mortgages. Often estate agents (as well as banks and brokers, such as NIB) cite the strong home equity cushion as a measure of support for the market, given that the equity component vastly outweighs the debt component. This is misleading, however, because it's based on averages. The calculation takes all homes in the country, including those bought thirty or forty years ago, that have no mortgage debt attached to them. Next it takes all outstanding property mortgages from Central Bank statistics and simply subtracts the total. It states the collective position but has no regard for the individual who may indeed now be suffering negative equity.

Since the peak in the property market in February 2007 the total value of the housing stock has declined significantly (see below).

Table 10 begins with the official number of dwellings in the country in December 2006, according to the Department of the Environment, Heritage and Local Government, namely 1.8 million. Using the latest CSO monthly completions data we can update this to 1.93 million dwellings by November 2008. Furthermore, we can show in the fourth column the national average home price, as calculated by the PTSB-ESRI home price index. We use this price data for two reasons, firstly to ascertain the total value of all Irish homes, which we do by multiplying quantity by price to give the latest value of about €509 billion. This is what it would cost you to buy up every home in the land. Secondly, as it's a moving target (both in the number of residences and their various prices), we use the last column to show the number of new homes coming on stream, albeit at lower market values, as prices fell before they were finished.

Table 10: Decline in value of housing stock, 2006–08

Period	Residences	Completions	Average price	Value (€ billion)	Added (€ billion)
Dec. 2006	1,804,000	8,364	€310,632	560	2.6
Jan. 2007	1,809,788	5,788	€311,078	563	1.8
Feb. 2007	1,816,840	7,052	€311,078	565	2.2
Mar. 2007	1,823,918	7,078	€309,071	564	2.2
Apr. 2007	1,829,882	5,964	€306,619	561	1.8
May 2007	1,836,714	6,832	€304,166	559	2.1
Jun. 2007	1,842,778	6,064	€302,605	558	1.8
Jul. 2007	1,847,840	5,062	€301,267	557	1.5
Aug. 2007	1,853,743	5,903	€300,375	557	1.8
Sep. 2007	1,860,105	6,362	€299,483	557	1.9
Oct. 2007	1,867,502	7,397	€295,469	552	2.2
Nov. 2007	1,875,198	7,696	€292,124	548	2.2
Dec. 2007	1,881,627	6,429	€287,887	542	1.9
Jan. 2008	1,886,485	4,858	€285,880	539	1.4
Feb. 2008	1,891,514	5,029	€283,650	537	1.4
Mar. 2008	1,895,537	4,023	€281,643	534	1.1
Apr. 2008	1,900,385	4,848	€278,521	529	1.4
May 2008	1,904,925	4,540	€275,176	524	1.2
Jun. 2008	1,909,163	4,238	€273,392	522	1.2
Jul. 2008	1,913,536	4,373	€272,946	522	1.2
Aug. 2008	1,917,141	3,605	€270,493	519	1.0
Sep. 2008	1,921,313	4,172	€267,594	514	1.1
Oct. 2008	1,925,140	3,827	€265,364	511	1.0
Nov. 2008	1,927,417	4,277	€264,026	509	1.1
Since peak		112,577	−15%	−59	34.7

The table shows that more than €1 billion worth of new stock has been added to the total each month, despite falling prices (and therefore values). The most important feature of this table is the €34.7 billion worth, or more than 112,500 new homes, that have been finished since the market peaked in February 2007. They in turn have dropped in value by at least €3.1 billion, along with the rest of the market.

If you were to take the number of residences today and calculate the drop in value of the housing stock, just by multiplying today's houses by the average, then compare that with the same figure for February 2007 (when the market peaked at €565 billion), you would be understating the total loss of value. You would have a decline of €56 billion (565 minus 509); but this ignores the fact that more homes had been added to the total housing stock in the interim. It's not fair to compare the total value of 1.8 million properties with the total value of 1.9 million properties. To make a like-for-like comparison you have also to add in the drop on the newer homes too. This takes the total fall in Irish property values to more than €57 billion from February 2007 to November 2008.

TOTAL WEALTH DROP WAS ALMOST €160 BILLION!

The combined loss of value of stocks and shares, at more than €98 billion, including the total drop in residential property values of about €59 billion over the same period, results in a drop in net wealth of almost €157 billion in a little over a year.

To put this figure in context, that amounts to roughly €35,600 for every man, woman and child in the country, based on the upwardly revised population figure of 4.41 million. That's the price of a new family saloon car or sporty hatchback for every resident in the land!

We don't see comments like this in the NIB report; but what we do see is a warning within the section on 'Managing wealth', which begins as follows:

> For many Irish households, wealth management remains unplanned. They now face a number of challenges, including lower returns on traditional investment vehicles like residential property, together with the challenges of managing wealth transfer.

Essentially, what this report is pointing out is that too many of us rely on investing in second or third properties as a form of financial investment for the future. Dr Ronnie O'Toole continues with the observation that more people are now taking control of their personal finances, in particular their wealth portfolios, and he quite correctly asserts that future growth in the euro area over the medium term will pale into insignificance when compared with the returns on offer in Asia. You have to agree with him on this and endorse the view that wealth management is really about diversifying risk. He puts it succinctly:

> The rapidity of Ireland's new found wealth has left Irish households with a much skewed distribution towards Irish property.

This overtly picturesque report, with its dramatic landscapes, beaches, lighthouses and Cliffs of Moher photographs, does contain some genuine nuggets of wisdom. There are some serious messages in it, chief among them the view that formal pension arrangements may not suffice and that people need to invest in other assets and diversify risk globally as well as consider the ramifications of wealth transfer from one generation to the next.

TIMING IS EVERYTHING!

As we mentioned earlier, timing is everything. It's precisely for this reason that financial advisers, such as NIB et al., advise people to invest regularly. That way you average out the investment price over time. This is the drip-feed approach. The purchase of residential property, however, is binary: it's all or nothing. Do I buy now or do I wait? Prices have dipped; do I buy that rental property and wear the haircut that I have to take when the rent won't meet the property costs?

These questions are being asked right now by people watching the recent market falls. For many, this decision will be made for them by the banks, which are now more reluctant to lend to people who can't put up a large deposit, or half the price in cash, to avail of the best interest rates on offer. Unfortunately for most people their biggest asset on their personal balance sheet is their home. It's certainly the biggest drain on their financial resources. But it doesn't have to be.

Consider for a moment the person who rents now instead of buying, saves an extra few thousand per year in doing so, and invests in overseas equities as well as some now-cheaper Irish ones (at 75 to 90 off the peak levels). If house prices continue their downward secular trend—and trust me: the momentum is still downwards—within a few years, say two to three years, that person will have accumulated a much bigger deposit for a significantly cheaper property. It's potentially a win-win scenario.

If my analysis of the property market is correct, those people will save not just tens of thousands but perhaps €100,000 or more, especially first-time buyers in Dublin. If I'm wrong, if the market turns in the latter part of 2009 and there's a shortage of housing (the estate agents' view) and prices resume an upward trend in 2009, but only by a couple of per cent, the additional cost would be minimal.

Which is worse—go on, ask yourself—the type 1 error, where the prospective buyer saves €50,000, €70,000 or €100,000, or the type 2 error, where the agents are correct and they have to pay another 3 to 5 per cent, so it costs them a few thousand more?

Now ask yourself, what is the probability of each occurrence? If it's fifty-fifty, it pays to wait. The cumulative probability is the sum of each outcome multiplied by the percentage probability. In short, you have to be at least 90 per cent sure that the estate agents are right to come out ahead on this bet. Investments, at least in the heavily regulated financial markets, come with a serious health warning: 'The value of your investment may go down as well as up . . . blah, blah'; but in the unregulated property markets, no-one tells you that home ownership may seriously damage your wealth if you pay near the top of the market—and let's face it, we've only seen the top less than two years ago. It's a very long way down to the bottom.

Chapter 7
| The new misery index

Back in the 1980s, economists often referred to the 'misery index'—a combination of the annual rate of inflation and the annual unemployment rate. The media loved to pick up this sort of information. It's easy to understand, and it accurately reflects how the populace at large feels when their cost of living is soaring yet their demands for wage growth are curtailed by the constraint or threat of high unemployment. After all, who among us wishes to join those already in the dole queues? The misery was further compounded by the traditionalists of the trade-union movement, who prefer to see job cuts than wage falls (what economists term 'labour being price-inflexible downwards'). Back then there was no social partnership to speak of.

If you travelled back to the spring of 1984, the conventional misery index of the day was in excess of 25, as both the unemployment rate and inflation were elevated to double-digit levels. Unemployment then was actually a lot higher than the growth in the price level. This pattern continued right up to the emergence of the export-led 'Celtic Tiger' period in 1994. For more than a decade the old-fashioned misery index remained at these high-teen levels; it wasn't until 1998 that it fell back to single-digit levels. It took the first four years of the tiger economy to get the unemployment rate down from the 15 per cent level to a more manageable 7 per cent. At the same time the annual inflation rate was reduced to about 2 per cent.

Using this traditional calculation for the misery index, Ireland in late 2008 has hit double-digit numbers again, as inflation was close to 4 per cent, while unemployment has ratcheted up by two full percentage points since the end of 2006, to 7 per cent. The slowdown in construction has made its presence felt in the growing dole queues, with a thousand workers per week being laid off during 2008.

Rather than use the traditional misery index, it would make more sense and be of more interest to add the annual growth in house prices to the equation, alongside increases in unemployment and the cost of living. This revised misery index has more appeal, because it reflects the three most important things to the individual salaried worker: their sense of job security, the reduction in the earning power caused by general price inflation, and their changing net worth caused by the change in value of the biggest asset on their personal balance sheet: their home.

Despite living in a new era of globalisation that has supposedly reduced chronic inflation, such as that experienced in the late 1970s, caused largely by the successive oil shocks back then, the general price level appeared to be on an upward tack once more. Furthermore, we had crude oil at $147 per barrel, and we appear to be adjusting as a society to generally higher energy prices, not to mention the knock-on effects on food prices as well. These food and energy prices have moderated, though, in part because of the stronger euro and in part because of reduced demand caused by the economic slowdown. It would be fair to say that declining inflation or 'disinflation' may be short-lived, lasting only one to two years (no economists are predicting outright price falls or 'deflation' other than a temporary phenomenon that may occur in the summer of 2009 because of year-on-year effects), reflecting lower interest rates. Thereafter, ECB rates and global economic growth are expected to begin rising again from 2010.

The simple equation for the new misery index is as follows:

Misery index = inflation + unemployment − annual change in house prices

The first two components are included because as they rise our wellbeing falls. The last component has a negative sign because as home values increase our misery falls, but when home prices drop our misery level rises. This makes perfect sense.

The other main reason for including the annual rate of change in the value of property is that it's such a strong overriding factor. For instance, if inflation and unemployment were both on the up but so too were house prices, the majority of people wouldn't care too much as long as they kept their job. Because if they had to pay an extra hundred a month at Tesco while their home was appreciating by €50,000 per year, would they really care? Therefore the house-price factor is highly intuitive, as it reflects the 'state of the wealth of the nation'. Conversely, if we take the situation that exists today, following two years of declining home values coupled with persistently higher inflation, added to a creeping increase in unemployment, then clearly things were not looking so good. Given too that Ireland has never experienced such a sustained decline in home values, more than twenty successive months by the winter of 2008, it might be interesting to compare the misery index today with where it has been over the past decade or so.

This is precisely what our next illustration shows. A cursory glance is all that's needed to see that the revised misery index sets a new record.

The starting date was chosen to coincide with the PTSB-ESRI house-price index, which began in the spring of 1996, so year-on-year annual movements could not be recorded until the beginning of the following year, 1997. Furthermore, four periods of interest have been annotated on the graph. The first was in the peak of the export-growth era of late 1998, when national output was increasing at double-digit rates, inflation was very subdued and the unemployment rate halved over the previous four-year period. Not surprisingly, then, capital appreciation in the housing sector was huge, as annual home price inflation was running between 25 and 30 per cent. This was the golden period, when misery was non-existent, and the chart illustrates this with a low −20 reading.

Fig. 7: Introducing the new misery index, 1997–2010

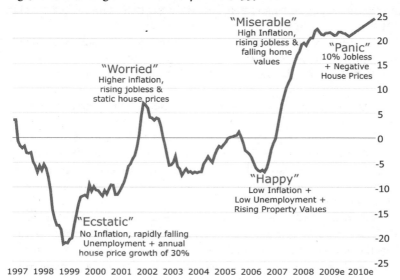

Source: Central Statistics Office, Permanent TSB-ESRI

Following the attack on the World Trade Center in 2001 the misery index became positive again, reflecting a period of greater uncertainty that was manifestly apparent with the drops in consumer sentiment indices at that time. The terrorist attacks occurred at a very inopportune time for the American economy, which was already slowing; the global equity bubble in technology shares had burst the previous year, and markets were still reeling from that shock. Nevertheless, as the picture shows quite clearly, happier times would return for the succeeding five years as interest rates were slashed and then cut again to rock-bottom levels.

Economies such as Ireland's back then were fully employed, and inflation was reasonably contained. House prices grew at double-digit rates once more. However, in March 2007 it all changed for the worse. Growth in house prices began to peter out, and annual growth fell to low single-digit levels and was in a definite downward trend. Not surprisingly, therefore, annual house-price appreciation would be negative by the summer. Compounding this situation, crude oil prices doubled in the same year, from $50 to more than $100 a barrel. Soft commodities and food prices followed suit, alongside increased mortgage interest payments due to rising European Central Bank base rates to combat this increased inflation.

All in all, then, inflation has remained considerably higher than virtually all the experts had predicted. Even Pat McArdle, the chief economist at Ulster Bank, who has a reputation for having his finger on the pulse of the constituents of the consumer price index and is the journalists' economist of choice when inflation data is due to be announced, was far off the mark with his forecasts for 2007 and 2008.

To make matters worse, the slowdown in housing resulted in greater unemployment, as housing completions began to tail off. It takes a lot more manpower to finish a house than it does to dig a hole and start the construction process, so we have yet to see the complete delayed impact of a big fall in the number of expected completions this year and certainly into 2009.

The preceding graphic has been extended to the end of 2010, using end-of-year forecasts from a consensus estimate for inflation and un-employment drawn from leading banks and brokers. These were an unemployment rate of 9 and 10 per cent for 2009 and 2010, respectively, while inflation is expected to fall back to nil in 2009 and then reach 2.4 per cent by the end of 2010 (but averaging just 1.3 per cent for that calendar year). A figure of −10 per cent was taken to be the consensus forecast for house-price growth in 2008 and similar falls predicted for 2009 and 2010. This would bring the national average home price, as measured by the PTSB-ESRI index, back to below €205,000, which represents a total cumulative price decline of 35 per cent from peak to trough, assuming that the housing recession will last four years. This is consistent with both the oversupply problem and the total experienced price falls to date.

WHAT WILL IT TAKE TO ELIMINATE THE MISERY?
So what will it take to get the misery index back to nil? Quite a lot, really, for we can expect higher inflation in 2008 and rising unemployment for at least another two years, possibly even more—especially when one con-siders that, as construction output (of which two-thirds is residential property) retrenches severely, the male unemployment rate will probably double, from 5 to 10 per cent, in a very short period. The total unem-ployment rate is therefore likely to climb to almost 9 per cent this year

alone. (Most forecasters were predicting an unemployment rate of 5½ per cent by the end of 2008, but it had reached 7 per cent at the three-quarter-year stage.) In 2009 it's highly probable that unemployment will hit the 8½ per cent mark at least; Professor Morgan Kelly of NUI, Dublin, believes we could see it hit 10 per cent eventually, and said so back in July 2007. This is the scenario outlined elsewhere in this book, where Irish unemployment rises significantly above that of the rest of the European Union. So much, then, for the pundits back in the summer of 2007 who extolled the virtues of the so-called 'strong economy', which we have been told will outperform our international peers!

Even if inflation were to drop back to a more modest 2 or 2½ per cent by 2010 and to remain subdued thereafter, given the higher unemployment rate it would take the return of double-digit house-price appreciation to return the misery index back to nil. It's extremely hard to imagine at this juncture that property growth would return to boom rates of growth within the next five years. A five-year time horizon is generally what is understood by economists and politicians when they talk about growth over the 'medium term'. But if you listen to the property market pundits, a recovery is just around the corner (just as it was supposed to be in mid-2007 after stamp duty was reformed).

It's highly likely that the residential property market will experience negative annual growth for a minimum of two more years, until the supply-demand balance is restored as well as price affordability being restored to reasonable levels.

This suggests that Éire Teoranta is poised for a prolonged period of economic misery for several years yet to come. It's entirely conceivable that the misery index could rise this year or next from its present elevated position. The future beyond the short-term (one-year) horizon is nigh on impossible to predict. However, what we can say with certainty is that absolutely nobody today is projecting double-digit house-price appreciation for 2009 or 2010. In fact the Panglossians and Über-optimists are forecasting negative price growth for 2008 and a return to low single digits in 2009. Even the most bullish property marketeer wouldn't claim that a return to this needed high growth rate is likely soon.

Only a fool, a liar or a politician would be stupid enough to claim that the misery index will drop back to tolerable levels in the short term. Of course nobody has an economic crystal ball, but the balance of probability is that at least two factors within the equation are conspiring to keep the misery index high.

We can expect to see persistent and prolonged uncertainty in prices and jobs and a continuation of the correction in the housing market as the property recession unfolds, leading to a sustained period of simply unprecedented 'misery'. We witnessed a dramatic turnaround in the misery index, from −20 to +20, over the last decade. Does anyone really believe that Éire Teoranta will return to full employment, with little or no inflation, as well as strong growth in house prices before 2012?

Not only will it take a decade for average house prices to return to the peak levels of 2006 but it could also take almost as long for our misery index to trickle back to where it spent most of the last ten years.

For those who are really interested, the last time the misery index was in the mid-to-low-20s level was during the 1992 slowdown. From a historical viewpoint, it took nearly half a dozen years for it to go back down below nil again. As the much-quoted saying goes, history has a habit of repeating itself. Even though those were very different times, the lesson that ought to be drawn from this experience is that the misery index can shoot up quickly but that it takes years, and not months, to correct itself.

The only difference today is that the economy is healthier, in that the recent unemployment rate had started from the low position of near full employment. Fifteen years ago both inflation and the fall in home prices were smaller. So, in real terms, the falling values in today's property market are substantially more severe.

It may be noted, purely as a matter of interest, that during the early 1980s property prices kept pace with inflation, so the misery index at worst would only have reflected the poor unemployment rate in the mid-teens but at best would have averaged around the low teens—only half the current level. If the unemployment rate goes above 10 per cent, even though inflation remains subdued, and we experience declines in house prices this year or next—similar to those experienced last year—we could see the misery index reach a new record around the 25 mark.

One thing is certain: an elevated period of misery is likely to persist for several years to come, even if the irresponsibly optimistic estate agents are correct in assuming a return to positive growth in home prices next year. Even in the best case scenario, the outlook is certainly not a rosy one.

Chapter 8

The stamp duty debacle

Nothing has become as polarised as the position of stamp duty reform within the VIP camp. The same Government who have been in power for more than a decade, precisely during the property bubble era and now bust, are entirely reticent about changing the status quo. They would prefer nothing more than to forget the debate and leave the stamp duty regime in place.

The reform of June 2007 was miserly, to say the least. In fact it did more to destabilise the market than anything else, because it made it easier for the first-time buyer not to buy a new home. Removing the requirement from first-time buyers on any home would have a negligible effect on receipts (because first-time buyers hardly ever paid stamp duty anyway, as they don't have the savings) but would kill off the new homes market that was already in dire straits.

Initially, refusing to budge on stamp duty was a mistake: it created another excuse for prospective home-buyers to remain sidelined. Having to do a U-turn in mid-year was a tacit admission of guilt by the then Minister for Finance, now Taoiseach, Brian Cowen. He was forced to by his predecessor. Needless to say, it has had hardly any impact on the market at all, other than being the final nail in the coffin for the ailing new-homes market.

The whole idea of paying a transaction tax to the state on your primary residence, beyond a nominal figure of, say, 1 per cent (the same as on stocks and shares), is ludicrous. Stamp duty should be abolished in the next Finance Bill. It should be replaced with a property-owner's tax, based on some conservative rateable value for each property. As we shall soon see, total receipts from stamp duty on property in 2008 will probably be around the €950 million mark, or about half what they were the previous year and a mere third of what they were in the boom year of 2006.

Taking the total value of the housing stock in late 2008 as about €510 billion, an annual property tax of 0.25 per cent would yield the exchequer stable annual revenue of about €1¼ billion. Politically it would be hard to sell, but it would be streets ahead of the present system in the equity stakes. It's unfair to punish young working couples seeking to trade up to bigger accommodation, often for personal or family reasons. At the same time, retired people with no mortgage debt living in larger homes would benefit enormously from rising capital values without any of the expense.

Will any of the opposition parties be brave enough to include some kind of substitute for property stamp duty in their next manifesto?

To be fair to the present Government, it was their predecessor in 1997, a coalition of Fine Gael and the Labour Party, in the person of Ruairí Quinn, then Minister for Finance, who introduced the top 9 per cent residential stamp duty on properties valued above £500,000, largely as a measure to deter speculators from crowding out ordinary buyers. That year it was expected that it would raise an additional £16 million for Government coffers; little did they guess that in the subsequent decade and a half it would generate billions in additional tax revenue.

Perhaps at that time it was construed as a temporary measure, or one that could be reversed at a future date or when market forces dictated. However, as the famous monetarist economist Milton Friedman was quoted as saying, 'There is nothing as permanent as a temporary government measure.' The 1997 residential stamp duty is another piece of legislation that was 'temporary' but still remains on the statute book and is voted in annually by Dáil Éireann.

Governments can and should change laws that are dysfunctional or have run their natural course. Perhaps the stagnant turnover in the property market, both residential and commercial, will facilitate this necessary change sooner rather than later. There may also be some political kudos in plugging such reform as a support mechanism for the sluggish market.

RECEIPTS ARE DOWN—WAY DOWN

As referred to already, tax revenue melted during 2008, and receipts from stamp duty began to vaporise. Indeed they would hardly be visible at all if it wasn't for the receipts from the stock market and other categories (including the 2 per cent levy on non-life insurance, cheques and ATM and credit cards, to name but some of this unusual grouping).

What a turn-up for the books! During the property bubble years of 2003–06 stamp duty receipts from residential property exceeded those from stock and shares by a factor of at least 2½ to 1. How things have changed since then! During 2007, property stamp duty was significantly down on the previous year. Admittedly that was the peak year, but it's a substantial decline nonetheless. That was the year the ISEQ overall index peaked at close to 10,000, so it's no great surprise that shares peaked in 2007.

Table 11: Breakdown of exchequer stamp duty receipts (€ million), 1995–2008

Year	Residential	Non-residential	Total property	Other	Shares	Total
1995	119	79	198	*n.a.*	*n.a.*	*n.m.*
1996	149	98	247	*n.a.*	*n.a.*	*n.m.*
1997	194	128	322	*n.a.*	*n.a.*	544
1998	213	174	387	138	161	686
1999	263	288	551	136	226	913
2000	282	392	674	201	231	1,106
2001	265	406	671	209	346	1,226
2002	349	317	666	170	303	1,166
2003	528	547	1,075	334	256	1,688
2004	752	709	1,461	348	261	2,088
2005	945	1,056	2,001	348	324	2,725
2006	1,311	1,679	3,112	218	386	3,716
2007 est.	1,096	1,340	2,436	204	546	3,186
2008	636	424	1,061	199	391	1,651

Source: Revenue Commissioners, Department of Finance, CBFSAI, Irish Stock Exchange

Both stock market turnover and property sales activity were sharply lower in 2008. By December, total stamp duty receipts were €1,651 million, against €3,187 million for the same period in 2007. It seems that stamp duty fell off a cliff in the latter part of 2007 and early 2008.

The full-year position shows a further decline of 48 per cent on the previous year, as the following annual table shows.

Table 12: Annual receipts from stamp duty, 2001–08

Year	Stamp duty (€000)	Change
2001	1,226,902	
2002	1,166,531	−5%
2003	1,688,382	45%
2004	2,088,454	24%
2005	2,725,210	30%
2006	3,716,501	36%
2007	3,185,602	−14%
2008	1,650,792	−48%

Source: Department of Finance

STAMP RECEIPTS UNRAVELLED

The exchequer doesn't provide a detailed breakdown of stamp duty receipts; but what we do know is that it largely consists of the 1 per cent duty payable on stock transfer (buying shares) and property conveyance as well as stamp duty payable on 'other' miscellaneous items. Therefore, if we know the total figure and one or more of the components, by a process of elimination we can work out the other. This is precisely what has been done here, using information on stock market turnover from the Irish Stock Exchange as well as historical monthly data on receipts from the Department of Finance. I have estimated stamp duty receipts on new credit cards, ATM and Laser cards, general deeds, bank cheques (30 cents per cleared cheque), as the payments are relatively consistent over time.

Luckily enough, the special €100 million bank levy was only for the years 2003, 2004 and 2005, so it doesn't enter into the equation for the subsequent estimated years. Fortunately, too, the Government abolished the companies capital duty (CCD) from 2006 onwards; so, like the old bank levy, we can put nil into the equation under that category.

The CCD that was levied on new companies listed on the stock exchange was considered to be a barrier to entry to the stock market. Likewise, the 1 per cent stamp duty levied on stocks and shares excludes market-makers who provide the continuous two-way (buy-sell) prices in quoted Irish companies, as this was always perceived to be a barrier to liquidity. However, as financial instruments based on those same company share prices, such as spread-betting or contracts-for-differences (CFDs), are provided by these same brokers, who are exempt from paying stamp duty (in effect on what could only be described to the lay person as their stock in trade), then only a certain proportion of actual stock-market turnover is liable for stamp duty.

At the peak of the stock market in early 2007, which coincidentally paralleled the peak in property prices, it was estimated that upwards of 50 to 55 per cent of total stock volume was facilitating CFDs bought and sold by Ireland's new, wealthier elite. For the purposes of extrapolation I have assumed that by 2008, because of lower CFD volume and higher initial margin requirements (caused by financial market turmoil), some 70 per cent of all Irish share turnover was to 'real-money' or end investors—in essence, back to 2004 levels adjusted for 2008 average volumes as reported by the Irish Stock Exchange. (For those wishing to delve deeper into the bowels of the mechanics of the revenue yield accruing to the state from stamp duties, please refer to my web site.)

The result is an aggregate stamp duty receipt time series for property— both commercial and residential. Although the residential rates vary, depending on the property price, stamp duty for the commercial property market is very easy to calculate: it is 9 cent on properties over €150,000, which is essentially on the full purchase price. In the same way that you can disaggregate property from stocks, you can disaggregate residential and commercial (although an estimated split was needed for 2007/08; I used the Department of Finance's budget estimate for 2007 at 45 per cent residential and 55 per cent commercial, and for 2008 I assumed that the split was 60-40, as commercial transactions have dried up more).

The following illustration is a graphical representation of the breakdown of stamp duty receipts in the two major categories over the last seven-and-a-half years.

Fig. 8: Stamp duty by major category, 2001–08e

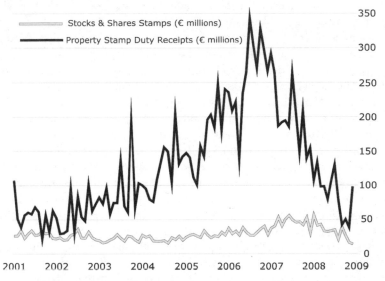

Source: Department of Finance, Irish Stock Exchange, Central Bank of Ireland

It's a very telling picture, for it gives us a reliable factual guide to the level of property turnover that the estate agents have experienced since the market downturn began. This is incredibly useful stuff.

We can see from the graph that the middle of 2006 was the boon period in terms of property stamp receipts. At one point the exchequer was raking in almost €350 million a month! That has fallen to levels averaging well below €88 million per month for the 2008 calendar year. (Property receipts fell to less than €40 million in November.) In essence, then, property transactions appear to be only a third of the levels of turnover experienced at the peak in 2006. However, adjusting for lower property prices as well as the recent reform in stamp duty rates, one can deduce that sales activity is effectually only about a quarter or a third, at best, of what it was a mere two years ago. Anecdotal evidence from estate agents' reports as well as news articles on auction activity suggest a fall of 75 per cent in sales turnover. So this reaffirms this deduction.

Okay, so 2006 was an exceptional year, probably a one-off. But the levels of turnover now being experienced are back below even pre-Bubble rates. In 2008, property transactions had dropped back to 2003 levels.

The pale line in the chart represents receipts from share trading. These have largely mirrored the overall performance of the stock market, as one would have expected, as stamp duty is a percentage of value. But the main reason that the figures for property stamp duty are important as a proxy for sales activity and therefore estate agents' turnover is that we need to understand where the market is so that we can work out how long it will take for it to clear the backlog of unsold homes.

For the record, the majority of property stamp duty receipts during the boom period arose from non-residential property conveyancing, a result of the larger deal sizes of the commercial property market, coupled with the higher rate of stamp duty rates (namely 9 per cent above €150,000). Notwithstanding this, during the bubble years, 2002–07, the exchequer took in almost €5 billion in residential property stamp duty alone! (Updates to this data will be posted on my web site.)

Suffice it to say that you don't need to be an accountant or a mathematician to see that the volume of property transactions needs to double or treble before any serious inroads are made into the unsold stock of homes. What is also worrying is that the commercial sector is really feeling the pinch too, and that will really depress the property stamp duty yield in the future.

As described at the beginning of this book, the oversupply situation and property recovery is a four-stage process. Stage 2 is a pick-up in sales activity, and a sustained one at that. It's highly unlikely that this will occur before the middle of 2009, especially now that the economic backdrop has deteriorated so rapidly.

Chapter 9

The creeping construction
conundrum

The Republic already has enough homes to house 5 million
people. According to the last census, approximately 15 per cent,
or one in six, lie vacant. The irresponsible commentators will
tell you that these are all either holiday homes or investment properties
purchased by buy-to-let investors. They are not. The stock of unsold
new homes has grown rapidly over the last three years; and many of
those vacant homes were sold to investors who failed to rent them
out.

What's more, despite the slowdown in the new homes market that
began in the summer of 2006—long before the general residential market
had peaked—builders kept building and finishing homes at a hectic pace,
despite the many warnings that prices were no longer affordable and
demand was simply not there. Property developers kept building and
planning new developments, because they thought the slowdown was a
temporary blip caused by rising rates and declining sentiment. Boy, were
they wrong!

Officially, house prices didn't begin falling until the spring of 2007; but
the industry insiders knew long before that—as early as the autumn of
2006—that the market was suffering. Estate agents had been busy selling
new developments like crazy during the first half of 2006; but the second
part of that year was as if somebody had flicked the 'off' switch.
According to the Central Statistics Office, in the two-year period from the
summer of 2006 to 2008 nearly 165,000 more dwellings were completed.
Even after prices began to tumble in March 2007, a further 112,500
new homes have been finished. How could the industry get the demand
estimate so wrong?

The housing optimists had completely misjudged the market. Many of
these irresponsible commentators, including the banks and estate agents,
misjudged the market because they believed it to be driven by economic
fundamentals. Some became convinced that the enormous ramp-up in
prices was justified by these fundamentals, such as population growth,

rising real incomes and, of course, the old chestnut of land scarcity. Add to this the historical evidence that big national price drops had never occurred in Ireland, and they believed that the worst case was that the growth in house prices would flatten for a couple of years.

The proof of this systematic misjudgement of true property demand is everywhere; it remains pervasive to this day. When you have senior political figures as well as industry spokespersons constantly referring to the 60,000 new homes that are required each year, it reinforces the public belief and perception. When you have stockbrokers such as NCB producing reports like '20:20 Vision' in March 2006, at the height of the boom, with neat little graphs of the number of young people in the country mapped to the quantity of new homes built and the relationship appears to be one to one, causality doesn't necessarily follow. Much of this growth in the over-25 population was in fact driven by immigrants, who typically rent accommodation and don't buy. Then there are outlandish population projections, accompanied by rhetoric and false claims over the record numbers of new PPS numbers being issued to non-nationals. These are then plugged in to the models, and it's inferred that huge demand was there and would follow a strong growth path.

In fairness to NCB it must be said that its projections of population growth did show a reduction in the number of over-25s over the next dozen years. It also tempered these estimates of housing demand by saying that they were based on the assumption of continued growth in immigration. However, it still didn't stop the VIPs from jumping on the bandwagon and proclaiming this to be sound evidence that many more new homes would be needed. (For a more detailed analysis of population growth and the expected demographic dividend see my web site.)

With regard to rising incomes, yes, real incomes doubled in the decade 1997–2007; but home prices trebled. In many parts of Dublin, house prices rose by a factor of ten during the same period. More than 600,000 new houses and apartments were built throughout the country over this decade. The housing stock increased by more than 50 per cent, from 1.25 million dwellings to about 1.93 million today.

Nobody disputes these numbers, as they're the official figures from the Department of the Environment, Heritage and Local Government. The total number of homes in the country expanded by 54 per cent, while the population grew by 22 per cent, to 4.4 million people. So Éire Teoranta built twice as many new homes as new people. It doesn't matter, then, if workers are earning twice today what they were earning back then: the excess supply should have kept a lid on prices. It didn't, because of the irresponsible commentary that all this was justified by economic fundamentals, which of course it wasn't.

Ergo, the classic definition of a housing bubble applies, where *supply exceeds demand, yet prices continue to rise.*

As regards land scarcity, only about 4 per cent of the 70,000 square kilometres of land in the Republic has been built on. There's no scarcity of land at all. Furthermore, there's no scarcity of zoned land for residential purposes either. The most recent figures from the Department of the Environment, Heritage and Local Government, published in its monthly housing statistics under the heading 'Supply of housing land', show that 15,100 hectares of zoned serviced land was available on 30 June 2007. It also informs us that this is suitable for building 469,837 homes. Very well: since then 86,600 have actually been built; but that still leaves a lot of available building land. Dr Alan Ahearne, economics lecturer at NUI, Galway, and a regular commentator on the housing market, has estimated that only 30,000 new homes per year are needed. This implies, therefore, that we already have ten years' supply of fully serviced and zoned land. So where is the scarcity?

In 2006 a record number of new homes—88,419—was completed. The construction industry and the estate agents would have us believe that this level of supply was justified to meet demand. But they would say that, wouldn't they? They're in the business of selling properties; the last thing they want people to know is that too many new homes have been built. Well, you might say, surely population growth has been increasing the demand for housing. Ireland was, after all, playing catch-up with the rest of Europe when it came to its housing needs.

Supply equals demand, one might think while reading an article by Marian Finnegan, chief economist of Sherry FitzGerald, in the *Sunday Business Post* in May 2007 entitled 'House-building boom steadies.' Furthermore, she asks the all-important question, 'Is Ireland still under-supplied with houses in certain locations?'

This is the usual marketing hype that's typical of the selling agents. The reality is that in 2006 our housing stock increased by 5¼ per cent, whereas the number of people resident in the Republic increased by only 2½ per cent, if we use the latest census data. Therefore, the growth in the number of new homes was more than double the pace of population growth. Even allowing for the fact that Ireland historically had larger average household sizes than other European countries, it now has a similar number of homes per thousand people, at about 437, compared with a European average of about 460. We still have more people on average per household than our neighbours: 2.5 in urban areas and 3 in rural areas.

'LIES, DAMNED LIES, AND STATISTICS!'
The average household contains 2.8 persons, compared with a European average closer to 2.2. There are three good reasons why the Irish average

is higher. Firstly, Ireland still has a comparatively high level of home ownership, at about 73 per cent, compared with 40 per cent in Germany and 56 per cent in the Netherlands, but it's only slightly above the United States, at 69 per cent, similar to Britain, at 72 per cent, but well below Italy at 80 per cent and substantially below central and eastern European countries, where owner-occupation rates are between 90 and 95 per cent. These figures may come as a bit of a shock to the many Irish people who were under the impression that Ireland has one of the highest home-ownership rates in the world. This is a myth perpetuated by VIPs and ill-informed individuals.

Secondly, because of the first point, twenty-somethings tend to live at home, in order to save a deposit for a house or apartment. There has not been a strong rental culture in Ireland, such as there is in the Netherlands or Germany, where almost half the population rents accommodation. The most recent figures from the Private Residents' Tenancy Board show that nearly 243,500 homes are now rented, out of a household total of less than 1½ million. One in six occupied properties is now a rental, seeing that almost 17 per cent of dwellings are let (with another 2.8 per cent holiday homes). So this picture is changing rapidly. From the end of December 2006 to November 2008 an additional 110,000 new tenancies were registered, while the total number of actual tenants rose from 238,000 to more than 410,000.

Thirdly, most of the population growth in recent years has been due to high net immigration—Polish, British, Lithuanian, Slovak and Latvian people coming here to work, who typically don't purchase a home but rather the opposite. Just ask yourself the following question: How many 25-year-old Latvians or Poles that you know have purchased a property in Dublin over the last five years? (Half the non-nationals resident in Ireland live in Dublin city and county.) I'll tell you the answer: fewer than 5 per cent of non-nationals have purchased a new home up to now (with the exception of British nationals, many of whom have an Irish partner, while others sold a home in Britain to buy in Ireland).

You see, the estate agents (and their economists) are extremely adept at putting a positive spin on the supply front; and the public, and in particular journalists, who feed us with a daily dose of useful information, are lazy when it comes to market information, just as the media are equally lazy in verifying these numbers. By the way, in case you're wondering why the estate agents and their analysts get so much coverage in both the property and business sections of the national daily newspapers, just pick up a copy of the *Irish Times* on a Thursday, or the *Irish Independent* on a Friday (or both on a Wednesday), and count the pages of property advertisements paid for by estate agents. If you took property advertising income away from the 150-year-old *Irish Times* the paper would probably be loss-making. At €15,000 for a full page (based on the number of property supplements and property classifieds), this adds up to about €25 million or more in advertising fees per year. In fact, given the housing slump, their property advertising income has halved in 2008, to €13 million; and the *Irish Times* responded by eliminating thirty jobs, with another thirty expected to go in early 2009.

Anyway, let's return to that very technical article, with all its references to build statistics by number of persons, population densities, stock levels and vacancy rates. Not really the kind of stuff you want to read on a Sunday morning or afternoon, is it? (By way of explanation, let me say that Marian Finnegan is not being singled out here from her peers, but she has been at Sherry FitzGerald now for almost two decades, so she knows the game better than anyone else. Moreover, her published article is entirely pertinent to the whole debate about the creeping construction conundrum.)

The article itself, though mind-numbingly boring because of the content and the plethora of statistics, was crafted very carefully. It began by raising a possible concern:

> Much has been said of late about the level of housing development in Ireland, with some concerns being expressed as to whether Ireland's housing market is oversupplied.

So she raises the question herself, just as a good salesperson will raise possible objections, without prompting. But then the rebuttal quickly ensues:

> With such a significant uplift in housing stock, it's perhaps not surprising that concerns are being raised about whether we have over-supplied our housing market. To address this issue, it is important that we view the housing stock level within the context of the population data.

We're a third of the way into the article and we get a repeat of the biggest problem facing the residential property market today, that of the huge oversupply. (We'll quantify this in a moment.) After this apparent repetition of the supply problem we're then bombarded with a plethora of housing and population statistics. I actually jumped ahead a few paragraphs on my first reading of this article, as I imagine did many a Sunday reader. We're subjected to a string of numbers that nobody is really interested in, moving from international comparisons to those along the eastern seaboard, essentially what is known today as the greater Dublin area. We're told that Dún Laoghaire-Rathdown, Fingal and South Dublin all have below-average densities of housing stock. How wonderful!

Such low stock levels suggest that the Dublin housing market is still undersupplied, a factor which will underwrite the performance of property prices in this location in the future.

So don't worry: there's apparently a supply shortage of housing in parts of the Dublin region. Or is there? Perhaps it's just that people can't afford to live there—particularly as house-price inflation in South Dublin has been several times that of the national average.

So Marian Finnegan's report made the leap from possible concerns of oversupply to concerns of a shortage of supply in one of Dublin's suburbs. This really is the argument of the glass half full rather than half empty; but it doesn't hold water. It is, in effect, a switch from defensive to offensive mode—because what agents really do understand quite well is that home purchase is hugely emotional. It's emotive because it's driven by fear—fear of being left behind or missing out.

Think about it. How many times have you heard your friends talk about their properties—how much they're worth and how much they've gone up in value? When was the last time you heard someone remark that they bought a property, paid too much, had to cut their losses and run? Probably never—though you may soon be listening to such horror stories.

The Sherry FitzGerald property guru continued:

This county analysis of housing stock also reveals a strong correlation between high housing stock and high vacancy rates in certain counties, while counties on the eastern corridor and the major regional centres display lower housing density levels and lower vacancy rates. This is perhaps best illustrated in South Dublin, where the vacancy rate is only 6.2 per cent.

She's done it again! Many readers may not make the association at first. A recent Government report, following the 2006 census, actually drew attention to the upswing in property vacancy rates since the last census was taken, in 2002. What the Sherry FitzGerald economist does here is, firstly, make a highly intuitive and very obvious statement: that higher level of stock equals higher vacancy rates. True. Most rational people would agree with that statement (so she's getting you on side). Next the report mentions the eastern corridor (the commuter belt of Cos. Dublin, Louth, Meath, Kildare and Wicklow) and the major regional centres—the cities of Galway, Limerick, Cork and Waterford—all being 'low-density' in terms of housing stock, thus implying low vacancy. This geographical grouping accounts for the majority of the population in the Republic. Finally, the reader is told that the best example of this geographical grouping is South Dublin, where the rate of vacancy is a mere 6 per cent—implying that more should be built, and right away.

Virtually all the time, estate agents revert to type and use the exception to the rule as the norm. They pick out of their considerable repertoire some isolated fact or statistic and present this to rebut any claims that nationally we may have a problem. If housing sales are down, they will tell you that viewings are up. They have an answer for everything, even when they're wrong. But you can do this only for a limited period—about one year or so. After that you get found out.

The article quoted above was a step-by-step example, in esoteric detail, of how easy it is for an estate agent to take a few facts and counter a much bigger story that nationally the vacancy rate has risen to worrisome levels. But the way that Marian Finnegan describes it one might be forgiven for believing that there's no vacancy problem. Indeed, once more you could easily be forgiven for assuming that a shortage is looming on the horizon.

Let's quash this notion once and for all. South Dublin is not Ireland, full stop. Vacancy throughout the land has risen; and when specific counties are mentioned, such as Cos. Cavan or Kerry, where the rates are 27 and 25 per cent, respectively, we're told that these are holiday homes, and isn't it great anyway that the booming economy has enabled many people to buy a second and a third home.

It simply doesn't wash. Fewer than 3 per cent of all properties in the land, or approximately 55,000 homes, are holiday homes, according to a recent Bloomberg report, citing data from the Economic and Social Research Institute—not to mention that vacancy rates have risen over the last five years in all the main urban areas too.

Then we come to the clincher, the answer to the original question posed under the title of the report.

> In conclusion, it would appear that the concerns about the housing supply levels in Ireland are largely unfounded—indeed, one could go so far as to say that there are still locations within the country that are significantly undersupplied.

There you have it. The conclusion: supply is not a problem. One can always cite an example of some location to prove a point. However, this is more likely to be the exception and not the rule. To add insult to injury, the article finished up with a patronising slap on the back to all and sundry.

> For the country as a whole, it is fair to say we have gone a long way to reduce this historical imbalance between demand and supply, a commendable achievement in a relatively short period of time.

As well as:

> Furthermore, the market has now clearly taken a more conservative view as regards the delivery of units, a factor which will underwrite the performance of the market in the medium term. Both of these factors bode well for the future price performance of the housing market, which is positive news for the economy overall.

So as a nation we have done very well to close the gap between demand and supply. Well done, everyone! But wait—there's more. Why has the market suddenly become conservative regarding the future rate of home-building? If the gap is only being closed, why do we need the rate of supply to fall sharply? Because it's more likely that supply exceeded demand—especially between 2005 and 2007—and that's why there are so many unsold new homes for sale, and why the vacancy rate nationally has increased to levels that give cause for concern.

There was enormous contradiction in this article in the *Sunday Business Post*. It read more like an advertorial than a serious story on the supply of new homes. The average reader who perused this article that Sunday with a cup of coffee in one hand and the paper in the other would finish with the thought that, Hey, the market is approaching equilibrium! So that's one less thing to worry about with regard to factors likely to affect the housing market.

The person who lives, eats and breathes housing statistics understands that too many new homes have been built, and a huge number remain for sale. Hence this article being published in the first place. At no point did the article discuss the most important factors relating to the supply of new homes, namely the price (seriously more expensive than second-hand homes of a similar size in the same area) and the quantity (especially the shortage of first-time buyers).

Meanwhile, new building continued at the rate of more than 1,500 homes per week during the first five months of 2007, up to the time this article appeared. The official figure from the Central Statistics Office for home completions during that full year was 78,027. In fact the number of new homes built in the first half of 2007 precisely mirrored the level of the first half of 2006, at 38,700 (when you eliminate the 5,000 properties that received ESB electricity meters during the first part of 2006 even though they were actually finished in 2005). So there had not really been a drop in the number of finished new homes (using the accepted measure of ESB connections) by the time the Sherry FitzGerald article appeared, though house prices had been falling and sales activity had been dead at that point for at least six months.

Sherry FitzGerald enjoyed a front-row view of what was going on at that time in the market. How responsible is this type of commentary? Whether or not it was intentional, it was possibly misguided and certainly over-optimistic.

Estate agents, of course, will argue that the continued high level of completions occurred for a very simple reason. These homes were started a year or more before, when the market was on fire and very buoyant. It takes at least nine months to a year from commencement to completion. This is correct with regard to construction logistics: it's stating the blindingly obvious. But everyone in the industry knew that the backlog of unsold new homes had been growing for at least eight or nine months at that point. Is it fair to the unsuspecting home-buyer to suggest that there was no over-supply problem?

One can't justify the unjustifiable. If supply wasn't such a problem, why was it imperative to halve the rate of new home-building from 2007 to 2009?

Interestingly enough, at the end of May 2007 Sherry FitzGerald received an awful lot of negative press attention when they hiked up their commission rates by half, from 1 per cent to 1½ per cent on residential property. Mark FitzGerald, group chief executive, said it was in response to the difficult trading conditions (read: nobody buying houses). Yet construction had not ceased! So one side of the equation (demand) had stalled, but the other side (supply) was pumping away. He received a sharp rebuttal from Senator Shane Ross, in his regular column in the *Irish Independent*. Ross criticised FitzGerald for saying that their stock of unsold homes had risen. He correctly pointed out that Sherry FitzGerald were brokers and didn't own the homes they were selling—a telling point.

To reiterate, one simply cannot justify the unjustifiable.

Chapter 10

Housing stock uncovered

To understand where Éire Teoranta is in terms of its present housing stock it's necessary first to take a quick look at how it got there.

From 1970 until 1995 the stock of residences rose from three-quarters of a million to slightly less than 1¼ million—an increase of half a million over a quarter of a century. A 'good year' for builders back then was when 20,000 new homes were built. The years 1974–75, 1979, 1981–82 and 1986 were good examples of boom building. In a bad year, fewer than ten thousand units were completed; those bad years were 1971, 1985 and 1987–88. Though the population of the Republic increased by a fifth over that 25-year period, from 3 million to 3.6 million, the number of new dwellings almost increased one-for-one in line with the population.

A central reason for this transformation was the change in average household size (a topic alluded to in the previous chapter but important here nonetheless). Back then, the average household was enormous by international standards. If you travelled back in time to when Éire Teoranta demerged from United Kingdom PLC you would be surprised at the number of people occupying each home. The following table from the Central Statistics Office shows this.

The average household used to be 4.5 persons per home; it has dropped quite significantly to a little over 2.8 persons in 2006. Back in the 1920s there were 200,000 homes that had six or more people in them. That's a third of all households.

At the time of the last census, Sunday 23 April 2006, there were 1.47 million occupied homes in the Republic, out of a total then of slightly less than 1.8 million homes. The vacancy rate was therefore estimated at 15 per cent.

The declining trend in household size may be attributed to economic success, less emigration and changing social values, such as the increase in divorce and the number of single people living alone. The first column in the CSO table shows that the number of one-person households has skyrocketed: it has virtually doubled within the last twenty years, to almost 330,000. Another factor that's equally important is the increased female participation in the work force, which goes hand in hand with declining fertility rates. More women are choosing a career over children. Many women have to work just to pay the mortgage.

Table 13: Average number of persons per household (000), 1926–2006

	One	Two	Three	Four	Five	Six+	Number of households	Average
1926	51.5	98.4	102.7	96.2	82.3	191.5	622.7	4.48
1936	60.6	111	111.5	100.1	82.9	181.3	647.4	4.31
1946	68.9	118.7	116.4	103.4	84.4	170.8	662.7	4.16
1961	85.4	137.3	116.9	98.2	78.4	160.2	676.4	3.97
1966	89	139.5	114.4	97.1	79.3	168	687.3	4.01
1971	103.6	150.4	116.6	102.8	84.3	172.8	730.5	3.93
1979	145	179	133	133.3	109.1	177.2	876.7	3.72
1981	155.7	184.1	136.4	140.3	117.2	177	910.7	3.66
1986	180.8	198	144.8	156.7	127.8	168.1	976.3	3.53
1991	207.6	218.5	157.8	170.9	130.9	143.4	1,029.10	3.34
1996	241.8	256.8	179.8	191.8	133	120	1,123.20	3.14
2002	277.6	333.7	227.8	223.2	134.9	90.8	1,288.00	2.94
2006	329.4	415.5	265.4	243.8	137.3	78.1	1,469.50	2.81

Source: Central Statistics Office

There are lots of reasons why homes today have fewer occupants. The main thing is not to get hung up on listing these different factors but to understand that this major social change was a one-off: it was playing catch-up with the rest of Europe and the developed world. The EU average household size today is 2.2 persons per home. Ireland has moved a long way towards that average.

Since the 2006 census more than 180,000 new homes have been built. Even assuming that all these homes were sold, and sold to single people living alone, the total number of households by mid-to-late 2008 would be approaching 1.6 million. We know too that the population continued to grow in 2007 and 2008, because of the record number of babies born and the continued net flow of immigrants (as evidenced by the PPS numbers), and reached the 4.4 million mark by mid-2008. So the average household size would remain unchanged, at 2.75 or 2.8 persons at most.

This assumption would be flawed, for a variety of reasons. Firstly, it assumes that all buyers are singletons—highly unlikely, given the affordability problems: it takes two incomes to pay the typical mortgage in the main urban areas. Secondly, it assumes that all new homes built were sold, which they were not, as evidenced by the slowdown in sales (not to mention both salary and job cuts at the estate agents). Thirdly, it assumes that most economic migrants that moved here purchased a home, or that one was purchased by an Irish person to let to them— highly unlikely too, given the low rental yields compared with higher mortgage costs. Fourthly, it stupidly assumes that existing homes had no new additions, i.e. babies. Fifthly, it erroneously assumes that credit was widely available for singleton first-time buyers. We know this not to be true also, because of the decline in the number of first-time buyers from the Irish Banking Federation's quarterly mortgage survey.

In other words, the chances are that average household size may have actually increased in 2008, closer to 2.85 people per home. This leaves the vacancy rate heading towards 20 per cent! Think about it for a minute. If the number of households increased by 50,000 per year over the last year and a half (a generous assumption, for the five reasons listed above) to 1.55 million, and there are now more than 1.925 million dwellings, that implies a vacancy rate of slightly more than 19 per cent, including holiday homes. Even excluding holiday homes, the vacancy rate has probably risen to above 16 per cent.

But what about the likelihood that Éire Teoranta moves more into line with other countries and that the average household size continues to decline? This may indeed happen; but most of the big movement has already occurred. More importantly, though, the high vacancy rate acts as a sort of buffer that may facilitate this trend anyway, without any further home-building. With the stock of unsold new homes growing by the month, there's less need to be building as many new homes as are now still being built (1,000 per week as recently as November 2008).

In fact, even if the population continued to grow and the number of households increased disproportionately (falling household size), Éire Teoranta could take a building break for five years and there would still be enough finished unoccupied units to house everyone, even under this wildly optimistic scenario.

THE DEMAND DEBATE

The debate about what the real, sustainable level of housing demand is has been raging now for almost a year. Before that the estate agents had their way with their sophisticated 'lick-your-finger and stick it in the air' model:

$$Demand = supply + whatever\ we\ say$$

The problem stems from the fact that 'supply' is known, whereas 'demand' is not. We have mountains of data on new-build completions, structural guarantee registrations and local authority commencement notices, as well as planning application statistics. We're not told sales figures. These are a closely guarded secret, with the estate agents and their umbrella organisations hiding behind the Data Protection Act. (Heaven forbid that a seller's privacy rights might be violated.)

This creates a lot of confusion in the market. The debate has become polarised, the academic economists versus the VIP economists (including the Construction Industry Federation and the Irish Home Builders' Association as well as the ruling Fianna Fáil party).

A regular writer in the *Sunday Independent* on the property market, Dr Alan Ahearne of NUI, Galway, wrote at the beginning of March 2008:

> But is there really an annual demand for 65,000 new homes? The answer is almost certainly no. On average 3 people live in each house. So our population would need to increase by 195,000 people each year to fill 65,000 new houses. That translates into annual population growth of about 4½ per cent. Such a rapid rate seems implausible. Our population has been growing about 2 per cent annually over recent years. Davy's economist Rossa White is pencilling in population growth of 1½ per cent over the next few years, as inward migration slows. From the discussion above, this implies annual demand of roughly 22,000 new units.
>
> The number of people per house may continue to decline, and there may be some demand for second homes and replacement homes. But adding in these factors still sees demand below 30,000. Worse still, the focus on new housing output ignores the houses that are currently empty. To calculate total supply, we need to consider them also.
>
> The reality is that all the spin in the world can't change the simple fact that at current prices the supply of homes vastly exceeds demand. Not for the first time, a bit of simple arithmetic casts serious doubts on vested interests' optimistic predictions.

What he says here is factually correct; the only assumption or guess is about expected population growth. He makes the point that supply exceeds demand, which it does—otherwise there wouldn't be the big supply cuts by the builders. He also makes the point that the VIPs, and the estate agents in particular, conveniently forget about the 350,000 vacant properties. If 55,000 of these are holiday homes, the balance, more than a quarter of a million homes, are lying vacant.

Some of these may be owned by wealthy Cork solicitors who like to keep a *pied-à-terre* in Ballsbridge for when their team is playing in Croke

Park or when they have to travel to the capital and spend a couple of nights a month there. But these professional types around the country that could afford a flat in Dublin are few and far between. There may be another 5,000 apartments around the country that are used for such purposes. The bottom line is that there are at least a couple of hundred thousand vacant homes, many still new and un-let because their owners bought them 'off plan', then refinanced them when 'built', as prices had risen, but have yet to sell them on and may be forced to rent them out to generate some income.

Whichever way you look at it, you cannot disguise the fact that the number of unsold vacant homes has grown to an unprecedented level. Worse, it's still growing.

A fortnight after the Ahearne article a rebuttal ensued. Dr John McCartney, head of research at Lisney, the estate agents, wrote a reply to the Ahearne article in the same paper. It began: 'Slowdown will help build stable future for our housing market,' with the tag line 'The shrinking size of the average household is [the] key to calculating future housing needs.' However, as we have already shown, the average Irish household size is no longer shrinking.

McCartney criticises Ahearne's methodology as over-simplistic:

Writing in the *Sunday Independent* two weeks ago, [the] Galway econ-omist Alan Ahearne suggested a continuing need for 22,000 housing units per annum. In arriving at this figure, his methodology was simple. He assumed 1½ per cent population growth, which equates to an increase of about 65,000 persons per annum. He then simply divided by three, as this approximates the average number of persons per household. Allowing for replacement houses and second homes, Dr Ahearne concedes that this figure could go a little higher than 22,000, but insists that our long-term housing requirement is less than 30,000. While the methodology underpinning these calculations is appealingly simple, it may also be seriously flawed. Surely, our additional housing requirement depends not on average household size, but rather on the size of newly formed households? This makes a critical difference to our sums.

So far so good. McCartney starts off by saying nothing new: we all know it's household growth and not population growth that determines the demand for new homes. The bubble period saw greater household growth than population growth; that's why the vacancy rate increased. However, the writer then goes on:

Between 2002 and 2006, the number of households in Ireland grew by 181,563. In the same period our population increased by 322,645. This means that new households are much smaller than the national average, with each consisting of 1.78 persons. Of course, this makes perfect sense; the people who set up new homes are typically singletons and couples. By dividing our 65,000 population growth by this figure of 1.78, we immediately get a requirement for about 37,000 new houses. But if we factor in a further 7,000 units every year to replace derelict properties (the estimate used by FÁS), and allow 15 per cent for second home demand, the annual requirement rises to over 50,000. Indeed, if we're a little more optimistic about migration and assume that population growth only slows to 2 per cent per annum from its current rate of 2½ per cent, it is easy to envisage a need for up to 64,000 new dwellings per annum.

To the lay person this may look like an innocent debate—two sides of the same story but with vastly different conclusions, based on varying assumptions. It's not. So let me explain why in greater detail.

McCartney began with some factual data (though he was slightly out on the demographic data, as the change in population was +315,726 between the census of 2002 and that of 2006; but who's going to argue over trivia like that?). It was factually correct to state that the number of new households was 181,500 or thereabouts, according to the CSO numbers. But he doesn't take into account the fact that half the population growth was among newborn Irish. From the first quarter of 2002 to the second quarter of 2006 (the period between the censuses) 278,000 babies were born in the country, while 128,000 deaths occurred. He took his figure of 1.78 persons per new household formed by simply dividing the increase in population by the increase in household number. But half the population increase was due to newborn infants, who don't live by themselves, and certainly don't buy homes!

He went on to say that the new homes were purchased by singletons and couples, which is highly intuitive. But he omits the number of new homes built over the same period. From 2002 to 2006 almost 300,000 new homes were completed, but McCartney argues that new households went up by only 181,563. That means that nearly 120,000 of those were left vacant—for whatever reason.

Mathematically, the way to estimate the difference in new household size is very straightforward. In the CSO table at the beginning of this chapter we can see that the last two rows of the last two columns on the bottom right tell us everything we need to know about the changing household size. First multiply the number of households by average size for 2002, then repeat for 2006, for each one gives a population estimate.

Next subtract the 2002 population figure from 2006, and then divide by the increase in the total number of households. Result: the average new household formed contained 1.9 people. If it didn't, the sums wouldn't add up and the official Government statistic of 2.81 persons per home would be inaccurate.

Next Dr McCartney makes the leap forward to projected population growth, using this new low average household figure; he gets a requirement for about 37,000 new dwellings. Again he completely ignores the fact that there are vacant ones already there, just crying out for carpets and curtains!

Another giant leap of faith he makes is that the replacement rate—the rate at which older homes need to be knocked down and rebuilt—is about 1 per cent of all the properties built before 1970, or about 7,000 every year. This is a clear over-estimation of the replacement rate. Homes are built to last a hundred years or more, especially those built in the nineteenth century: they were built to last centuries and are certainly of superior quality to the cavity-block, stud-partition interior-walled homes of today. He attempts to give the number a stamp of respectability by stating that it's the same estimate used by FÁS, the employment and jobs agency. If I wanted to get specific information on construction data, FÁS wouldn't be my first port of call.

He takes the biscuit when he makes the outlandish claim that one out of six Irish people have two homes or are in the market for a second one when he asks us to allow 15 per cent for second-home demand. Curiously enough, 15 per cent is precisely the proportion of all vacant homes in the country, including holiday homes, according to the CSO data from the 2006 census. The Lisney guru has developed a new mathematical model for vacancy rate:

Vacant property = holiday home

Someone should probably tell those wealthy Cork solicitors that they shouldn't be using their family's 'holiday home' as a *pied-à-terre* for work purposes!

Once again, it's a classic case of the estate agent making giant leaps of faith between supply and demand, and making erroneous assumptions to justify present reality.

But it didn't end there. John went on to become even more optimistic, suggesting that population growth will probably slow to only 2 per cent per year (incredibly optimistic for a country heading into recession) and that as many as 64,000 new homes would be required each and every year. It gets worse:

This figure, it has to be said, is consistent with the estimates of most economists, as well as with the figures attributed to the Tánaiste and the Construction Industry Federation. It would be wrong to dismiss these arguments as pedantic or trivial, because their implications could be immense. On the employment front, the difference between 64,000 and 22,000 housing completions per year is about 77,000 construction jobs. But there are also implications for the corporate sector. The prospects for our construction, materials and financial services companies, not to mention the pension funds that invest in them, must surely depend on our long-term house-building requirement.

Most importantly, however, there are implications for the property market. On the basis of my calculations, current house-building levels appear to be below our long-term requirement. Everything else being equal, this should support residential property prices in the medium term.

So there you have it. If the Taoiseach and former Minister for Finance, Brian Cowen, agree with McCartney, as well as the Construction Industry Federation, it must be true.

The present head of the Construction Industry Federation is Tom Parlon, a former Government minister who lost his Dáil seat in the 2007 general election. Tom Parlon has been consistently banging the drum, on radio and television, that 60,000 new homes per year are needed.

The statement by Dr McCartney that it would be wrong to dismiss these arguments as trivial because they're so vitally important for the economy is an understatement. Of course it's true. But he also asserts that many economists' predictions of housing demand are similar to his own and that of the Construction Industry Federation. These are the very same VIP economists who got it wrong on the way up; why should we believe them now on the way down?

SUPPLY-TAP THREAT IS NO THREAT AT ALL!

The VIPs always resort to fear tactics and threats. The supply tap can be turned off quite easily and very quickly but takes a long time to come on stream again, they say. Therefore, as supply is cut now, this could lead to a scarcity—demand exceeding supply—which could squeeze prices up sharply. This is absolute nonsense; utter nonsense.

Supply is being cut because it's considerably greater than demand. And if equilibrium is reached within the next five years (the 'medium term') and it does necessitate increasing supply again, it won't be an immediate problem because of the big cushion of vacant homes that will have to be sold first.

Or are the VIPs assuming that these vacant homes are all holiday homes, or that they will be sold very quickly, thus eliminating the backlog within a couple of years? If this is true, they should stop firing employees and start hiring more in preparation for the increased sales activity that's looming on the horizon.

Here are some examples of the propaganda used by the industry umbrella organisations, beginning with the director of the Irish Home Builders' Association, Hubert Fitzpatrick, writing in the *Sunday Independent* on 3 February 2008:

> Another factor to be considered is the very rapid supply-side response to the uncertainty in the housing market. House builders have significantly scaled back activity. Registrations, for instance, which are a useful indicator of housing starts, fell by over 50pc last year, with the decrease even more pronounced in key growth areas.
>
> Based on the above, the likelihood is that 45,000 new homes will be built in 2008, about half of the 88,000 built in 2006 and significantly below the estimated medium-term demand for housing in Ireland. The Department of the Environment, Heritage and Local Government estimates that 600,000 new homes will be needed in Ireland over the next 10 years. Output below this figure creates the prospect of demand once again exceeding supply in our main urban centres.
>
> The signs are that this imbalance is already occurring. During 2007, rents rose by 12pc nationally and by in excess of 20pc in some parts of Dublin. This is a direct consequence of the fall off in rental properties coming to the market and the fact that people who would previously have bought have opted to rent.
>
> The combination of very good value, continuing strong demographic growth and falling output, allied with certainty around issues such as interest rates and stamp duty, are likely to underpin a more positive and stable housing market in 2008.

First of all, registrations are not as reliable an indicator of housing starts as they once were (we cover this in more detail in the next chapter), as fewer builders are buying new-home structural warranties.

Secondly, who in their right mind believes that by 2018 we need 2½ million homes (600,000 new plus the existing stock of 1.9 million)? Even if the average household size fell further, to 2.5 persons per dwelling, this would imply a population of 6¼ million. It's totally bananas to even suggest that—especially when you consider that using the present average household figures this would necessitate a population increase to 7 million from the 4.4 million in 2008, or, put another way, a consistent growth in population of a quarter of a million persons per year.

Thirdly, the signs of a demand deficit are already occurring, because rents rose in 2007 as a delayed reaction to the doubling of interest rates by the European Central Bank, from 2 per cent to 4 per cent. Rents have actually been falling since the beginning of 2008, precisely because too many new homes were built, could not be sold and subsequently flooded the rental market. How are landlords supposed to cope when their tenants opt to rent a brand-new flat for the same or less money every month? This is exactly what happened.

His last point doesn't even merit criticism, it is such blatant and unashamed marketing for the developers. What's so positive about the 2008 housing market?

This article appeared under the heading 'A good year really does lie ahead.' Hot on its heels, one month later, more positive spin appeared in the *Irish Times* on 12 March. The title said it all: 'CIF says housing shortfall may drive up prices.' This time the article included a photograph of Hubert Fitzpatrick of the Irish Home Builders' Association with Tom Parlon of the Construction Industry Federation, below which was the opening statement:

A mismatch between housing supply and demand could see 'high levels' of house price inflation return in some parts of the Republic in the short-term, claimed the CIF yesterday.

High levels of house-price inflation returning within a year! Yippee! Sorry, it was just more CIF attempts to talk up the market. It's actually more dysfunctional to talk up a declining market than to talk it down. The latter gets you there more quickly, so recovery can begin sooner; but persistently talking up a weak and falling market just raises false hopes and expectations that may continually be dashed, again and again. Moreover, it eradicates all semblance of credibility. Here is a new equation for the construction industry pundits (VIPs please note):

$$Credibility = believability$$

If your claims are so incredible, no-one will believe you. Then they will stop listening to you.

The chairman of the Irish Home Builders' Association, John Moran, told the media gathered at the briefing that day:

Improved affordability coupled with stamp duty reforms for first-time buyers and mortgage interest relief had combined to produce 'the first shoots of recovery' in the housing market.

What country was he talking about? Surely not Ireland!

For the first time in many years it is cheaper to buy a new home than rent a new apartment.

No, he definitely wasn't referring to Ireland. Average Irish rental yields vary between 3 and 4 per cent, whereas the cost of money then was still around 5 per cent. So, it remained much cheaper to rent than to buy, not even allowing for further drops in house prices (and nominal rents, which fall as prices do).

He then said:

House builders were 'gearing-up' to meet renewed demand later this year but conceded [that] this would be unlikely to feed through into higher completions until 2010.

That's the tap being turned back on, which takes a couple of years. He followed that with the projected cuts in supply:

As few as 45,000 completions were being forecast by the IHBA this year, falling to 37,000 in 2009. This figure compared with average demand of 60,000 houses a year, implying that a shortfall could emerge as developers scrambled to boost supply into a rising market.

Again, the ubiquitous 60,000 new homes needed per year. I suppose if you say it often enough, people will believe it. Perhaps if you wish for it hard enough it might even come true. This is a common technique used by salespeople at important meetings with clients: say one thing, keep repeating it, and the client will leave believing it.

Moran then made the following strange comment:

National house price inflation over the longer term, however, would return to equal or near to levels seen elsewhere in the economy as housing supply rose to meet demand, probably in 2010 or 2011.

So what is that price growth figure, the 'level seen elsewhere in the economy'? Maybe matching the growth in unemployment? No: if people lose their job they can't afford to buy a new home. Perhaps we shall never know what he really meant.

Supply will rise again once more, to meet demand in two years' time. Ergo, the recent slashing of output will be only a temporary blip. It's funny how every problem the construction industry is faced with is seen as temporary. Perhaps the journalist who wrote this article misquoted him. There's a popular saying that when you're in a hole and hit rock-bottom you should stop digging.

Hubert Fitzpatrick was then quoted as saying

the stock of unsold houses nationally was 'playing catch-up' but said the effect of this overhang to the market had been overplayed. He said a large number of these houses were occupied by 'would-be vendors' who, when they did sell, would generate demand for new homes— providing an additional unrealised fillip to demand.

You might have to read that sentence a couple of times before you really get it. First of all, he refers to the stock of unsold homes nationally—so all homes for sale, including of course existing pre-owned houses. He admits a supply overhang but blames it on the second-hand homes market. Strange; what about all the unsold new homes? Does the Irish Home Builders' Association not care about those any more? He then proceeds to say that when these existing home-owners sell—if they're able to sell— they will want to trade up to new apartments and houses.

So the Irish Home Builders' Association—a cousin of the Construction Industry Federation—believes that first-time buyers can no longer afford to buy new homes. Only existing home-owners with properties to sell can.

It wasn't just the industry associations that were threatening us with scarcity and supply shortfalls but the estate agents as well, in particular Hooke and MacDonald, an agency that deals almost exclusively in new homes sales and doesn't sell second-hand residential property. This time the article appeared in the *Irish Independent*, written by the property journalist Donal Buckley, on 20 February 2008. The ominous heading was 'fall in residential building may lead to homes shortage,' with comments from the new homes agency's economist, Geoff Tucker.

He began with the usual guff that a decline in residential building activity could lead to shortages in important urban areas, such as Dublin, within the next eighteen months (by the summer of 2009). According to the agency, its predictions for new home starts were 35,000 nationally but only 6,000 in Dublin—quite aggressive supply figures, then.

During the first eleven months of 2008 there were 10,762 home completions in Dublin but only 4,441 starts from January to October. Total completions in Dublin in 2007 were 17,725, with total commencement notices of about half that number. All things being equal, this would suggest an ultimate drop of about a third in final completions for 2008.

Tucker went on to criticise the census vacancy figure, even the fact that Dublin had the lowest vacancy rate, of 9.7 per cent.

And yet even this is an overestimate. This figure includes second homes, properties vacant due to refurbishment, re-lettings and re-sales, and old local authority schemes that are vacated for rejuvenation.

But this data was two years old by then, and didn't include all the vacant unsold new homes that had been completed in the intervening period—homes that Hooke and MacDonald had difficulty in shifting. On this front Tucker was very upbeat, as reported by Buckley.

> In contrast Hooke & MacDonald estimate that there are about 5,500 new homes completed and available for sale in Dublin, which is less than six months of normal demand.

We shall explore this figure in the next chapter, particularly in the light of the number of unsold new houses and apartments available back in 2007 for which Hooke and MacDonald were either sole or joint agents. The article continued:

> Geoff Tucker economist with the agency points out [that] those completed and unsold properties in Dublin would be much higher if it were not for the fact that there was a very high level of pre-sales from plans during 2005 and 2006, and that a number of builders have opted to rent out units rather than leave them empty. Referring to the possible shortage he says: 'It will be at least 2010 before it is possible to get production back to required levels.'

What a shocking revelation: that the unsold number would have been greater if they hadn't been taking deposits on new schemes at the off-plan phase! Back in 2007 Hooke and MacDonald reported to the national press that they had sold 122 apartments in one development—Wyckham Point in Dundrum, Dublin—at the launch weekend in March. According to a senior director at Savills HOK, 95 of these were pre-sales from September to October 2006; they counted the pre-sales in the launch weekend to flatter the sales figures. The subsequent revelation by Tucker leaves one to conclude that this was common practice.

He mentions too that developers were now renting out vacant unsold units. Indeed, in the *Sunday Independent* on 22 June 2008 there was a feature article by Ray Grehan of Glenkerrin Homes. He spoke about one of their developments—the Grange, near Stillorgan, Co. Dublin—stating that 190 units were occupied. However, he didn't elaborate or say how many had been sold and how many had been let by Glenkerrin Homes, if any. As always, we're kept guessing.

Finally, we get the last comment that the possible shortage may occur. If it does, it could take at least two years, until 2010, to get new supply back on track. They must think the public are all congenitally stupid. There is oversupply—they admit that much. They tell us that builders can't sell new homes but have been forced to rent them. Then they expect us to believe that there may be an imminent shortage as new building ratchets down. Well, if that does occur and demand suddenly picks up, the developers can sell into the market all the new units that have been rented out, as tenants leave in the rush to buy new homes.

This article closed with the following comments:

> The reduced new home starts will put pressure on rents in the next two years in key urban locations, as will the recently reduced investor activity. Although home-buyer confidence is low at present, demand for accommodation is strong as evidenced by the buoyancy in the rental market with rents rising on average by 12pc per annum.

Once more we have the dreaded analogy drawn between rental demand and supply as buyers opt to rent rather than buy. We're told that demand for accommodation is 'strong' because of this rental demand. However, the magic figure of 12 per cent (which we will explore later in the chapter on rents) actually comes from the cso data on consumer prices. It's derived from the housing sub-component of the consumer price index and is both out of date (backward-looking, as reported several months in arrears) and based on a notional index of imputed rents.

If you're not totally confused by this you're probably an economist. If you are, don't worry about it: it's just a theoretical rental index used by the cso to estimate what rent home-owners *would have to pay if they didn't own their own home*. You're now probably even more confused. Suffice it to say that it's not based on actual rents in the market.

Right at the end of this article is the acknowledgement that the market is facing tough times for at least another year but, as always, an imminent recovery is waiting around the corner.

> New homes enquiries and viewings have increased since the start of the year, which should lead to a reduction in available properties between now and the autumn. However, it is not expected that the market will return to normality until spring 2009, but a good level of sales will probably be transacted in the final quarter of this year.

So from February (the time of the article) to October (the beginning of the final quarter) don't expect much but hang on: 'viewings' are up, and sales activity might be good towards the end of the year. Sure, they might be if prices keep falling and potential buyers are tempted from the side-lines.

By now you ought to have a good idea where Éire Teoranta stands with regard to existing housing stock. You should also have grasped the fact that there's oversupply, and that new-home sales activity is at a low ebb.

Having uncovered the housing stock situation, in the next chapter we look at the extent of the supply overhang, and the outlook for the future.

Chapter 11

New-homes supply lookout

The biggest issue facing the Irish economy in 2008 was the impact of the declining new-homes supply on jobs, growth, tax revenue, consumer sentiment and, not least, property-buyers' confidence. Don't be fooled by what anybody tells you: Ireland's house party culminated in a new-homes supply bubble that could take years to unwind. This is one serious hangover that has spilled over into the rest of the economy.

WHEN THE OUTLOOK BECAME 'LOOK OUT!'
It was the first week of July 2007. It was also my last week at Savills HOK, as I was leaving the firm on Friday 6 July. I had spoken earlier in the week to Rossa White, chief economist at Davy's, and had told him I was leaving. He wanted me to talk to a couple of his firm's clients, so we booked the meetings for that Wednesday and Thursday. Both clients were American hedge funds, based in London.

The first meeting, on 4 July, was with Ziff Brothers. They wanted to know all about the Irish property market, particularly from the viewpoint of the banking industry. Having worked at an investment bank for more than a dozen years, I had met a lot of hedge-fund managers in the past. I knew at once that they were fishing for data to support their view that the best way to 'short' (i.e. sell) the Irish property market was to execute the trade by 'short-selling' Irish financials, namely the four main banks.

The meeting went on until quite late, almost 8 p.m., having begun at about 5:30 p.m. They asked a lot of pertinent questions, the thrust of which concerned new-homes supply estimates. They wanted to know just how bad the supply problem was. I had prepared a lot of data for them, probably much more than they were expecting. Even though Rossa himself was not in attendance, they were accompanied by Ronan, an institutional salesperson from Davy's. He didn't say too much: he let them ask the questions; but I could tell that he was more than a little surprised, especially by the sheer number of new developments in Dublin, where sales had stalled. And all these guys were probably taken aback by my candour.

One of the Ziff Brothers people said to me when I went through the list of new housing schemes, pointing out the scale of each, putting the figures too into a historical context, that none of the other estate agents (and they'd been to three or four of the major ones earlier that same day) had told them about potential oversupply. Needless to say, I was astonished. It was the number 1 driving factor in the market: the pipeline of new properties completed was continuing unabated, while sales activity had fallen off a cliff. He said that the other agents had painted quite a rosy picture!

The following evening was a repeat performance. Again it was a hedge fund, Centauris. They came in with Ronan, just as before. These guys were even keener to find any negative theme they could on Irish financials. The meeting went on until 8:30 that evening.

The following day, in the financial review section of the *Irish Times,* there was the comment in an article by Laura Slattery that there had been a big seller of Irish financial institutions that day in the stock market. My guess is that it was one of the two hedge funds.

GLUT OF NEW HOMES

At that fateful meeting in July 2007 we discussed the oversupply problem facing the Irish residential property market. What the Americans call the *inventory-to-sales ratio,* the number of months' worth of sales represented by the backlog, had crept up in Ireland to pandemic proportions, and this was something the Americans fully understood. Unlike Ireland, where everybody quoted in the press is an expert, without any substance, the Americans are statistical maniacs. You only have to watch one of their baseball or football games to learn why. They love the nitty-gritty: they like granularity—down to the lowest possible detail. For the devil is indeed in the detail. It's where you learn the true picture of what's going on.

So a list of 252 new housing developments was produced. The total number of new apartments and houses in these new schemes was a massive 38,200. No, this wasn't for the whole of Ireland but only for the greater Dublin area, including the commuter-belt counties of Louth, Meath, Kildare and Wicklow. Remember too that this was in the summer of 2007, a long time ago.

There were two important caveats with that particular list that need to be covered now or else the VIPs will be up in arms, attempting to discredit this analysis, though it is based on real empirical evidence. Firstly, many of these schemes were multi-year schemes, because of the sheer scale and size. Secondly, some units in some of them had already been sold.

In the summer of 2007 the top 60 new development schemes—those with more than two hundred homes each—were as follows (the complete list would take up too many pages):

Table 14: Sixty largest new development schemes, 2007

Agent	Development	Developer	Units	Location
Hooke and MacDonald	Delmayne	Stanley Holdings	2,650	Dublin 13
Hooke and MacDonald	Phoenix Park Racecourse	Flynn and O'Flaherty	2,300	Dublin 15
Savills HOK	Abbeystone	Albany Homes	1,800	Malahide-Swords
Hooke and MacDonald	Stocking Wood	Deane Homes	850	Dublin 16
Multiple	Clancy Quay	P. Elliot	700	Dublin 8
Gunne Residential	Adamstown Castle	Castlethorn	630	Adamstown
Hooke and MacDonald	Northern Cross	P.J. Walls	600	Dublin 17
Savills HOK	The Grange	Glenkerrin Homes	550	Blackrock
Savills HOK	St Edmund	Glenkerrin Homes	525	Dublin 20
Hooke and MacDonald	Alliance Building, Ringsend	Danninger	520	Dublin 4
Multiple	Wyckham Point	O'Malley/Dorville	515	Dublin 14
Sherry FitzGerald	Hunterswood	Ellier Developments	500	Dublin 24
Coonan Real Estate	Moyglare Hall, Maynooth	Mycete Homes Ltd	500	Kildare
Hooke and MacDonald	Prospect Hill	McCabe Builders	500	Finglas
Sherry FitzGerald	Lusk Village	McGarrell Reilly Homes	438	Lusk
Hooke and MacDonald	Eden Gate	Cosgrave Group	400	Delgany
Multiple	Herberton	Maplewood Dev./Elliot	400	Dublin 8
H. T. Meagher O'Reilly	Marrsfield	Pierse Homes	400	Dublin 13
Sherry FitzGerald	Vantage	Lalco	400	Dublin 18
Hooke and MacDonald	Tullyvale	William Nevill and Sons	390	Dublin 18
Sherry FitzGerald	Castle Grange	E. P. Lynam	387	Dublin 15
Hooke and MacDonald	Parkview	Fleming Construction	386	Stepaside
Sherry FitzGerald	Farmleigh Woods	Menolly Homes	363	Castleknock
Hooke and MacDonald	Carrington	P. Elliot	360	Dublin 9
Sherry FitzGerald	Steeplechase	McGarrell Reilly Homes	355	Meath
Savills HOK	Heathfield, Cappagh Road	Manorpark	351	Finglas

Agent	Development	Developer	Units	Location
Savills HOK	Adamstone-District Centre	Castlethorn	350	Adamstown
Hooke and MacDonald	Elm Park	McNamara	332	Dublin 4
Sherry FitzGerald	Dunboyne Castle	Menolly Homes	330	Meath
McPeake Auctioneers	Cruise Park	Twinlite Developments	320	Tyrellstown
Sherry FitzGerald	Smithfield Market	Fusano Properties	314	Dublin 7
Kelly Walsh	Meadow Vale	Noonan Construction	313	Arklow
Multiple	Castleforbes Square	Danninger	311	Dublin 1
Hooke and MacDonald	Longboat Quay	McNamara	295	Dublin 2
Coonan Real Estate	Ryebridge	Merlon Dev.	294	Kildare
Savills HOK	The Village	Castlethorn	291	Meath
Hooke and MacDonald	Carrickmines Green	Hanly Homes	277	Dublin 18
Savills HOK	Levmoss Park	Park Homes	267	Dublin 18
Gunne Residential	Adamstown Square	Castlethorn	265	Adamstown
Hooke and MacDonald	Loreto Abbey	Danninger	260	Dublin 14
Gunne Residential	Parkview, Poppintree	Lyndonbarry	254	Finglas
Coldwell Banker	Island Key, IFSC	Ellen Construction	250	Dublin 1
Sherry FitzGerald	The Kilns	Ravenshall Developments	248	Port-marnock
Hooke and MacDonald	Arena Court	P. Elliot	235	Dublin 24
Sherry FitzGerald	Ashewood	Logancourt Dev.	233	Meath
Finnegan Menton	Peyton, Stoney Lane	Blackchurch Homes	232	Rathcoole
Sherry FitzGerald	Oldbridge	Springwood Ltd	224	Naas
Other	Bremore Pastures	Monkspark Dev. Ltd	223	Balbriggan
Kelly Walsh	Lis na Dara	Lisnamere Developments	222	Dundalk
Sherry FitzGerald	Belmarine	Castlethorn	220	Stepaside
Other	Newcastle Lyons	Maplewood Developments	220	Dublin
Savills HOK	Earlswood	Capel Developments	216	Rathborne
Gunne Residential	Old Chocolate Factory	Lalco	210	Dublin 8
Sherry FitzGerald	Brennanstown	Tudor Homes	200	Cabinteely
Sherry FitzGerald	Olcovar	Tudor Homes	200	Shankill
Hooke and MacDonald	Tallaght Cross	Danninger	200	Dublin 24
Hooke and MacDonald	The Gasworks	Danninger	200	Dublin 2
Sherry FitzGerald	Westfield	Emdan Developments	200	Kells
Hooke and MacDonald	Priors Gate	P. Elliot	198	Dublin 24

Source: various newspapers

In case you were wondering what the total was just for this incomplete list, it exceeded 26,450!

Let's put some of these numbers into the context of both history and expected demand. In chapter 2 there was a chart with the annual level of new homes built to date, plus estimates for expected levels for 2009—assuming that new home-building drops 66 per cent from the 2006 level to 30,000 by the end of 2009, as told to us by the Construction Industry Federation. This is only a guestimate: the construction industry collectively has to reach this new low level.

BELMAYNE OR BUST!

You can challenge an estate agent on affordability and interest rates and they will probably agree with you. The latest rhetoric from the vips is that it's a good thing that prices have come down to more sustainable levels (though they weren't saying that last year, or the year before that). The same goes for the entire issue of stamp duty reform and the negative sentiment that it has caused in the market. Both of these they have blamed for the slowdown in the market and the general malaise that they refer to as 'poor sentiment'. But they fail to realise that prices are still too high.

But ask them about supply, or the level of unsold homes, or indeed the heady pace of new development that continues unabated, and they will see red. They don't wish to come clean on the one issue that will cause customers to sit on their hands and wait for the market to cheapen. After all, this is their future fees we're talking about. Their important big developer clients' backs are against the wall with the banks on this one. They have to shift the product, or at least get the unsuspecting buyers to sign contracts and complete as many transactions as possible, before the inevitable happens and they have to—Heaven forbid—cut prices again.

The biggest new scheme on the market—Belmayne, on the Malahide Road, Dublin—had already slashed prices for two-bedroom apartments down to €315,000 just before the 'summer 2007' launch. That was a significant discount on the original price talk. Now Belmayne is noteworthy on a variety of fronts. First of all, it's the largest continuing residential development in Ireland. It's close to the 'Darndale Hilton' (the Hilton Dublin Airport Hotel) and 'Darndale Opera House' (the large Tesco superstore with the high glass roof). It has been marketed as 'Malahide Road' and is also called 'Balgriffin'. As always, a 'postcode licence' was used when marketing the scheme. (Another development in Poppintree, Dublin 11, called 'Parkview' was marketed by the developer as 'Glasnevin North, Dublin 9' in advertisements and even as 'North County Dublin' in others; but it's Dublin 11—the same as Finglas and Ballymun.)

Not only is Belmayne the biggest development, at 2,600 units, but it achieved notoriety because of the racy advertising campaign that was used: hoardings in train stations with bikini-clad women and muscle-toned guys draped over granite-topped kitchen islands drinking champagne. The newspaper advertisements were the same. The ads received more attention for their flamboyant style than for the development itself. According to one newspaper, during the first half of 2007 about €750,000 was spent on this marketing and advertising campaign. Did it work? No, not really. Informed sources (predominantly two architects, to be precise) said that only about fifty units had been sold during the first half of 2007. This was after it was widely publicised that about 300 units had been sold the previous year. By mid-2008 a spokesperson on a radio programme said that 800 units had been built so far and that 600 had been sold. That leaves just another 2,000 units to go!

At the beginning of July 2008 there was a generic advertisement on the property web site www.daft.ie for a new two-bedroom apartment in 'Belmayne, Balgriffin, Dublin 13,' placed by the selling agents Hooke and MacDonald, still at the €315,000 price. However, at the top of the property description (just below features) was the following: 'Number of units in development: 10.' This low figure might persuade potential buyers that those flats were part of a small development. The agents were probably referring to ten apartments in one block; but a block of flats doesn't constitute a development where there are fifty or more blocks in a scheme.

Watch this space, folks! Another 1,990 are available, or yet to be completed.

REDUCED SUPPLY FORECASTS

In January 2007 I was the first person to predict that the number of new homes built that year (75,000 forecast) would be 15 per cent less than the previous year; the actual outcome was 78,000. Obviously those that had been started needed to be finished, so the pipeline that year was still quite full. At that time I had the lowest new home-building forecast in the country. Davy's had ratcheted down their forecast from 87,000 to 84,000, then to 82,000, and by the summer they had dropped it to 80,000. It was becoming apparent to all market analysts that the number of new housing starts had begun to drop off sharply.

By the late autumn of 2007 it was apparent to everyone that new-home supply was going to be a big problem for the market. At this point it was evident too that the second-hand home sales activity had stalled. On 22 November 2007 an article appeared in the *Irish Times* with the following heading: 'Builders hold finished units to wait and see.' The writer of the report began with:

> With an estimated 10,000 empty apartments in the Dublin area, builders are opting to rent them out rather than try to sell them, says Fiona Tyrrell.

The estimate of 10,000 was on the conservative side. But there were also reports that a big backlog of unsold second-hand homes was brewing too, as the article continued:

> Meanwhile, Dermot O'Leary, economist from Goodbody's, says that stock levels of unsold homes in Ireland have risen steadily. There are now 42,000 second-hand homes for sale—equivalent to a 12-month supply of housing stock, he says

Again this was on the conservative side, according to the numbers being posted on property web portals, such as Daft and MyHome. Figures for unsold properties for sale back then varied from 65,000 to 80,000. The problem with duplicate advertisements made it very difficult to ascertain the true number.

Nonetheless, by the end of that year the market pundits and journalists had begun to put together the pieces of the jigsaw to reveal that there was at least one year's supply of unsold new and second-hand homes on the market. Compared with the American property market, the Irish market was in more serious trouble: the American housing sector is only suffering a backlog of nine to ten months' supply.

As we saw in chapter 6, declining stamp duty receipts, particularly on property (both commercial and residential), mean that estate agents' turnover is running at best at a third of the 2006 peak, but probably more like a quarter. Even if sales activity doubles it could still take two years or more to clear the backlog.

THE FOUR INDICATORS OF FUTURE SUPPLY
Broadly speaking, in Ireland there are four main indicators of prospective home-building activity. The obvious starting-point or first indicator is planning applications. Secondly, there are commencement notices sent to each local authority. These are only one component of 'housing starts', because each local authority may record commencement notices differently. (One may record multiple starts as one commencement notice.) The other component of starts is 'structural guarantee registrations' or the new-home warranties, as most people would call them. However, there's no legal requirement for builders and developers to purchase these. Typically, when times are good and when more homes are being built, most come with a ten-year structural warranty. Also, they tend to be a more common feature of apartment buildings than of one-off housing. As most apartments are built in urban areas, you would expect to find these with structural guarantees but perhaps less so for rural houses. The fourth main indicator is, of course, the finished property as reported by the cso, with data compiled by the Department of the Environment, Heritage and Local Government, based on esb meter connections.

PLANNING APPLICATIONS RUNNING HIGH

The beauty of planning applications data is that it sets a ceiling for what potentially may be built. Technically, no new properties may be built without planning approval. Obviously, not everything that's applied for is approved, so the rejection rate is an important indicator of the overall planning environment.

Planning is quite cyclical in nature. Local authority planners react to the economic environment, allowing less to be granted in a downturn, and vice versa. In addition, undoubtedly less is applied for when growth is weaker, and planning applications usually increase when growth is higher. It's all common sense really, not rocket science!

Actual building and completions are less cyclical, though, because of the longer lead times, so projects have to be finished even after things begin to slow down—just as in 2007 the number of completions remained high, at 78,027 for the calendar year. This also fed into the construction employment figures, and we didn't see the big drop in the employment of building workers until 2008.

The total number of planning applications, despite what you might think, has remained high throughout 2007 and well into 2008, even though the refusal rate has increased in recent times: now roughly one in every four planning applications is refused. The next illustration shows that, though completions began to fall in 2007 by 15 per cent, to 78,000, and are expected to fall further in 2008 to less than 52,500, or 33 per cent fewer, the number of homes granted planning permission has remained high. The VIPs and the Construction Industry Federation had been trumpeting an even lower level of completions than this, at 45,000 units.

Fig. 9: Granted planning applications v. completions, 1975–2008

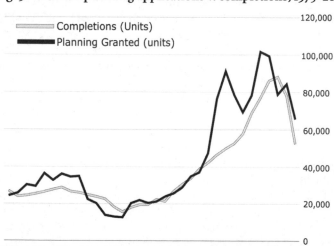

The reality is quite different, though. The number of planning permissions granted in 2007 was up on 2006—the peak year! From the chart you can see that applications precede completions by two years or more, which is normal, but the level of permissions for new dwellings approved in 2007 is more consistent with completed levels of 60,000 to 70,000 for 2009 or 2010. This doesn't bode at all well for future supply if those permissions were all followed by completions.

But of course the builders and developers don't have to build once planning is approved: they can wait. But the point is that all the rhetoric about the supply tap being turned off quickly and being slow to turn back on is nonsense. It could actually be the opposite. When you have started a building you have to finish it, in order to pay the banks, etc. That takes a year or so at least (turning off the tap). But if you have land, planning permission and a lot of unemployed construction workers you can have the tap back on again just as quickly, or quicker!

In the chart, the number of houses (one-off and scheme housing) for which permission was granted declined by 25 per cent in the first nine months of 2008 compared with the same nine months in 2007, and this decline has been extended for the remaining half of 2008. Therefore, if we took the year-to-date 2008 and annualised the granted planning permissions it would be close to 50,000 units—just houses, excluding flats!

What is more worrying is that the number of new apartments approved during the first half of 2008 was up 18 per cent on the previous year, at 12,625 (634 separate developments). The annual rate of permissions for apartments peaked at the end of 2004 at a little more than 33,000. It fell back to an annual clip of 17,600 at the beginning of 2007 but has since increased steadily to 21,000 units approved in the twelve months to September 2008. The number of planning applications for apartments is on the rise again. This is contrary to the recent stamp duty reform, which made it easier for young people to live where they want and to buy what they want: a property with its own front door.

The completion statistics of the Department of the Environment, Heritage and Local Government for the first eleven months of 2008 show that 12,252 apartments were built, or 26 per cent of all dwellings finished by type. It was the highest proportion since records began in 1994. Ireland is getting more new apartments at a time when there's a glut of unsold new homes that are predominantly—you guessed it—apartments.

So how do we justify all this? How do we make sense of all these figures? There's only one possible solution. The developers and builders have amassed enormous land banks. They have continued seeking planning approval on large quantities of prospective new housing, especially flats. Obviously, back in 2007, when the market turned in terms of price, or as far back as late 2006, when the new homes market dried up in terms of sales, they believed the other VIPs when they said that all of this was a temporary blip. The estate agents and other VIPs assumed it was all due to finance and interest rates, with a dash of negative sentiment thrown in. Boy, were they all wrong! What if this property slump turns into a multi-year 'bear' market? They have not planned for this event. Wishful thinking has been the dominant factor here. The bottom line is that they don't have to build on this land for many years, as long as they bought it, say, ten years ago. Any developer who bought development land since 2004 has paid top dollar for it and will be in hock to the banks in a big way. They may just chance it when they think everyone else is cutting back supply; but what if lots of builders think the same, all at the same time? To put it more succinctly, 'You can stop some of the builders all the time, and all the builders some of the time, but you can't stop all of them all of the time . . . from building like crazy.'

HOUSING STARTS: 'YOU WOULDN'T START FROM HERE!'
Accurate data for housing starts doesn't exist for the residential property market. Instead we're told that 'commencement notices' (which we touched on earlier) are recorded differently by each planning authority. There exists no centralised planning register that could compile all planning data using a standardised approach. Therefore, all figures for commencement notices need to be treated carefully, to be taken with a pinch of salt. Due credit to the CSO: they're flagged with a visible health warning.

So far during 2008 commencements are down sharply on 2007, by about half, which would be consistent with at least a 40 per cent forecast drop in new-home supply for 2009. The biggest proportional drops (more than two-thirds) were in Cos. Carlow, Kilkenny and Westmeath, or the new 'outer commuter belt' for Dublin, as they have lately come to be called. Rising fuel costs have probably put paid to the expansion of the greater Dublin area; however, in Cos. Clare and Wicklow the numbers have only nudged down slightly, by about a third on the previous year. Clearly, then, it's still easier to commute from Co. Wicklow, which probably has more to do with improved transport links, both road and rail.

Cos. Waterford, Cork and Limerick have all witnessed a drop in the rate of new building, very similar to the national average including Dublin. During the first half of 2008 this was not the case. It seems there was a 'Munster effect': possibly success on the rugby pitch at the international tournament level raised optimism in the southern part of the country.

The problem with all these figures is that they're base-case scenarios. Just as the planning approvals were effectually the ceiling, the total of commencement notices is the floor, as each start is one or possibly more homes. It still helps to know what this floor is or is likely to be in 2009, as what is started this year will probably be completed next year. For the sake of simplicity, though, in the next graphic we assume there's a nine-month build period between start and finish, in other words a nine-month lag.

Fig. 10: Housing starts v. completions, 1970–2010

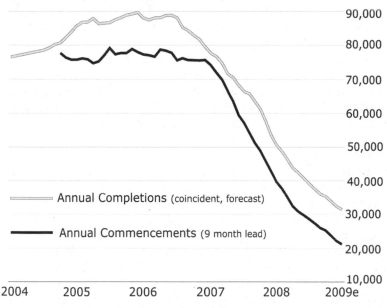

Source: Central Statistics Office

The lighter shaded line represents the annual rate of finished homes, whereas the solid dark line is the annual rate of housing starts (based on commencements) lagged or delayed by nine months. The relationship appears quite strong and would appear to support the VIPS' claims. However, there's one strong caveat. The number of commencements acts as a floor or minimum number, which is the same as saying that it assumes that all commencement notices were for single, one-off dwellings. The reality is that they are not; so you have to multiply this commencement number by some factor to adjust it upwards—but there's no way of knowing by how much. It varies from year to year, so there's no point in even trying.

What we can say is that it will be at least this figure. My own best guess is that the 25,000 new homes predicted for 2009, based on previous commencement notices, is an absolute minimum and could be a lot higher, possibly even 30,000 or more.

HOUSING REGISTRATIONS: A PROXY FOR STARTS, OR SO WE'RE TOLD

Because of the inherent flaws in the local authority commencement notices data, many market analysts have turned instead to new-home 'structural guarantee registrations' as a better proxy for the number of starts. Only two companies in Ireland provide these insurance warranties: Homebond and Premier (Coyle Hamilton Willis).

A bit of background information first, to explain these structural guarantees. When builders decide that they wish to offer their finished homes with a structural warranty, primarily as a marketing or selling feature, they approach either of the two aforementioned companies. Having agreed a price, the companies send out inspectors to inspect the construction at the three main stages, namely the foundations, the walls, and finally when the roof is put on. When the developer registers their development for these warranties, the registration is recorded after the first inspection. These registrations are collated and compiled by the Central Statistics Office, as well as the two insurers.

Some people in the property market view these registrations as a good proxy for housing starts, possibly even better than commencement notices. But they have their own flaws too. Unlike a local authority commencement notice, which is a legal obligation—you can't start building without telling the local authority—you may begin construction by choosing not to register your development. So, not all properties have these structural guarantees, but multi-dwelling buildings (i.e. apartments) should have. Secondly, it's often assumed by certain property analysts that these structural guarantee registrations don't include 'one-offs' in rural areas, for example in remote areas of Co. Donegal. The insurers themselves deny this. They provide them to anyone willing to pay, whether it's a developer building 250 apartments in Dundrum, Dublin, or a builder building two bungalows in Glenties, Co. Donegal.

As our thirty-year illustration below shows, registrations peaked in 2006 and have fallen very sharply since then. Indeed the annual total fell by 43 per cent in 2007 to fewer than 38,000, and during 2008 the annual level dropped another 67 per cent to the 13,275 mark. These drops have been widely reported in the national newspapers and on the television news. They're always reported as 'new housing starts', and very rarely are they qualified beyond that inaccurate description.

By November 2008 the total number of registrations had dropped to less than 500 per month. If that monthly total were to persist until the end of the calendar year, annual registrations would decline to 12,500—almost a 70 per cent drop on the previous year—implying that output for 2009 would be two-thirds less than the expected lower figure for 2008. If registrations did fall to below 13,000 this would take us back to 1993 or pre-'Celtic Tiger' levels. Who said we're not returning to the bad old days?

Fig. 11: Annual new home guarantee registrations, 1979–2008
Source: Homebond, Coyle Hamilton Willis

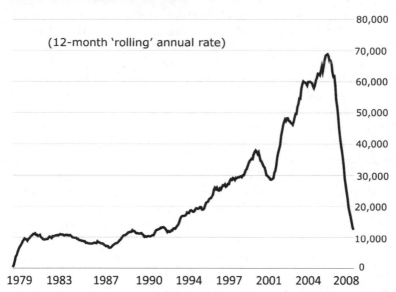

One thing is certain: if they're still a good barometer of housing starts, the new-build rate will probably contract just as sharply. These registrations on their own appear to suggest that new-home supply could fall to 50,000 units in 2008 and even less than 20,000 in 2009. This would be a level more in keeping with the natural, sustainable demand for new homes as recommended by Dr Alan Ahearne, a regular commentator on this topic.

But there are two worrisome areas that may give rise to concern about the reliability of registrations in a downturn. First of all, they're more associated with the building of apartments, which has remained high, with apartments representing an increasing proportion of total new homes. This is counter-intuitive compared with the actual data. If more apartments are being built, the level of guarantee registrations should not be falling more rapidly than all the other supply indicators—well, not if builders and developers were still subscribing to them.

This brings us to the other area of concern. Based on the historical data, the proportion of all new homes that were accompanied by a struc-tural guarantee has consistently been in the 60–70 per cent range from 1993 to 2000. From 2002 to 2004 it was even higher, at the 70–75 per cent level. At the market peak in 2006, eight out of every ten new homes were sold with one. In 2007 this number fell to two-thirds, and in 2008 it fell further, to below 50 per cent. To arrive at these figures correctly we take last year's registrations as a percentage of this year's finished units. Conceivably, if the monthly rate of new registrations was to average just 600 to 700 per month during 2009, and only 25,000 new homes were constructed in 2010, we could witness a situation where fewer than one in three new homes comes with a structural warranty.

It would appear that there's a declining propensity to pay for these structural guarantee products. But wait a minute. They don't cost that much: just a few euros per square metre, or a couple of hundred per flat. The marketing benefits easily outweigh the costs, even in a downturn. Why would developers slash €25,000, €50,000, €70,000 or even €105,000 off the price of a new home and then skimp on a selling feature that costs in the hundreds of euros?

There's no straight answer to this question. It has been put to the largest of the insurers, Homebond, but no answer has been forthcoming. Understandably, they don't wish to comment on speculation about the declining sales of their product, a published fact—the reduced sales figure.

A conspiracy theorist could be forgiven for thinking that perhaps as everyone—market analysts and commentators—was using them as proxies for new housing starts, then if builders stopped purchasing them everyone would naturally assume that new starts were falling at a much faster rate than they were (the supply tap being turned off).

This may appear quite tenuous to some, but the biggest fall so far has not been in planning applications, commencement notices or even completions but in structural guarantee registrations. It's this that receives most attention in the media. Completions are not as relevant today, as they reflect what was started a year ago or before. Planning approvals don't necessarily result in new properties: they're not always built; while commencements are not a like-for-like comparison throughout the country.

Only time will tell us what the real answer was. It's intriguing, all the same. Just out of interest, during the first eleven months of 2008 the counties where new-home structural guarantee registrations declined most were Cos. Clare (−87 per cent), Cavan (−79 per cent), Longford (−93 per cent), Leitrim (−76 per cent), Roscommon (−83 per cent) and Westmeath (−90 per cent). The national average fall was 65 per cent. Many of those counties are, of course, holiday counties.

ANNUAL COMPLETIONS
Housing completions data is based on electricity meter connections. Once more we're resigned to using data that may be fundamentally

flawed. First of all, some builders have the meter and electricity installed during the construction process; later they transfer the account to the home-buyer's name. This means that four walls and no roof but power on site equals a completion.

Another hiccup that actually occurred between 2005 and 2006, because of the enormous building activity, was that there was a backlog of homes built in 2005 that had to wait until the ESB could get around to connecting them in 2006. To be precise, 5,000 units were affected, 2,000 of which had meters installed in January, February or March 2006, with the remaining 3,000 installed during the second quarter. This resulted in the erroneous reporting of 93,419 homes built in 2006, when the real figure was 88,419. It also means that the figure for 2005 was under-reported, at slightly below 81,000 instead of 86,000 homes.

Anyway, virtually all property analysts account for this mistake and have amended their data accordingly. Figures for the first eleven months of 2008 have already been released, and they show that a total of 48,190 new homes (including conversions) were built. If this pattern was to continue, more than 52,500 new homes would be finished in 2008 (although completions for the last month of the year are likely to total no more than 3,000 units, thus taking the annual build for the year as a whole to 51,000). This is a considerably higher number than the figure of 45,000 that Tom Parlon of the Construction Industry Federation has been repeating incessantly in the media during the first six months of 2008— though on a television news interview in late June he murmured a figure of about 50,000 new homes to be built in 2008. Was it a slip of the tongue? Was it only rounding up by a mere 5,000 units here or there?

Recall that the economists at all the leading banks and brokerage houses have informed us that every reduction of 10,000 units equals 1 per cent off GDP growth. Given that by mid-2008 the Minister for Finance and the Government altered the official GDP forecast for 2008 from 3 per cent to 0.5 per cent when the June exchequer statement was published, these extra 5,000 new homes could have effectually doubled the Government's economic growth forecast for that year! So perhaps it could be positive news for the tax man. Not so for the housing market, however, as supply really needs to fall sharply to allow time for dwindling sales to catch up with non-existent demand.

Those who are interested in a regional view of the completions data can be reliably informed that the counties where new-home supply has dropped least are Tipperary North (−6 per cent), Meath (−17 per cent), Kilkenny (−26 per cent), Louth (−17 per cent), Sligo (−22 per cent), Kerry (−25 per cent) and, of course, the city of Dublin (−16 per cent). Nationally, the annual average decline (based on the first eleven months of 2008) has been 33 per cent.

It's a bit of a surprise to see Cos. Kilkenny and Meath appear again with less of a drop in new building, especially as they have witnessed greater declines in commencements (both down by two-thirds). Perhaps one-offs have been replaced by flats. Or, most probably, we're still witnessing a comparatively high completion rate into a weaker market, which is why the number of new starts has fallen off a cliff.

The biggest drop in completions has been in Cos. Cavan and Longford, at 49 and 62 per cent, respectively. Probably these were holiday homes. This ties in with the registrations data, so expect even further falls there in finished units in the year to come. Only five homes were registered with Homebond in Co. Longford in the first half of 2008 and 19 up to the end of November, compared with 156 in 2007, and no new Co. Longford homes at all have been registered with Coyle Hamilton Willis ('Premier Guarantee') in 2008, as against 123 the previous year!

Finally, Co. Mayo has produced an interesting statistic. Although finished new homes were down by eight hundred units in 2008, a 27 per cent decline, the number of new home starts has hardly fallen at all, with a drop of just 13 per cent. New home starts in Co. Mayo will probably fall by only 200 compared with the previous year. One possible factor could be that prices were always lower there, so those areas may not be so affected by the downturn.

If supply doesn't fall enough, the outlook may soon become 'Look out!'

Chapter 12

Land values determine house prices, not the other way around

There are two schools of thought when it comes to the value of land. The first group believes that land is one of the most valuable scarce commodities known to humanity; as Mark Twain famously said, 'Buy land. They've stopped making it.' The second group believes that land of itself has very little appeal other than utilitarian worth, such as for growing crops for food or as space for building factories, shops or houses on. The second group doesn't believe either that these buildings themselves have that much value, again other than their intrinsic worth, given their function.

The first group sees land as an indicator of wealth, a measure of substance and success. The second camp sees land purely as another factor of production, the same as money, machinery, people and intellectual property. To them it's not important if land is not even owned: it can be rented or leased. In fact they may even prefer it that way, as it's often more tax-efficient to do so.

Property has always featured prominently as a store of wealth for the rich, or 'high-net-worth individuals,' as they now like to be called. To be sure, throughout history super-wealthy people have always held much of their assets in land and property, and not just for economic reasons. Partly this is for show, as property, and particularly because land is highly visible; partly too it's because they can derive an income from it through rent; but it's also because land is a very secure form of investment. It's not a *wasting asset*, like cars, racehorses or yachts; and it's very difficult to steal. Wars have been fought for less.

There is another, perhaps less well-known reason, and that is that buying land is quite uncomplicated and doesn't require any formal education. Many affluent people have acquired a tremendous fortune through the acquisition of property and land over long periods, despite being functionally or even totally illiterate. All it took was graft and perseverance.

Then there are the unimaginably wealthy people, the industrialists, investors and software and internet billionaires, such as Lakshmi Mittal (steel), Roman Abramovich (oil), Warren Buffet (investing), Bill Gates (software), Michael Dell (computers), Carlos 'Slim' Helú (telecommunications), Ingvar Kamprad (IKEA), Sheldon Adelson (hotels and casinos) and Bernard Arnault (Louis Vuitton Moët Hennessy), all of whom are worth $20 billion and more. Even Asia's richest man, Li Ka-Shing, derives most of his wealth not from real estate, as many may have thought, but from Canadian oil (40 per cent) as well as two of Hong Kong's largest listed companies, Hutchison Whampoa and Cheung Kong (mobile phones, container ports and electricity). In fact, whether one uses the *Sunday Times* Rich List for Britain and Ireland or the *Forbes* Rich List for the wealthy of the planet, land and property doesn't really feature that much.

The fabulously wealthy are often more fascinated by intellectual property than by physical property. They made their vast fortunes by being really good at doing whatever they do and what they specialise in, rather than merely accumulating assets or property; 'For 'tis the mind that makes the body rich,' as Shakespeare put it. The super-rich are driven people, driven to succeed, and wealth is seldom the primary motive. When has anybody heard Warren Buffet, the 'Sage of Omaha', ever talk about buying land? In truth, he doesn't. He comes from a part of America where land is both plentiful and comparatively cheap. For instance, today one can buy a quarter-acre plot in Omaha for $20,000. The city of Omaha has a population of nearly 420,000 people, with the same population density as the greater Dublin area or Co. Cork.

Closer to home there have been widely publicised power struggles between the Irish billionaires, such as the continuing feud between Denis O'Brien and Dr Anthony O'Reilly for the control of Independent News and Media PLC. Both men have made their vast fortunes from a variety of sources, none of which include large land sales or divestment of large property portfolios.

Similarly, Ireland's richest man, Seán Quinn, who at one time had an estimated wealth of €4.7 billion, is more concerned with the acquisition of a major stake—15 per cent—in Anglo-Irish Bank, Ireland's fourth-largest bank by market value, than in buying the land that the bank has been so quick to lend on during the boom years.

Sometimes the only land these billionaires are interested in is the country homes and estates that they own. Increased wealth in Ireland has directly led to an increase in the demand for period homes with considerable acreage attached—so much so that this phenomenon has had a big impact on the price of agricultural land.

IRISH FARMLAND, THE DEAREST IN EUROPE

In May 2007, together with David Ashmore of Savills HOK, I wrote an article specifically tailored for the *Irish Farmer's Journal*. The tag line in the title was that Irish agricultural land values were approaching €60,000 per hectare. The article began as follows:

> During 2006 average agricultural land values appreciated in Ireland by nearly two fifths, from C13,300 per acre to about C23,600 per acre today. On a price per hectare basis (more commonly used for international comparisons), this represents a figure of €58,450 per hectare. One of the main driving forces behind this recent development is the increased personal wealth in the country prompting many businessmen to purchase 40–60 acre farms as a lifestyle choice. Another equally significant factor has been the incremental selling of small tracts of agricultural land for development purposes, with the resultant proceeds of such land sales being reinvested into an increasingly scarce commodity, namely more farmland. This virtuous circle has been further compounded by the chronic lack of supply. We estimate that land sales of approximately 8,000 hectares per year represent a mere 0.18% of the total stock of farmland in the country.

The exceptionally low turnover of agricultural land was identified as a major factor in driving up land prices. Indeed, thanks to David's diligent research and the excellent transparency provided by the *Irish Farmer's Journal*, we were able to make the following observation:

> In 2006 only 100 farms in excess of 100 acres came to the market. Of those 26 farms were larger than 200 acres, whilst a further 74 farms that were sold were between 100 and 200 acres.

We contextualised the turnover of farmland by using a direct comparison with France, the largest agricultural country in the European Union. France has a total area devoted to agriculture of about 135 million acres. With the turnover of farms there and the matching acreage it was possible to estimate that on average each piece of farmland changes hands once every seventy years (based on annual turnover of 1.4 per cent of farms). The corresponding statistic for Ireland was that each field changes hands on average every 555 years!

The article went on to discuss the differences between population densities and land values, the broken linkage between farm incomes and land values, and the increased demand from 'hobby' farmers. Included was a graph of the meteoric rise of agricultural land values since 1999. (The chart began in 1973.) There was also a large map of Europe, with each country shaded from pale pink, as 'cheap', to deep burgundy, as 'expensive', the most expensive being Ireland. This received a lot of attention in the media at that time.

There was an interesting parallel, though, between farmland values and residential property prices since the turn of the century.

Prior to 1999, Irish farmland values were on a par with those in England—at about €10,000 per hectare—now values in Ireland are five times that of England. Farmland prices have trebled since 2004. On a pan-European basis, Ireland now has the highest land values and they are set to rise further!

Clearly the increased wealth in the country, coupled with the scarcity of land caused by exceptionally low turnover (i.e. availability), contributed to agricultural land values having risen 500 per cent over a relative short period—less than a decade. Most of this price explosion occurred during 2005 and 2006, the same time that property mania gripped the residential market. Evidently, profits in one market trickled down to the other.

We summed up the results of this occurrence with a regional snapshot of typical farmland prices around the country.

Agricultural land values exploded during 2006. Average prices per acre in Dublin are now more than €45,000, in Kildare €36,000 and in Meath, Wexford and Wicklow prices range from €23,000 to €25,000 per acre. For the rest of the country, typical farmland values are averaging around the €20,000 per acre mark, with the exception of the West or Northwest, and Roscommon where prices are still around the €13,850 an acre level.

Those who are interested in farmland prices should read the *Irish Farmer's Journal*, in particular Shirley Busteed's round-up of auction results, sales prices achieved and what is coming on the market. Estate agents, take note: the *IFJ* doesn't hide behind the Data Protection Act, and agricultural land sales are a unique area where there is real transparency in property prices.

The main conclusion of the research was that Irish farmers should look abroad for better returns. Indeed it's possible to rent farmland in eastern Europe in 2008, such as the new EU countries of Bulgaria and Romania, for as little as €45 per acre per year, though crop insurance would be strongly recommended. It's obviously considerably cheaper for Irish farmers to buy farmland in Scotland or England than in Ireland if they don't wish to stray too far from home.

However, just as property prices (both residential and commercial) have fallen over the last year and a half, so too have agricultural or farmland values. At the peak of the market, Irish farmland was regularly achieving €15,000 to €20,000 per acre, but by the end of 2008 those prices have dropped by €5,000 an acre. It appears that even unzoned agricultural land prices are not immune to the vagaries of the retrenchment in the market and have fallen by a third already. Note that farmland values have dropped by more than double the decline registered up to now in residential property (as measured by the PTSB–ESRI index).

DEVELOPMENT LAND
The joys of the metric system: all advertising of land for sale must, under EU rules, contain a measurement in hectares (followed by acres, if so desired). The younger generation have no problem with the metric system, as they have grown up with it; older people, including many of today's property developers, prefer the traditional 'imperial' system of acres, square feet and square yards. As a rule of thumb, 1 acre is a shade more than two-fifths of a hectare; in other words, 2½ acres equals 1 hectare. We shall use either unit, or both, in the following section on development land.

If you thought residential property prices experienced spectacular growth over the last decade, this pales in comparison with the increase in the price of development land. The best way to see how much land prices have appreciated is to use Dublin city prices as an example, especially the most sought-after postal districts of Dublin 2 and Dublin 4.

In 1992, before the 'Celtic Tiger' era was even thought of, a 5½-acre site in Ballsbridge, Dublin 4, fetched a record price for the time of £5.6 million, the equivalent of €7.11 million (though back then the Irish pound bought considerably more than the euro today). The price per acre then was €1.3 million, which would be €2.15 million in 2008 terms, given the 165 per cent increase in the consumer price index in the intervening decade and a half.

That particular piece of development land was the old Johnston, Mooney and O'Brien bakery site. Anyone brought up in Dublin over the last two or three generations would be intimately familiar with their products, having grown up eating them daily.

Four years later, in the middle of 1996, and not a million miles away, the 7.8-acre site of the old gasworks in Barrow Street, off Grand Canal Street, came on the market with an estimated guide price in the region of £5 to £7 million. It was sold for somewhere between £9 and £10 million, which would be the equivalent of about €1.63 million an acre then, or €2.7 million an acre in 2008 terms. Later, Iarnród Éireann built a new DART station, Grand Canal Dock, next door to this development. It's also adjacent to the European offices of Google, the internet search engine company. A decade later land in this more industrial part of Dublin 4, such as Merrion Road and Leeson Street—the office-type locations, as opposed to the more up-market Ballsbridge embassy area—was selling for at least €32 million per acre in 2006. That's twenty times the price of development land ten years earlier or, in annual return terms, the equivalent of +35 per cent per year compounded.

Another good example of how much Dublin development land has appreciated, at a multiple of the rate of growth in house prices, and using the same location, was a 12.2-acre site in South Bank Road, Ringsend, Dublin 4, sold by AIB in November 1998 for £23 million, generating a profit of £20 million on its original purchase price back in 1988 of £3 million.

The biggest development-land sale in the history of the country occurred on the same road in October 2006 when the Irish Glass Bottle Company's 24-acre site attained a price of €412 million, or €17.2 million per acre. (AIB bought its South Bank Road site in 1988 for a mere €312,000 an acre. Its selling price in 1998 equalled €2.4 million an acre.) The Glass Bottle site fetched fifty-five times the price per acre achieved eighteen years earlier. This is a good like-for-like comparison, and it represents an annual average growth in capital appreciation of 25 per cent every year, continuously! Contrast this with the national average home price in 1988 of €51,028, rising to €309,206 over the same period (using the house-price index of the Department of the Environment, Heritage and Local Government), which was an average price gain of only about 10 per cent annually. Still, that was impressive by international standards; but land for building houses on increased in value at two-and-a-half times that rate.

Earlier in this book it was mentioned that estate agents are fond of the saying that 'house prices drag up land values.' It was shown that the reverse is true: land prices push up new-home prices, because they're an inevitable cost of construction and development. Professor Maurice Roche at NUI, Maynooth, has written extensively on this subject. He found that the price of development land for residential purposes had more to do with differential zoning and planning use, as well as density, than what existing homes were selling for.

During the spring of 2007 I recall a discussion with my boss, the former managing director of Savills HOK, on his return from Leinster House following a briefing by several of the large estate agents to a cross-party group of TDs. He remarked to me that the penny didn't drop with the politicians about how home prices drive up land values. It didn't drop with me either, because that afternoon I was going through the firm's extensive data-base of development-land sales over the previous three-year period and I found that land prices—not just in Dublin but nationally—had risen by several hundred per cent in many instances from 2004 to 2006, yet house prices had appreciated by only a small fraction of that.

If house prices really did dictate development-land prices, why did land appreciate by more?—consistently more, as we have just seen in a couple of illustrations. The short answer is that home prices rarely go up by that much, but the land they sit on does. Land is more valuable than the buildings that sit on it. Land has scarcity value. So, land prices are more volatile than building prices.

DUBLIN'S GOLDEN TRIANGLE

The most expensive land in Ireland, including Aylesbury Road and Shrewsbury Road, is in Dublin 4, closely followed by Dublin 2. In particular, there's a 'golden triangle' of the most sought-after and therefore priciest land in the city. The vertices of this triangle stretch from the famous Ha'penny Bridge at the south side of the River Liffey to George's Quay (opposite the Financial Services Centre), across to Leeson Street Bridge and down to Ballsbridge.

To walk this golden triangle one would begin at the Ha'penny Bridge, walk up to Dame Street by the Central Bank, stroll across Drury Street to St Stephen's Green Shopping Centre and along the green to Ely Place, then to Lower Leeson Street. From there you would travel along the bank of the Grand Canal, down Wilton Terrace, back to Upper Baggot Street, out to Ballsbridge, and back across by Merrion Square (included), just missing Lower Mount Street and the National Maternity Hospital in Holles Street.

This takes in Lincoln Place as well as Clare Street and the main section of Pearse Street; it includes Townsend Street, and so back to George's Quay. It therefore encompasses Trinity College in its entirety, as well as the main shopping districts of Grafton Street, Dawson Street and of course Kildare Street, the home of Leinster House and some of Government Buildings.

A good method of comparing the price of land is to look at the price per acre. The newspapers do this all the time: they love to eulogise about how much someone paid for a particular site, especially if it sets a new record for that area.

Our top 30 price-per-acre chart below shows that the top 15 sites in price paid per acre were almost all in Dublin 2 or Dublin 4, with two notable exceptions: Dún Laoghaire and the city of Galway. Most went for a substantial premium over the guide price, with the sole exception of the Eyre Square site in central Galway, which had been expected to reach €15 million.

Table 15: The most expensive Irish land ever sold

Street	Area	Acres	Hectares	Quoting price	Sale price	€/acre	Premium	Agent	Sold
Franklin House	Dublin 4	0.19	0.08	25,000,000	25,000,000	133,000,000	n/a	H. T. Meagher O'Reilly	Jun. 2006
Allianz, Burlington Road	Dublin 4	1	0.40	75,000,000	100,000,000	100,000,000	33%	Lisney	Feb. 2007
Tara Street	Dublin 2	0.5	0.20	40,000,000	48,000,000	97,124,555	20%	Harrington Bannon	Feb. 2006
Shelbourne Road (OPW)	Dublin 4	0.378	0.15	27,000,000	35,891,000	95,000,000	33%	Lambert Smith Hampton	May 2006
Carrisbrook House	Dublin 4	0.52	0.21	45,000,000	46,300,000	89,223,549	3%	Savills HOK	Dec. 2006
40–47 Fleet Street	Dublin 2	0.4	0.16	30,000,000	33,200,000	83,972,271	11%	Lisney	Nov. 2006
UCD Veterinary College	Dublin 4	2.05	0.83	100,000,000	171,500,000	83,618,781	72%	Lambert Smith Hampton	Nov. 2005
Hume Street Hospital	Dublin 2	0.37	0.15	25,000,000	30,000,000	80,937,129	20%	CBRE	Nov. 2006
Lad Lane	Dublin 2	0.38	0.16	23,000,000	30,000,000	78,326,254	30%	Savills HOK	Dec. 2005
Burlington Hotel	Dublin 4	3.8	1.54	250,000,000	288,000,000	75,681,471	15%	CBRE	Apr. 2007
Adelphi Centre	Dún Laoghaire	0.193	0.08	10,000,000	13,000,000	67,275,107	30%	H. T. Meagher O'Reilly and Hooke MacDonald	May 2006
Berkeley Court Hotel	Dublin 4	2.0	0.81	100,000,000	119,000,000	59,453,817	19%	Jones Lang LaSalle	Nov. 2005
Eyre Square	Galway	0.25	0.10	15,000,000	14,500,000	58,679,418	–3%	O'Donnellan and Joyce Auctioneers	Nov. 2006
8–16 D'Olier Street and 24–27 Fleet Street	Dublin 2	0.44	0.18	25,000,000	25,000,000	56,206,340	n.a.	CBRE	Jun. 2006
Jury's Hotel	Dublin 4	4.8	1.95	250,000,000	260,000,000	53,958,086	4%	Jones Lang LaSalle	Sep. 2005
North Circular Road	Dublin 7	0.1	0.04	5,000,000	5,000,001	52,969,336	0%	Quinn Agnew	Oct. 2005

Percy Place	Dublin 4	0.2	0.10	8,500,000	12,000,000	48,659,597	41%	Ganly Walters Ltd	Jul. 2005
Ranelagh Road	Dublin 6	0.1	0.02	1,800,000	2,250,000	44,547,099	25%	Turley and Associates	Apr. 2006
High Street	Dublin 8	0.0	0.02	1,700,000	1,750,000	42,407,178	3%	GVA Dónal Ó Fuachalla and Co. Ltd	Nov. 2006
Warner's Lane	Dublin 6	0.0	0.02	1,400,000	1,520,000	41,008,145	9%	Lisney	Jun. 2005
Wilton Place	Dublin 2	0.2	0.08	6,500,000	7,000,000	37,078,528	8%	CBRE	Jun. 2004
Grosvenor Square	Dublin 6	0.1	0.03	2,000,000	2,500,000	35,749,615	25%	Sherry FitzGerald	Sep. 2005
Great Longford Street	Dublin 2	0.1	0.03	1,350,000	2,260,000	35,176,521	67%	Savills HOK	Jun. 2004
City Quay	Dublin 2	0.1	0.04	2,000,000	3,000,000	34,102,723	50%	Jones Lang LaSalle	May 2004
Bow Street	Dublin 7	1.1	0.43	35,000,000	35,000,000	32,939,529	0%	Savills HOK	2006
Gloucester Street, South	Dublin 2	0.1	0.05	2,750,000	4,000,000	32,374,852	45%	Jones Lang LaSalle	Jun. 2005
Merrion Road	Dublin 4	0.5	0.20	8,000,000	16,000,000	32,374,852	100%	Savills HOK	Feb. 2006
Northumberland Road	Dublin 4	0.2	0.09	4,500,000	7,125,000	32,037,614	58%	H. T. Meagher O'Reilly	Dec. 2004
Bride Street	Dublin 1	0.2	0.10	7,000,000	7,200,000	29,137,366	3%	Lambert Smith Hampton	Oct. 2003
Stillorgan Road, Donnybrook	Dublin 4	1.8	0.72	50,000,000	50,000,000	28,103,170	0%	Jones Lang LaSalle	Oct. 2006

Top honours go to the five-storey building at 140 Pembroke Road, Dublin 4, known as Franklin House, which went for €25 million for less than one-fifth of an acre in June 2006, thereby setting a new record price of €133 million per acre. It was bought by the developer David Daly, managing director of Albany Homes, in a private transaction arranged by James Meagher of H. T. Meagher O'Reilly. Fifteen months later Daly acquired two shops in Grafton Street for €115 million, River Island and the adjoining Wallis, and at the time of purchase the 'reversionary' yield (essentially the yield following a subsequent rent review) was 2.4 per cent. Nine months later CB Richard Ellis, a large commercial property agency, reported that in June 2008 investors wouldn't buy in Grafton Street for less than a 4 per cent yield. If true, that would imply a value today of both properties of about €69 million. Daly was setting records not only for Dublin 4 redevelopment sites but for prime retail sites as well.

Coming in at no. 2 is the Allianz building in Burlington Road, which achieved a €100 million price for a 1-acre site behind the Burlington Hotel. It was bought by Bernard McNamara through his company Glasbay in February 2007.

A site in Tara Street of only half an acre attained a 20 per cent premium over the *advised minimum value* or guide price of €40 million in February 2006 when it went for almost €97 million an acre.

It was closely followed by the Office of Public Works building in Shelbourne Road, Ballsbridge, which achieved a record price of €95 million an acre for Dublin 4—a record that was to last only a month. The 0.378-acre site, close to Jury's Hotel and the Berkeley Court Hotel as well as the former site of the NUI Veterinary College, also in Shelbourne Road, was listed by the agents Lambert Smith Hampton with an advised minimum value of €27 million; in fact it achieved a sale price of €35.891 million, or 33 per cent above the guide price. That was in May 2006, at the peak of the new-homes market, and it was bought by David Courtney and Jerry O'Reilly.

This set a new record for Shelbourne Road and Dublin 4 by beating the previous record, set in November 2005 when Glenkerrin Homes purchased the 2.05-acre site of the Veterinary College for €171.5 million, equivalent to €83.6 million per acre, and made it no. 7 on our top 25 list. That piece of land on the corner of Pembroke Road and Shelbourne Road was sold by the state through the same agents as in the previous example, which had placed a guide price of €100 million on the land. Ray Grehan of Glenkerrin Homes paid almost a 72 per cent premium above the guide price, around the same time that Seán Dunne bought the Berkeley Court Hotel and only two months after he paid €30 million an acre less for the Jury's Hotel site. These appear on the top 25 chart at numbers 9 and 11, respectively.

By the end of 2006 near-record prices were still being achieved for development land in the Dublin 4 area. In December that year a consortium headed by Bernard McNamara and Gerry O'Reilly paid €46.3 million for Carrisbrook House, an eight-storey building in Pembroke Road opposite Jury's Hotel. The size of the site was 0.52 acres, so the price per acre was €89.2 million (despite being reported in the *Irish Times* in January 2007 as €92 million an acre: those fractions in plot size really do matter!). Anyway, Carrisbrook House made it to the no. 5 spot on the list.

In at no. 6 was 40–47 Fleet Street, on the corner of Parliament Row adjacent to Westmorland Street and extremely close to both Trinity College and the premier shopping district. Lisney put the 0.4-acre site up for sale with a guide price of €30 million, and it achieved €33.2 million, or €83.97 million per acre, a shade more than the Veterinary College site at no. 7 in the chart.

The 3.8-acre site of the Burlington Hotel in Dublin 4 went up for sale in the spring of 2007, listed with a guide price of €250 million by Savills HOK. It was purchased shortly thereafter by Bernard McNamara for €288 million, or approximately €75.7 million per acre, a 15 per cent premium over the guide price. McNamara was strongly tipped as the preferred buyer because he had paid so much for the adjacent Allianz site two months before. This is what is known in developer jargon as 'site accumulation', but in this instance it was over a relatively short period, and considerable premium prices were being paid above both advised minimum values and earlier land prices of a year or so previously.

The 0.193-acre Adelphi Centre in Upper George's Street, Dún Laoghaire, was sold by tender in May 2006 for €13 million, or 30 per cent above the €10 million guide price set by the joint agents, H. T. Meagher O'Reilly and Hooke and MacDonald Commercial. This was a whopping €67.3 million per acre for an outer suburban site. Previously it was a five-storey-over-basement office development, but it was sold with full planning permission for a mixed-use development, comprising 676 square metres of retail use, 1,389 square metres of offices and fifteen residential units from floors 2 to 6. A revised planning submission to decrease the commercial property sizes and increase the number of residential units to thirty-one was made just before the sale. Even taking into account the fifty-two parking spaces in the basement, this was a record price for Dún Laoghaire, especially when one considers that nearby Blackrock, also close to the seafront and even closer to Dublin city centre, was selling for about €20 million an acre. It was definitely a premium price for the no. 9 position on the list.

At no. 10 was a half-acre site in Lad Lane, Dublin 2, that achieved €30 million in December 2005 or an equivalent price per acre of €78.3 million—impressive, considering that the same agents, Savills HOK, achieved €22.5 million for the 0.39-acre OPW site in Lad Lane a year and a half earlier, corresponding to a little less than €57 million an acre then, so roughly 24 per cent per year growth rate, or capital appreciation, as the aficionados like to say.

Indeed this has been a consistent theme of the Dublin development-land market since 2002, that is, capital values appreciating at 25 per cent per year right up to 2007.

Although higher prices have almost always been recorded in Ballsbridge, Dublin 4, and this is where many of the larger development-land sites have been sold in recent years, the average price per acre is similar to that of the more central Dublin 2 area. The problem, though, is that fewer smaller sales have taken place in Dublin 2 and only one tiny one during 2007, as the following summary shows.

Table 16: Sales of land, Dublin 2 and Dublin 4, 2004–07

	Dublin 2			Dublin 4		
	Number	Acreage	Price per acre	Number	Acreage	Price per acre
2004	9	6.34	€16,669,978	3	1.93	€17,186,169
2005	9	2.22	€33,628,363	11	14.34	€43,657,134
2006	8	2.44	€64,319,948	11	29.54	€20,955,131
2007	1	0.22	€21,968,649	3	5.28	€73,972,951

Source: *Irish Times*, Independent Newspapers

Total acreage sold over the four-year development-land boom in Dublin 2 was 11 acres, plus 51 acres in Dublin 4, so a grand total of 62 acres in fifty-five sites.

That may not seem like a lot, but when you put it in money terms, a total of €2,011,203,300 was spent on Dublin 2 and Dublin 4 development-land sites from 2004 to 2007. The split was €342 million for Dublin 2 and almost €1.7 billion for Dublin 4 alone. So 83 per cent of all that money was spent acquiring Dublin 4 sites, the largest of which was the €412 million paid for the Irish Glass Bottle site in South Bank Road, Ringsend. Considering that this site sold for €17.2 million an acre, and it was a 24-acre site, it really dragged down the Dublin 4 average for 2006, as seen in the previous table.

With so few sites dominating the league tables, it does make nonsense of average prices. However, taking these figures for 2004, both areas were selling for approximately €17 million an acre. Within two years Dublin 2 prices had rocketed by 286 per cent and three years later Dublin 4 prices had risen by 330 per cent. This puts it all into some kind of perspective, especially when you consider that over the same period the average

Dublin house price rose from €300,000 to €425,000, or 40 per cent, according to the PTSB-ESRI index. A similar gain was recorded in the Dublin second-hand home price index published by the Department of the Environment, Heritage and Local Government, with average prices gaining from about €360,000 to a peak of €520,000 in early 2007.

It may seem odd to non-Irish or even non-Dublin people to concentrate almost exclusively on such a small area of Dublin; but when you consider that €1 billion worth of development land was sold throughout the country in 2004, another €2 billion during 2005, a further €1.4 billion in 2006 and about half a billion in 2007, these two city districts dominate the development-land results.

The final table in this section on the value of development land lists the top 20 sites that have been sold. To make it into this top 20 a developer or consortium had to have paid €50 million or more. Seven of these top 20 sites were in Dublin 4, including the top 5.

We have already discussed most of the €100 million sites sold already. There's one caveat, however, on the Burton Hall Road site that was sold for about €75 million at the end of 2006, and that is that the final payment was never made. A deposit of €15 million was paid to the owners, Irish Life, by John Lally's company Karleigh, part of Lalco Holdings, but the remaining €60 million has not been paid, and now the case has ended up in the High Court. Irish Life claims that Karleigh has been unable to raise the funds, having agreed to purchase the site in November 2006. Karleigh has counter-claimed that there's a Traveller community living on the site and that it's covered with rubbish. We shall have to wait and see what develops.

Lalco already owns another Dublin 18 site (no. 7 in our table), the former FAAC Electronics site, for which it paid €110 million in June 2006. That price was slightly more, at €22 million an acre, than the later purchase of below €19 million per acre. At the peak of the market, prices for Sandyford Industrial Estate ranged from €20 million to €25 million per acre. Since then the market price of development land has dropped by at least 20 per cent from the spring of 2007 to the spring of 2008 and probably a good deal further since then, given the liquidity crunch, higher rates, and the continual decline in both residential and commercial property prices. In fact, some market commentators have ventured to say that development land prices have collapsed by 40 to 50 per cent, or more than double the official 15 per cent drop in national house prices.

Rather than describe each of these development-land transactions in turn, which would be beyond the scope of this book, I thought it would be interesting to focus on the large residential development sites that were purchased back in 2004.

Table 17: Twenty most expensive development sites sold, 2003–07

Street	Area	Hectares	Price sold (€)	Price per acre (€)	Premium	Agent	Date sold
South Bank Road	Dublin 4	9.7	412,000,000	17,188,710	65%	Savills Hamilton Osborne King	Oct. 2006
Burlington Hotel	Dublin 4	1.5	288,000,000	75,681,471	15%	CBRE	Apr. 2007
Jury's Hotel	Dublin 4	2.0	260,000,000	53,958,086	4%	Jones Lang LaSalle	Sep. 2005
UCD Veterinary College	Dublin 4	0.8	171,500,000	83,618,781	72%	Lambert Smith Hampton	Apr. 2007
Berkeley Court Hotel	Dublin 4	0.8	119,000,000	59,453,817	19%	Jones Lang LaSalle	Nov. 2005
Thomas Street (Digital Hub)	Dublin 8	2.3	118,000,000	21,129,604	18%	Finnegan Menton	Dec. 2005
Leopardstown Road	Dublin 18	2.0	110,000,000	22,037,337	38%	H. T. Meagher O'Reilly	Jun. 2006
Naas Road (An Post)	Dublin 22	5.8	107,000,000	7,530,672	34%	Jones Lang LaSalle	May 2006
Allianz, Burlington Road	Dublin 4	0.4	100,000,000	100,000,000	33%	Lisney	Feb. 2007
The Grange, Stillorgan	Co. Dublin	4.6	85,000,000	7,510,541	0%	CBRE	Nov. 2004
Westgate, St John's Road, West	Dublin 8	3.3	79,263,000	9,661,626	32%	Jones Lang LaSalle	Jun. 2005
Celbridge	Co. Kildare	26.7	77,600,000	1,176,165	11%	McDonald Brothers Ltd	May 2005
Burton Hall Road	Dublin 18	1.6	74,500,000	18,610,544	24%	HWBC	Nov. 2006
Poppintree	Dublin 11	16.5	63,000,000	1,543,293	5%	James Synnott and Company Ltd.	May 2004
Swords Road	Dublin 9	2.7	55,000,000	8,243,596	10%	GVA Dónal Ó Buachalla and Co. Ltd	Jul. 2006
Rathborne, Ashtown	Dublin 15	5.0	55,000,000	4,451,542	0%	Savills Hamilton Osborne King	Jul. 2006
M50 Business Park, Santry	Dublin 9	20.2	55,000,000	1,100,233	10%	Savills Hamilton Osborne King	Apr. 2004
Little Connell, Droichead Nua	Co. Kildare	104.0	53,000,000	206,234	18%	Savills Hamilton Osborne King	Jun. 2005
Thomas Street	Dublin 1	3.0	50,618,500	6,828,193	0%	Savills Hamilton Osborne King	Jul. 2003
Stillorgan Road, Donnybrook	Dublin 4	0.7	50,000,000	28,103,170	0%	Jones Lang LaSalle	Oct. 2006

THE GRANGE: A CASE IN POINT

The Grange in Stillorgan, opposite the Galloping Green pub at the junction between the N11 road, Newtown Park Avenue and Leopardstown Road, comes up a lot in this book, because it's a prime example of a large residential scheme (550 units) that has been caught by the property slump. In a recent article in the *Sunday Independent* by Ray Grehan, joint owner (with his brother Danny) of Glenkerrin Homes, which built the Grange, he stated that 190 units were now 'occupied'. Presumably this means that some have been sold and many now have been rented out, as their advertisements have flooded the rental market in obvious web portals, such as www.daft.ie. Accordingly, the same development appears in the section on rents and yields.

It's also a good example because the land was bought several years ago and the construction phase is largely complete. Another reason why it's an excellent barometer of the poor health of the property market is its location. Within the Blackrock postal district, it's close to Dublin and to all possible amenities (schools, universities and shopping centres, such as Dunne's Stores at Cornelscourt as well as Ireland's first, Stillorgan Shopping Centre); and it's within half a mile of where I grew up and lived for twenty-two years, so I know the area well. It's a highly sought-after residential area, and there are no negative circumstances or drawbacks because of location.

Glenkerrin Homes bought the 11.32-acre site with full planning permission in November 2004 for a reported €85 million from a consortium headed by Derek Quinlan. Quinlan Private had bought the same site in 2000 for €31.74 million, without planning permission; but Grehan managed to secure planning permission for 525 flats in blocks rising from three storeys at the front, adjacent to the main road, to six storeys at the rear, backing onto Leopardstown. Before Quinlan acquired the site it had been owned by the Royal and Sun Alliance Insurance Group for forty years and was formerly rented by ESSO Ireland Ltd. (I worked for a year in 1987–88 for ESSO, so this was another reason why this particular site holds some interest for me.) The insurance company decided to sell the site, having failed to get planning permission from Dún Laoghaire-Rathdown County Council for a private hospital or clinic.

On the evening of the announcement of the sale the *Evening Herald* published a feature article with the heading 'The man who made €1 million a month,' a reference to the €52.26 million profit made by Quinlan and his group by flipping the land (buying with the intention of reselling for a substantial profit without occupation) after four-and-a-half years for a then record of €7½ million per acre for a suburban site.

When I began working for Savills HOK, two months after I returned to live in Ireland, I did contemplate getting onto the property ladder. It's true what they say about where most people would like to live, within a two-mile radius of where they were brought up. This was a Savills HOK development, and because its director of new homes, Catherine O'Connor, had forged a close working relationship with Ray Grehan and Glenkerrin Homes she was subsequently responsible for selling all his developments. So in March 2007 I asked her what price the two-bedroom 80-square-metre flats (approximately 850 square feet) started at, and she told me at that time they would be pricing the next phase at €750,000 upwards! She thought that was good value at the time, but I certainly didn't.

Later, after I had left the firm, phase 3 was launched in mid-July 2007 with prices from €660,000 for the smaller two-beds up to €685,000 for the 80-plus square metres (considerably less than the previously mentioned aspirational price and back in line with phase 2 pricing levels). By the end of the year, according to the Savills HOK web site, the two-bedroom flats had been reduced to 'from' €635,000, even though there was one available for sale (number 5 at 'The Onyx', the first block next to the dual carriageway) for €60,000 cheaper than that, at €575,000. And so this particular development made it into chapter 15, 'Top of the Drops', too (by mid-2008 prices had been reduced further, to 'from' €525,000).

On 28 November 2004, in the *Sunday Tribune*, Helen Rogers quoted Catherine O'Connor as saying there was a long list of potential buyers at likely prices of €400,000 plus. Even back then she wrote that the estimated price per flat on completion could be half a million plus. In late 2004 the PTSB-ESRI new-home price index stood at €250,000 and by market peak in early 2007 it had increased by a fifth, to €306,000. So, allowing for this general market rise, one could reasonably have expected two-bedroom units to be launched at €450,000 to €480,000. But Glenkerrin Homes were seeking as much as €550,000 or more for the two-beds (70 to 83.9 square metres) when phase 1 was launched on 17 November 2005. By September 2006, when phase 2 was launched, the asking price for the two-beds ranged from €605,000 to €685,000.

The *Irish Times* reported on 1 December 2005 that the Grange had yielded sales of more than €100 million by then, with more than 100 units sold in phase 1 and 60 units sold in a single weekend. These were for occupation by the end of 2006, whereas the phase 2 sales in September 2006 were for occupation by the end of 2007, so presumably the phase 3 launch in July 2007 was for units to be completed and occupied by the end of 2008.

It's an interesting case study, because the initial euphoria and property fever mirrored precisely what was going on in the general residential property market. It's also noteworthy because resale prices on units that were sold in phase 1 and completed first were now 'for sale' at below the initial launch price in November 2005. If only 190 units are occupied, which represents about a third of the development, and some of these may actually be rented by Glenkerrin, it raises the question, How many cancellations have there been? How many purchasers paid the deposit and failed to complete? Or did they all sign contracts in time?—in time for the developers, that is. Only time will tell.

As a side note, it's worth mentioning that I asked one of my colleagues who set the initial prices, the developer or the agent. I was told that for many years the developers went along with what the agents recommended as what the market would bear, but that in recent years the developers often increased the asking price. By way of example, in another South Dublin development, it was recommended that two-bedroom flats be priced from €450,000 but the developer overruled this and insisted on €535,000 instead. Interestingly, one year later the same flats were reduced to €435,000 and by September 2008 they were on offer at a little less than €395,000.

In 2004 when the Grehan brothers bought the Stillorgan site opposite the Galloping Green pub, they paid €31½ million for the 22-acre site (8.9 hectares) of St Loman's Hospital in Palmerstown, Dublin 20, now marketed as St Edmund's. The guide price for that site, with planning permission for 640 apartments at €300,000 a piece, was only €17 million (given by DTZ and Sherry FitzGerald). The premium paid over this guide price was 85 per cent.

In December 2003 Glenkerrin paid €51 million for the 24.3-acre site at Ballinteer Avenue, Dublin 16, a full €16 million or 46 per cent above the guide price of €35 million. At the time it set the record for a period home in that part of Dublin. In total, some 505 units have been built there; some are one, two and three-bedroom flats, others are duplexes and town houses. Most have now been sold, as total sales have exceeded the €250 million mark. All that's left for sale are fourteen apartments and the original listed house dating from the 1820s, which had to be left intact. Planning permission had been sought for twelve apartments for the 6,600-square-foot mansion on an acre of grounds with a private driveway, surrounded now by all the newer properties, but permission for only four units was given, so Glenkerrin put the house up for sale in November 2007, with a guide price of €3½ million.

All these illustrations reflect accurately what has gone on in the development-land market in the suburbs of Dublin since 2004, as well as the direct link between the cost of residential development sites and their impact on the price of new homes. It also represents an excellent model of market timing as well as market pricing strategies. The Glenkerrin story was one of remarkable success, just like the market, until quite recently following the market collapse.

THE IMMEDIATE OUTLOOK FOR DEVELOPMENT LAND

As development-land sales have all but dried up since the middle of 2007, it's difficult to say with any accuracy where land prices are today. What is clear, and what the pundits who are closest to all the intriguing of the property market sectors tell us, is that there's little or no appetite for residential 'ready-to-go' sites at present. Figures of 35 to 40 per cent declines in infill residential sites, not just around Dublin but throughout the country, are commonplace. With the supply overhang persisting, if anything that situation can only worsen.

During July 2008 Paul Puryear, a well-known house-building analyst at the New York investment brokerage firm of Raymond James and Associates, went on record at the media giant Bloomberg about the drop in land values in the United States. He said that the country was now in its third year of the downturn (remember that Ireland is a year behind, in its second year of its downturn), and that land values for home-building purposes had dropped as much as 40 to 60 per cent in large metropolitan areas, such as Detroit. He mentioned that the United States had 2 million homes too many and that this 'excess' represented a backlog of eleven to twelve months' supply—or, to put it another way, it was the equivalent of a full year's building at the peak year, which was 2005.

The backlog in Ireland is greater than one year, and thanks to really low sales activity it could be as much as sixteen to eighteen months' supply. Putting a rough figure on that, it could be as much as 80,000 to 100,000 new homes too many (given that about half of these are in the hands of investors who bought to flip).

Puryear also revealed that on any given night 18½ million American homes lie vacant, out of a total of 129 million housing units, and that includes second homes. (The figures include 7 million holiday homes as well as 1.4 million 'vacant for rent' homes.) This 14 per cent vacancy rate, he said, is the highest rate in living memory.

The census of April 2006 revealed that the vacancy rate in Ireland then was 15 per cent, even higher than the American level, and Ireland is a full year behind the United States in the property cycle. Since that time, from May 2006 to November 2008, an additional 188,316 homes have been completed, according to the Central Statistics Office. On census night, that 15 per cent vacancy equalled 270,000 homes. If only two-thirds of what has been built since then has been sold and one-third remains unsold there would be another 60,000 vacant homes, bringing the total to 330,000, or 17 per cent vacancy, of the 1.9 million Irish homes in existence.

If, however, only a quarter remained unsold, or about 40,000—an optimistic figure, really—then the vacancy rate would be still higher, at about 16¼ per cent. Worse still, if only half have been sold over the last two years, the vacancy rate may have risen to a whopping 18½ per cent!

Whichever way you look at it, the vacancy rate has gone up, and that's a disaster for the price of new homes, and calamitous for the price of development land.

Whatever about the correction that's now taking place in the property market for houses and apartments, there is still a plentiful supply of zoned and serviced land. The Department of the Environment, Heritage and Local Government has listed 15,100 hectares of zoned and serviced land—enough for 469,937 homes—as being available in June 2007. If we subtract the 86,639 that have been built since that time we're left with a figure close to 383,300, which is possibly enough to meet the country's housing requirement for the next eight to ten years.

That too is ominous for the future fortunes of the Irish development-land market. Whatever about the price of homes falling by 30 to 40 per cent (some market commentators suggest 50 or even 60 per cent), the drop in development land could be even larger than that. Remember, it's land values that drive home prices, and not the other way around.

So far the falls in house prices nationally, as measured by the official house-price index, have paled in comparison with the anecdotal evidence that site values have already fallen 40 per cent. (There's no reliable index of either commercial or residential land values in Ireland.) What is certain is that, as long as site values are falling more rapidly than home values, there's little hope of recovery in house prices until such time as site prices hit bottom. Until builders and developers are confident that the slump is well and truly over and they begin paying premium prices for 'ready-to-go' infill sites, take it as a portent of things to come that the housing market remains fragile.

Chapter 13

Residential bail-out and buy-back

SEPTEMBER 1992

It was 1992 and I was working as an econometrician (that's the person who builds the economic factor models—models for the bond and equity markets, among others) for the chief economist at Barclay's, Michael Hughes. Not long after I joined the economics and strategy team of BZW (now called Barclay's Capital) another new person was hired. He was Robert Barrie, a Scot educated at a public school who had worked at Her Majesty's Treasury. He was a very amiable chap, like all the others in our group.

It was a small team, only fifteen people. Robert had spent his time in the civil service at the Treasury—what we in Ireland would call the Department of Finance. He had made the leap from a £20,000-a-year job to one with a basic of about £60,000 plus generous bonus as well as the opportunity to double, treble or even quadruple his income within a few years. He had jumped from the public-sector cruise ship to the private-sector battleship. Not such a surprise, really—but it was more than that: it was market timing; and, as we shall soon discover, timing was one of Robert's skills.

He had been at the Treasury during the Nigel Lawson boom years. During Lawson's tenure as Chancellor of the Exchequer (Minister for Finance) in the mid-1980s he had slashed interest rates and manufactured an economic boom, fuelling the fires of Thatcherism and the new reality of home ownership. The construction industry boomed; this was the last time that more than 450,000 new homes were built in a single year. (In 2006, Britain built only a third of this quantity.) It spawned new television comedy characters, like Harry Enfield's 'Loadsa Money', a plasterer who had money to burn—not very unlike the economic miracle in Ireland attributed to membership of European Monetary Union, according to Dan McLaughlin at Bank of Ireland. The similarities are frightening. They had ultra-low interest rates when they didn't need them, and money supply growth and a credit boom—well, just like Ireland's, really.

They built a record number of new homes, and the banks relaxed lending criteria.

That sounds familiar, doesn't it? But of course Ireland was totally different, if not unique: it had massive net immigration. Hang on a minute: so had Britain. During the Thatcher years, according to the Irish census data, 200,000 young Irish people emigrated to Britain between 1979 and 1990. I know, because I was one, as were 90 per cent of my school friends and fellow-graduates. When I was a forced economic migrant in the late 1980s more than 40,000 young people per year were fleeing the country. To put that into perspective, there were about 55,000 school-leavers per year back then.

Robert had been there, through all the boom times, watching the figures roll in. He knew they were scary. He knew where it would all end. He had to do something about it. Like many others of his generation, he had bought property in the mid-1980s. He had bought a two-bedroom flat in Clapham Common, just off the communal green space. He paid about £80,000 for it. He had done well, because when he decided to sell it five years later he got £285,000. He'd cleared a cool £200,000 in a few short years; in fact he had made more each year on the value of his appreciating home than he had earned at the Treasury. The capital value of his flat rose by more than his gross salary each year. Again, how familiar does that sound? Could be Dublin between 2000 and 2006, couldn't it?

So Robert knew, like others at the Treasury, that something was amiss and that the numbers they were crunching were not looking good. The writing was on the wall; the market was about to turn. He needed to sell, and quickly; so he did. He took profit, sold into a strong market and decided to rent another flat in the same street. He moved his wife and daughter into rented accommodation. Shortly afterwards he also decided to change jobs, and in this way he joined BZW just after I did.

Not only did we both start working there the same year but the following year we both bought properties. It was September 1992, and all the house-price indices, like those of the Nationwide and Halifax building societies, had fallen considerably, and British home prices appeared to have value again. You see, from 1990 to 1992 the average house price had fallen by more than 20 per cent, and in parts of London it was more like 30 to 40 per cent.

I had bought a one-bedroom flat in Grange Road, off Tower Bridge Road, very close to work and the City. Robert, on the other hand, had told me he had his eye on a house facing the Common, two streets from where he was living and a stone's throw from where he had sold his first flat. He bought that four-bedroom house for a quarter of a million—that is, about £35,000 less than what he sold the two-bedroom flat for two years earlier. He had done it. He had timed it to absolute perfection: he had sold right at the top of the market and then bought again closer to the bottom.

Economists don't usually get it this right. But Robert knew more than the average bear. He had been right at the heart of it. He knew that interest rates would have to rise steeply to counteract inflation and to curtail the enormous credit boom. He also knew that the house-price appreciation was unsustainable. Meanwhile estate agents were telling people to buy or miss the boat for ever. Property fever had gripped the country and it was the only thing people talked about.

Not like Ireland. It's just a quadruple coincidence that we got super-low rates when we joined the euro, had strong economic growth that required lots of migrant labour, and had a booming construction industry with record additions to the housing stock, coupled with 30 per cent growth in private-sector credit. This was pure coincidence. Ireland's story is different. Ireland had to play catch-up; or had it? Ask yourself this question: is there such a thing as quadruple coincidence?

A party is a party in any country or any economy. And a hangover is a hangover too. Will an Irish hangover be different from a British one, or a German one, or a Japanese one? The one commonality among all property bubbles is that you know it was a bubble only after it has already burst.

We move forward in time, as history attempts to repeat itself.

We begin this part of our story at the beginning of 2007—Wednesday 10 January, to be precise. It was a breakfast conference held by Bank of Ireland at its offices in Ballsbridge, Dublin. The subject was, of course, the Irish economy, and the seminar was opened by Frank McDonagh, commercial manager at the new Ballsbridge branch. The great and the good were all in attendance. It was structured as a debate, though I don't think that was the idea. Yes, they had an impartial chairperson in the form of Moore McDowell of NUI, Dublin, but the choice of speakers was designed not just to entertain but to pit the perennial economic optimist against a well-known property bear. I refer to Dan McLaughlin, chief economist of Bank of Ireland, versus the independent and highly amusing David McWilliams, whose wit and charm didn't fail to impress. But there's the rub. David could be relied upon to be outrageous, to be extreme in his views, to be pedantic in a light-hearted way.

It was his extreme view that the housing market was fundamentally overvalued. His views would be shown up for what the audience knew they were: more prophecies of doom and gloom. The doomsayers—sure we all know they've been saying that for years, and getting it wrong for years too. Sure the Irish property market is a virtuous circle, as we all know: a never-ending economic miracle. (It's no surprise that English people look down on us with the puerile level of debate that occurs in this land.)

To question the economic miracle was heresy. And economists who do are said to be practising the black art of the 'dismal scientist'. Those who denigrate economics using this rhetoric are usually uninformed, half-educated eejits, who really don't know why things really happen at all. Or, put it another way, they're referred to as 'experts' on current affairs television programmes. The most misused word in the Hiberno-English vocabulary is the term 'expert', in my humble opinion. If you don't believe me, keep listening to the RTE main evening news for 'Experts say the housing market is set to recover very shortly.' Who are these so-called experts? Depending on the topic, anyone working for an industry-related organisation—myself included. (I was quoted as an expert in a national newspaper less than two weeks into the job!)

Anyway, David McWilliams didn't fail to impress. Indeed he surprised all and sundry by cleverly structuring his thoughts and views on the market into a thought-provoking challenge. He asked if anyone present would oblige him with a 'sale and lease-back' deal on his primary residence. You got it: he threw down the gauntlet and said to all there that morning that if you believe that 'Ireland PLC is the envy of Europe,' as it was according to Dan McLaughlin, and that Irish house prices would increase by 3 per cent in both 2007 and 2008, with single-digit growth rates thereafter or, as Dan put it, 'nominal increases in line with incomes,' then accept his offer and buy his house, and he would rent it back at the prevailing market rate. David began his speech with his challenge, essentially saying: put your money where your mouth is.

I want to short the Irish housing market. Okay, I want to sell my house. I have a house in Killiney. Sherry FitzGerald tell me it's worth two million quid—whether they're right or wrong I'm not too sure. I want to sell it to somebody in the room, but I want to do what the banking system is doing. I want a sale and lease-back arrangement, because I have two young kids who live beside the school they go to. My missus doesn't know I'm saying this, so clearly it's going to cause all sorts of ructions. [She knows now.] But this is a very serious challenge. I want to offer somebody in the room a detached house in Killiney, right beside the DART. I want a sale and lease-back operation with a two-step clause in it, one at five years, to see if we want to go again, and another at ten years. I want tenancy for ten years, and I'll give you a stream of income for ten years. The stream of income will be the rate at which we would rent the house today. Okay, I believe that rate is somewhere around two-and-a-half grand a month. Okay. That's the challenge if you believe Dan.

Nice try, David. That would be a gross rental yield of 1½ per cent or about half the prevailing rate for south Co. Dublin in early 2007. To be fair to David, he did express it as an absolute monetary amount and not a given yield, and he did say the market rate, so we shouldn't really nit-pick too much on that front.

On another level he was quite accurate. The reality is that people will pay only two to three thousand a month for a typical, say, four-bedroom home in the suburbs, irrespective of where it is. Even a nice big property in sought-after Dalkey would fetch only about €4,000 a month maximum. Beyond this level, normal people are just not willing to shell out that kind of dead money in a rising market. In effect, there's a rental ceiling for each and every property.

This is why a really smart professional investor would buy five properties in Ballyfermot for the same two million instead, rent out each for a thousand a month, thereby netting twice as much rental income, and have greater diversification of risk to boot. In a strong, rising market the Killiney house would probably appreciate by more, as a percentage; but on the other side of the equation the smaller west Dublin properties would be easier to rent (and to sell) in a declining market.

Let's return to the debate.

It's a very serious challenge. I want to short the market, but I want to live where I want to live. It's exactly what Bank of Ireland is doing, and AIB has done. They want to short the market, but they want to keep their properties and their staff where they are. I don't want to move home, so there you have it. Who's game?

The challenge was made, but would there be any takers?

A sale and lease-back operation. Dan's right: the economy is going to be kosher, everything is hunky-dory. You'll probably have doubled your price in ten years' time. I'll underwrite your funding by paying the rent with a stream of income, and we're all happy.

There was total silence. David pauses for ten seconds or so to gauge the reaction. A few murmurs and quiet giggles down the back. Maybe they don't think he's serious—perhaps a misguided and early April fool joke, though it's only January. David breaks the silence himself.

Rarely have I seen this in a bunch of investors! [Silence again.] Is that not the best deal you've heard all year? So you don't believe the housing market? Okay, I think Killiney is a fairly good location.

Some laughter resonates.

I really do. Here we have an audience of investors and a bank to finance the deal. They're my bank as well—okay. I want to get out of the market for the next six to ten years. There's the deal of the century.

There's no risk for you, 'cause I'm underwriting your financing by paying today's rent—whatever the market will bear. You're getting the asset at a time when Dan thinks it's not near the top of the market, and I take a few shekels off the table. That's really what I wanted to say today. Because if you believe Dan, then you've got to go for this. If you don't believe Dan, I'll tell you why maybe it's not the best investment. I'd like to see a show of hands. Anybody interested in a house in Killiney?

More laughter, but more subdued this time—nervous laughter, really, as one tentative arm is raised. 'I think it's time to get out of this market . . .'

That was it in a nutshell. To be perfectly honest, I'd have preferred it if David had arrived in and said he had sold his house in Killiney and had rented another in the same area. That would really have shaken them up and put the cat among the pigeons. For later on, during the same seminar, David made a reference to one of J. P. Morgan's famous quotations, that 'nothing clouds one's financial judgement more than the sight of one's neighbour getting rich.' This works both ways.

Investors are just as concerned about not losing money as they are about making it, perhaps even more so. How many times in the past few years have you heard people talking about how much they made on buying property? When have you ever heard of someone making a loss? You possibly never have. However, in the future you will undoubtedly hear tales of those who got out in time, or just before the decline. These will be the heroes of tomorrow.

What if David had turned around to the salesperson from Sherry FitzGerald who valued his home at €2 million and said: 'Hey, listen, do you want to make a quick €200,000? Just give me €1.8 million and it's yours!'

I bet you all the tea in China the response would have been, 'Oh, no, sir, we don't buy properties, we're just the selling agents.'

I'll leave that one up to you to decide.

Anyway, this brings us full circle, back to my original story, that of a British economist who did precisely what David McWilliams was trying to do at the beginning of 2007. Eight weeks later, house prices nationally began to fall.

Chapter 14

House-price bonanza (or should that be 'bananas'?)

The old joke about asking an Irish person for directions and being told 'If I were you I wouldn't start from here' is pretty corny but has never been as true as it is of the property market. You really wouldn't start from here if you had a choice to begin with. Unfortunately, Ireland doesn't have that luxury of choosing and is stuck with an oversupplied housing market, falling prices, negative sentiment and, worst of all, an erosion of confidence.

Before we look to the future price prospects for the housing market it's essential to take stock of where the market is today. To do that we need to examine the extent of the run-up in prices that led to Ireland outperforming internationally.

THE GREAT IRISH PROPERTY BULL MARKET, 1994–2007
Actually, the best way to describe the tremendous run that residential property has enjoyed over the last decade and a half is by way of illustration. A good comparison is with the changing cost of money, the doubling of real wages, and the rising costs in the general price level (including building costs) over the same period.

New-home prices quintupled since 1991 and more than quadrupled since the emergence of the 'Celtic Tiger' era in 1994. During the same period the average new-home price in the United States doubled, from $154,500 to $305,900, while the British average trebled, from £61,600 to £190,500. So the Irish performance was truly spectacular, from an existing home-owner's viewpoint. Not so for those younger people who had to scramble to get onto the property ladder. As the following table shows, despite a halving of mortgage interest rates since 1992, and a doubling of wages since 1990, neither kept up with the enormous ramp-up in new-home prices.

Table 18: New house prices relative to mortgage interest, average industrial wages, building costs and consumer price index, 1990–2007

	New house price	Mortgage interest rate costs	Average industrial wage	House building costs	Consumer price index
1990	98	99	99	98	98
1991	100	95	103	102	101
1992	103	100	106	104	105
1993	104	80	111	107	106
1994	109	60	114	110	109
1995	116	64	116	114	111
1996	130	57	121	116	113
1997	153	60	125	120	115
1998	187	59	129	124	118
1999	222	41	137	131	120
2000	253	45	144	140	126
2001	273	48	155	161	132
2002	296	39	163	170	139
2003	335	31	170	175	143
2004	372	29	178	180	146
2005	412	29	184	186	150
2006	457	35	189	193	156
2007	480	44	197	200	164
2008e	456	45	203	207	170
2009f	410	35	209	205	173
Base: 1st quarter 1991 = 100.					

Source: Department of the Environment, Heritage and Local Government

Even the cost of constructing a property doubled, beating the general cost of living index (the consumer price index). But realistically, the value of any property is not the home itself but rather the land it occupies. Homes in the traditional sense don't really appreciate in value: it's the site that becomes more valuable, as is evidenced by many older, smaller properties with large gardens having fetched ridiculous prices at auctions. For instance, a 1940s bungalow in dire need of repair on one acre of ground in a desirable built-up area will achieve a much better price in a strong market than a modern five-bedroom detached house on a sixth of an acre in the same street. Most people recognise this to be true, but the estate agents believe that house prices drive land values and not the other way around.

This is a topic that we have already addressed in chapter 12, which dealt specifically with the Irish love affair with land. Suffice it to say that land values have risen even more than house prices. Land became such a hot commodity during the property boom that there were people going from door to door asking property-owners with a larger than average side or back garden if they would part with some of their garden in exchange for a substantial consideration. In mid-2007 one such example was a local builder in Bray, Co. Wicklow, who put leaflets through letterboxes offering €300,000 for a suitable site for him to build a new home for his daughter so that she could remain living close to her parents. The same builder went on a local radio station to appeal for somebody with enough land adjacent to their home to oblige him. He said he would pay the full market price.

A similar thing occurred in the 1980s property bubble in Japan. By late 1989 the area occupied by the Imperial Palace in Tokyo was said to be worth more than the entire state of California or even the whole of Canada. Following the bursting of the Japanese housing bubble the economy experienced four recessions in a little over a decade and it took fifteen years to stabilise home prices, despite official base rates being slashed to a mere 0.15 per cent. Japan actually suffered from 'deflation' at that time. Before that, urban land prices in Japan from 1985 to 1990 increased in value by 20 to 35 per cent per year, just as they did in Ireland from 2002 to 2007. Annual growth or change in land values was negative, year after year, from 1991 right up to 2006. On average, prices fell by 5 to 10 per cent per year. The biggest cause of the mega-boom, then mega-bust, in Japan was excessive bank lending.

The Japanese banks' share prices collapsed shortly after the bubble burst in 1990, and the share price of Irish banks followed a similar path in 2007–08. Japan was the most extreme case and is probably the worst case for any economy. There are lessons to be learnt, though. It's good to begin with the worst possible case and then look to the best case to get a handle on the range of potential outcomes.

In recovering after a burst bubble, Sweden enjoyed the quickest turnaround. It took only five years (three years of falling prices and two years of static prices). Ireland could and should have learnt from the Swedish example when the liberalisation of credit and bank deregulation occurred in the early 1990s. In 1985 the Swedish monetary policy authorities abolished lending controls on banks. House prices jumped by a quarter, even allowing for inflation, which was running at a rate of 5 to 10 per cent. Swedish inflation shortly thereafter hit double-digit levels, and the central bank was forced to raise interest rates while trying to maintain a currency peg. By the time the crisis was over and home prices began to rise again, in 1996, typical mortgage rates were still as high as 9 per cent.

It's worth mentioning, though, that in the Swedish experience the investment purchase of rental properties or 'quick-flipping' was not a common theme of that market, though it has been a prominent feature of the Irish experience, particularly since 2002. The proof of this was the jump in the national vacancy rate.

CHOICE OF HOUSE-PRICE INDEX
Again, given the optimal choice you wouldn't really start with either of the principal home-price indices in use in Ireland today. As mentioned earlier, there are only two, and neither of them is really adequate for the job. Both national sets of indices are based on home loans.

The Department of the Environment, Heritage and Local Government produces a series of national house-price indices for both new and second-hand homes, as well as for the Dublin area. It also produces additional indices for the other cities, namely Cork, Galway, Waterford and Limerick, as well as 'other areas'. It gives a further breakdown of properties with and without apartments. None of these house-price indices is 'mix-weighted': that is, they don't separate out the types of dwelling or their sizes as reflected by the number of bedrooms.

Therefore, a big problem exists when more five-bedroom detached houses appear on the market and sell, because when the home loans are processed and drawn down they can distort the average price for that area. Let's use an example of Cork. If the average new-home price in Cork was €325,000 in 2007 and a major development was launched with larger homes selling for, say, €600,000 in the same year, then their selling price was slashed by €100,000 to half a million euros, and they're all sold, they would actually bring up the Cork average, because they would still be selling for €175,000 more than the average, despite the price reduction. If you can follow that illustration you will understand why the Government's home-price indices are a reliable indicator only of general trend. In effect they lump two-bedroom flats with three-bedroom semi-detached houses, along with bungalows and larger detached properties.

The second and more widely used national average home-price index is based on only one mortgage lender's loan portfolio (Permanent TSB), though it's constructed in conjunction with an external organisation, the Economic and Social Research Institute. This is the PTSB-ESRI index. Though this index is indeed 'mix-weighted' for property type, and even gives a breakdown for 'commuter' homes and 'three-bed semis', it's based on only about a fifth of the home loan market. It doesn't have the regional or city breakdown of the official government series, but it does break out Dublin from the rest. It also features a 'new' home index.

There's an old saying that 'in the land of the blind, the one-eyed man is king.' And so it is with the PTSB-ESRI national average. In short, it's better than nothing. Another drawback with the PTSB-ESRI index is that it begins only from March 1996, so it covers only a bull-market period. Unlike the Government index, which goes back as far as 1970, the PTSB-ESRI index has a very limited history, and one that was dominated by a single phase in the market (the land of the blind). Another big problem with both indices is the considerable time lag between actual measurement and the reporting of monthly data. For instance, the PTSB-ESRI index is reported almost two months in arrears. This means that you get, for example, June data either at the end of July or in early August. There have been reporting periods when the ESRI has had a clash between the IIB-ESRI (now called KBC-ESRI) consumer sentiment index (which is normally reported at the beginning of the following month) and the PTSB-ESRI national average house-price index. In such circumstances it has not been unusual to find that the house-price index is reported later (meaning last).

As alluded to earlier, the PTSB-ESRI house-price index is akin to looking in the rear-view mirror of your car. Because it's based on actual mortgage draw-down on a property, this usually occurs eight to ten weeks after 'sale agreed' (after the seller accepts the buyer's offer and a deposit is paid), so—back to the June example again—it can relate to sales that were arranged in March or April. If so, and the June monthly figure is not reported until August, because of holidays or a queue of data releases, it's probable that the user of the index is using stale data, which may be four or five months old. Not least of its shortcomings is the fact that the Permanent TSB is only one mortgage lender and so represents a narrow view (hence the analogy of squinting in the rear-view mirror), at best a fifth of the total market, and it could have a more regional or rural bias, or indeed possibly a smaller-home bias, as suggested by the fact that the average price is much lower than anecdotal evidence suggests, for Dublin at least.

To provide an example of this last point, let's look at the average Dublin house price. The PTSB-ESRI index for Dublin in June 2008 was €371,000, having peaked in April 2007 at a shade under €430,000. On the other hand, the house-price index of the Department of the Environment, Heritage and Local Government for Dublin peaked in the third quarter of 2006 at €549,000 for second-hand homes and €426,000 for new homes, later dropping to €455,000 and €390,500, respectively, by the second quarter of 2008. The official government series incorporates all mortgage lenders, both banks and building societies.

It's also highly likely that the borrower profile of your Permanent TSB customer is significantly different from that of, say, a Bank of Ireland or AIB one. Indeed, evidence on loan-to-value ratios suggests that AIB customers borrow proportionately less of the purchase price, though they

may borrow a larger absolute amount. They tend to be long-time customers of the bank (and so may be 'trader-uppers'). Permanent TSB, on
the other hand, has lent aggressively to buy-to-let investors, and its
mortgage profile is vastly different (and this is the main reason why its
share price has been pummelled more than AIB during the first half of
2008; institutional stock market investors are an unforgiving bunch).

The next chart is an illustration of the PTSB-ESRI home-price index,
broken down into national (excluding Dublin) and Dublin city and
county.

Fig. 12: PTSB-ESRI home-price index

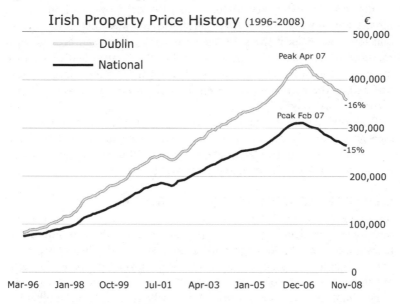

Source: PTSB-ESRI House Price Indices

The biggest problem I have with the PTSB-ESRI house-price index, for
Dublin especially, is that during early 2007, at the peak in the series, there
was precious little you could have bought in Dublin at that time other
than a two-bedroom flat. And some of those in the biggest new areas,
such as Sandyford and Dundrum, were selling for half a million plus.
Even three-bedroom terraced former council houses in less desirable districts were achieving €650,000 and more at the height of the property
boom. In March 2007 an 850-square-foot two-bedroom terraced former
council cottage at the back of the car park of the Queen's Pub in Dalkey
sold for €950,000, or more than a million if you include stamp duty. Of
course one can always find exceptional cases, but the exception here was

the PTSB-ESRI index itself, because to find a family home in Dublin in 2006 for €430,000 would have been nothing short of a miracle. Every two-bedroom terraced cottage in the city had a price tag starting with at least half a million back then.

NATIONAL HOUSE-PRICE INDEX DELAYED

Figures for the national house-price indices of the Department of the Environment, Heritage and Local Government for the first quarter of 2008 were still not available in July 2008, and the second-quarter numbers did not materialise until 23 October with the October release. Furthermore, for the full time that I was employed as head of research at Savills HOK, from January to July 2007, the department's house-price indices were not revised at all, not once: the data was stuck at the second quarter of 2006 until the summer of the following year, because of a revision of the index. The department and the Central Statistics Office drew attention to this at the time. It also occurred at a most inopportune time, when the market was turning. It couldn't have been worse if you planned it that way.

Can you imagine in Britain if the Nationwide or Halifax building societies suspended their national average home-price index for more than twelve months or in the United States if the S&P/Case-Shiller twenty-city house-price index went unchanged for that length of time?

LOST OPPORTUNITIES ARE BEST FORGOTTEN

It's a pity that none of the Irish residential estate agents didn't team up with an independent organisation, perhaps a university or technical college, a couple of decades ago and create a more reflective house-price index. A good example of a microcosm of the property market throughout the boom and before is the 'Gallops' near Leopardstown Racecourse in Dublin 18. A series of new starter-home schemes was launched there in 1991, and new developments are continuing. It's one of the few places in the country that have seen considerable home-building throughout the property boom. Another important factor there is the uniformity of properties, most of which are your typical three-bedroom semi-detached starter family homes. The Gallops house-price index, if it existed, would have been infinitely superior to both the PTSB-ESRI index and that of the Department of the Environment, Heritage and Local Government.

Presumably the estate agents were too busy making money to be bothered with building an objective benchmark or true barometer of house prices for a given area. For this is what banks and brokerage houses do all the time. However, part of the problem is the deliberate lack of transparency in the market. Valuers would probably have taken such indices as an affront to their experience and professionalism, notwithstanding that such short-sightedness on the part of all the bigger agencies prevented them making their jobs and their lives so much easier. It would also have meant that we, the public, would have more reliable indicators of home prices and in a more timely fashion. Is that too much to ask? (Don't answer that. The last thing we want to hear is the dreaded 'Data Protection Act' excuse.)

ANNUAL AVERAGE HOUSE-PRICE GROWTH

Fig. 13: Residential house-price growth

Real house price growth adjusted for inflation

Annual house price growth (nominal terms)

Source: PTSB-ESRI, Central Statistics Office

The graphic illustrates the house-price growth experience of the residential property market, based on the PTSB-ESRI index, over the last decade. Property prices have fallen for twenty-one months in succession, from April 2007 to November 2008, with a total fall of 15 per cent. Adjusting for inflation, the average drop has been 21 per cent; but, as mentioned earlier, there are inherent delays in the index, not to mention that it doesn't reflect asking or 'aspirational' price drops at all. Real prices adjust for the cost-of-living index, because inflation erodes your fixed debt over time and puts upward pressure on your wages, both of which should improve affordability over time.

Although market commentators, especially those on RTE (such as the 'Ear to the Ground' programme), constantly refer to the 30 per cent drop in home prices, we shall show later in chapter 16 that they're talking about declines in asking prices and not official index price falls. Nevertheless, they are referring to more up-to-the-minute home prices. My own analysis of thousands of falls in asking price illustrated that the average drop from the market peak was about 18½ per cent in late 2008. The difference between this number and the cumulative decline shown by the PTSB-ESRI index probably reflects the time lag in reporting that was covered in extensive detail earlier.

Chapter 15

The negative-feedback price loop

During 2001 the Irish property market experienced a bit of a price wobble. For five months, from September 2001 (after the attacks on the World Trade Center) to January 2002 (after interest-rate cuts), the PTSB-ESRI house-price index fell as the national average home price dipped from €186,000 to €180,000, a decline of about 3 per cent. Global confidence was temporarily knocked by the fateful events in New York in 2001. To use market terms, that was a minor 'price correction'. All markets suffer these price corrections regularly.

Then fast forward to 2007, when the national average Irish home price peaked at €311,078, according to the PTSB-ESRI index, or €331,947 for a new home and €386,989 for an existing one (in the second quarter of 2007), according to the whole-country index of the Department of the Environment, Heritage and Local Government. Taking only the PTSB-ESRI index, the national average house price soared from €75,000 to €311,000 in little more than a decade. With such high growth as that it's nigh on impossible to engineer a 'soft landing', as opposed to a prolonged property slump, especially now that interest-rate policy has been ceded to a foreign body, namely the European Central Bank in Frankfurt. Without the ability to use monetary policy as a weapon with which to combat falling prices, the Government has only fiscal policy at its disposal.

The problem with this is that it was excessive fiscal policy that fanned the flames of the property boom all along. All right, the number 1 factor behind the massive run-up in property prices was the relaxation of monetary policy—the slashing of interest rates to unprecedented low levels—after 2001 and lax credit standards by the banks. That was beyond the control of the Government; but tax factors were not. The raising of mortgage interest relief, the introduction of tax incentives for landlords, such as section 23 of the Finance Act (1981) and the reduction in capital gains tax to the new low rate of 20 per cent (together with exemptions on inheritance), all combined to perpetuate the boom. In effect, it was a state-sponsored property boom.

The Government may well argue that other taxes, such as stamp duties (paid on conveyancing), were there to prevent speculation and so reduce the likelihood of a speculative bubble; but they would be wrong. Firstly, stamp duty at the old higher rate of 9 per cent was there almost from before the boom, since January 1997. Secondly, stamp duty is a universal property tax, applied in most industrialised countries. Essentially it acts as a 'liquidity tax', as it is based on transactions and is a one-off payment to the exchequer. It is therefore factored in by buyers and sellers alike, just as other conveyancing costs are, such as solicitors' fees. In a rising market, stamp duty is simply paid for by capital appreciation for those with existing properties, whereas first-time buyers never paid stamp duty anyway, because they're exempt (or, under the old regime, were forced to buy new and so were exempt on new homes below 125 square metres). Stamp duty never came from savings; banks and mortgage lenders never lent money for stamp duty. Furthermore, as Alan Cooke of the Irish Auctioneers' and Valuers' Institute has constantly reminded us, the abolition of stamp duty would merely have enabled sellers to ratchet up their asking prices.

Going back in time to when the property slump first emerged, in early 2007, we were told by way of incessant media spin, primarily instigated by the estate agents and their lobbyist organisations, that there was not going to be a property crash but rather that a 'soft landing' was the most likely outcome. This is what is known euphemistically and affectionately as the 'big river in Africa' phenomenon (pronounced, in an appropriate Dublin accent, 'denial').

THE 'SOFT LANDING' SCENARIO

What exactly does a 'soft landing' mean? This is a much-abused term, but it means a price correction downwards of approximately 10 per cent—in other words, a decline in value of one-tenth from the peak to the bottom. This is the definition most widely used by central bankers and practitioners in the world's financial markets. It hasn't often been associated with property markets, because it rarely applies. In stock market parlance a soft landing would be called a 'technical correction'. It really means that the market gives back some of the froth.

If that is so, how do you define a 'crash'? Well, this is really an arbitrary term but it usually means a fall in price of at least 20 per cent. Accordingly, using these definitions, a soft landing would imply a reduction in the national average house price to €280,000—a fall of about €30,000. We've already passed that milestone back in April 2008. On the other hand, a crash implies a fall of approximately €70,000 or €75,000 to about €235,000 for the national average price as measured by the PTSB-ESRI index. Even if the national average price doesn't fall that low, it will still

feel like a crash to everyone, as indeed it does already. We are only
€30,000 away from that level now.

OVERVALUED METRICS

It's widely accepted that a house is usually the largest asset of a household. It's not a financial asset, as it doesn't throw off a stream of income,
which is why your primary residence is exempt from capital gains tax. A
second property that's let for rental income may be perceived as a financial asset, and that's why it's subject to capital gains tax. At the beginning
of housing booms, prices are often justified at first by the economic fundamentals, such as growth in household income and demographic shifts
as well as tax incentives designed to encourage home ownership.

Contrary to popular belief, it can be shown by much empirical evidence (research conducted by academics published as working papers by
various central banks) that incomes don't really matter that much when
it comes to explaining the driving factors behind large swings in house
prices over the typical housing cycle, which is usually about fifteen years.
Studies have shown that only about a tenth of the gains in house prices
can be explained by rising salaries and household incomes. What is
important is the size of the monthly repayment in relation to take-home
pay, rather than the absolute loan amount in relation to gross household
income.

This may appear counter-intuitive at first. You might think, surely
a person's salary depends on how much they can pay for a home. In
reality, it doesn't matter as much as you may have thought. Let's use a
simple concrete example. Joe earns fifty thousand a year and wants to buy
an apartment for €150,000. He applies to a bank for a loan, and they say,
sure, they will lend him two-and-a-half times his salary, €125,000.
Fortunately, Joe's parents have given him a gift of ten thousand ('parental
assistance' in real-estate jargon) and he already has almost twenty
thousand in savings for the deposit and legal fees. But Joe had applied to
more than one mortgage lender for a loan, and he receives an offer of
four times his salary from a building society. He can now pay up to
€225,000 for an apartment. Perhaps he can buy a bigger one in the same
complex, top floor with roof garden, or perhaps a property in a more
desirable area. The net result is that more money is now available for
buying properties, and prices continue to rise.

But wait a minute. Joe's income is unchanged: he still earns €50,000 a
year. As long as he can afford to make the higher monthly repayment on
the bigger loan there's more money (or credit) available to buy property.
Multiply this story by 200,000 Joes and you have the Irish property
experience since 1992.

Economists and stock-market analysts always look at the overvaluation of the property market in terms of income multiples: the average home price divided by, say, the average industrial wage. It's not wrong to do so: it's just not a reliable metric over the long horizon ('long' being greater than ten years). However, in the short term it does provide a useful insight.

Fig. 14: House prices in terms of income multiples, 1990–2010e

Source: Department of the Environment, Heritage and Local Government, Central Statistics Office

These heuristic maxims of how many times your salary your home price should be vary over time, depending of course on which economic era we're talking about. During the inflationary high-interest-rate 1980s these income multiples were small. Throughout the 90s they increased, largely as inflation subsided, and corresponding rates of interest fell too. At the peak of the property bubble, average home prices were more than ten times the average industrial earnings, or four to five times the average household income for a dual-income household. The latter has become the new norm, especially with increased female participation in the labour market.

Given that home prices have been falling for a year and a half now, just how far can we expect them to fall according to the 'income multiple'? Well, our graph illustrates what it would take to bring house prices back in line with the more recent historical average (since the liberalisation of credit from 1990) of about six times the average industrial wage. It would take a fall in house prices of 30 per cent over a three-year period, accompanied by a 10 per cent increase in wages over the same period. That would be totally consistent with the 2008 national pay deal.

Because homes are usually financed with external debt, it's important to understand the three essential ingredients of mortgage finance: credit availability, short-term interest rates and bank margins. All three home-finance variables can, and do, adjust very rapidly, unlike the supply tap, which is rather sluggish, because of the long lead times in building new homes—often one to two years. We covered this in the earlier chapters on supply, but it's worth reiterating. Don't believe the estate agents when they say, 'It's quicker to turn off the supply than it is to turn it back on again.' This is utter nonsense. All the empirical evidence, as well as the factual data from the Central Statistics Office and the Department of the Environment, Heritage and Local Government, proves that new-home supply moves at a glacial pace. Why else would the rate of finished homes still be so high in 2008 after twenty successive months of falling national home prices and two years of new-home sales being in the doldrums?

With the availability of bank credit and short-term rates changing daily, and following the global bank liquidity crunch that began in August 2007, banks everywhere are sitting on their cash piles, seeking out new depositors by offering spectacularly high deposit rates. They're also rebuilding their margins, or 'spreads', as they're called in banking circles.

These 'de-leveraging' pains are being felt right now in the property market. Irish banks, like their international counterparts, are in the process of rebuilding their margins by following a crude strategy. This involves lending less, to a smaller and more select group of people, as well as increasing the margin between where they fund themselves and what they ultimately charge the customer. Back in early 1999, when Ireland joined the euro bloc, Irish banks typically earned 2¼ per cent above base rates for home-loan credit. At the peak of the market, in 2006, this spread had fallen to about 1 per cent or less. Take this former spread as the new target and you won't be far wrong in guessing where banks would like to see their margins again in the not-so-distant future.

This means that they will be paying more attention to 'borrower quality', which is the new catchphrase. It actually takes Ireland back to the days of pre-liberalisation or 'pre-postcode' property credit.

Two other characteristics of the mortgage market are relevant to this discussion. The first is that Ireland has always been a 'variable-rate' mortgage market. Three out of every four mortgages are 'tracker' or variable-rate mortgages, which means that they adjust monthly, depending either on base rates or on the three-month European inter-bank offered rate (Euribor). The second characteristic is that of the maximum loan-to-value ratio. At present there's no statutory maximum loan-to-value ratio in the home-loan market. Perhaps there should be. This was another feature of the property bubble, particularly in the consumer boom era of 2003–07, when 100 per cent mortgages became commonplace. Actually they should be renamed or reclassified as the no-deposit or no-savings home loans.

THE HOUSE-PRICE FEEDBACK LOOP

Everyone knows that if you own a property and its value increases a lot over time, perhaps doubling or trebling, you can borrow more money secured on the property itself. This is an example of the 'positive' house-price feedback loop. There's a reverse, however—the negative feedback loop—and it works the same way, but in the opposite direction. As valuations fall in response to drops in house prices, the amount of credit available for home purchase will contract; this in turn means less money available for home-buyers who offer less, so house prices fall, and so on.

Fig. 15: The house-price feedback loop

This is what happened in the latter part of 2007 and since then. It will continue to occur until a nadir in property prices is reached. Once a confirmed market bottom has occurred, the house-price feedback loop will turn positive once more. A simple definition of a price bottom for Irish property would be six successive monthly price increases, to be accompanied by a rising number of sales and a definite increase in turnover.

It should be noted that alongside the increased availability of credit and the preponderance of the 100 per cent loan-to-value mortgage, another contributing factor to the property price bubble was the illusion of affordability conjured up by ever-increasing loan tenures. Put simply, going back to our earlier example, Joe's defining affordability criterion was the monthly repayment in absolute or money terms. Merely extending the loan period, to reduce the size of the monthly mortgage repayment, increases the total amount of interest payable and delays the inevitable, when price affordability is pushed beyond the reach of the average buyer. For decades the average tenure of a home loan in Ireland was only 20 years. At the height of the boom, 30, 35 and 40-year loans became commonplace. This was totally irresponsible behaviour by banks and their mortgage brokers. Why did the financial regulator, which in Ireland is the Central Bank and Financial Services Authority of Ireland (CBFSAI), not stop this!

Purely as a matter of interest, this phenomenon was neither new nor unique to the Irish situation. In Germany, for instance, 40-year home loans have been the norm for many years now; but mortgages in that country are predominantly fixed-rate, so they are not sensitive to movements in short-term interest rates. The best example of home-loan tenure lunacy was in Japan in the 1980s, when 'century' mortgages became popular. Yes, they were bequeathed from father to son, or daughter. The children not only inherited the property but inherited the mortgage too!

If any bank provides a forty-year home loan to a 25-year-old it means that the institution accepts that the borrower will be paying a mortgage in their retirement. The social costs and consequences should be obvious to all. But many young Irish people took 100 per cent loan-to-value forty-year mortgages (some with interest-only initial periods) at the height of the property boom (late 2005 to early 2007) in the mistaken belief that future capital appreciation, combined with rising incomes, would allow them to refinance later on at more advantageous terms. How wrong they were! Those young potential home-buyers who in recent years failed to get onto the property ladder because of reduced credit availability have been inadvertently saved from their own ignorance. That may not sound nice, but believe me, it's a good thing.

SECURITISATION SAVES

Part of the improved credit availability during the bubble period was due to new legislation passed in 2001 that enabled specialist credit institutions (such as the banks and building societies) to pool together large bundles of mortgages as bonds and then sell them on to professional and institutional investors. These bonds, called 'asset-covered securities', are commonly traded in other European countries, including Germany, France and Spain. Indeed when I was European credit strategist at Morgan Stanley and later at UBS (the financial services company) I used to cover this market segment from an analysis viewpoint. These 'covered' bonds are heavily regulated and often have far less credit risk than the banks that issue them. The incentive for the mortgage lenders who issue them is that they receive favourable risk weighting from the Bank for International Settlements, the global financial regulator—often called the central bankers' bank—and they allow banks to transfer some of the credit risk associated with home loans to the debt capital markets—a sort of stock market for bonds rather than equities, though the same group of professional investors invest in both.

Bank of Ireland has been a big issuer of asset-covered securities, so far removing about 5 per cent of all its home loans off its own balance sheet. In essence, this reduces the bank's sensitivity to the house-price feedback loop. But since the global credit crisis began, investors' appetite for these securities has dried up. This puts added pressure on lenders such as Bank of Ireland in the form of available capital for making new home loans.

Securitisation not only saves money for the issuing bank, in lowering the amount of capital reserves needed to be put aside against mortgage loans, but in this instance also saves the prospective and willing mortgagee from acquiring more credit through higher effective mortgage costs. Sometimes unsuspecting customers need to be saved from themselves, especially when it comes to credit.

INFLATIONARY DRIVERS

Believe it or not, inflation is actually good for something. Houses are perceived as a hedge against future inflation, because they're financed with fixed nominal debt. Inflation may cause the value of your house to rise (in nominal terms anyway) but not your outstanding mortgage balance. Householders have caught on to this fact over many years of experience, and it's one of the attractions of home ownership (especially as, in the long run, inflation drives up rents too). The academic research does indeed support this conclusion. However, as Irish property prices are more sensitive to nominal rates (the money rate you pay) than to 'real' rates (inflation-adjusted downwards), persistently higher rates of inflation can have a negative impact on house prices, particularly as short-term interest rates (like the European Central Bank rate) have to be raised to counter this threat.

This is why the European Central Bank had been in rate-raising mode from December 2005 until October 2008. (We explore this shortly in chapter 18.)

CONCLUSION

Potential home-buyers may be confused by mixed messages received from the objective and largely independent academics on the one hand and the vested-interest parties—our 'vIPs'—on the other. If you find yourself in this situation and you don't know who to believe, err on the side of caution. Do nothing! Wait and see what happens. You needn't worry: the market won't run away from you, as it did in the late 1990s. There were genuine reasons for the large price increases back then. Not so now.

It's still a buyer's market. That means that the potential purchaser has the balance of power. It also means that home-buyers can negotiate better prices. But don't go bananas either way: the bonanza may be gone but the recovery is a long way off. The recovery period has always been longer than the initial price-fall period.

Oh, yes, and the agents will now talk about prices in the 'medium term' and not about prices this year or next. The medium term is a five-year horizon, so time is definitely on the potential buyer's side.

There have been many property booms in many countries around the world. Often they have been characterised by individual years when property prices rise by as much as 20 to 40 per cent. But just as there are booms there are also busts, and these always begin with falls between 8 and 15 per cent in the initial down years, just as Irish residential property prices officially dropped by 7.3 per cent in 2007, according to the backward-looking house-price indices. The true decline in asking prices was closer to 15 per cent.

A good example of the pattern of price falls and of how things may pan out was provided by the Netherlands in the early 1980s. In 1980 house prices there fell by 8.7 per cent, then by another 10.3 per cent in 1981, followed by a further 10 per cent fall in 1982. In Finland in 1991 and 1992 home prices fell year on year by 15 and 17 per cent, respectively. Even in Japan in 1992 house prices only dropped by 8.7 per cent.

This is how property slumps begin, following a major housing bubble.

Nominal house-price falls usually run for three or four years from peak to trough. In the past it has taken between three and seven years for these markets to recover in 'real' terms; some have not yet regained their former glory in nominal terms. The length of the recovery period is directly proportional to the size of the bubble, as one would expect.

This doesn't bode well for the Irish residential property market. As we have shown elsewhere, nominal house prices may not regain their 2007 peak until 2016 or beyond. Three years of 'famine' (price drops of about 10 per cent or more) followed by seven years of 'feast' (price gains of 5 per cent per year) would still leave nominal prices lower than they were a decade earlier. That, dear reader, is just sums.

POSTSCRIPT

Charles Kindleberger, in *Manias, Panics, and Crashes: A History of Financial Crises* (second edition, 1992) offers an alternative definition of a speculative bubble, which he describes as

> a sharp rise in price of an asset or a range of assets in a continuous process, with the initial rise generating expectations of further rises and attracting new buyers—generally speculators interested in profits

from trading in the asset rather than its use or earning capacity. The rise is usually followed by a reversal of expectations and a sharp decline in price, often resulting in financial crisis.

It was certainly true of the Irish property bubble that initial increases gave rise to the belief in further price gains. It was also true that the number of speculators entering the market, at one point becoming as important as traditional first-time buyers (according to mortgage data and the Bank of Ireland loan portfolio in June 2007), were more interested in flipping properties or refinancing them once values had increased. The increased national vacancy rate is further evidence that these speculators didn't purchase for utilitarian use or even to rent out in many cases.

The last point is equally compelling, as the reversal in fortune of the property market has indeed had disastrous financial consequences for the share prices of Irish banks.

It remains to be seen whether this reversal manifests itself as a full-blown financial crisis. For that to happen, a major property developer would have to go bust, or the banks would need to be fully recapitalised. As the British banks learnt in a severe lesson in 2008, the market can be a very unforgiving place. Just ask Northern Rock, Bradford and Bingley, Barclay's, Halifax Bank of Scotland and Royal Bank of Scotland (owners of Ulster Bank) how the reversal of fortune in the British housing market decimated their balance sheets, not to mention their share prices.

As the traditional warning goes, the value of your property can go down as well as up.

Chapter 16

Top of the Drops

It's no secret that house prices have fallen substantially over the last year and a half. The official figures suggest that Irish property values declined only 7.3 per cent in 2007, as measured by the PTSB-ESRI house-price index and by almost 10 per cent so far in 2008. However, we now know that using the PTSB-ESRI index is like squinting in the rear-view mirror of your car and trying to see what's going on several miles back.

Earlier in the book we explored the reality of this index and its inherent problems, both being backward-looking and representing only a fifth, at best, of the market in terms of mortgage loans drawn down. We still don't know how prices really fared in the closing months of 2008, and we won't find out until March or even April 2009, when we're told what the February 2009 average house price was, and that will reflect 'sale agreed' deals done just before Christmas.

We also know, just by looking around at what's for sale in our own localities—what people like to call anecdotal evidence—that asking prices on second-hand homes are seriously down on the previous year, indeed by at least double the official fall in the average home price. Nobody is a better judge of true property valuations than ourselves and what we witness with our own eyes. Even the VIPs, and the estate agents in particular, have not shied away from telling us that in some areas asking prices have been reduced by 20 to 30 per cent. Serious discounts, then, are to be had.

Take some time off to do some research—and, let's be honest, how many of us like to browse the property classifieds or surf the property web portals, having a sniff of what's out there and what kind of money people are asking for? Honestly, isn't everybody interested in property?—especially when we've seen the market ramp up for so many years and now the opposite is occurring. Remember when your neighbours sold their house and got €250,000, or half a million, or even a cool million? Some Dublin people not so long ago, much to the disgust of others around the country, were asking themselves, sure what would you get for a million nowadays? A three-bedroom end-of-terrace in Killester!

One of the most popular television programmes back in the bad old days of the 1970s and 80s was a weekly BBC chart music show featuring the latest bands and musicians, ranked according to their weekly record sales. It was called 'Top of the Pops' and was probably the most popular television show of its day among teenagers and pre-teens. You have to remember that this was BMTV (before MTV) and long before satellite or cable. Streets were cleared at twenty past seven on a Thursday as teenagers flocked home to sit in front of the box to see who number 1 was in the charts and to see their favourite group perform live. It was compulsive viewing, not just because it was aimed at young people or had all the latest songs but rather because you hadn't really made it until you appeared on it. It was *the* popular-music league table; and we, as human beings, have always been fascinated with league tables.

Just as today we're all still interested in popular music, sports and other league tables, it seemed a good idea to compile a chart of property price falls—a sort of 'Top of the Drops', if you'll excuse the pun. This is not at all meant to be mean to those sellers who have found themselves in the unfortunate position of having to knock serious lumps off their asking prices. In fact most can be and are in the fortunate position of being able to do so, because they bought so long ago that, even allowing for significant price discounts, they're still far ahead in money terms. Many people when they learn what these owners originally paid for these properties that are now for sale may be tempted to use the G-word. (Hint: sounds like 'creed'.)

The best place to begin our Top of the Drops chart is not with the new housing schemes, though they're widely publicised in the media in recent times, but rather the far more expensive second-hand homes market. Why do we use the term 'second-hand' homes? Why don't we just call them 'existing' or 'previously lived in', particularly as there's nothing wrong with a property that has been somebody else's home for any amount of time? Older or 'period' houses have far more character than the pebble-dashed breeze-block rectangles that have been built in recent years; and people are often willing to pay a big premium for these properties, especially when they're of historical interest or significance, as we shall soon see. This is probably one reason why they went up so much in the first place.

Just as that television show was made around a top 40 music chart, we begin with Ireland's top 40 price drops of 2007 and 2008, inasmuch as one can measure these things. It's difficult to compile completely accurate figures, as many properties are withdrawn at auction and then later sold privately. (One seminal feature of the residential property market in 2007 was the death of the property auction and the near-universal move to sale by private treaty.) Where possible, multiple sources have been used to confirm both the original selling price, often from newspaper reviews at the time of listing, and the latest price from estate agents' web sites.

Needless to say, when the dreaded 'POA' (price on application) appears next to a property, we can no longer consider it for the price-drop charts, or we just have to use the last known published price. Also, the 'sale agreed' symbol (usually and appropriately in red, for some reason) often appears after a property has spent some considerable time languishing on the market. When the selling price disappears, again we can't accurately assess whether or not it achieved the asking price, unless, of course, the agents say so—and how truthful or forthcoming are they?

It's not an easy task to compile such lists—despite such wonderful new tools as internet search engines and web sites like irishpropertywatch. com, as well as well-known property web portals such as www.daft.ie and myhome.ie or even blog sites such as www.thepropertypin.com—firstly because of the duplication of properties between sites but secondly also because properties may be listed, then removed for a period, then listed again, usually with a significantly reduced price. One can only try to uncover as much truth in the price discovery process as possible. It's worth the considerable effort, however, as the result makes for fascinating reading.

To make it into the Top of the Drops Top 40, the asking price of a house has to have been slashed by at least €1 million. To buy all forty of these properties at the full asking price today would cost you more than €228 million, but back in the spring of 2007 the same motley collection would have set you back more than €328 million—in other words, there's been a total reduction in price of more than €100 million, or an average drop of €2.5 million per house. That's a lot in anyone's book—representing an average fall of some 30 per cent. But that average disguises the fact that some have been reduced by a mere sixth (similar to the drop in the overall national house-price index up to now), whereas others have had the price cut by half or more! It shows how much fat was there in the first place if sellers can slash prices by that much and still be ahead in the money stakes.

Others might claim that it's just a reflection of how weak the market is, lacking the confidence of prospective buyers and lacking financial support from lending institutions. Perhaps what went before in recent years was abnormal, it wasn't justifiable, and we're now returning to reality, with corresponding prices coming back down to earth. You can judge for yourself.

Table 19: Top of the Drops: The forty biggest fallers

Rank	Property	Location	First price	Latest price	Drop	Percentage drop
1	Sorrento House, 1 Sorrento Terrace	Dalkey, Co. Dublin	€30,000,000	€20,000,000	−€10,000,000	−33%
2	53 Aylesbury Road, Ballsbridge	Dublin 4	€60,000,000	€50,000,000	−€10,000,000	−17%
3	Monte Alverno	Dalkey, Co. Dublin	€25,000,000	€17,500,000	−€7,500,000	−30%
4	Moyglare Manor, Maynooth	Co. Kildare	€10,000,000	€3,750,000	−€6,250,000	−63%
5	Trefleur, Westminster Road	Foxrock, Dublin 18	€13,000,000	€7,000,000	−€6,000,000	−46%
6	An Cúlú, Kenmare	Co. Kerry	€15,000,000	€10,000,000	−€5,000,000	−33%
7	Kinnitty Castle	Co. Offaly	€13,000,000	€9,800,000	−€3,200,000	−25%
8	Jamestown Court, Castletown Geoghegan	Mullingar, Co. Westmeath	€7,500,000	€4,500,000	−€3,000,000	−40%
9	20 Burlington Road, Ballsbridge	Dublin 4	€7,500,000	€4,750,000	−€2,750,000	−37%
10	Fairlawn House, Saval Park Road	Dalkey, Co. Dublin	€6,250,000	€3,700,000	−€2,550,000	−41%
11	Ballycarbery, St George's Avenue	Killiney, Co. Dublin	€4,500,000	€2,250,000	−€2,250,000	−50%
12	Bellingham Castle, Castlebellingham	Co. Louth	€6,750,000	€4,500,000	−€2,250,000	−33%
13	Knockrobin House, Knockrobin	Co. Wicklow	€7,000,000	€4,800,000	−€2,200,000	−31%
14	Mount Henry, Torca Road	Dalkey, Co. Dublin	€8,000,000	€6,000,000	−€2,000,000	−25%
15	Gerrardstown House and Stud, Dunshaughlin	Co. Meath	€15,000,000	€13,000,000	−€2,000,000	−13%
16	Eirene, Marino Avenue, East	Killiney, Co. Dublin	€6,000,000	€4,150,000	−€1,850,000	−31%
17	Monalin House, Newtown Mount Kennedy	Co. Wicklow	€6,300,000	€4,500,000	−€1,800,000	−29%
18	Ashroe, Malahide	North Co. Dublin	€6,500,000	€4,800,000	−€1,700,000	−26%
19	51 Nutley Road, Donnybrook	Dublin 4	€3,500,000	€1,900,000	−€1,600,000	−46%
20	Glenlion House, Thormanby Road, Howth	Co. Dublin	€6,500,000	€4,900,000	−€1,600,000	−25%
21	Rockview House, Port Laoise	Co. Laois	€3,000,000	€1,500,000	−€1,500,000	−50%

22	Killenure Castle, Dundrum	Co. Tipperary	€2,750,000	€2,250,000	-40%
23	Lower Cove, Kinsale	Co. Cork	€2,750,000	€3,300,000	-53%
24	Kilcolman Rectory, Enniskeane	Co. Cork	€3,200,000	€1,750,000	-45%
25	34 Belgrave Road, Rathmines (4-bed)	Dublin 6	€3,800,000	€2,395,000	-37%
26	18 Sydney Avenue	Blackrock, Co. Dublin	€3,350,000	€2,000,000	-40%
27	Clonacody House, Fethard	Co. Tipperary	€7,000,000	€5,650,000	-19%
28	Kilbarron, 4 St Matthias Wood	Killiney, Co. Dublin	€3,750,000	€2,450,000	-35%
29	Lios na Mara, Saval Park Road	Dalkey, Co. Dublin	€4,500,000	€3,250,000	-28%
30	Dunkellin Street, Loughrea	Co. Galway	€2,200,000	€1,000,000	-55%
31	Killymard House, Donegal	Co. Donegal	€2,500,000	€1,300,000	-48%
32	Lairaken, Banagher	Co. Offaly	€6,700,000	€5,500,000	-18%
33	Lois Bridges, Greenfield Road, Sutton	Dublin 13	€2,800,000	€1,650,000	-41%
34	Baywood House, Glandore	Co. Cork	€2,500,000	€1,400,000	-44%
35	Rushanes, Glandore	Co. Cork	€2,500,000	€1,400,000	-44%
36	Garrylough, Screen, Castlebridge	Co. Wexford	€2,600,000	€1,550,000	-40%
37	7 Claremont Road, Howth Road	Dublin 13	€4,800,000	€3,750,000	-22%
38	Sea Haven, Coast Road, Portmarnock	Co. Dublin	€4,000,000	€2,975,000	-26%
39	Brandy Hall House, Castletown Bearhaven	Co. Cork	€2,700,000	€1,700,000	-37%
40	Glengarriff	Co. Cork	€2,900,000	€1,900,000	-34%

NO. 1
'Sorrento House', Dalkey, Co. Dublin

Coming in at no. 1 in our charts for the biggest drop in asking price is none other than 'Sorrento House' or number 1 Sorrento Terrace, Dalkey, Co. Dublin. It appeared on the market for a staggering €30 million in September 2006, which was then reduced to €25 million and subsequently in 2007 to €20 million. For those who are not familiar with the area, Sorrento Terrace is a small row of stucco-fronted houses, only eight in total, with a south-facing view of Killiney Bay and the Wicklow Mountains. These highly sought-after nineteenth-century houses have gardens that run down to the sea, are five minutes' walk from the centre of Dalkey and two minutes' walk from Coliemore Harbour. The area is a favourite weekend walking spot for many Dubliners, who like to stroll over Killiney Hill, down to Vico Road and Killiney beach. It's truly a beautiful place, and walking down Vico Road towards Sorrento Terrace you could be forgiven if you thought you were in the south of France. This stretch of coast, from Bullock Harbour up to the top of Vico Road, has indeed been called the Dublin Riviera. (The similarity between Killiney Bay and the Bay of Naples is where the Italian name Sorrento is derived from.)

The present owner of number 1, Terry Coleman, bought the house in 1998 for what was then the record sum of £5.9 million (a little less than €7½ million), outbidding Lochlann Quinn (brother of the Labour Party TD Ruairí Quinn) in the process. This was a lot for an old house that was in need of complete renovation, especially as the previous owners had kept the property in their family for more than half a century. The 96-year-old seller was Dorothy Lavery, the widow of an eye surgeon. Obviously Mr Coleman has done a lot to the property over the last decade to warrant such an exorbitant asking price. The house seemingly lay vacant for the first couple of years while wrangling went on with the planning authorities and An Bord Pleanála. Despite planning refusal in July 2000, the house was eventually renovated.

Although Terry Coleman was born in Ireland, he made his fortune in Britain in the car alarm and mobile phone businesses. The Scorpion car alarm was originally manufactured in Manchester by Mr Coleman's company, though it was put into receivership five years ago.

Generally speaking, properties in this road would be expected to fetch at least €5 million, and for this the lucky buyer could expect to rub shoulders with such neighbours as Neil Jordan (film director), Robin Power (property developer), Glynis Robins (Dalkey Design Company) and Colm Barrington (a former executive with Guinness Peat Aviation). Other former neighbours at one time included no less than three senior counsels, while Ronnie Robins SC still lives at number 2. The first to sell up and move was Eoin McGonigal SC (who represented the former Taoiseach Charles Haughey in the beef tribunals). He paid £450,000, or €571,000, for number 3 in the early 1990s, later putting it on the market in 2000 with a guide price of £2.2 million. Back in 1993 another barrister, Frank Clarke SC, bought number 5 for £470,000, or about €600,000. He sold in 2004, and the house was placed on the market with a guide price of €3.8 million.

The legal connection goes back further and has been a continuing theme at this address. When the barrister Hercules Henry Grave MacDonnell and his family eventually sold Sorrento House in the early 1900s it was to Judge Thomas Overend. Perhaps it will take the income of a senior counsel today—maybe one working in the Mahon Tribunal—to be able to afford such an ostentatiously priced house at one of Dublin's most salubrious suburban addresses, though at twenty million it may be beyond even their reach. This would explain why both agents, Knight Frank and Sherry FitzGerald, are marketing it as an 'international' property, one for the international jet-set.

Number 1 is different from the rest. It's the end of the terrace, therefore semi-detached. Like the others, it's four storeys, but it comprises more than 8,000 square feet of interior living space, as well as 1½ acres of gardens, including a small private harbour and even enough space for a helicopter pad. The house was built in 1845 and was the first and the largest of the series of residences owned by the MacDonnell family, who had purchased the land and built Sorrento Cottage in 1837. They laid down strict criteria for how they wanted the site developed: the rest of the houses were to be built to the same design, by the architects Frederick Darley and Nathaniel Montgomery. Each house had to cost at least £1,000, and permitted colours and proportions were set out in the lease: namely, they were all to be the same. The last house to be finished, number 8, was not built until 1874. All eight were built by a local builder, Edward Masterson, who had a reputation at the time for building fine houses in Dún Laoghaire and Dalkey.

By the early years of national independence the value of these properties had plummeted, to £650 in 1925. It took until 1968 for the price to rise, when one was sold for £7,500. Another was sold in 1979, this time fetching about £200,000 or a little more than €250,000. In 1991 Neil Jordan spent £400,000 on number 6, which at the time was the highest price paid for a mid-terrace house in the Dublin area. Then seven years later, in 1998, he bought the house next door for £1.8 million from the Forsythe family, who had spent the previous decade restoring the property from flats to a full house. Jordan turned number 7 into his work space and office.

And the rest, as they say, is history.

What is noteworthy is that both Terry Coleman and Neil Jordan bought properties here in the same year, 1998. The former bought for nearly €7½ million, the latter for €2.3 million, or roughly a third of the price of the big house at the end. Assuming this logic still holds true, you would reasonably expect numbers 2 to 8 to fetch about €7 million today, provided number 1 is fairly valued at €20 million.

What if one of these houses was to come on the market with a guide price of, say, €6½ million but make only €5 million? Then logic would dictate that Sorrento House would be worth only €15 million, wouldn't it? We shall have to wait and see.

NO. 2
53 Aylesbury Road, Dublin 4
This Dublin 4 residence has also been cut in price by €10 million but was pipped to the post for top drop by virtue of the fact that its price cut, though large in money terms, was a mere 17 per cent off the original asking price. Number 53 is technically a little bit of the French Republic for sale, as of course it's the French ambassador's residence. (Perhaps, then, if it's bought by an Irish person the territory of Ireland would officially expand by 1¾ acres when ownership reverted back from foreign-soil status.)

This eleven-bedroom 11,000-square-foot mansion, built in 1900 and in French hands since 1930, was originally put on the market at the beginning of 2008 for megabucks. A staggering €60 million was the initial asking price. If it had sold for that money it would have achieved the dubious status of being the most expensive house ever sold in the history of the country. (That honour went instead to 'Walford', a seven-bedroom house in nearby Shrewsbury Road that went for a record €58 million in 2005.) Despite the accompanying 1.8 acres of grounds on Ireland's premier road (yes, Shrewsbury Road pips Aylesbury Road—recall those rainy days spent as a child playing Monopoly), it's still a horrendous amount of moolah for a home. Maybe as a hotel or a shopping centre one might be forgiven for spending that much, but for a private residence to cost upwards of $100 million you would expect substantially more.

According to the property team at the *Irish Times* it's rumoured that 'Walford' is back on the market, with an asking price of €75 million, but they also reveal that at least one property insider reckons it wouldn't fetch anything more than €40 million today—a decline in value of some €18 million in less than three years, or a loss in value of half a million per month. These telephone numbers being bandied about for house prices are truly repulsive and are a sad indictment of the crass *nouveau-riche* class that comprises Ireland's new super-rich.

Aylesbury Road was built in the middle of the nineteenth century on land owned by George Herbert, Earl of Pembroke, whose daughter married the Marquis of Aylesbury, hence the naming of the street in his honour. Aylesbury Road was the longest straight road in Dublin, running from the church at Donnybrook to the railway at Sidney Parade. The designs called for a combination of red brick and granite, with granite steps leading to the hall door, and all residences were bordered by iron railings. Numbers 1 to 27 were all built by Alderman Joseph Meade, whose designs were always characterised by circular granite pillars at the entrance gates. His own home on Merrion Road (now St Michael's College) bears testament to this compulsion.

Aylesbury Road is without argument one of Ireland's premier addresses. It's right in the centre of the embassy belt and not too far from Dublin city centre. If you were to count the number of houses on this road that have changed hands over the last couple of years you'd run out of fingers very quickly. Even Albert Reynolds, the former Taoiseach, managed to offload his Dublin 4 pad here for €14 million, though Sherry FitzGerald had put it on the market with an initial asking price of €15 million. With hindsight, this may prove to have been quite a shrewd move. Albert paid £625,000 in 1993 for number 18, 'Avonmore', equivalent to a smidgen below €800,000. Fourteen years later he sold it for seventeen-and-a-half times the purchase price. The capital appreciation over this period amounts to 23 per cent per year, an unprecedented level of price growth.

The financier and former tax inspector Derek Quinlan bought number 43 in 2006 for more than €8½ million. Number 41 was withdrawn at auction in early November 2007 at €8½ million and is still for sale. Number 61 sold in the first half of 2007 for a staggering €15½ million. Several properties changed hands between 2006 and 2007, many achieving prices above €10 million. In early 2008 number 39, the French embassy offices, a two-storey building on one acre, went up for sale at €20 million. (That's in addition to number 53, the ambassador's residence, mentioned above.) Do the French know something we don't? Are they attempting a sale and lease-back, like what a big Irish bank did in Ballsbridge a year earlier?

NO. 3
'Monte Alverno', Sorrento Road, Dalkey, Co. Dublin

Meanwhile Sherry FitzGerald had another house for sale in Dalkey, in Sorrento Road, just up the hill from Sorrento Terrace and at an even higher price. 'Monte Alverno' was up for sale at €25 million, having been on the market since April 2007. It was more than a year on the market at that price, even after its neighbour down the hill had dropped the price of his 'des. res.' by ten million. So it was definitely on the cards that this Dalkey delight would succumb to the general property malaise and suffer a similar fate. In the summer of 2008 the auctioneer's gavel gave way to the estate agent's scalpel and, lo and behold, €7½ million was whittled off the asking price.

This six-bedroom mansion on 1.2 acres, next door to Van Morrison and Michelle Rocca, was bought by the present owners, Alphonsus and Claudia O'Mara, in 1992 for £1.01 million, or a tad under €1.3 million, from Renata Coleman. Incidentally, this was more than double what Neil Jordan paid for number 6 Sorrento Terrace about the same time, and he later paid a third of what Terry Coleman paid in 1998 for Sorrento House for number 7. But Monte Alverno was more expensive and on a smaller plot than Sorrento House, and it shares a driveway with the neighbours, which has led to High Court and Supreme Court action over privacy and plans to widen the driveway.

Monte Alverno is a superb dwelling, built about the same time as the other Dalkey mansion, in 1835. It's large, at more than 8,000 square feet, has a pool and a tennis court, manicured gardens and an elevated position with magnificent sea views, but it doesn't have a private harbour. Was it worth five million more than Sorrento House? Undoubtedly not, hence the subsequent drop to €2½ million below Sorrento House. This is what investment bankers call relative value—the market price of one compared with the other, accounting for subtle differences, of course. In a downturn some sellers trim or slash their asking price. Others simply don't: they play the waiting game instead. At the beginning of 2008 a lot of properties fell into the latter category, even after they had appreciated at 22 per cent per year for fifteen years, or nearly twenty times the original price paid. An annual return of 20 per cent would result in an asking price of €20 million, whereas €15 million would equate to an annual return of 18 per cent since 1992.

Greed is a terrible thing. It clouds people's judgement. Is 18 per cent compound return per year for fifteen years on the trot necessarily a bad result? Let's put this in perspective: even €10 million would still equate to a compound return of 15 per cent per year. Not bad if you can get it, eh?

Even if further big falls occur at the top end of the property market (prices halving is not an unrealistic assumption), these sellers remain big winners, whichever way you look at it. But some people simply don't get it. Jim Sheridan's concrete box, 'Martha's Vineyard', overlooking the sea on Coliemore Road, is another example of a Dalkey house on the market for more than a year with no price movement. Mr Sheridan is seeking €8 million for this ultra-modern home. Perhaps this property may make the price drop charts in the not-so-distant future.

NO. 4
Moyglare Manor, Maynooth, Co. Kildare
At €6¼ million off the original €10 million advertised by the agents, Savills HOK, back in 2007, this Georgian residence on 13 acres in Maynooth has the biggest proportionate price drop in the top 40 at a whopping 63 per cent off. At present Moyglare Manor is run as a country-house hotel and restaurant, but, as the agents' original advertisement, said,

> Moyglare Manor is ideally suited to future use as a luxurious private residence, particularly given its wonderful location on the edge of Dublin, in the heart of Ireland's top bloodstock region.

They have pitched this property not as a commercial entity, as it is today, but towards the 'high net worth' individual with a penchant for horse-riding or perhaps even horse-breeding. This may have been a mistake, as there are many larger country houses, stud farms and estates with purpose-built equestrian facilities elsewhere in Cos. Meath and Kildare, and with a lot more land attached too. Moyglare Manor is in the commuter town of Maynooth, adjacent to the university, only sixteen miles from Dublin. Most prospective buyers would probably wish to continue to run it as a hotel and restaurant of some renown and might be attracted by the substantial price cut, first from €10 million to €7½ million in June 2007, then towards the end of the year by another €2½ million. Next, at the end of March 2008, the €5 million price tag was shaved down to €4.9 million, only to be cut once more in May to a price of €4 million; and then later, in early October, a further quarter of a million was snipped off the asking tag.

Given that everyone likes a bargain, or at least a substantial discount, there must be many interested parties who have looked at this one. Perhaps it hasn't sold because of the inability of buyers to obtain a mortgage. The role of banks in the price-drop stakes shouldn't be underestimated, for they caused most of the spectacular price increases during the boom years with their reckless lending practices.

NO. 5
'Trefleur', Westminster Road, Foxrock, Dublin 18
Another €6 million drop at no. 5 for Trefleur, on two-thirds of a hectare (approximately 1.65 acres) in Foxrock. This five-bedroom 3,000-square-foot period house doesn't command the €7 million price premium but rather is being sold as development land, with a large frontage (more than 100 metres) onto snobbish Westminster Road, though it's only 150 metres from the N11 Stillorgan dual carriageway. This was another Savills HOK property, which was originally on the market for €13 million. Some

real arm-twisting must have occurred for the agent to persuade the seller to drop their asking price by 46 per cent. This property is still a private residence and could be kept as such, though at €7 million it would be a lot of dough per square foot, even for this Dublin 18 address.

NO. 6
'An Cúlú', Kenmare, Co. Kerry

If anyone asks you again what you would do if you won the euro millions lottery you should reply that you would buy a castle in Co. Kerry. 'An Cúlú' is truly one of those unique properties—a bit of a paradox really. It's a modern 'castle' with six bedrooms and five bathrooms, built over four floors, surrounded by a moat and entered by way of a drawbridge. Inside, the driveway is flanked by one wall with a cascading waterfall. It's extravagance in the extreme, but a contradiction too. For instance, the exterior is presented in a gothic style, yet the interior boasts an indoor grotto-style swimming pool. Access to this contemporary dwelling is even available by boat via a private harbour, as it sits adjacent to the water not three miles from Kenmare. A magnificent floodlit picture of this anachronistic house appeared in the *Irish Times* in July 2007. Originally it came on the market in March 2007 at €15 million. Obviously the agents, Knight Frank, believed it to be worth that much back then. One year later it can be had for a mere €10 million. As the Lotto slogan goes, 'It could be you!'

NO. 7
Kinnitty Castle, Kinnitty, Co. Offaly

According to the Offaly Property web site, Kinnitty Castle is a neo-gothic castle dating from the tenth century. 'Tastefully restored, the property is situated in a very central and accessible location in the middle of Ireland'. The site listed the price as approximately $21 million, obviously seeking an American buyer who requires a 28,000-square-foot residence on 61 acres. Americans do like bigger homes, but surely not this big. However, the web site also explains that

> the Castle is the ancestral home of the O'Carroll's who ruled this territory for almost a thousand years. They were dispossessed by Oliver Cromwell in the 1630s at which time they were granted huge estates in Maryland, USA where they remain to this day.

So that's the American connection. That $21 million is the approximate equivalent of €13½ million, taking an exchange rate of 1.55 (which is conservative, as one could reasonably argue that it was more than €14 million according to the lower value of the dollar when it first went up for sale).

Kinnitty Castle today is more famous as a hotel that caters for weddings and is marketed as the 'gateway to the Slieve Blooms.' It also achieved notoriety because of the court battles over its sale. The most recent owner, Con Ryan, apparently agreed to sell the property to the Hanly Group, a Roscommon construction and development firm that paid a deposit of €2 million in 2006. According to the *Irish Independent*, the sale was agreed for €14 million; however, the *Sunday Business Post* reported in June 2007 that the proposed sale was for €16 million. (Needless to say, the papers often get the numbers wrong, but the added confusion of quoting the sale price in a foreign currency hasn't helped.) It has been on the market subsequently for varying amounts. It would appear that in recent times the asking price has been cut by several million, to slightly less than €10 million by mid-2008. The agents, Knight Frank, have listed the castle on a British web site, www.primelocation. com, at £7,856,660, a rather spurious degree of precision. It's also listed as €9.8 million. This is a clue to when the price was last dropped, because it represents an exchange rate of 80.2 pence to the euro, and the only time the euro was worth that much or more against the pound was the week of 15–22 April 2008. That narrows it down quite a bit, then. Consequently, Kinnitty Castle earns the no. 7 spot in the top 40, with a recorded reduction of some €3.7 million.

Stop the press! The latest news in November 2008 is that Kinnitty Castle is now in receivership. That means another price drop could be in the offing!

NO. 8
Jamestown Court, Castletown Geoghegan, Co. Westmeath

Sticking with Knight Frank Ganly Walters—which, we're informed, is a member of the Luxury Portfolio group of estate agents—we come to a country house of true distinction, which slides in at no. 8 on our top 40 price-drops chart. Jamestown Court in Castletown Geoghegan, Co. Westmeath, appeared in *Country Life* on 22 May 2008 with a guide price of €4½ million and with the comment 'A far cry from last summer's launch price of €7½ million.' This house sits on 29.5 hectares (62 acres), just south of Mullingar, close to the new N6 dual carriageway at Kilbeggan. This eight-bedroom, eight-bathroom property is approached by a half-mile driveway and includes a two-bedroom guest cottage as well as a one-bedroom gate lodge, not to mention a sunken garden that was once an old chapel. Jamestown Court was built in 1720 with materials taken from Carne Castle. It was later extended by Sir Richard Nagle, who was the member of Parliament for the county at that time. All in all, this is a lot of property with a lot of history for €4½ million. Not exactly cheap by most people's standards but a realistic price drop nonetheless.

NO. 9
20 Burlington Road, Ballsbridge, Dublin 4
For those in the know, this is the heart of the embassy belt in Dublin. Ballsbridge itself is an important business district, close to Dublin city centre. Houses in this area don't come cheap, and many have been converted to offices by the professional classes. Number 20 Burlington Road is a 3,500-square-foot five-bedroom two-storey-over-basement period house with a detached stone coach-house (read: 900-square-foot garage) at the side of the property. In 2007 it went up for sale at €7½ million, but by the middle of October the same year the price had been dropped by three-quarters of a million, only to be reduced again in late February the following year by another half a million. Six weeks later, in early April 2008, another €300,000 was lopped off, taking the new price down to €5¾ million. By the middle of May, again within another five to six weeks, despair had evidently set in; this time the price was cut by another €1.2 million, bringing the total reduction to €2¾ million, or nearly two-fifths off the first asking price. At €4¾ million in June 2008 this property is still no bargain, but it serves as a good illustration to us all of how quickly overpriced properties can and do fall. Burlington Road thus makes it to no. 9 in our top 40.

NO. 10
'Fairlawn House', Saval Park Road, Dalkey, Co. Dublin
The South Dublin enclave surrounding Killiney Bay features prominently in the Top of the Drops—not surprising, really, as this is one of the areas that appreciated most during the boom-and-bubble years. 'Fairlawn House', a large period residence on one acre in trendy Saval Park Road, first came on the market in mid-2007. It failed to sell at auction, and the Lisney *For sale* sign remained in situ. Then, in February 2008, the price was dropped from €6¼ million to €5 million in an attempt to shift the property. The *Irish Times* reported the fall and noted that this was the type of property that developers were keen to get their hands on. It said: 'The property slump is not going to last forever, and as soon as there's a lift, buyers may be regretting not having moved in time.' Well, they would have regretted snapping up Fairlawn House at five million, because the seller reduced the price by another €0.5 million in May, then another €0.8 million in early September. All told, the reduction was €2.55 million, which earns this Dalkey home no. 10 place in our drops chart.

Interestingly, an article in the property section of the *Sunday Tribune* on 24 June 2007 stated that this house had been withdrawn from auction and was now going for €6.5 million, so the true drop in asking price could be €2.8 million (or it may have been a misprint in the paper). Still, it wouldn't make a great deal of difference to this property's position in the top 40 price drops.

NO. 11
Knockrobin House, Knockrobin, Co. Wicklow

In at no. 10 with a price drop of €2½ million, almost a third off the initial asking price, is Knockrobin House at Knockrobin, Co. Wicklow. This large (5,000-square-foot) period residence on ten acres of grounds near Rathnew had been run as a country-house hotel up to 1993 but was subsequently renovated and converted into what the previous agents, Lennox Estates, described as a comfortable family home. It was put up for sale three years ago at €7 million. Whether it sold then or not isn't known, but what is known is that you could have bought it for a little more than €4.8 million in early 2008, according to the new agents, McDonnell Properties in Ashford. However, by the end of July another 300 grand was lopped off the asking price.

NO. 12
'Ballycarbery', St George's Avenue, Killiney, Co. Dublin

A late entry to our Top 40, Ballycarbery appeared on the market in the spring of 2008 with an initial asking price of €4½ million. Then, at the end of May, the sought-after price was reduced by €650,000; then a further €350,000 reduction occurred just one month later. Finally, in early October, panic obviously set in and another €1¼ million drop appeared to be on the cards, taking the total decline in asking price to 50 per cent.

NO. 13
Bellingham Castle, Castlebellingham, Co. Louth

Registering a total price reduction of €2¼ million, or a drop of one-third, was Bellingham Castle at Castlebellingham, Co. Louth. This well-known property was a recent addition to our list, having been put on the market only in 2008, with an asking price of €6¾ million. That was cut in early September to an even €5 million, only to be chopped by a further half a million one week later, making it another latecomer to Top of the Drops.

NO. 14
'Mount Henry', Torca Road, Dalkey, Co. Dublin

This was the home of the singer Lisa Stansfield, in a quiet cul-de-sac overlooking Killiney Bay. You can't really miss it, as it's painted pink and so tends to stand out against the foliage on the hillside, as well as being one of the houses closest to the top of Killiney Hill—in fact if you stand at Killiney DART station, about one-and-a-half miles away, you can clearly pick out Mount Henry because of its distinctive colour. This six-bedroom nineteenth-century house was originally put on the market in May 2007 for €8 million, later to be reduced to €7.4 million. In early 2008 the asking price dropped by a further €1.4 million and it then dropped to a 'round' €6 million. It sold not long after for an undisclosed sum. The dogs in the street in Dalkey were barking that the agents, Knight Frank, had received offers around the €4½ million mark. It probably achieved something closer to €5 million, but we'll never know, unless the new owner spills the beans. Anyway, we've left the last published price, €6 million, in place, so that's a drop of €2 million on the initial asking price.

Mount Henry could very well have sold for another million less but, in Dublin estate agents' parlance, 'in the region of six million' might easily include a price of five million. Recall that the *Irish Times* property editor, Orna Mulcahy, complained to the National Consumer Agency that a property in Dublin was sold for €625,000 while the agent quoted 'in the region of €950,000.' So, in other words, plus or minus 50 per cent—who's counting, anyway?

This property is big, but not enormous, approximately 511 square metres inside (or 5,500 square feet) and sits on three-quarters of an acre. This part of Dalkey has been called 'Bel Éire' by journalists because so many musicians and celebrities have lived here. Many have now moved on. Robin Palmer of Ganly Waters (now Knight Frank) put an 'advised minimum value' on Mount Henry of €8 million in 2007. When he was interviewed by Cliodhna O'Donoghue on the 'Property View' programme on City Channel that summer he summed up the property by stating that the prospective buyer would be paying €4 million for the wonderful view and the other €4 million for the property! Well, the view hasn't changed in the last year, but the price obviously has. Was Lisa tempted to let it go for substantially less than the asking price?—so that's about a million for the house and grounds and the balance for the view!

Even though the eventual selling price was a massive drop on the €8 million guide of yesteryear, it was no doubt a massive price gain on the original purchase price fifteen years previously. Lisa Stansfield bought Mount Henry in 1993 for around the £400,000 mark, or slightly above €500,000. A €5 million sale would still be ten times the original price paid, or a gain of 17 per cent per year for fifteen years compounded. Not bad, not bad at all!

NO. 15
Gerrardstown House and Stud, Dunshaughlin, Co. Meath
Gerrardstown House in Dunshaughlin, Co. Meath, is a 180-acre stud farm with all the usual trappings one would expect to find at a professional stud: stable yard with twenty-one boxes, indoor training arena, tack room, paddocks and of course a three-bedroom staff cottage. The

main residence is a nineteenth-century two-storey-over-basement house, but there's also an older, eighteenth-century farm residence that serves at present as a home for the estate manger. This property appeared in the *Irish Times* in September 2006 with an asking price of €13 million. It appeared again in the *Irish Farmer's Journal* on 28 October 2006, having been unsold at auction at €12 million (the auction opened at €8 million) and failed to reach the guide price. However, the *Irish Independent* a week earlier, on 20 October, had reported that it had been withdrawn at €10 million. But then in early 2007 the same property appeared on www.privateseller.ie, marketed by the present agents, Jordan Auctioneers, for €15 million. It was later dropped back to €13 million. So a €2 million price drop, back to a price that it failed to sell at two years earlier! This is definitely one to watch as a barometer of the general state of the country-home and estates market.

NO. 16
'Eirene', Killiney, Co. Dublin

This mid-1880s residence on half a hectare was not long on the market before the auctioneer's scalpel was ruthlessly applied. Placed on the market with Savills HOK in Dún Laoghaire, it featured in the property section of the *Irish Times* on 20 March 2008, listed at €6 million. Three months later the price was reduced by three-quarters of a million. Not long afterwards, on 19 June, it featured on the RTE television programme 'Capital D', with Ronan O'Hara of Savills HOK giving the viewers a tour of the house.

It has to be said that the best part of this property is the couple of acres overlooking Killiney Bay. It seems that O'Hara thought so too, as during the interview he kept looking out the window. Perhaps he was admiring the view, or maybe he just didn't want to be there. Only four days later, despite having featured on national television, the price was cut again, this time by a massive €1.1 million, taking the new sale price down to €4.15 million. The total price drop therefore was €1.85 million, more than 30 per cent down in little over a month. This property was used in the Savills HOK Property Outlook, summer 2008, as a backdrop to the Irish residential property section, at the higher price tag. It seems that no amount of publicity will shift a property at the wrong price.

NO. 17
Monalin House, Newtown Mount Kennedy, Co. Wicklow

This six-bedroom country house on 22 acres and only twenty-two miles from Dublin was a late entry at the time of writing, because on 31 August 2007 it had the asking price reduced from €6.3 million to €5.7 million, a drop of €600,000, just missing the top 40. However, during July 2008, a year later, the asking price was reduced again, this time by a further €1.2 million to €4.5 million, so earning it a place in our Top of the Drops chart at no. 17 with a total average fall of 29 per cent.

NO. 18
'Ashroe', Malahide, Co. Dublin
A late addition to the top 40 national property price drops was this dormer-style bungalow, which had its asking price slashed in September 2008 by a whopping €1.7 million. Surprisingly, it's the only entry from Malahide in a list dominated by south Co. Dublin and west Cork. Nevertheless, proportionally speaking, the reduction of a quarter in asking price was very much in keeping with falls in other parts of north Co. Dublin, such places as Sutton and Howth and, of course, Portmarnock.

NO. 20
Glenlion House, Thormanby Road, Howth
This house has already been sold, but it deserves a place in our top 40 and certainly necessitates a mention if only on the grounds of infamy. This was the unoccupied property (for only one year) of the rogue solicitor Michael Lynn. Glenlion House, on 4¾ acres, sits high on the Hill of Howth, overlooking Dublin Bay in the most sought-after address of north Co. Dublin. It came on the market in June 2006 at €6½ million but failed to sell at auction. A couple of months later, in January 2007, Michael Lynn and his wife, Bríd Murphy, bought Glenlion House for more than €5 million (with a €10 million mortgage!). A bad joke, really. But probably not altogether surprising, considering that Lynn was struck off by the Law Society for giving fraudulent undertakings and obtaining multiple mortgages on the same properties. Not surprising, then, to learn that a year later Glenlion was repossessed and sold at auction but achieved a sale price of only €4.9 million. That represents a drop of €1.6 million in a year and a half or, to put it another way, a reduction in value of €100,000 per month.

TOP OF THE NEW HOMES DROPS
Top of the Drops wouldn't be complete without the latest release charts, and we have these in the form of the 'New Homes' price drops. Even though the wealthy builders and developers were initially reluctant to cut prices, preferring instead to reduce supply and sell less, it was only a matter of time before they had to throw in the towel and bring the price of new homes at least some of the way back towards affordability.

Table 20: Largest drops in 'new' home prices

Rank	Property	Location	High price	Last price	Change	Percentage drop
1	Block of 12 apartments, Donabate	North Co. Dublin	€6,500,000	€3,500,000	-€3,000,000	-46%
2	Barnston, Hainault Road, Foxrock (6-bed)	Dublin 18	€4,200,000	€2,350,000	-€1,850,000	-44%
3	Hainault, Foxrock (4-bed det.)	Dublin 18	€3,500,000	€1,730,000	-€1,770,000	-51%
4	Cragside, Hainault Road, Foxrock (5-bed)	Dublin 18	€3,800,000	€2,350,000	-€1,450,000	-38%
5	Dalle Cottage, Hainault Road, Foxrock	Dublin 18	€3,800,000	€2,350,000	-€1,450,000	-38%
6	Fortfield Grove, Terenure (5-bed)	Dublin 6W	€2,800,000	€1,950,000	-€850,000	-30%
7	Thornwood, Booterstown (3-bed)	South Co. Dublin	€1,500,000	€975,000	-€525,000	-35%
8	Brighton Square, Foxrock (4-bed det.)	Dublin 18	€2,500,000	€2,000,000	-€500,000	-20%
9	Hollybrook, Brighton Road (2-bed)	Foxrock, Dublin 18	€1,289,030	€975,000	-€314,000	-24%
10	Blackthorn Bay, Greenhill Road	Co. Wicklow	€1,250,000	€995,000	-€255,000	-20%
11	Killiney Court, Killiney (ground floor)	South Co. Dublin	€1,200,000	€950,000	-€250,000	-21%
12	Eden Gate and Wood, Delgany (5-bed)	Co. Wicklow	€1,395,000	€1,150,000	-€245,000	-18%
13	Holywell, Kilcoole (4-bed det.)	Co. Wicklow	€780,000	€550,000	-€230,000	-29%
14	The Nurseries, Delgany (houses)	Co. Wicklow	€1,650,000	€1,450,000	-€200,000	-12%
15	Old Chocolate Factory (2-bed)	Dublin 8	€545,000	€355,000	-€190,000	-35%
16	Carrickmines Green (4-bed)	Dublin 18	€1,000,000	€830,000	-€170,000	-17%
17	The Grange, Galloping Green (2-bed flat)	Stillorgan, Co. Dublin	€585,000	€525,000	-€160,000	-23%
18	Forbes Quay, Sir John Rogerson's Quay (1-bed)	Dublin 2	€550,000	€395,000	-€155,000	-28%
19	Dunboyne Castle (3-bed town house)	Co. Meath	€500,000	€360,000	-€140,000	-28%
20	Ballintyre, Ballinteer (2-bed)	Dublin 16	€535,000	€395,000	-€140,000	-26%

Rank	Property	Location	High price	Last price	Change	Percentage drop
21	Forbes Quay, Sir John Rogerson's Quay (2-bed)	Dublin 2	€635,000	€495,000	−€140,000	−22%
22	Stocking Wood, Rathfarnham (4-bed)	Dublin 16	€690,000	€550,000	−€140,000	−20%
23	Carrickmines Manor, Glenamuck (3-bed)	Dublin 18	€710,000	€575,000	−€135,000	−19%
24	Phoenix Park Racecourse, Castleknock (2-bed)	Dublin 15	€435,000	€310,000	−€125,000	−29%
25	Dunboyne Castle (4-bed det.)	Co. Meath	€600,000	€475,000	−€125,000	−21%
26	Ivory Building (3-bed duplex)	Dublin 2	€650,000	€525,000	−€125,000	−19%
27	The Pierre, Victoria Terrace (2-bed)	Dún Laoghaire	€685,000	€560,000	−€125,000	−18%
28	Stocking Wood, Rathfarnham (3-bed)	Dublin 18	€595,000	€475,000	−€120,000	−20%
29	Dunboyne Castle (1-bed)	Co. Meath	€285,000	€170,000	−€115,000	−40%
30	Dalriada, Knocklyon (4-bed)	Dublin 16	€575,000	€460,000	−€115,000	−20%
31	Elmpark, Merrion (2-bed apt)	Dublin 4	€585,000	€470,000	−€115,000	−20%
32	The Meadows, Swords (3-bed end of terrace)	North Co. Dublin	€454,950	€340,850	−€114,100	−25%
33	305 South Block, Longboat Quay (2-bed)	Dublin 2	€598,000	€485,000	−€113,000	−19%
34	Camac View, Kilmainham	Dublin 8	€500,000	€392,000	−€108,000	−22%
35	Carrig Court, Citywest (3-bed)	Dublin 24	€475,000	€370,000	−€105,000	−22%
36	Churchfields, Delgany (3-bed semi)	Co. Wicklow	€700,000	€595,000	−€105,000	−15%
37	The Oaks, Dundrum	Dublin 14	€600,000	€498,000	−€102,000	−17%
38	Waltrim Grove (2-bed), Bray	Co. Wicklow	€400,000	€299,000	−€101,000	−25%
39	Weavers' Hall, Clonsilla (2-bed)	Dublin 15	€306,000	€206,000	−€100,000	−33%
40	Dunboyne Castle (2-bed)	Co. Meath	€335,000	€225,000	−€100,000	−31%
41	Millrace, Saggart (2-bed)	Co. Dublin	€345,000	€245,000	−€100,000	−29%

42	The Waterfront, Tarmonbarry	Co. Roscommon	€399,000	€299,000	−25%
43	The Meadows, Swords (2-bed)	North Co. Dublin	€399,950	€299,950	−25%
44	The Crescent, Ashtown (3-bed)	Dublin 15	€460,000	€360,000	−22%
45	Millrace, Saggart (4-bed)	Dublin 24	€485,000	€385,000	−21%
46	Adamstown Castle (4-bed houses)	Dublin 22	€525,000	€425,000	−19%
47	Longboat Quay, Hanover Quay (2-bed)	Dublin 2	€700,000	€600,000	−14%
48	Auburn Park, Castleknock (3-bed duplex)	Dublin 15	€750,000	€650,000	−13%
49	Fairview Close, Fairview (3-bed apt)	Dublin 3	€555,000	€459,000	−17%
50	Priorsgate, Greenhills Road (2-bed)	Tallaght, Dublin 24	€370,000	€275,000	−26%

Some of these discounts on new homes have been incredible. Take, for instance, numbers 28 and 30 Fortfield Grove in Terenure, Dublin 6W. These were the two remaining five-bedroom detached houses in this small gated development where initially asking prices were €2.8 million. The agents, Sherry FitzGerald, were asking €1.95 million in April 2008; that's a drop of 30 per cent. A similar thing happened with our two top-spot entries from Foxrock, Dublin 18. Four new homes had prices slashed by a significant €1.5 million! Not quite 50 per cent but, in absolute terms, the biggest decliners.

A late entry from Co. Wicklow was Blackthorn Bay, new five-bedroom houses that were cut by more than a quarter of a million each.

The top 50 new-home price drops average more than €285,000 per unit. The cost of buying one property in each of these new developments at their previous high figures would have been €50 million; a little over a year later the same portfolio would cost €35 million, a saving of €15 million or 29 per cent. From the table it's pretty clear that price cuts of 15 to 25 per cent are the norm. If this is not evidence of a major supply overhang, then what is?

Unfortunately for the developers, this is only the first round of cuts, and—contrary to the lyrics of a famous song, 'the first cut is the deepest'— we can expect even bigger cuts to follow in 2009. On the other hand, it's very fortunate for the prospective home-buyer, as it shows that the wait-and-see strategy has in fact paid off handsomely.

To merit inclusion in the top 50 new-scheme price drops the builder has had to slash the price by a minimum of €95,000. That just goes to show what is gained by adopting a wait-and-see stance.

As long as rental yields remain below mortgage rates, this strategy would continue to reap dividends. Given that national average rental yields were still around 4 per cent, yet the average mortgage rate remains above this level, even another round of price cuts of the same magnitude would only bring property prices back to a level where annual rents would be equivalent to nearly 5 per cent of the purchase price. This would be closer to the cost of a mortgage, notwithstanding the fact that rents are falling because of the oversupply of unsold new homes that have flooded the rental market. It's a 'lose-lose' situation for the builders and developers but a 'win-win' for Mr and Mrs First-Time Buyer.

One of the first developments to show substantial price cuts, and one of the best known, was the €105,000 discount on new three-bedroom semis in Delgany, Co. Wicklow, in September 2007. Prices were dropped from €700,000 to €595,000, much to the displeasure of those residents who had already bought at the higher price. Only eight houses were left for sale, those that had been completed last during the summer. The developer, Jim Wood, decided that if it was going to be a 'race to the bottom' he who goes first wins. This is precisely what occurred. All eight remaining houses were reserved at the new, lower price the following weekend. However, a precedent had been set.

Price cuts do indeed work, especially at the beginning of a property recession, as people don't psychologically possess an innate sense of value but rather base their decisions on what others are doing, or what others have paid. In the Delgany example, prospective purchasers saw more than €100,000 being knocked off prices in a development where many of the houses had already been sold and were occupied by residents who had paid the higher price. In essence, buyers saw a bargain. After all, they were getting a €700,000 house for less than €600,000, weren't they?

There has been much empirical evidence, conducted by eminent psychologists around the world, that human beings allow price to determine value, and not the other way around. Think of it this way. What if the last buyers in Delgany had actually paid €105,000 less than their neighbours for, say, a house that is really only worth €400,000? Where's the bargain now?

The unfortunate reality is that just because you purchase something for less, even a lot less, than somebody else within a similar time frame it doesn't necessarily follow that prices will stop falling. Often they do keep falling. Remember, the momentum is always with the existing market direction. Turning points are impossible to predict, hence the financial market maxim 'The trend is your friend.' People soon catch on to this fact. It explains why initial price cuts may tempt some people while merely whetting the appetite of others for future and possibly bigger cuts. It also explains why property prices often overshoot on the way down, just as they did on the way up! This latter point has been laboured to death by Morgan Kelly of NUI, Dublin. Perhaps people should start listening to this professor, who earned his PhD studying at Yale University, the same one that Robert Shiller (the number 1 American property guru) teaches at.

TOP OF THE COUNTRY-HOMES DROPS

Just as in the world of music, there are always alternative market segments to suit different styles and tastes. Urban dwelling is not for everyone. The country-homes market may appear to be a niche segment for the affluent, but it's very important to the country's estate agents, as it's where large commissions can be earned on single properties, not least those great properties in their glossy brochures. We can refer to this section of Top of the Drops as the 'life-style charts', as many of these big houses are bought by wealthy individuals in order to make a statement about their life-style choice.

As with other parts of the property market, the country-homes segment has fallen. Price drops have ranged from 13 to 66 per cent. Some of these country-homes fallers have already appeared in our general top 40 decliners; however, from the next table you will notice that Dublin hardly features at all, as one would expect, but Cos. Cork and Wicklow are most prominent, along with Cos. Limerick and Kildare. Here are the latest top 50 country-homes asking-price drops:

Table 21: Largest drops in prices of country homes

Rank	Property	Location	High price	Last price	Change	Percentage drop
1	Moyglare Manor, Maynooth	Co. Kildare	€10,000,000	€3,750,000	−€6,250,000	−63%
2	An Cúlú, Kenmare	Co. Cork	€15,000,000	€10,000,000	−€5,000,000	−33%
3	Kinnitty Castle	Co. Offaly	€13,500,000	€9,800,000	−€3,700,000	−27%
4	Jamestown Court, Castletown Geoghegan	Co. Westmeath	€7,500,000	€4,500,000	−€3,000,000	−40%
5	Knockrobin House, Knockrobin	Co. Wicklow	€7,000,000	€4,500,000	−€2,500,000	−36%
6	Bellingham Castle, Castlebellingham	Co. Louth	€6,750,000	€4,500,000	−€2,250,000	−33%
7	Gerrardstown House and Stud, Dunshaughlin	Co. Meath	€15,000,000	€13,000,000	−€2,000,000	−13%
8	Monalin House, Newtown Mount Kennedy	Co. Wicklow	€6,300,000	€4,500,000	−€1,800,000	−29%
9	Rockview House, Port Laoise	Co. Laois	€3,000,000	€1,500,000	−€1,500,000	−50%
10	Killenure Castle, Dundrum	Co. Tipperary	€3,750,000	€2,250,000	−€1,500,000	−40%
11	Lower Cove, Kinsale	Co. Cork	€2,750,000	€1,300,000	−€1,450,000	−53%
12	Kilcolman Rectory, Enniskeane	Co. Cork	€3,200,000	€1,750,000	−€1,450,000	−45%
13	Clonacody House, Fethard	Co. Tipperary	€7,000,000	€5,650,000	−€1,350,000	−19%
14	Lairakeen, Banagher	Co. Offaly	€6,700,000	€5,500,000	−€1,200,000	−18%
15	Baywood House, Glandore	Co. Cork	€2,500,000	€1,400,000	−€1,100,000	−44%
16	Rushanes, Glandore (7-bed)	Co. Cork	€2,500,000	€1,400,000	−€1,100,000	−44%
17	50 Eagle Valley, Enniskerry	Co. Wicklow	€2,500,000	€1,450,000	−€1,050,000	−42%
18	Garrylough, Screen, Castlebridge	Co. Wexford	€2,600,000	€1,550,000	−€1,050,000	−40%
19	Sea Haven, Coast Road, Portmarnock	Co. Dublin	€4,000,000	€2,975,000	−€1,025,000	−26%
20	Brandy Hall House, Castletown Bearhaven	Co. Cork	€2,700,000	€1,700,000	−€1,000,000	−37%

21	Glengarriff (4-bed house)	Co. Cork	€2,900,000	€1,900,000	-34%
22	Kilbrennal House Stud	Co. Tipperary	€3,400,000	€2,400,000	-29%
23	Ballybrada House, Cahir	Co. Tipperary	€6,000,000	€5,000,000	-17%
24	Janeville, Slane	Co. Meath	€6,500,000	€5,500,000	-15%
25	Black Hall, Termonfeckin	Co. Louth	€7,000,000	€6,000,000	-14%
26	Glebe House, Croagh	Co. Limerick	€1,950,000	€1,000,000	-49%
27	75 Garden Courtyard, K Club, Straffan	Co. Kildare	€1,400,000	€475,000	-66%
28	Ballycummisk, Schull	Co. Cork	€1,650,000	€790,000	-52%
29	Crooked Wood	Co. Westmeath	€2,000,000	€1,195,000	-40%
30	Period country residence, Mullingar	Co. Westmeath	€1,800,000	€1,000,000	-44%
31	Crockeendranagh House, Rathcoole	Co. Dublin	€2,000,000	€1,200,000	-40%
32	Crann Síóg, Church Hill, Letterkenny	Co. Donegal	€2,400,000	€1,600,000	-33%
33	Togher House, Monasterevin	Co. Kildare	€4,500,000	€3,700,000	-18%
34	Waterside Residence, Carrick-on-Shannon	Co. Leitrim	€1,200,000	€450,000	-63%
35	Bayview House, Clonard	Co. Wexford	€1,500,000	€750,000	-50%
36	Sean-Bhóthar House, Belmont	Co. Offaly	€1,500,000	€750,000	-50%
37	927 Ladycastle, K Club, Straffan	Co. Kildare	€2,000,000	€1,250,000	-38%
38	Ossory, Knockmaroon Hill, Chapelizod	Co. Dublin	€1,800,000	€1,100,000	-39%
39	Teach Nollag, Fromoyle, Broadford	Co. Clare	€1,900,000	€1,200,000	-37%
40	Littor Strand, Ballybunnion	Co. Kerry	€2,500,000	€1,800,000	-28%
41	Leoville House, Dunmore Road	Co. Waterford	€3,000,000	€2,300,000	-23%
42	Hollon House, Straffan	Co. Kildare	€3,450,000	€2,750,000	-20%
43	Crag Lodge, Claremont Road, Howth	Co. Dublin	€3,500,000	€2,800,000	-20%

Rank	Property	Location	High price	Last price	Change	Percentage drop
44	Glencullen House, Glencullen	Co. Dublin	€3,700,000	€3,000,000	−€700,000	−19%
45	3-bed house and farmyard on 6 acres, Naas	Co. Kildare	€1,200,000	€535,000	−€665,000	−55%
46	Wyanstown House, Togher, Drogheda	Co. Louth	€1,500,000	€850,000	−€650,000	−43%
47	2 The Vale, Kilmacanogue	Co. Wicklow	€3,300,000	€2,650,000	−€650,000	−20%
48	Whiddy Island, Bantry (4-bed)	Co. Cork	€1,100,000	€490,000	−€610,000	−55%
49	Seacrest, Roscam	Co. Galway	€1,600,000	€995,000	−€605,000	−38%
50	Carrig House, Ballylusk, Ashford	Co. Wicklow	€1,500,000	€900,000	−€600,000	−40%

The first twenty houses in our country charts have been covered earlier in the general top 40. No. 9—Rockview in Port Laoise, Co. Laois—was the home of the Odlum family (of the flour and breakfast cereals) and has been on the market for more than two years, hence the 50 per cent price drop. Another property that has languished on the market for two years or more is Kilcolman Rectory in Enniskeane, Co. Cork, which has also been reduced by nearly half.

Some of these properties have now been sold. For example, Glencullen House in Co. Dublin was reduced by €700,000 to €3 million but was then withdrawn at auction at €2.1 million and later sold. It could easily have sold for less than the €3 million shown in the no. 44 slot it occupies in our charts above. Castlefleming House and Coach House in Co. Laois sold in November 2006, probably for €100,000 less than the €1.3 million guide price, according to some reports. That drop would have been only €450,000, not enough to gain entry to the country top 50, where the minimum price slash was a cool six hundred thousand euros.

Other houses that failed to make the list but have seen substantial price falls include Creek Lodge in Belgooley, Kinsale, Co. Cork (home of the celebrity chef Keith Floyd), which has been reduced in price by nearly a fifth. The former home of Eddie Hobbs, Summerhill House, near the Curragh, Co. Kildare, is back on the market, this time with a 10 per cent reduction of €250,000.

Quite a few of the Co. Wicklow properties have seen their price slashed several times, such as Granmore in Valleymount, close to Ballymore Eustace, south of Blessington and adjacent to the reservoir. Its price has been cut three times, a drop totalling €400,000 or 27 per cent of the original asking price. Lisardboula in Tralee, Co. Kerry, has also been cut twice, by €350,000 to €900,000, another 28 per cent fall.

Taking the sum of all fifty of our country-homes price drops, the original cumulative asking price was €204 million; by the winter of 2008 you could purchase the lot for €139 million. This is a total reduction of €65 million or 32 per cent. That's an average price drop of €1¼ million per property.

To recap, the top 40 are down in price by 30 per cent, new homes are 29 per cent lower, while the country-homes segment has seen prices fall by 32 per cent. All these reductions are far greater than the 15 per cent drop in the national average according to the PTSB-ESRI house-price index, from the price peak in February 2007 to November 2008.

We learn two important things from this. Firstly, the index is a very narrow view of the property world and realistically is only a true measure of the cheaper end of the market. Who goes to the Permanent TSB for a mortgage on a €10 million house? Secondly, these price drops are reductions in the asking or aspirational price. These houses probably never traded at those inflated prices anyway, so there are probably more and potentially greater falls yet to come.

How low can they go? You may well ask. Until prices eventually come, as the tuneful and unforgettable Soul2Soul song goes, 'Back to life, back to reality.' Okay, then, enough obfuscation. The real answer is that, as we're half way through the property slump and have yet to see any light at the end of the price tunnel, we're probably also half way done in terms of price falls. To some people that may seem totally bananas: that after reductions in asking prices of 20, 30, 40 and even 50 per cent we could see further falls of a similar magnitude. Short answer: Of course we could. Each subsequent 10 or 20 per cent fall is a smaller money amount. Perversely, then, each new drop of a hundred thousand in asking price is a greater percentage of the most recent price. This is what's known as increasing volatility in a declining market. You want proof? Just look at the stock market for your evidence. Granted, home prices are not going to fall as much as stocks and shares have, but the principle is the same—with more modest amplitude.

In a recent documentary on TV3, 'Credit Crunch: The Property Crash', on which I appeared as well as Morgan Kelly, I stated that official (read 'PTSB-ESRI index') house prices will probably fall by at least a third or by 35 per cent nationally. Morgan stated that homes in the better parts of Dublin that had traded at €800,000 to €900,000 could end up eventually selling for €220,000 to €300,000, or, in other words, a fall of at least two-thirds! Both statements are factually correct in terms of probability, and there is complete consistency between them.

Let's illustrate this by way of an extreme but simple example. On the one hand we have a three-bedroom semi in Foxrock, Dublin 18, at €900,000, and on the other hand we have a similar-sized property in Inchicore, Dublin 8, on the market at €440,000. The former has already seen a price reduction of seventy thousand, while the latter has been cut by thirty thousand so far. Assume that by 2011 Dublin prices have fallen on average by two-fifths from the peak; this would put the Dublin 8 home at around €282,000. But let's also assume that the Dublin 18 property fell by three-fifths (from a peak of €970,000), to €388,000. Finally we assume that all non-Dublin property prices fall by a third. The national average house price index in this instance would show a total fall of around 35 per cent, using the PTSB-ESRI index.

Obviously there are more homes outside Dublin than in Co. Dublin itself. Their percentage drop would be only slightly smaller than that of the capital city but would be far smaller in money terms, as prices are cheaper in the rest of the country. So the bigger drops in the salubrious suburban areas are diluted in the national average calculation.

If you still have problems understanding the mechanics of this, think of it another way. For every one expensive home in Dublin 2 (City Docks) or Dublin 4 (Ballsbridge, Donnybrook) there are a hundred cheaper homes in Dublin 22 (Clondalkin, Adamstown) and in Dublin 24 (Firhouse, Citywest, Tallaght). Even if the expensive Dublin 2 and Dublin 4 homes fall by 75 per cent, while the others drop by 39 per cent, the Dublin average fall may be recorded as only a 40 per cent decline.

Ergo, when commentators talk about house price falls, qualify whether they are referring to 'asking' prices or 'recorded' prices. Secondly, are they using location-specific examples, or are they using national averages? It makes a big difference.

POSTSCRIPT

The house that I grew up in, in Blackrock, Co. Dublin, has been on the market since the spring of 2007. It was first listed by Gunne Residential at €1.6 million. They reduced the price twice before the seller (the same seller who purchased the house from my parents in 1996 for £188,500) switched to a different agent, Allen and Jacobs. They too have reduced the price, from €1.395 million to €1.195 million and more recently to €895,000. In total, that's a drop of €705,000 in a year and a half. In percentage terms, it's a reduction of nearly half already. However, it's still three times the price that the seller paid only a dozen years ago. Even if they are forced to cut the price by another €120,000 to €675,000, which would be considered cheap today for a five-bedroom detached house in Newtown Park Avenue, they would still have made an annual compound return of 9 per cent per annum for twelve years. Allowing for consumer price inflation, they would still have made +4.8 per cent in 'real' terms on their money each and every year, yet it would equate to a total price drop of nearly 60 per cent on the original asking price.

In investment terms, they would still have beaten every Irish managed pension fund over the same period.

I rest my case.

Chapter 17

Money supply and the end of the consumer boom

For the next few years there's going to be less money chasing more houses. That means one thing only: a further drop in prices. Here's why. (This explanation entails a little basic but easily understood economics. So stick with me: it clarifies how the system works and will be explained later in this section.)

One of the most famous Abba songs of the 1970s contained the lyrics 'Money, money, money, must be funny in a rich man's world.' They weren't far wrong. There's an interesting parallel between that era, characterised by rampant inflation, and today, now that inflation has been on the up again. We may not reach the absurd double-digit rates that prevailed back then, and inflation has waned in recent months, but there's one important lesson to be learnt. That lesson is that another way of looking at inflation is to examine the supply of money in the economy. Central bankers and economists do this by adding up all the different measurements of money, whether they be simply notes and coins, also known as 'narrow money' (as it's a narrow view of how much money there is in circulation), or include broader measurements, such as deposits in banks, in addition to loans advanced to people and businesses, otherwise known as credit.

One of the leading monetarist economists was Professor Milton Friedman, who said that monetary policy authorities (i.e. central banks) ought to spend more time looking at the total amount of money circulating in the economy, as this was a predictor of future inflationary pressures. Not everyone agreed with Friedman's thesis, especially those free-market thinkers who don't believe that governments should attempt to control the money supply. Primarily this is because they don't want central bankers attempting to manage asset-price inflation (the best-known type of which is, of course, our old friend rising property prices).

But the simple fact is that if credit is growing too rapidly and the total growth in money supply is high (double-digit annual rate), more money will be sloshing around in the economy to facilitate higher prices for goods and services. There's a direct relationship between growth in money supply and inflation. This is why the European Central Bank is mandated to maintain 'price stability', using a 'two-pillar' strategy, one being an inflation ceiling of 2 per cent, the other being a target for growth in broad money supply of 4½ per cent (though since the inception of the European Central Bank and the introduction of the euro the measurement of broad money growth—called M3—has exceeded this target nearly all the time, except for November 2002 to October 2003). By the middle of 2008 the euro zone M3 was more than double the target, as was inflation, at 4 per cent, which is why the European Central Bank hiked up interest rates on 3 July 2008, before it was forced to cut rates aggressively because of the collapse of some banks in the financial markets (most notably Lehman Brothers in the United States).

Returning to the whole issue of Irish money supply, this is directly related to property prices, because it paints a picture of how much money is in the economy and, of course, is a big clue to credit availability, which is really important for property, as most new homes are purchased with a mortgage loan. If you've ever heard the old adage that a 'picture is worth a thousand words,' cast your eye over the following chart. It's the annual growth in Irish money supply since 1972, so it includes several business and economic cycles.

Fig. 16: Annual growth in money supply, 1972–2008

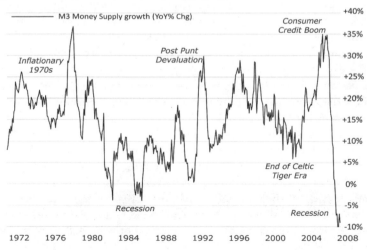

Source: Central Bank and Financial Services Authority of Ireland

What's really scary from the recent vertical descent is that between November 2006 and July 2008, according to the official figures, Irish money supply growth has gone from +35 per cent per year to −10 per cent. In other words, it has been shrinking and in negative territory since April 2008 and was still falling by a tenth at the end of October.

This recent trough is lower than anything ever experienced before, even in the torrid 70s and bad old 80s. The growth from 2004 to 2007 was astounding, and this is why that period deserves the title of the 'consumer boom' era—a period of exceptionally high credit growth, much of which went into our old friend bricks and mortar!

This rapid 35 per cent growth in money during the consumer era occurred at a time when the Irish economy was experiencing 6 per cent real growth a year on top of inflation of about 3–4 per cent, so in money terms (what economists call nominal or price terms) Éire Teoranta was expanding at roughly 10 per cent per annum. But wait a minute; the growth in the volume of money was three times that annual rate, so how can money growth persistently exceed economic growth? It can't. It was simply unsustainable, and all the clever people knew that, but they were ignored.

Usually when the total amount of money in an economy shrinks, inflationary pressures subside. There's less money chasing the same amount of goods, and so on; that's the argument. However, just as Éire Teoranta has witnessed the vanishing money and credit supply trick, consumers are being forced to pay more for food and fuel (oil prices in eoros per barrel are back to where they were in February 2000, but diesel and petrol prices at the pump remain a quarter higher than they were back then), because of global inflationary forces. The poor Irish consumer is also facing higher domestic inflation, principally because of the state-owned monopoly utilities, i.e. gas and electricity. These utility bills were expected to increase in 2008 by large double-digit rates (close on 20 per cent). Even though disinflation (falling inflation) is now the order of the day, those higher utility prices have been ratcheted up and will stay at those higher levels. Just look at the 10 per cent hike in public transport fares in January 2009.

At the same time the trade union movement is seeking higher pay for private-sector workers, to compensate them for the loss in earning power or 'real incomes' of about 10 per cent over the last two years, caused by persistently high inflation of about 5 per cent per year. And who can blame them? Inflation has often been likened to a mugger who hits you over the head and takes a fifty-euro note out of your wallet and replaces it with two twenties.

So, returning to the introductory paragraph, what does all this 'money supply' talk mean for the residential property market? It means there will be less money chasing more homes. Therefore, there will probably be further downward pressure on prices. The negative feedback loop is just as strong in a downturn as the positive one was during the boom. Higher credit growth during the property bubble meant there was more money (credit) available for people to bid up the prices of properties to exorbitant levels. This force is now firmly in reverse, and it won't alter course very dramatically or very quickly, irrespective of interest rate cuts.

The other big issue Irish people may not be aware of is that money growth throughout the euro zone countries is still very strong, at 8 per cent—close to a record—at a time when Éire Teoranta is in reverse gear while the other fourteen countries are in higher gears.

So this 'one-size-fits-all' monetary policy may have suited France, Germany and the other euro area economies earlier in 2008, but it's the last thing that we needed then. But there's nothing we can do about it, especially now that Éire Teoranta has ceded those powers to the European Central Bank in Frankfurt. Swapping the Irish pound for the German mark may have seemed like a great deal back in 1998 but it's turning into a headache for Irish people just at a time when they're already suffering a hangover from the house party.

Warning! As we shall explore in the next chapter, Irish credit growth remains positive, yet total money (cash plus credit) growth is negative. By inference, therefore, Irish businesses and individuals are rapidly running out of cash. People and companies are spending more and more of their spare cash and accumulated savings on rising costs. If this situation persists there will be a cash crisis as well as a credit crunch. Indeed this phenomenon had already begun, with calls by the Irish Congress of Trade Unions to the Government to nationalise the six domestic Irish banks, as well as cries of foul from the Small Firms Association and organisations such as ISME complaining that small and medium-sized companies are unable to get sufficient credit to maintain their businesses.

Most normal businesses that operate within the country, which provide all the goods and services that consumers avail of, are short of cash, and things are getting worse as the economy shrinks. Trade credit is the new funding of choice for non-banks; and if credit growth turns negative in 2009 we're all in trouble. Cash doesn't lie.

Chapter 18

'Help! I'm a debt addict. Get me out of here!'

If ever RTE wanted to make a reality show about consumer finance and people with debt issues they could do worse than copy the 'I'm a celebrity—get me out of here' formula. They could even bring in a panel of judges that might include the financial ombudsman, Joe Meade, and the consumer advocate Eddie Hobbs as well as Brendan Burgess, the founder of www.askaboutmoney.com—all regular pundits on the perils of finance.

In chapter 5 we touched on the fact that private indebtedness has reached endemic proportions, as total private-sector credit reached €402 billion by October 2008. That figure is more than double Irish GDP, which was approximately €190 billion in 2007 and is expected to be even smaller in 2008. Public-sector debt fell dramatically in the early 90s, before Ireland adopted the euro; at one point in the mid-80s it was more than 120 per cent of GDP. In 1980 Charles Haughey appeared on television to inform the nation that we were all living beyond our means and that a period of belt-tightening was in order. Two decades later total government debt was slightly over a quarter of annual GDP. It has since begun to rise rapidly.

But if one was to combine public-sector and private-sector debt today, it's two-and-a-half times our national income. Back in the bad old days of the 1980s it was only one-and-a-half times. Éire Teoranta has never been more highly leveraged than it was in 2008. Leverage or debt is a double-edged sword: it acts as a lever or amplifier of profit or return when times are good, but it can be a killer when times are bad.

Take an investor with €100,000 to invest. They buy a property in 2002 for €400,000 by borrowing €300,000 from a bank and put their own €100,000 down as a deposit. Four years later, in 2006, the same property is worth, say, half a million. They haven't made a 25 per cent return if they sell that property for €500,000: because of that 3:1 leverage or gearing they actually doubled their money and made 100 per cent. They began with €100,000 and a few years later, having sold the property for 25 per cent more (€500,000 selling price divided by €400,000 purchase price), they've ended up with €200,000 in the bank. This is the joy of gearing—of using someone else's money—in a rising market.

Conversely, let's take a different example, this time a young married couple. They buy the same €500,000 property off this investor in 2006. They have only €50,000 in savings, including parental assistance, as well as €5,000 borrowed from a credit union. So they take out a 90 per cent loan of €450,000, secured on the property. They can do this because one of them is a nurse and the other is a garda, so their combined gross income is €90,000. Their mortgage, therefore, is five times their combined income. This would be a reasonable mortgage-income multiple assumption at that time. In effect, their gearing was much higher than the investor who sold them the property. Their gearing is not four times but ten times: they put down only a tenth of the money required to buy the property.

Now let's jump forward three years to 2009. Property prices fell in 2007 by 7.3 per cent; there was another 10 per cent drop in 2008 and a further, say, 7.5 per cent decline in 2009. All told, their property is now worth 25 per cent less than what they paid for it. The property is then valued at €375,000 (€500,000 minus €125,000, or 25 per cent). They have 'negative equity', in other words, as the house is worth €75,000 less than the mortgage secured on it. Forget about their €50,000 deposit or initial equity, which is completely gone. The net result is that their original investment of €50,000 became an unrealised loss of €75,000 within three years. The correct way to view this is a loss of 150 per cent (−75,000 ÷ 50,000), caused by the very high gearing they used to get onto the property ladder in the first place.

This example is a perfectly realistic one. It also reveals the folly of high gearing when asset prices are at a record figure. By that we mean that they should have known that prices had run up in previous years: they would have witnessed the large increases in prices from 2002 onwards. There would have been other clues too: the bank would have said that the €450,000 was the maximum loan they were willing to offer that particular couple, based on their combined salaries. The surveyor's report for valuation purposes (a requirement for getting the mortgage) may have included such comments as 'the purchase price was at the top end of the valuation scale for similar-sized properties in that locality.' Ignorance is bliss, but it's no excuse: the onus was on them to do their homework. If they believed estate agents who said that property prices were likely to rise further in that particular area, more fools they. If their families and friends had encouraged them to buy and to borrow lots of money to get onto the property ladder, it wasn't their money they were spending, nor would it be them making the monthly mortgage payments.

The bottom line was that they probably didn't care about any of those warning signs. They just wanted a new home, and the banks offered them finance. Why go hungry when you can eat tomorrow's lunch (as well as next week's) today?

Two words apply more than any others when you're purchasing a property. They are the Latin phrase *Caveat emptor*—'Let the buyer beware.'

Our little didactic parable serves as a useful illustration of the fact that consumers will inevitably succumb to pressure and will see credit as 'having today what they would have had to wait until tomorrow to get,' if the credit is forthcoming.

One of the advantages of the present credit crisis and the dwindling availability of credit is that it may actually serve to protect consumers from their own ignorance. That's not meant in a disparaging way for those who have already fallen into this trap but rather to serve as a dire warning to those who may be about to.

Credit is a two-way street: it can work for you and it can work against you, depending on which way the market is heading. Just because it was a one-way street for fifteen years doesn't mean that will always be so.

Credit is also a little bit like alcohol: taken in moderation it can be quite beneficial; taken in excess, however, it can destroy lives.

TWIN PEAKS IN PSC

Despite the shrinking money supply, the rate of credit growth is still very much positive. Although the growth rate in private-sector credit—in other words, borrowings by businesses and individuals—has moderated from its peak of 30 per cent year-on-year growth in April 2006 (when the property market was on fire) back to 9.5 per cent in October 2008, it's still high. The residential mortgage component of PSC is a big chunk of the total, some €148 billion of the €402 billion total, which also fell from its peak of 36½ per cent annual growth in July 2004 to a little over 7½ per cent by October 2008. The total outstanding balance (new less redemption or repayments) mortgage lending growth has averaged slightly more than €770 million a month throughout 2008. People are still borrowing money to buy new homes and trade up. Figures from the Irish Banking Federation for the first nine months of 2008 show that 91,600 mortgages were issued, totalling some €19½ billion.

However, most market observers have predicted a continued fall in the annual pace of credit growth as the economy slows. My own view is that total growth in PSC should slow sharply during the last quarter of 2008 to an increase of less than €500 million per month, or half the recent monthly changes. Credit growth should remain subdued during 2009, possibly increasing by only €1 billion per month. This would imply that total PSC rises to approximately €415 billion by December 2009 (excluding securitisation), at which point the annual rate of growth would slow to about 3 per cent. As our long-term chart shows, this would be roughly equal to the low rates of credit growth that were experienced during past recessions, such as the mid-1980s and early 1990s. It could actually be worse: there could be outright credit contraction; but so far there's no evidence of that, despite the property slump. However, Rossa White, chief economist of Davy Stockbrokers, had just published an article at the time of going to press. He outlined a scenario where there is outright 'credit contraction' (negative growth), whereby banks continue to lend out money but just not as much as the money that they're receiving from borrowers as capital repayments on loans that were taken out many years ago. If this does occur it would be a disaster for the home-loans market. However, considerably lower European Central Bank rates by mid-2009 should stave off this possibility.

Fig. 17: Annual growth in private-sector credit, 1984–2008

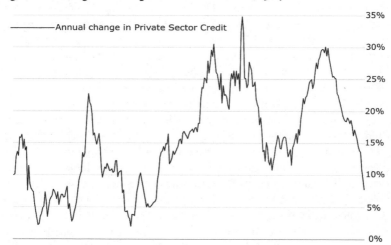

Source: Central Bank of Ireland

In residential mortgage lending, excluding 'securitisation', there have been months when loans for home purchase have actually contracted, for example December 2006, March and December 2007, and March 2008. It would be unrealistic to assume that new mortgage lending would dry up completely. The banks have to lend some money to some people to buy homes. They're like sharks moving through the water: if they stop moving they die, because they're not oxygenating their blood by moving water into their mouths and out through their gills. Banks have to lend to make money. Their loans to you and me are their assets, their life blood. The measure of a bank's importance and size is determined by its total assets.

Even if the banks only advanced the same level of mortgage loans that they did during 2002, which was about €800 million per month, the total of outstanding residential mortgages would increase to approximately €158 billion by the end of 2009 (or €134 billion excluding securitisation, a net increase of about €10 billion on the year). That would still be an annual growth rate of 6½ per cent. All of this assumes that the securitisation market for repackaged mortgages remains closed to the Irish banks because of the global liquidity crunch. Nobody expects the credit crisis to be over soon and certainly not by the spring of 2009.

Whichever way you look at it, credit growth will continue to slow in the second half of 2008 and in 2009 as a whole. Demand for credit will fall as home prices do. The banks have started down the path of a return to more normal lending practices (not lending too much and increasing their margins at the same time). During 2004 Irish mortgage lenders lent out an additional €1½ billion each month on new home loans; to put things into perspective, they lent an extra €2 billion per month on average during the heady years of 2005 and 2006. Even during the weak year of 2007 an additional €16½ billion in residential mortgage lending was forthcoming. Up to the time of writing, in late 2008, it averaged less than €800 million per month, effectually back to early-2003 levels.

So a word to the wise, especially those home-owners seeking to offload their properties, or those prospective home-buyers wishing to trade up and take advantage of what some might see as better value in the market: price pressure remains downward, and don't expect large swathes of credit to bail out the market. A smaller pot of money will be made available to the total universe of prospective borrowers. That in turn means that sellers will have to be more realistic in their asking price (as many have no doubt discovered, having entered into a sale agreement only to see the purchaser pull out because of inability to get enough credit), and purchasers will have to save a bigger deposit as loan-to-values are reduced by the lenders.

The reference to the twin peaks of private-sector credit was made because the last time the growth in Irish private credit peaked at 30 per cent was in 1998. It too fell sharply as the global economy slowed in 2001 and 2002; but this time the economy is facing completely different economic circumstances. Éire Teoranta weathered the last storm quite well. But this time there are not enough umbrellas to go round. Credit is a privilege extended to some, but not all; it should be treated as such.

There are those who see reduced credit availability as 'the' problem for the property market. It is not. It is a symptom of the underlying problem of too much household debt. It is actually part of the ultimate solution. Anyone who says otherwise simply cannot see the wood for the trees. Debt junkies will have to go 'cold turkey', and credit 'alcoholics' will need to 'dry out'.

Chapter 19

Rate expectations: Follow the money trail

On 1 January 1999 the new EU currency, the euro, was launched, and Ireland was one of the first eleven countries to join the euro area (now sixteen). Ireland ceded its powers over monetary policy—the ability to set its own interest rates—to a new body, the European Central Bank in Frankfurt, in effect a new über-Bundesbank.

Back then we knew there would be tremendous advantages in joining this new currency bloc. First of all, we would have a stable currency, and, hopefully, some way down the road it would become a global reserve currency, like the British pound or the American dollar; and to a large degree this has happened, as the euro now constitutes more than a quarter of the foreign-currency reserves of the world's central banks. Secondly, we would benefit from German-style low interest rates, in effect 'cheap money'. Thirdly, there would be a big boost to trade for our exports to the rest of Europe, especially as all our goods and services would be priced in the same currency. And lastly, at the individual level, we didn't have to get ripped off by the bank or by the bureau de change at the airport when we went on our holidays. (The last point is a trivial one but to some people perhaps it's the most important one, especially the *nouveau-riche* who were buying holiday homes abroad.)

It all sounded great; and as the official European Central Bank base rate was only 3 per cent in January 1999, that meant that average Irish mortgage rates would eventually fall. They did. In fact the average home-loan rate was more than 7 per cent in the two years before the introduction of the euro; five short years before, in 1992, the monthly average mortgage rate had been as high as 12 per cent.

So what happened to home-loan rates after the introduction of the euro? Well, for 1999 as a whole the average mortgage rate was 4.9 per cent. That's a 2 per cent reduction for a country that constituted less than 2 per cent of the euro area. Thus was born the 2 per cent nation—a member-state whose size didn't really matter when compared with the likes of Germany, France, Italy and Spain. Ireland was a minnow. It didn't matter if our growth or inflation diverged substantially from the rest of the pack:

we were going to get the one-size-fits-all interest rate; and didn't we just revel in it.

During 1999 the European Central Bank rate went as low as 2½ per cent, but it didn't stay there for long. By 2000 rates were on the rise again, and by October that year they peaked at 4¾ per cent. In effect they had almost doubled, as they did again from 2005 to 2007. Nonetheless, if you had examined the monthly average mortgage rate here in Ireland you would have seen that during 2000 it averaged only 5½ per cent and in 2001 only 5¾, despite higher base rates. Competition had entered the Irish mortgage market, and the banks and building societies had dropped their margins for home loans. On top of this, inflation had risen to 5 per cent, so in 'real' terms, loan rates adjusted for cost-of-living increases were less than 1 per cent (today real rates are similar). The economy had been flying: growth had averaged 10 per cent over the four-year period 1997–2001. Unemployment hit a new low, below 4 per cent for the first time in 2001. The 'Celtic Tiger' was roaring ahead. Ireland was growing faster even than China.

In chapter 5 we said that the person who coined the term 'Celtic Tiger' was a British economist working at an American bank. This was Kevin Gardiner, an economist at Morgan Stanley, in a paper he wrote in 1994 that predicted the phenomenal growth ahead for Ireland because of European monetary union. I worked with Kevin at Morgan Stanley between 1997 and 2000; both of us were vice-presidents and we often sat beside each other at Monday afternoon sales meetings. Kevin always spoke first, as he was one of the European economists, then I usually followed, as I was a strategist who covered the European bond markets.

So whenever you hear commentators say, 'Sure who could have predicted the boom we had?' you now know that it was widely predicted (from afar) that Ireland would have an enormous boom.

It was during those years working in London for global investment banks on the trading floor that I developed my knowledge of the interest-rate markets and of how they work. Moreover, and more importantly, I learnt how to interpret the bets investors make with regard to the likely future path of interest rates. This is something that should be of interest to the average Irish home-owner with a large mortgage, or anyone who needs to borrow money for that matter.

By May 2001 rates had begun to decline, but then the infamous incident of September 2001 occurred when two hijacked airliners were flown into the twin towers of the World Trade Center in New York. No-one could have anticipated that event. (I was in the South Tower two months before that event, visiting two clients, Putnam Associates and Fiduciary Trust. Putnam was on the 32nd floor, while the other had a suite on the 97th and 98th floors, with a staircase and mezzanine level in between.)

The ripples spread across the globe, and confidence was shaken. Central banks around the world reacted quickly to provide liquidity and restore confidence. They did this in the best way they knew how: they slashed interest rates. In the United States the Federal Reserve System (as the central bank is called) cut rates by half a per cent within the week; the following day the Bank of England eased by a quarter of a point and reduced the Bank of England base rate. The European Central Bank followed suit on 18 September 2001 and cut by a full half point, from 4¼ to 3¾ per cent. Then, in early November, it added another half-point cut for good measure.

So by the end of 2001, moving into 2002, rates had fallen back to 3¼ per cent. Remember that this was at a time when Éire Teoranta was absolutely booming. The unemployment rate fell to what economists call full employment, which is when 96 per cent of the work force is in work or effectually when everyone who wants a job has one. Rates stayed at this lower level until Christmas 2002, but the average monthly mortgage rate for this period fell to only 4.7 per cent. The week before Christmas that year the European Central Bank provided an early gift for all householders; yes, you guessed it, they slashed rates by another half point, to 2¾ per cent.

By the summer of the following year base rates had fallen all the way down to 2 per cent. With hindsight, this could only be described as 'manna from Heaven' for the 2 per cent nation; but therein lay some of the seeds of destruction as far as the present housing recessions are concerned.

For the next three years the Irish home-loan rate averaged a mere 3½ per cent. Banks had cut their margins on tracker mortgages to the European Central Bank rate plus 1½ per cent or lower. Interest rates were now 'ultra-low' and money was never so cheap, really cheap. What followed next—asset price inflation in the shape of the housing market—should not have surprised anyone. A housing bubble is a bubble, whatever way you look at it. Builders responded to this new artificial demand driven by cheap money (investor-driven and not utilitarian), and supply took off while prices continued to rise. This is the classic tell-tale sign of a housing bubble when the fundamentals are reversed.

House prices, as measured by the PTSB-ESRI house-price index, rose 40 per cent in three years following the post-tech bubble correction and subsequent wobble in late 2000. By 2004 you could get very little for a quarter of a million euros in Ireland by way of accommodation, especially in Dublin.

WHERE TO FROM HERE?
So much for the history lesson. What about now? We all know that interest rates had more than doubled, with eight successive increases from 2 per cent in December 2005 to 4 per cent in June 2007 and a further hike to 4¼ per cent in July 2008. Interest rates were no longer 'ultra-low' but

only 'very low'. Yes, they were still low. It may be of little comfort to those who bought a property a couple of years ago and watched their monthly mortgage payment increase by 50 per cent. A middle-income couple may have been spending a fifth of their take-home pay on servicing the monthly home loan three years ago; two years later the same mortgage was eating up a third or more. This may reflect the actual experience of a typical couple in, for instance, the commuter belt, but a similar couple who bought in Dublin would have had to borrow a lot more and there fore could easily be paying out two-fifths or nearly half their combined net salaries—just to pay for the same loan on the same property. It's important to remember that they were not getting any additional value for their money. All right, it's still their home, but it was now costing them a lot more.

Although European rates had remained reasonably low, at 4 per cent, for more than a year, inflation had remained stubbornly high, and despite the fact that growth in the euro zone appeared to be slowing, the scope for interest rate reductions was seen as limited. However, all that changed dramatically in October 2008. The global recession came to the euro zone, and even Germany entered recession. Oil prices collapsed from nearly $150 per barrel to just a third of that level, and the core inflation measure so favoured by the European Central Bank, the harmonised index of consumer prices (HICP), halved between July and November to just 2.1 per cent, a touch above the ECB target rate. What a difference a few short months make! Really, what it showed was that the ECB was behind the curve in appreciating just how quickly the economic slowdown was occurring. Everyone is familiar with the adage that when the world's largest economy sneezes the rest of the world catches a cold; but this time around the United States has caught a severe cold and the rest of the world is probably suffering from pneumonia (as American consumers stop buying goods and world trade slows).

European Central Bank rates were cut by a full percentage point in less than a month, and the balance of probability now is that the ECB will con-tinue slashing rates until mid-2009. However, it's still too early to get excited, as it's cutting for a reason. That reason is recession, slumping demand and rising unemployment. All told, then, lower rates will help the Irish home-owner, but on their own they are certainly no panacea for what's ailing the property market.

It's the outcome that many estate agents had hoped for; but will it make that much of a difference? The present correction downwards in house prices is a necessary adjustment in the process of eliminating the backlog of excess supply, and it's also necessary to the process of bringing prices back down to affordable levels. All interest rate hikes did two years ago was to hasten the process, which was no bad thing really.

Fig. 18: Bank base rates, 1945–2009e

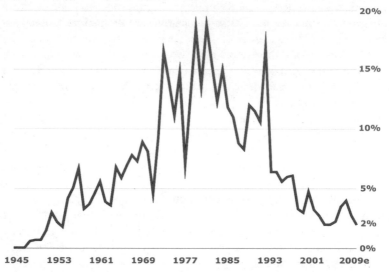

Source: Central Bank and Financial Services Authority of Ireland

The preceding chart illustrates the history of Irish banks' base rate since the end of the Second World War. The period just after the war is very relevant, as base rates were below 1 per cent until 1951. The whole point of this long-term graphical representation of base rates is to prove that the 2 per cent rates prevalent for two-and-a-half years from 2003 to the end of 2005 were not just low but ridiculously low. Rates not seen since the 1950s were totally inappropriate for the Irish economy of the late 1990s.

Over the last half century the Irish bank base rate has averaged 7 per cent. We're still far below this long-term average. Fortunately for those with large borrowings, we're heading again below the 3 per cent average since we joined the euro. But Ireland had been spoiled, almost to the point where we could say that such cheap money sowed the seeds of our own destruction. Rates have been so low over the last half a dozen years because Europe, especially Germany, has been in the economic doldrums. However, this situation was reversed in 2006 and 2007, and German growth was higher than Irish growth in the first part of 2008. The former sick man of Europe seemed to be the economic powerhouse once again.

Cast a thought back to December 1989, when the news was all about the dismantling of the Berlin Wall and the subsequent talk about German unification. When East German territory was absorbed by what we used to call West Germany, the country's national debt trebled almost overnight, from 40 billion to 120 billion marks in January 1990. Nobody anticipated how long it would take for Germany to bring its new eastern provinces up to their western levels. A special unification tax of up to 13 per cent of income had to be imposed to pay for the cost. This process today is still far from complete, but German unemployment has fallen sharply, and high global prices for crude oil were actually a boon to the German manufacturing machine over the last couple of years.

What has all this to do with Irish bank base rates? Well, the German economy is 30 per cent of the economy of the euro area. Add in France and you have half. Germany was reeling from those extra costs of unification and soaring unemployment. France had its problems too, principal among them a weaker trading partner and socialist governments imposing shorter working weeks etc. Basically, what happens in Germany still determines what interest rates are needed for the euro zone as a whole. German economic weakness lasted for a decade and a half, resulting in a boon and ultra-low rates for the Irish economy. Like it or loathe it, Éire Teoranta is totally dependent on 'core Europe' for its interest rates, and you don't get more core than Deutschland.

Furthermore, all of this occurred in the midst of an economic boom in Ireland, as export growth was among the highest in the world, new jobs were being created, wiping out unemployment, net migration had turned positive from 1996 onwards, and construction exploded to meet all this new demand. It was an economic virtuous circle, fuelled further by the advent of super-cheap money, just at a time when what Éire Teoranta really needed was a return to 7 per cent or higher rates, and certainly not the 2 per cent rate it actually got.

One of the basic points made by David McWilliams in his book *The Pope's Children: Ireland's New Elite* (2005) was that Ireland benefits more when the American economy is strong and the rest of Europe is weak. This is precisely what occurred during the eight years of the 'Celtic Tiger', 1994–2001. McWilliams described very well the interesting social types and the changing social fabric of Ireland as a consequence of that period of high growth.

So we know why euro area rates were subsequently raised, because of a resurgent German (and global) economy, helped in large part not just by renewed consumer confidence and a more price-competitive work force but by high energy prices. The price of oil had quadrupled in the last few years, touching $147 per barrel. So how does this help the Germans? Well, the Germans make things: they manufacture precision machinery; German engineering is the envy of the world. (Just ask any aspiring professional why they want to buy a bmw car.) Germany has been exporting like crazy. Its exports in 2007 alone amounted to €969 billion, while imports came to €770 billion for the same calendar year: that's a trade surplus of almost €200 billion, more than the size of the

Irish economy. In November 2007 Germany's surplus for one month was almost as big as the Irish trade surplus for 2006 or 2007. Granted, it has twenty times the population, but it's still impressive all the same to have almost a trillion euros in exports. Who wouldn't want trade figures like that?

Meanwhile the Americans are having a tougher time of it. Their manufacturing has slumped to levels not seen since the early 1980s, unemployment has surged above 6½ per cent because of the economic downturn, and there are huge problems with the housing sector. Consequently, the United States has cut its official target rates back to just 1 per cent—in fact it appears that the monetary policy authorities there are pursuing a 'zero interest rate policy' (ZIRP), especially as short-term money market rates have fallen to absolutely nothing: three-month US treasury bills were changing hands in November at yields of just 0.04 per cent! That's almost nil. This has paved the way for other central banks, such as the Bank of England and the European Central Bank in the euro zone, to also aggressively cut rates to counter the new economic slowdown, especially now that inflationary pressures are diminishing.

The bad news is, don't expect anything radical from the Irish mortgage lenders. It's likely that European Central Bank rates may fall back to the really low 2 per cent level once more and then remain at that level for a year. But if new mortgage lending remains tight, as it needs to because of the excessively high household indebtedness, then this cyclical downturn could feed on itself, and last even longer than it would otherwise if lending were to return to normal (like, say, the pre-boom days of 2002). And standard variable rates may not fall below 3½ per cent and could remain even higher.

One does not need a crystal ball to look into the future to see where European Central Bank rates are likely to go, because all we need to do is 'follow the money', or those wagers on the other interest rate, the three-month Euribor rate. These financial futures contracts are traded every day in the European futures markets. (See appendix A for a detailed explanation.)

At the time of going to press you could place a bet on where you think rates will be as far ahead as December 2014. Realistically, however, most of the bets are placed on March, June, September and December of the current year or the following year. We know this because the futures exchange tells us every day how many outstanding bets there are for each contract. As each single contract has a notional value of €1 million (market value is this amount multiplied by the price expressed as a percentage), we can work out how much money is actually riding on each outcome.

Jolly useful stuff, really. I mean, if you don't believe it then bet against it. You can bet on these Euribor futures with any of the spread betters (including Worldspreads, Delta Index and Paddy Power Trader). There's always the indisputable argument of 'put up or shut up,' in other words, put your money where your mouth is.

The beauty of using the follow-the-money argument is that we can then plot these expected or implied rates, the professionals' wagers on likely future rates of interest, on a chart alongside historical base rates. Then we plot the likely European Central Bank rate based on the forecast for the three-month rate. Our chart below does exactly this.

Fig. 19: Predicted European Central Bank rates, 2006–14

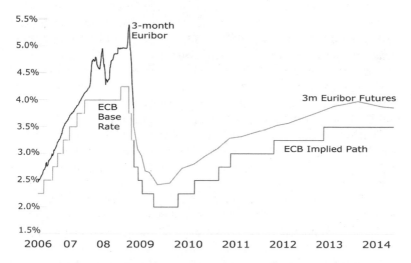

Source: EuroNEXT Financial Futures, European Central Bank

We begin the chart at the beginning of 2006, highlighting the last nine increases in interest rates since 6 December 2005, taking the European Central Bank rate from 2 to 4¼ per cent by 9 July 2008. Furthermore, the chart shows that the short-term futures are pointing to possibly one or two more rate cuts this year and then an even-money chance that they will stay at this rate for a year or so, possibly only returning again to 3 or 3½ per cent some time between 2013 and 2014.

Another misnomer and misconception about interest rates is that they're mean-reverting. That means that if they go up they should immediately begin falling again. This is a totally erroneous assumption. Estate agents are always talking about interest rates as if they were like the tides. The tide comes in, then it's on the turn, and then it goes out again straight away. It doesn't work like that at all.

Central bankers change a level of interest rates in an attempt to fine-tune the economy, to rein in borrowing and to maintain price stability.

But monetary policy is analogous to steering a supertanker: you make small adjustments at the helm, and two miles later (or two years later in the case of the economy) the ship turns back on course. If you listen to some commentators you would think that interest rate movements are like a speedboat that can turn on a sixpence. Monetary policy is not like that. Nor is it a rubber band that becomes stretched and then inevitably returns. It took the calamitous events of major bank failures and a sharp global recession not witnessed in more than a quarter of a century to force the hand of the world's central bankers. What the pros are telling us (through their wagers) is that rates will fall back to their lows in 2009 and will stay at this level for a good while before they begin rising once more. However, the message that these large rate cuts send out to ordinary folk is that the world is in big trouble, and they smack a little of desperation. That can knock consumer confidence further.

One other problem with this fallacious assumption is that it's assumed that interest rates were normal before, at 2 per cent, and then they were high because they had more than doubled to 4¼ per cent. Clearly in a historical perspective they were not that high at 4 per cent. In fact they were then at what many economists would call the neutral level—the level at which they're neither stimulatory nor contractionary, in economic terms. This 'neutral' level is about 4 to 4½ per cent. They were ultra-low before and then they were just low, and now they're heading back down again.

There's only one major caveat when you're using these investors' bets for forecasting rates: the bets themselves change over time and may do so quite dramatically. For example, in late 2007 the Dutch bank ABN Amro was predicting a European Central Bank rate of 5 per cent in 2008, whereas the American investment banking giant Goldman Sachs, as well as Bank of America, were forecasting rates of at least 4¾ per cent. The market generally was predicting that rates would peak at 4½ per cent, before the bank liquidity crunch as a result of the American sub-prime debt crisis.

If we examine where the March 2008 Euribor futures contract was back then, it was very different from today. During July 2007 this contract was telling us that March 2008 rates would be 4.72 per cent for three-month Euribor, which would be more consistent with a 4.5 per cent European Central Bank rate. But by 17 August 2007 it had dropped quickly, within a month, to 4.15 per cent, more or less implying that European Central Bank rates had peaked and would be falling by the spring of 2008. What a huge turnaround! By February 2008 investors had bet heavily that the European Central Bank would cut rates at least two to three times that year, to 3¼ per cent, because of the rapid global economic slowdown. But three months later those views had altered and their position reversed course, back to assuming rate increases to 4½ per cent by the end of 2008.

Right now the March contract is trading at an implied rate of 2.25 per cent, consistent with the current 2.5 per cent European Central Bank rate being cut by half a point to 2 per cent, thus maintaining a quarter-point differential between these two rates. However, the June 2009 contract, at 2 per cent, implies that base rates may be below 1.75 per cent again, thereby hinting that the European Central Bank rates will trough during the middle part of 2009 and then may begin moving back up again after the summer or early next year, depending on the global credit crunch.

So these bets change over time. Do we really care? No, not really. We should take the market average, as it's the collective view. Usually the average view of many individuals is far superior to that of just a few. The debate will always be polarised among the views of economists of the leading international banks.

We should go with the flow, as the money is usually right. Rates will stay at these lower levels while GDP growth projections for the euro area have been revised downwards, from positive growth in 2008 to negative figures for 2009.

Using the figures available at the end of December 2008 (see appendix A) we arrive at a notional total value of all bets on all Euribor futures contracts of €2.95 trillion. However, the individual investors are liable only for the difference in price between where they bet and the outcome. For example, if interest rates end up 0.25 per cent lower than where they were when the bets were placed, the total value of all outstanding bets would increase by €8 billion (as prices shift up to reflect these lower rates: *price = 100 − rate*). Likewise, if rates fail to go this low and ended up ¼ point higher, then the value of all outstanding bets would fall. Therefore for every rise or fall of a quarter of a point that the pros get wrong they stand to lose or make €8 billion, the winners being those who made the correct prediction. This is not fantasy stuff but real money we're talking about. The sums involved are considerable.

CONCLUSION

Altogether, billions would be wiped off the value of these wagers if this occurred and the European Central Bank just refused to change rates or did not move as much as the market has wagered. This is a very powerful argument. You see, you don't have to second-guess interest rates, or lick your finger and stick it in the air and say we think interest rates are going down or up or whatever. All you need to do is look at the financial section of the newspaper or go on line and look at the financial web sites and find out where the professional investors are putting their bets about where rates will be, this year or next. Then just follow the money.

POSTSCRIPT: 'FUTURE SHOCK: IDIOCY'

One of the most frustrating parts of the RTE programme 'Future Shock: the Property Crash' in 2007 was the interview with a young woman who had taken out a mortgage to purchase a flat on the outskirts of Dublin three years earlier, when the European Central Bank base rate was 2 per cent. What was annoying was that she complained that no-one told her that rates would rise—utter madness, considering that bank base rates were at a fifty-year low. Had she no family or friends who told her about 14 per cent mortgages a decade earlier or the 19 per cent home-loan rates two decades ago?

It's incredible that someone would believe that a 3.1 per cent mortgage rate was the norm. Moreover, was she not paying attention when her mortgage broker gave her the obligatory risk warning that rates may rise as well as fall (which they're legally required to do under guidelines set by the financial regulator)? Anybody can take your mortgage application details, but only a registered person can administer the risk warning at the end. Perhaps she was asleep for that part, or just too excited at getting her own pad. Ignorance is bliss, yet it's no excuse for ignoring the most important part of a home loan: what the monthly repayment would be using the 2 per cent stress test.

Anyone who can borrow at 4½ per cent or below today is getting a great deal on the cost of money. Heaven help the poor first-time buyer if base rates ever go back to the forty-year average of 7 per cent.

It now appears likely that Ireland may soon experience 2 per cent base rates once again. Will people learn the lessons from the past, that just because credit is cheaper it doesn't follow that one needs to avail of more of it (if banks are willing lenders, of course)? Leverage itself is risk. And what will the VIPs say when lower rates fail to kick-start the housing market because of all of the other problems? We shall explore in the next chapter why interest rates are not all they're cracked up to be!

Chapter 20

The interest-rate fallacy unravelled

Estate agents will undoubtedly herald the latest decreases in the European Central Bank rate as the much-needed catalyst for the recovery of the property market. The same estate agents' ranting was that rate increases were apparently to blame for the housing recession in the first place. So does this mean that the end is in sight if rates are slashed back to 2 per cent? No, definitely not.

They got it wrong in the first place about what brought on the Irish housing recession. They blame rising rates; in fact rates went from ridiculously low to just very low and are still well below trend rates. They also blamed poor sentiment caused by confusion over stamp duty. If this was so, why did first-time buyers stop buying new homes completely, without having to pay any stamp duty at all?

The twin causes of the Irish property correction were oversupply and excessive valuations. The latter destroyed affordability, as prices simply went up too much too quickly. However, the former caused the developers to shoot themselves in the foot. They were building not for genuine demand but for speculators who could buy second or third homes as rental properties. They have now realised this, as evidenced by the reduction in new-home starts, and they have begun to take serious lumps out of the stupidly high asking prices with serious price discounts.

Why have estate agents involved in selling new homes cut staff numbers and wages by 10 per cent? In the middle of June 2008 two of the larger agents, CBRE Gunne New Homes and Lisney, began serious cost-cutting. The story was reported by Barry O'Halloran in the *Irish Times* on 21 June 2008 and included a direct quotation from Aidan O'Hogan, chairman of Savills HOK, who stated, 'It's all purely a function of finance.' The journalist went on to say: 'Mr O'Hogan said that the difficulty for everyone involved in the property market in borrowing money from the banks was the main reason for the Republic's slowing property markets.' Having worked with the man in question, I can confirm that this was indeed a regular complaint of his.

It's very worrying that those employed in the construction industry, and a former president of the Irish Auctioneers' and Valuers' Institute to boot, actually believe that it's all due to credit availability and the unusually low level of interest rates. To blame the entire Irish property crash on Jean-Claude Trichet and the European Central Bank doesn't even merit comment. We shall show in this chapter that interest rates play a very small role in determining property prices. When the International Monetary Fund said that Irish property was 32 per cent overvalued at the end of 2007, after the fall in prices of 7.3 per cent that year, it didn't mention interest rates.

The most important factor in price affordability is of course price itself. If you're faced with a choice in purchasing a property in Dublin between two similar-sized properties in the same street and one is €100,000 cheaper to buy than the other, interest rates don't even enter the decision-making equation. If estate agents actually believe that interest rates are the sole problem for the property slump, then God help them, because they will be bewildered when they see ultra-low European Central Bank rates of 2 to 2½ per cent again and property prices still falling. If they built their businesses on the basis of those exceptionally low rates they actually deserve to go out of business. If your business can sell its products only when the climate is rosy you're a 'fair-weather' trader. Every business undergraduate is taught in management theory that even the most ill-conceived business strategies do well on the crest of a bull-market wave, but when that wave recedes and the tide is on the way out those ill-conceived strategies are left very exposed.

The next time an estate agent says that lower interest rates will equate to higher home prices, ask them the following question: Why did house prices keep rising rapidly in early 2006, when the European Central Bank was increasing interest rates? Why did house prices fall each and every month from June 2007 to June 2008 while interest rates were left unchanged by the European Central Bank? Why would lower rates not stop the secular decline in average home prices?

The answer to all these questions is that interest rates now account for only very small changes in home prices. The scientific and empirical evidence behind this is overwhelming. It may run counter to what most people think if they think that lower rates mean they can borrow more, and vice versa, but all the statistical evidence shows that rates are very far down the scale when it comes to the principal factors that drive home prices.

Back in the mid to late 1990s interest rates were a principal determinant of the increased demand for housing when Ireland joined European monetary union and adjusted to the new interest-rate regime created by the single currency. That was a one-off event and will not be repeated. It was also a unique era because of explosive growth in population, rising real incomes (prosperity), rapid economic growth and uncharacteristically low annual inflation rates. Then, unlike now, housing demand exceeded supply.

The biggest problem with Irish estate agents is that they assume that 'supply equals demand' all the time. They never speak of the oversupply problem, yet the dogs in the street can see the unsold new homes. The other problem with Irish estate agents (and it's unique to Irish agents, because American and British agents differ in this area) is that the asking price is always correct, it's always right . . . until they begin chopping it. Then the property is correctly valued at the new, lower price. When have you ever heard an estate agent talk of overvaluation? Well, I can reliably inform you that Savills in Britain do have research staff that not only talk about 'stretched' or 'overvalued' properties but make that point in their research and their presentations to customers and the media. It's such a pity that in Ireland there's a virtual police-state mentality when it comes to talking about the real problems facing either the property market or the general economy.

Almost a decade ago, because of the massive increases in property prices, the Government commissioned three consultancy reports on the property market. As Dr Peter Bacon was involved in all three, they subsequently became known as the Bacon Reports.

BACON III, JUNE 2000

The third and final Bacon Report, *The Housing Market in Ireland: An Economic Evaluation of Trends and Prospects*, published in June 2000, contained a very important fourth chapter on an econometric analysis of the housing market and projections for the future. This chapter not only contained some very important analysis on the supply side of the housing equation, by modelling new-home completions using forecasts by the Economic and Social Research Institute and the Central Statistics Office, but it also specified a model for estimating house prices, or the demand side. The biggest factor in determining supply is—surprise, surprise—prices. We could all have guessed that one. But what are the main determinants of house prices? The study identified the major factors on the demand side of the equation as (in order of importance):

- the size of the existing housing stock,
- the size of the housing stock the previous year,
- the level of personal disposable income,
- the price of second-hand homes the previous year,
- the population aged between twenty-five and thirty-four, and
- the base mortgage rate.

The interest-rate variable not only had the lowest coefficient but also had the smallest 't-statistic' as well, which in mathematical terms says that it was the least reliable variable.

What this model said was that the prices of second-hand homes were far more dependent on supply (the total size of the market and the increase in the housing stock), income (the amount of money people had to spend), prices (where prices were previously), demography (the changing size of the population of younger first-time buyers) and, last *and* very least, rates (the rate of interest on mortgages).

The quarterly bulletin of the Economic and Social Research Institute published an article in July 2002 by the ESRI economist David Duffy entitled 'A descriptive analysis of the Irish housing market.' (See appendix B for a more detailed discussion of this report.) He made two important points. Firstly, he referred back to an earlier analysis of the market in 1998 ('An economic assessment of recent house price developments' by Bacon, MacCabe and Murphy), which found the four principal drivers of the market to be

- economic growth,
- demography,
- the cost of finance, and
- the speed at which supply responds to changes in demand.

The 1998 report had estimated in broad terms, looking not just at mortgage interest rates but also at anticipated capital appreciation. It found that from 1992 to 1998 the cost of housing to buyers had fallen dramatically, despite higher prices. In short, low interest rates plus expected capital gains on personal property drove a rising market.

Ten years later, in 2008, real interest rates are still very low by historical standards but demand is greatly lowered, because of expected future capital losses. People stopped believing in the boom. Instead they began believing that houses were overpriced.

Duffy also discussed the ESRI model for estimating 'fair-value' housing prices. He found that the principal factors, in descending order of importance, were

- demography (25 to 34-year-olds as a proportion of the working population),
- the stock of houses divided by the population,
- the increase in real disposable income, and
- interest rates.

Not only were interest rates the least important, they registered only half the predictability of the income variable. In short, they were of little relative importance.

The first two factors make perfect sense. If you have more young workers in the country you need more homes, and prices may rise; and if the stock of homes in the country increases faster than the growth in population, prices will fall. With regard to changes in real disposable income, just ask any salaried taxpayer and they will tell you that their real income is falling, thanks to higher inflation, especially higher prices for food and energy. With the exception of lower rates, all the factors in the ESRI model for new home prices point to lower prices in the future. Yet the VIPs and estate agents kept saying (in 2007 and the first half of 2008), parrot fashion, that 'the fundamentals are good'!

The analysis by David Duffy was broadly endorsed by work done over many years by Professor Maurice Roche. In 2003, in an article in the *Quarterly Economic Commentary* headed 'Will there be a crash in house prices?' he wrote that the two biggest factors were disposable income and land costs. Both make perfect sense, especially when we consider that back in 1995 land costs represented 13 per cent of the price of a new house, a figure that had risen to 23 per cent by the time Professor Roche wrote his article eight years later. In 2007 it was almost 50 per cent.

A quick example is needed to prove this point. Let's take Blackrock, a suburb in south Co. Dublin where land prices peaked at €20 million per acre in 2007. We assume that the local authority, Dún Laoghaire-Rathdown County Council, would give planning permission for fifty-five large two-bedroom and three-bedroom apartments (averaging, say, 100 square metres) on a hypothetical one-acre site, which would be considered high density. At the peak of the market those new apartments might have fetched as much as €750,000 each. Let's say they did; then the total sales revenue from the one-acre sample site would be €41¼ million. But land was half that.

Those figures are not fictitious: they are based on real numbers. A half-acre site in front of the Blackrock Clinic (the former Texaco service station, now the consultants' car park) sold for €10 million, while apartments next door in Sion Hill and Frascati were for sale at those asking prices in early 2007. As Maurice Roche warned five years ago, 'trends in land costs are the most important factor explaining the trend in new house prices and it is perhaps here the government should be directing more attention.' Unfortunately, Government policy on land has been lacking and appears to have been made on the hoof (excuse the pun) in a tent at the Galway Races.

CONCLUSION

Interest rates only play one part in the demand for housing. The availability of credit is more important than the rate of interest; and real interest rates—those deflated by consumer price inflation—are more important than nominal rates.

The following table summarises the Irish experience of inflation, mortgage rates and house prices over the last decade. All the figures are percentages.

Table 22: Comparison of inflation and interest rates, 1998–2008

Period	Inflation	Mortgage rates	Real rate	House prices
Dec. 1998	+1.7	+5.6	+3.9	+29.8
Dec. 1999	+3.4	+4.0	+0.6	+17.9
Dec. 2000	+5.9	+5.9	−0.0	+21.3
Dec. 2001	+4.2	+4.5	+0.3	+4.4
Dec. 2002	+5.0	+4.3	−0.7	+13.3
Dec. 2003	+1.9	+3.5	+1.6	+13.7
Dec. 2004	+2.6	+3.4	+0.8	+8.6
Dec. 2005	+2.3	+3.6	+1.3	+9.3
Dec. 2006	+4.9	+4.8	−0.1	+11.8
Dec. 2007	+4.7	+5.3	+0.6	−7.3
Oct. 2008	+4.0	+5.2	+1.2	−10.4

Source: Central Statistics Office, Central Bank of Ireland, PTSB-ESRI

There you have it in figures. There is, at best, a tenuous relationship between the third column of figures, 'real' inflation-adjusted mortgage rates, and annual growth in house prices. In fact during the best year ever for property prices, 1998, real mortgage rates were 'high'! That was because of the failure to predict the level of demand for new homes, so prices went up too quickly. Contrast this with the time of writing, late 2008, when real rates were the same as 2004 but the opposite was occurring with respect to annual inflation in home prices. This time supply is once again to blame, but too much rather than too little. Also, when the European Central Bank began the last round of rate increases in December 2005, real Irish mortgage rates had fallen by half a point, because of the doubling of domestic inflation.

Real Irish mortgage rates are still *low*. Don't be fooled by estate agents.

Credit is still available but has simply been restricted back to more normal levels, such as a loan-to-value ratio of 80 per cent for first-time buyers and a 70 per cent cap for buy-to-let investors. Some lenders have completely stopped buy-to-let or speculator loans. That's a good thing, as the market had become over-dependent on speculators and amateur landlords instead of real property-buyers. Dangerous 100 per cent mortgages have been restricted to the professional classes, such as doctors and dentists, solicitors and barristers, accountants and even architects, as well as to some segments of public-sector employees. Again, no property market should be reliant on 'no-savings' finance to ensure a property purchase.

The negative feedback between credit and the property cycle when prices are falling is further reinforced when bank lending is highly dependent on collateral values, as it is in Ireland in 2008.

Banks will lend; they will extend credit. They're just not happy lending into a declining market. They don't want to catch a falling knife, as the expression goes. But banks were the main culprits (after the politicians) in causing the property bubble in the first place.

You see, dear reader, it's not about finance at all. It's about quantity and price, the two principal determinants of demand and supply.

Chapter 21

'Please mind the gap': The negative-equity trap

W hen I'm on a train that pulls alongside the platform and a voice comes over the loudspeaker system with the ubiquitous phrase 'Please mind the gap,' I always suffix to it the rhyme '—the negative-equity trap!'

Passengers are always warned of the perilous gap that may exist between the carriage doors and the platform. It's a pity that first-time buyers are never afforded a similar courtesy when they're offered 100 per cent mortgages at the height of a property bull market. Home loans that exceed the value or purchase price of a property are indeed a late bull-market cycle phenomenon. When the only way that new buyers can enter a market is with a no-savings loan, then that surely is the best indicator that the market in question has got ahead of itself in terms of price affordability. Bring back the statutory maximum loan-to-value home loan, that's what I say.

For the purpose of clarity, we need to define simply the concept of negative equity. News bulletins of late have talked about negative equity in the same breath as home prices falling below the price paid by purchasers. Negative equity exists only when the size of the loan is greater than the value of the property.

Basically, there are two ways that a home-owner may be saddled with negative equity. One is when they 'over-borrowed' or borrowed too much initially to purchase the property; the other is when there's a major property crash. In the latter scenario—the one most likely today in Ireland—property prices decline so much during the slump that even those who bought homes with a modest degree of leverage in the first place are affected. Anybody who bought an Irish property after 2003 but borrowed at least three-quarters of the purchase price may well fall into this camp.

Negative equity doesn't creep up on you like a debilitating illness. It just appears one day, and by then it may be too late. You may feel fine, look well and have the outward appearance of normality, but then, *Bang*, like the commercial for a household cleaning product, you have negative equity. It has never really been a feature of the Irish property market, but it has now arrived on the scene.

NEGATIVE EQUITY: A TUNNEL WITH NO LIGHT

In 1992 I bought my first property, a new one-bedroom flat in London. I waited until September of that year, until the Nationwide and Halifax greater London home-price indices had fallen 25 per cent from the end-of-1988 peak (though history now shows that London prices fell for a further six months—another 4½ per cent down—and then moved sideways until 1996). So I thought I had timed it well and had got in close to the bottom after the recession. Wrong! By Halloween, two months after I moved in, one of my neighbours threw in the towel after the freehold was sold to an unscrupulous managing agent. The annual service charge was doubled and threatening letters were sent to all leaseholders that their mortgage lenders would be informed that they were in breach of their lease if they failed to pay the new exorbitant charge. So she panicked and handed the keys back to the Bradford and Bingley Building Society. They duly sold the property within a week and, lo and behold, my new neighbours and I all had 35 per cent negative equity. Every estate agent in the locality knew what price my neighbour's flat had sold for before we did. The problem was that it was sold into a falling market.

Suddenly, you find yourself trapped in a place you had previously imagined as a short staging-post. After all, who wanted to live in a tiny one-bed for more than a year or so? I sold the flat eventually, six years later, for exactly what I had paid for it. But I was one of the lucky ones. You see, the 95 per cent mortgage I had taken out was less than a year's salary then. Therefore, within a couple of years I was in a position to borrow more money and buy a bigger, two-bedroom flat and rent out the first one. During the interim four-year period it was rented out for the equivalent gross yield of 14 per cent, which was considerably more than the mortgage interest rate at the time, which was about 7 per cent by the time the flat had been let. I had to pay a letting agency one month's rent in commission, plus a service charge, which they took in advance. But paying them the high annual service charge, and the mortgage lender, still left me with a couple of hundred quid profit at the end of each month.

The biggest problem is not financial but psychological. When you're thrust into the position of negative equity there's no light at the end of the tunnel. There's nothing to look forward to. You begin to resent your own home, often to the point where if things break you leave them that way. It's difficult to explain to someone who has never experienced it. It's a horrible time. Even though you may be quite happy living in the house or flat and happy with the surrounding area, you're stripped of one important human element, the element of personal choice.

Don't underestimate the sacrifice of not having freedom of choice, because negative equity in many cases is like a prison sentence. It impairs your credit standing. You can't trade up, unless you have the funds to cover the shortfall between the value of the property and the outstanding mortgage loan. For many salaried workers who had to borrow a large multiple of their basic income just to get their first home it's a trap, a pernicious one at that.

SOCIAL CONSEQUENCES OF NEGATIVE EQUITY

Negative equity should never be played down or belittled with phrases like 'It doesn't really matter as long as the home-owner can afford to keep making their monthly loan repayments,' or 'perhaps they're already living in their ideal home.' The fall-out from negative equity among the younger population is severe. All surveys and corresponding empirical evidence, both in Britain and Ireland, have shown that it's the younger home-buyer, in the 22–34 age cohort, who are most afraid of the spectre of negative equity. And with good reason too. These are the people of starter-family age. If a 32-year old woman is trapped in a two-bedroom flat for seven or eight years, until the negative equity has disappeared or until she and her partner have saved enough to clear the shortfall, she may face the prospect of having her first child in her forties, when the risk of Down's syndrome has trebled. Many couples may not make it through negative equity, especially when one considers the economic backdrop that usually accompanies it—rising unemployment, for example, or plummeting real incomes. Although lenders may be sympathetic when one partner loses their job, they will have to weigh up the odds of letting arrears build up or cause prices to fall further by foreclosing. This is the same dilemma that the Irish banks are now facing with the big developers and their large stocks of unsold new homes.

A former colleague of mine bought a new two-bedroom apartment in London in 1991 for a quarter of a million pounds, jointly with his Australian girl-friend. A year later, as prices dropped, she moved back to Australia. He couldn't afford the mortgage repayments on his own, so he gave the keys to the bank and walked away—or he thought he would. The bank, Barclay's, immediately sold the flat at auction for £180,000 and then chased James for the £70,000 shortfall—just him, not the other mortgagee. You see, two or more people who take out a home loan are 'jointly and severally' liable. That legalese means that the lender can chase one party for the whole of a joint debt.

The last story should not be lost on the thousands of young Irish people who now settle into partnerships but no longer consider it necessary to marry. A notable feature of social change between the census of 2002 and that of 2006 was that about 125,000 couples married during that four-year period but almost 147,000 couples lived together without getting married. The point is that it's easier for a person who is not legally married to walk away. There's no waiting around for half the assets when negative equity is in town.

LENDERS' LUNACY

The fastest route to negative equity is to simply borrow more than the property is worth in the first instance. Lenders should never have countenanced such madness, and the financial regulators and central banks should never allow them to offer loans that put the borrower into a negative-equity situation from day 1. It's not clever to borrow the full price of a home: this is tantamount to infinite leverage. A quick illustration of this point would be if I want to buy all the houses in Aylesbury Road in Dublin and I want a consortium of banks to lend me all the money needed to buy them, on a 100 per cent finance basis. The banks' interest payments will be met by the rent I will charge the embassies and all my other tenants in this street. It would be a 'neutral cash flow' transaction.

The banks would just laugh at that; yet in July 2005 Bank of Ireland launched its 'Quickstart 100', a 35-year loan where the 10 per cent deposit was lent at 6 per cent and the balance of the loan at the prevailing mortgage rate. It just copied the British mortgage lenders. It has to be said, though, that the British home-loan providers were far more reckless. The Bradford and Bingley Building Society had 'Max 130', where 130 per cent of the purchase price could be borrowed (subject to a maximum of £30,000 over the valuation). It was tailored to provide first-time buyers the extra cash to buy furniture (a feature that many Irish developers already included in the purchase price, through incentives, so the home-buyer is essentially borrowing for those anyway, which explains the higher prices for starter homes in Ireland). Needless to say, this goes a long way towards explaining why Bradford and Bingley's share price collapsed in July 2008, from 418 pence to 34 pence—that and the fact that it also lent heavily to the buy-to-let sector.

But Bradford and Bingley were not alone. Northern Rock, Coventry Building Society and Halifax Bank of Scotland all offered 125 per cent loan-to-value mortgages where essentially the first 95 per cent was secured on the home, with the balance of 30 per cent as an unsecured loan. (This sets an important precedent for a possible solution for home-buyers caught in the negative-equity trap, which we shall explore further shortly.) Suffice it to say that banks have been willing in the past to modify loan terms to allow an 'unsecured' component.

How big a problem will negative equity be for Irish people? One of the most important aspects of negative equity is quantifying the problem, trying to establish the likely numbers affected, based on varying degrees of property price falls. In effect, what we're attempting to do here is set the parameters for the possible extent of the fall-out from negative equity. We do this by ignoring the phenomenon from a 'mover-up' or 'trader-upper' viewpoint and look at the group in society likely to be hardest hit by the negative-equity scenario: the first-time buyers. We zoom in on the first-time buyers primarily because quantifiable data is available for this high-risk group.

Table 23: Negative equity, 2005–08e

Quarter	Number of FTBS	PTSB-ESRI FTB price (€)	IBF FTB loan (€)	Average LTV	Negative equity (€)
2005, q1	7,139	222,635	187,309	84%	n.a.
2005, q2	9,394	228,641	199,593	87%	−3,921
2005, q3	10,062	238,080	209,174	88%	−13,502
2005, q4	11,284	247,651	212,709	86%	−17,037
2006, q1	8,789	253,855	212,053	84%	−16,381
2006, q2	9,407	264,416	227,454	86%	−31,782
2006, q3	9,884	275,109	231,514	84%	−35,842
2006, q4	8,984	279,135	240,151	86%	−44,479
2007, q1	7,919	279,531	222,023	79%	−26,351
2007, q2	7,883	273,459	239,416	88%	−43,744
2007, q3	7,817	267,452	248,068	93%	−52,396
2007, q4	6,850	261,380	243,232	93%	−47,560
2008, q1	4,329	254,387	251,831	99%	−56,159
2008, q2	6,106	247,783	249,844	101%	−54,172
2008, q3	5,553	242,569	238,064	98%	−42,392
2008, q4e	4,500	231,806	230,000	99%	−34,328
30% fall		195,672			

Source: Irish Banking Federation, ESRI, Permanent TSB

Our table above shows the number of first-time buyers each quarter since the beginning of 2005, using data from the Irish Banking Federation. The second column is the average price of a new first-time buyer's home as provided by the PTSB-ESRI home-price indices. (Well done, Permanent TSB and ESRI, for doing a first-time buyer break-out or sub-index!) The next column shows the average loan-to-value ratio. It's quite revealing. It shows that in recent times the poor first-time buyer has been borrowing increasingly more of the purchase price of the property. This is interesting because, although the average first-time buyer typically borrows 85 to 90 per cent of the price of a new home, back in the first quarter of 2007, when the market peaked and prices began falling, the number of first-time buyers tailed off sharply in line with the zenith in the market. This was also a period of considerable uncertainty, while at the same time consumer sentiment had begun to plunge. Also in that first quarter of 2007 first-time buyers borrowed significantly less proportionately—less than 80 per cent of the new property price. Caution was the operative word back then.

The big price slashes by the developers that began in the third quarter of 2007 obviously attracted first-time buyers in their droves, for although their total numbers have dwindled in each successive quarter the proportion borrowed jumped to 90 per cent and more. This tells us that those who could get credit availed of it; those who still couldn't get enough credit have been protected from their own stupidity. Thus the total number of first-time buyers is down, but those who were still buying were tempted by the big apparent price discounts and jumped in with both feet. These are the people most at risk from the spectre of negative equity.

The final column shows how much negative equity, on average, each first-time buyer who bought at each period would have if prices fell 30 per cent from peak to trough. This figure is taken from Dermot O'Leary, chief economist at Goodbody's (a subsidiary of AIB), published in its *Irish Economic Commentary: 2010 Vision* on 10 July 2008. If this gloomy but rather conservative prediction does unfold, the price for the average first-time home will fall to a little less than €196,000, or about €50,000 less than the corresponding figure for May 2008. I myself think the market could fall more, perhaps by 40 per cent in nominal terms, because of the increasing stock of unsold new homes and the likelihood of further price slashes in the autumn of 2008. I use the Goodbody's forecast because it is independent and so more objective.

The net result of the prices of new first-time-buyer homes falling by this amount would be to place about 119,000 relatively recent first-time buyers (since the second quarter of 2005) in a negative-equity situation. Assuming a 30 per cent decline in new homes purchased by first-time buyers, this would result in more than €3.8 billion of total negative equity, or approximately €32,000 per first-time home affected. Let's not forget that the first-time-buyer home-price index peaked in March 2007 at €279,795, and the figures in the table above are quarterly averages of monthly data. So by that reckoning, based on the PTSB-ESRI first-time-buyer index for November 2008 of €230,094, a drop of nearly 18 per cent has already occurred.

The next short table provides a useful illustration of how damaging negative equity could potentially be to the first-time buyer, based on differing scenarios with respect to possible price falls.

Table 24: Expected negative equity based on home price falls

FTB home price drop	FTBs with negative equity	Total negative equity (€ million)	Average negative equity (€)
−15%	47,500	297	6,200
−20%	79,200	1,104	14,000
−25%	99,300	2,267	22,800
−30%	118,800	3,828	32,200
−35%	148,300	5,640	38,000
−40%	173,800	7,931	45,600
−45%	192,000	10,563	55,000

The 30 per cent fall shaded area represents the Goodbody scenario. It would be a disaster if prices fell by 40 per cent or more (that is, if first-time-buyer prices dropped to below €168,000), because then it would affect almost 174,000 new homes that had been purchased since September 2003, and total negative equity could amount to €8 billion—a staggering amount, which would leave the average first-time buyer with negative equity of more than €45,000. Those who purchased since the third quarter of 2007 would end up in the red to the extent of €75,000 to €85,000 on average, depending on when they bought, whereas those who purchased during 2004 would probably only be in the red between €10,000 and €20,000, depending on whether they bought at the beginning or during the second part of that year. (Those number-crunchers who are really interested in the pre-2005 data methodology can review appendix C for a complete description of the method used to extend the Irish Banking Federation series back to 2003.)

THE FIRST DECILE DOESN'T COUNT
It may appear strange at first, but the first 10 per cent drop in new-home prices doesn't really matter. It doesn't create many cases of negative equity, apart from the obvious ones (those who bought at the peak using 100 per cent loans). All property slumps begin with a 7–10 per cent drop in the first year. Usually this doesn't create much negative equity; it's the second year of the crash—the one we're in now—when prices fall by more than the first year that does the real damage. At the time of writing, these estimates of annual decline in home prices by the banks and brokers for 2008 average between −10 and −12 per cent, depending on who you speak to. Evidently, the first 10 per cent fall eats up the existing equity that was there because of the initial home-buyer's deposit upon purchase.

What is important to remember, though, is that, as explained earlier, negative equity appears quite suddenly. Often it's sparked by panic selling.

In the Irish case this could be prompted by buy-to-let investors looking for the door, but the more likely catalyst is the big developers slashing prices to eliminate the backlog of unsold homes, particularly if the banks capitulate and fire the starting-pistol for the ultimate 'race to the bottom'.

MEANINGLESS MISINFORMATION AND THE ART OF SPIN

Undoubtedly the vested-interest parties, and the estate agents in particular, will play down the whole negative-equity problem. They will spin stories that it will affect only a small minority of home-owners, as they will refer to meaningless national averages, including wealthy solicitors and accountants with valuable properties and no mortgages to speak of.

I'm reminded of a conversation I had with one of Ireland's largest estate agents in the spring of 2007. It was one of those brief chats when you bump into someone while going for coffee. I raised the spectre of negative equity. His reply was blasé: it would affect only about 1½ per cent of home-owners, and, as he put it, 'the market can live with that.' That's great if you're in your fifties, have sold your company for €50 million, have pocketed €5 million and already own your own home. Not so great if you were one of the unlucky first-time buyers who borrowed heavily to get onto the property ladder since 2003. I recall thinking at the time that about 950,000 homes in Ireland had loans secured on them, and 1½ per cent of those would be more than 15,000 homes, each with two incomes to pay the mortgage. That's 30,000 people adversely affected by negative equity, and it's a lot of people in anyone's book. But I also thought to myself, if negative equity does become a prominent feature of the property market it will probably affect a lot more people than that, because of the sheer number of those who were buying new homes each year, especially during the property boom of 2002–07, with nearly half a million new homes completed during that six-year period.

It also struck me that the figure of 1½ per cent had been plucked out of the air. No property market ever faced a major slump with 98½ per cent of mortgage-holders getting off that lightly.

Another ruse to watch out for will be the estate agents putting negative equity within the general context of the home equity cushion. Again using national averages, if negative equity turns out to be about €4 billion—the Goodbody scenario—then they will say that this represents less than 1 per cent of total home equity of about €365 billion (*1.9 million homes × national average price − total mortgages*). Beware of these meaningless statistics, for they hide the real truth, as many homes in the country have no mortgage attached to them as well as those that have, and of course the biggest home loans are skewed towards the younger generations who have bought in recent times. It's worth remembering that 5 per cent of the home-owners who buy in a given year set the prices for the 95 per cent who don't move house or buy their first home. If a large chunk of those recent purchasers end up with negative equity it will cast a shadow over the entire market for years to come. And it will devalue all homes nationally.

WHAT TO DO IN A NEGATIVE-EQUITY SITUATION?

The best advice I can give, having suffered negative equity myself for six years, is to repay the loan as quickly as possible by making additional payments; or, if your finances allow, rent out the property to cover the mortgage payments (or most of them) and wait it out. But remember, it will take years to erode negative equity.

Those who are paid weekly could switch from monthly mortgage repayments to bi-weekly, because this results in the equivalent of thirteen monthly payments a year instead of twelve (or twenty-six half-monthly payments really).

Those with an irregular income, or those who earn commission or bonuses, could use them to make one-off capital repayments. But find out when the lender accounts for capital repayments. If it's 31 December it would be better to set up a parallel savings account and then make the balloon payments just before the end of the year.

If you're young and single you can avail of the rent-a-room scheme and not pay tax, or you can rent out the whole property and move back in with your family. Though this is not ideal it allows for the individual to make double the monthly repayments.

If you're on an interest-only mortgage, switch immediately to a repayment one. It will cost a lot more, but the sooner you begin making capital repayments the better.

If you like your home and don't care about its monetary value, and you have a good income, just make your regular loan payments and forget about it. Life's too short to be worrying about money all the time.

However, there will be those who are doubly hit by negative equity and the economic downturn at the same time. They need to retain control of their personal finances and rely on the art of negotiation.

NEGOTIATE YOUR WAY OUT OF MISERY

The worst possible decision in a negative-equity situation is to succumb to temptation, capitulate and hand the keys back to your mortgage lender. They might sell your beloved property for a lot less than the open-market valuation, at a distressed auction, and then chase you for the balance (including fees and additional interest) for years to come. Pragmatic realism is far more important than knee-jerk panic.

One interesting development in the United States recently has been the emergence of the 'deed-in-lieu foreclosure' (even if it sounds like throwing your deeds into the loo—which is what many home-owners with negative equity may feel like doing). This happens when the home-owner is in arrears with significant negative equity, but they retain control of their situation. They know they have to sell to repay the bank, and they know there will be a shortfall. So they agree with their mortgage lender that they will sell the property themselves (thereby ensuring a proper price), pay the bank the proceeds, then negotiate a settlement for the balance as an unsecured or personal loan. This loan may even be less than the shortfall.

For example, say you bought a new home for half a million, with a 90 per cent loan of €450,000, but three years later the property is worth only €380,000, so there's negative equity of €70,000. You would agree with your mortgage lender that you will sell the property for the best possible price. You do so, achieving the market valuation figure that leaves a funding shortfall of €70,000. Then you agree to pay the bank back €50,000 over ten years as a personal unsecured loan at a slightly higher rate of interest than the standard variable rate normally charged on a home loan. In this way you kill two birds with one stone: you get yourself out of a bind and put yourself in a position to buy another home at a vastly cheaper price and, secondly, you assist the bank in recovering most of the loan and help them to avoid repossession (and its legal costs).

You may ask yourself why someone would go to such extreme measures. Well, they might need to move home to start a family or to provide a bigger home for a growing family. It also allows them to take advantage of the lower home prices in the market. There's a value trade that outweighs the burden of the additional personal loan.

Would the banks participate in such schemes? Initially they would be reluctant, but they have already set the precedent of using unsecured loans as part finance of a property, as mentioned earlier. It would be seen as the lesser of two evils.

CONSTRUCTIVE SOLUTIONS

It's probably a good idea to finish a chapter on such a sensitive topic with lessons that may be learnt and prospective solutions that may prevent negative equity from becoming a regular feature of the residential property market.

First of all, the financial regulator could impose a statutory minimum loan-to-value ratio for first-time buyers and second-time buyers—probably something in the region of 80 per cent loan-to-value for a first-timer and 75 per cent for a 'mover' (who should already have a bigger deposit or savings because of existing home equity). Then they need to monitor financial institutions properly to ensure that this is enforced and not just send them letters saying *Please don't lend too many times a person's income including overtime etc.*, as they did regularly in the early 1990s. Those letters were ignored.

Secondly, the Government should abolish stamp duty on property altogether, or make it a flat rate of 1 per cent—the same as stocks and shares. Stamp duty on property could be replaced with individual property taxes, payable by all home-owners. I know this would be unpopular at first, but it's infinitely fairer than the present system, which is nothing more than a 'liquidity tax' on property transactions. Turnover would improve, and the backlog of unsold homes could clear quickly, which in turn would have a beneficial impact on the stock of unsold new homes.

Both these measures would serve to smooth out the property cycle in terms of property prices. The proposed property tax based on rateable values would reduce the vast price ranges between property types within a given area. This would make it easier for young families to trade up. It would also deter property speculators who have no utilitarian interest in a home.

Thirdly, the banks should have work-out specialists or teams set up before negative equity became a big problem. They should also be looking at potential problems of loan modification in the light of the new regulatory capital regime under the Basel II accord. And they need to identify potential restructuring solutions with regard to the heavy mortgage securitisation that has already taken place. Central Bank statistics suggest that approximately €23 billion or more of Irish residential mortgages has been repackaged and resold to international investors. The home-owners and therefore mortgagees may not realise that their mortgage loan has been sold to a Dutch or German pension fund or Italian insurance company. Under the covenants attached to these securitised mortgage loans the banks may have their hands tied with respect to loan modification as a result. Perhaps they could explore the avenue of possible mortgage substitution as an alternative solution.

Fourthly, the banks could take a leaf out of the Australian banks' book and offer a 'no negative equity guarantee' mortgage for first-time buyers. It could be structured as an insurance product, whereby the prospective home-buyer takes out their first mortgage, pays a one-off premium for the 'no negative equity' protection, then will never have to worry about a funding shortfall when they come to move home, as the bank will accept full sales proceeds as final payment for the outstanding mortgage. Already there are private organisations offering home-owners in Britain and the United States 'lock-in-value equity' or, put another way, a guaranteed minimum purchase price for their home over the next ten years, that is, above their outstanding mortgage balance.

Lastly, negative equity is a trap, but it doesn't last for ever. It's a feature of a declining market that causes prices to fall further, but it should be recognised by the state that the primary goal ought to be to keep those people in their homes who are willing to make some form of repayment.

This may necessitate setting up a state-backed entity that would purchase distressed home loans from the banks—at a discount, I may add (there has to be some benefit to the state, and some cost to the lenders)—and would enable loan restructurings and not simply add arrears to the outstanding mortgage balance as deferred capital payments, as the lenders did when interest rates went up in the early 1990s and banks allowed mortgagees to make the same monthly repayment but deferred the additional interest payments onto capital. This only makes the problem worse, as the borrower ends up paying interest on the interest.

One thing is certain: there are choppy waters ahead for the homeowner, and it only remains to be seen if the Government, the regulator and the banks can rise to the challenge.

POSTSCRIPT, 24 JULY 2008

An article appeared in the *Irish Times* on 24 July 2008 reporting that Mary O'Dea, consumer director at the financial regulator, gave evidence to an Oireachtas committee. She explained that 7 per cent of the value of all new mortgages taken out during 2007 were 100 per cent loans. The total value of these amounted to €2.36 billion, but in the intervening period official house prices had fallen by about 10 per cent. It was also reported that in volume of loans some 5½ per cent, or 8,695 mortgages, were 100 per cent loans.

According to the latter figure, and knowing that most mortgages are taken out by couples, as it takes two incomes to service the average mortgage, we can see that approximately 15,000 people were already in a negative-equity situation one year ago. The total amount of negative equity on this basis would have been about €230 million.

This endorses the views expressed earlier in this chapter about the likely numbers affected after the first year in the property slump, and it ties in with the quantum shown in the summary table representing the potential extent of the problem. If anything, indeed, these figures are worse, because they show that a smaller number of people have the same level of negative equity with a smaller property price fall of 10 per cent and not the 15 per cent shown in the first row of the table.

However, the obvious caveat is that those mortgages were spread across the year and were not all taken out on 1 January. Therefore, the figure for the total number of borrowers would be absolutely correct, but some of them would have little negative equity so far (those who purchased in the final quarter of 2007 or the first quarter of 2008). On balance, then, this suggests that the earlier table is probably a better representation of the average negative-equity experience.

It's nice to know, though, with regard to statistical accuracy, that the numbers suggested at the beginning of this chapter do hold up well to scrutiny, as well as the strong supporting anecdotal evidence that has subsequently been made available. It's encouraging with regard to a realistic appraisal, though obviously not for the people affected.

Lastly, five months after I had originally conducted this statistical analysis of the quantum of negative equity, Dermot O'Leary of Goodbody's told the media in mid-October 2008 that he expected that about 170,000 home-owners would probably end up in a negative-equity situation. I didn't see his report, as their web site is password-protected and available only for 'institutional clients'; but I'm guessing that his research includes not just first-time buyers but all home-owners with mortgage debt. Using data from the Department of the Environment, Heritage and Local Government on home prices and loan approvals to 'existing' home-owners historically, I calculated that under a base-case scenario of a 30 per cent drop in property values a further 140,000 home-owners could potentially be facing another €2.8 billion of negative equity. Suffice it to say that for a bigger decline from peak to trough in home values the negative-equity balloon expands exponentially.

Chapter 22

Similarities between the American and Irish property markets

On 16 October 2007 the Secretary of the Treasury, Henry Paulson Junior, gave a speech at Georgetown University Law Center in Washington. What was interesting about his speech was that it centred largely on the American economy and the impact the housing recession there was having on the country. At the beginning of his speech he made some comments that could have applied to Ireland just as much as they do to the United States.

> The ongoing housing correction is not ending as quickly as it might have appeared late last year, and it now looks like it will continue to have an adverse impact on the economy, capital markets and many home-owners for some time yet. Even so, I believe we have a healthy diversified economy that will continue to grow.

This sounds very similar to the situation here, especially with regard to the 'temporary blip' that was foretold to us all by estate agents in 2007: that the housing market would recover after the stamp duty changes in the summer of that year; but this predicted recovery failed to materialise. The debate has moved on, and there's now much talk about lower economic growth this year and next. Everybody then was still predicting that the economy would continue to grow, just as Paulson said the American economy would, despite what was going on in their housing market. His speech continued:

> The housing correction has its roots in a multi-year period of exceptional home price appreciation, which was fuelled by an increased demand for and an abundant supply of easy credit. Speculation also played a significant role as the share of buying activity by investors buying second homes more than doubled from 2000 to 2005.

Home-builders responded to the extraordinary demand for more and larger homes as if it would last forever.

Let's take this step by step. Firstly, he talked about the huge extended period of high capital value appreciation. In the United States it was eight years and in Ireland it was actually longer, at twelve years. He talked also about the abundant supply of easy credit. The mortgage market and bank lending were liberalised here with deregulation in the early 1990s. Subsequently, credit growth took off, and then there were the exceptionally low interest rates we got after 2001, especially in 2002 and 2003, with a European Central Bank base rate of 2 per cent, which created enormous demand, not just from 'real' or buy-to-live home-buyers but also from investors buying second or third homes as investment properties to rent out—in other words, speculative investors. Just as Paulson said that speculation played a significant role in their market in the last few years, the same could very well be said of the Irish property market over the same period.

His last point too, about builders responding to this extraordinary demand, believing that this situation would continue, could just as well be applied to the Irish situation and the ratcheting up of expectations that occurred here. Because this is precisely what happened: builders and developers stepped up the output of new homes to the point where they were building houses not just for people to live in but because of cheap credit and because speculators were buying properties.

The figures support this interpretation. The quarterly mortgage figures from the Irish Banking Federation show that first-time buyers and buy-to-let investors (or what the IBF refers to as 'residential investment let' investors) became equally important in the house market over the three years or so from 2004. In fact the average investor usually borrows on average €100,000 more than your typical first-time buyer. They have savings already (particularly equity in other properties), so they don't need to borrow as large a proportion of the purchase price as a first-time buyer normally does. The first-time buyer typically borrows from 85 to 92 per cent upwards of the price, whereas the average investor takes out a 75 to 80 per cent loan-to-value mortgage. This not only makes it easier for speculative investors to purchase than those attempting to get onto the property ladder for the first time but it makes them infinitely more attractive to the developers of new schemes, as they can move quickly—not forgetting too that they may also purchase multiple units. From the lender's viewpoint, speculators have a larger pool of assets (more collateral) and more equity. So it's no surprise that they favour them also.

In essence, the Irish situation is really only about a year or so behind the American one. (The American housing bubble peaked in the summer of 2006, whereas the Irish one peaked in the spring of 2007.) Further proof of this increased demand by investors is self-evident in the statistics of the biggest residential mortgage lenders, namely Bank of Ireland. The proportion of its total residential loans outstanding was the same, at 28 per cent, for first-time buyers financing the purchase of a home as it was for speculators buying additional properties on their total loan book in mid-2007.

But let's return to Paulson's speech, because he went on to make some other interesting points that are not just a coincidence as regards the Irish situation. The American experience holds lessons for Ireland, particularly in the pattern or process of how a housing recession unwinds. This could very well be a good guide to what is likely to happen here. Now, I believe that the American scenario will differ from Ireland's experience in two main respects. The American housing recession will be deep, but it will also be shorter-lived than the Irish one. There are many reasons for this; primary among them is the additional transparency (and hugely superior information flow) in that market, combined with greater acceptance of market conditions by sellers. Back to Paulson:

> The inevitable correction began in early 2006. Today average nation-wide home prices are barely up in the year to June. Sales of existing single-family homes are down nearly 5 per cent from the peak in 2005, and the inventory of unsold homes has increased to levels last seen in the early 1990s. Housing should be analysed by local or regional markets, as averages can be misleading. Areas of the greatest price appreciation before the correction, such as Las Vegas, San Diego, central California and a number of cities in Florida, have seen declines, and prices are falling in other parts of the country where economic growth is slower. Working through the housing correction will continue to take time.

Again the parallels are astounding. He says first that the correction he talked about would take longer because turnover or sales had abruptly fallen off. We have seen this situation occur here. The new-homes market was very busy in 2006 up to May, became quiet in the summer months, and then in the latter part of that year activity dried up completely. Then in the fourth quarter of 2006, partly because of comments from politicians regarding the possibility of reform in stamp duty, coupled with the half-dozen increases in interest rates from the European Central Bank, but largely because of exorbitant prices, demand dried up in the second-hand housing market; in other words, the normal market activity of people trading up and down dissipated.

This is precisely what happened in the United States. Paulson makes the point too that we should look at the market with regard to regional differences, and he also emphasises the fact that the areas with the greatest price appreciation before the market began to correct have seen the biggest declines or are now beginning to see the biggest declines. He also finishes on the point in this paragraph that the housing correction will continue and will take some time.

Next he turned his attention to the impact on the real economy.

In addition to affecting individual home-owners, the housing correction is also having a real impact on our economy. Annual housing starts peak at an annual rate of almost 2.3 million units in early 2006 before falling off more than 40 per cent through August of this year. Employment in residential building, including specialty trade contractors, has dropped by almost 200,000 since early 2006, offsetting about one-quarter of the jobs gained in the housing boom. It looked like housing construction had reached the bottom in the first half of this year, but starts have declined again since June, and data on applications and inventories of unsold homes suggest [that] further declines lie ahead.

When again we return to the Irish situation, the fact is that the housing correction is having a real impact on our economy too. If we examine the housing figures in the United States we note that they built 2¼ million homes in 2006, a record number (just like Ireland), when there was a demand for only about 1½ million. I distinctly remember an article in the *Economist* in late 2005 warning of this impending demand-supply imbalance. Therefore supply exceeded demand in 2006 by a significant margin, just as in Ireland when the total number of new homes built in the twelve months to November 2006 reached almost 90,000 units.

By my reckoning (and I'm certainly not alone in this respect) market demand was for, at most, 60,000 units for that year. I don't know about you, but I don't believe there's such a thing as a triple or quadruple coincidence in life, nature or even the universe. Indeed a pattern is emerging here between the American housing downturn and the continuing Irish correction. It would be folly to ignore these similarities, and only a fool would try to suggest that we're in an entirely different position. No doubt the usual pundits will spout some nonsense about demographics and the like, completely ignoring basic economics: supply versus demand, the most potent economic forces known to humanity.

Remember this: to justify 80,000 to 90,000 new homes per year, where an average household contains 2.8 people (the number of people resident in the country divided by the total number of households in April 2006), Ireland would need an addition of almost a quarter of a million to the population per year, or 200,000 new immigrants when one strips out babies being born and people getting older each year. And this is against the backdrop of a declining total fertility rate, now down to 1.9, whereas every country needs a total fertility rate of 2.1 for the population just to stand still. (This is explained in one of the extra chapters, on demographics, available on the web site.)

However, even adjusting these figures for smaller, Continental-style household sizes of just over two persons, let's assume that all new properties are occupied by only two people (it takes two to pay the mortgage or the rent), and further assume that the natural population increase (births minus deaths) remains at 40,000 per year. We still arrive at a figure of at least 120,000 new non-nationals per year. If you believe there are more than 10,000 immigrants arriving here each month over and above those who are leaving, then and only then may you begin to justify these levels of housing output.

The fact is that in the period 2004–06, alongside the near-doubling of credit from €162 billion to €318 billion, housing output became unsustainable—so much so that projections for future housing output for 2008 have been halved by the Construction Industry Federation, down to a mere 45,000 units. If this is not an admission of oversupply, I don't know what is. When the body that should know, the one that represents builders and property developers, acknowledges that an oversupply exists, and suggests that next year's output will have to be below normal demand levels, and possibly for several years to come, at least until the imbalance is removed, this tells us how dire the situation really is.

Paulson mentions the falling off in housing starts, and we have seen precisely the same thing here in Ireland. We have seen housing starts as measured by local authority commencement notices drop to slightly over 22,150 for the period January–November 2008, but on an annual basis, for the twelve months to November, they dropped a little more than 24,000 —a significant fall on the three years 2004–06, when starts averaged around 77,000 per year.

Unfortunately, like most Irish statistics, quite a time elapses before we get the data. So, as a more up-to-date proxy for housing starts most commentators use new-home guarantee registrations instead. These registrations have dropped by more than two-thirds as well in the first eleven months of 2008; so we're seeing a similar situation there. I mentioned earlier that the United States is at least nine months to a year ahead of Ireland in its property cycle, and it has already witnessed a huge decrease in construction employment, which we're only beginning to see now in the second half of 2008.

Paulson also mentioned that a number of market commentators had already judged that the American market had reached a bottom in early 2007. It's no surprise to many of us who follow and have been following the unfolding events in the Irish property market, as we heard a similar story on a number of occasions. The truth is that housing starts continue to decline, and there's a large stock of unsold homes.

Again, this whole bottoming process is going to take some time. As I mentioned before (and I apologise for repeating myself, but it's too important to let it go unsaid), one doesn't get from A to F in an instant or without first going through B, C, D and E. It's a clearly defined process, based on published housing statistics and sales activity (which we will pick up through the mortgage statistics) and resulting in a confirmation of a turnaround reflected in positive price growth over a reasonable period. Probably three to six months' consecutive positive price growth will be needed to provide this evidence. All told, it's a multi-year process.

Furthermore, in the United States it's estimated now that the stock of unsold homes is still around the ten months' supply mark. My own research has led me to believe that Ireland is actually in a worse situation, because the unsold stock here could be as high as two years' supply, given the accepted churn rate of about 5 to 7 per cent in housing transactions each year. This is an accepted rule of thumb on the likely size of sales (both new and second-hand), widely used by estate agents. We know that the total housing stock is 1.93 million properties, therefore this equates to annual sales of approximately 120,000. In recent years this has consisted of almost equal proportions of new and second-hand homes, but over the last year it has been skewed more towards existing home sales, particularly as the new-homes market has died a death.

Nobody is suggesting that Ireland's housing downturn will follow religiously that of the United States; however, does anyone really believe in double, triple or quadruple coincidences? That the American housing recession is under way is not in question, and undeniably our market is following a similar pattern in almost every respect. Perhaps it's the same forces acting out in each market, although with varying degrees of influence.

Another point that Paulson spoke about is something that confounded me for several months at the beginning of 2007 until I realised what was happening and that this event had actually occurred before. Let me elaborate on this. Paulson talked about the economy still being strong and remaining in positive territory despite negative growth in the residential property market. First we examine his exact words.

We confront these current challenges against the backdrop of a strong economy, not just in the United States but globally. Indeed, this is the first housing downturn in the past three decades in which American GDP growth has not turned negative. Business investment has expanded in recent months, our exports have been boosted by the strong economic growth of our trading partners, and a healthy job market has helped consumer spending continue to grow.

Strangely enough, this is precisely the situation that Ireland has found itself in. An economic recovery was still under way in Europe and the euro zone, the global economy was still growing at a good clip, a rate of 3½ per cent or more per year now, having grown at 5 per cent for the previous five consecutive years (something that hadn't happened in more than thirty years), and the Irish economy remained robust, with good growth of 6 per cent in 2007.

In effect, a 'decoupling' appeared to have occurred between the real economy and house-price appreciation. Although economic growth is certainly a precondition of a vibrant housing sector, it seems that a buoyant housing market is not necessary for a growing economy. Obviously there's the one-off shock of an abrupt decline in new home-building, but this will wash through the economic output statistics within two years.

If you look at 'real' house-price growth, taking the nominal house-price increases minus the rate of inflation, and examine this relationship over the last thirty-five years, from 1971 to 2006, a clear pattern exists between growth in real GDP (or GNP or national income—it doesn't matter which) and the real house-price changes. In other words, the two have followed each other closely in magnitude and in turning-points. This is highly intuitive and what one would expect. One would naturally expect that rising economic growth would be reflected in rising house prices and for the housing market to follow the real economy.

Over the past decade and a half, when estate agents failed to predict accurately the strength of the housing market, perhaps what they were really failing to pinpoint was the enormous growth that occurred in the real economy, especially during the late 1990s. Who would have thought that the Irish economy would expand at double-digit levels between 1997 and 2000 on average (certainly above this rate in both 1997 and 1999)? During this period Ireland actually grew faster than China and all the other ASEAN countries, including South Korea and India.

Returning to the point at hand, we saw in 2007 a decoupling of the real economy from the housing market. This was just a delayed and temporary phenomenon, as it took time for the construction industry to reduce its output, as evidenced by the 78,000 new homes built during 2007, despite falling prices. It takes just as long, or possibly longer, to turn off the supply tap than it does to restart it again.

The recent drop in expected economic output is based on the huge decline in construction output that materialised only in 2008. It took until October 2008 for the twelve-month running total (annual pace) of new home building to fall below 60,000 units. From November 2007 until October of the following year new home completions averaged 4,800 per month. Yet the industry insiders bragged about how quickly the supply threat would retreat, given falling home prices. They were wrong, totally wrong.

The reason I mention all this here is because the criticism that it's possible to talk oneself into a downturn or recession—that it may become a self-fulfilling prophecy—had little credibility and was an argument that doesn't hold water. And this was the criticism widely levelled at the 'economic bears' by the 'perennial bulls' (market insiders).

However (and I can't help feeling here like a judge delivering a judgement), it's also possible to talk up the housing market and therefore the economy so much that one becomes wedded to the view that any serious housing slump or crash must equate to a depression, thereby creating the very same self-fulfilling prophecy. This is the notion that consumers react badly or overreact to the continuing slump in house prices following repeated calls by the banks, brokers and estate agents that all is well and that things will recover soon. The 'credibility gap' is just as dangerous a factor in causing a recession as is talking down the economy—probably more so, as it raises false positive expectations as opposed to true negative ones.

The case for pragmatic realism has never been stronger.

Paulson points out that this strange decoupling between the property market and the economy has happened before in the United States, but you have to go back in time, more than three decades in fact. So this is not a totally unusual event, as there's a precedent for it, where the housing market can detach itself from the real economy. Of course it will have a big impact on economic growth and can bring growth down to much lower levels (at the initial stage of the property crash), but it doesn't necessarily mean that negative growth in house prices equals a recession all the time but only if we let that happen through our collective actions.

This is very important stuff.

Paulson also mentioned the fact that in the United States the healthy job market has helped consumer spending to continue rising. Here in Ireland too this has been a salient feature of the economy. Both economies were close to full employment back then, with almost identical unemployment rates of about 4.7 per cent. By October 2008 both rates had jumped to around 7 per cent.

Although Irish export growth had tapered off in 2007, the economy was driven by domestic demand, fuelled by domestic consumption and high rates of consumer spending, and the country continued to add jobs.

The point I'm trying to make here is also the point that Paulson was making: that the economy was strong and robust, that the housing decline and the emergence of a housing recession, which is still unfolding, will of course have an impact on the economy, as the two are inextricably linked, but it doesn't necessarily mean that, as house prices decline, future economic growth will stay negative too. Growth will be lower, in Ireland's case, for at least two years; but the contraction due to declining construction will have worked its way through the economic statistics by 2010.

This is a hugely important point for the debate on the Irish property market; because if we allow house prices to adjust downwards—a correction in asset-price inflation—housing prices will return to affordable levels and the economy can continue to grow in the long term, and that to me is a 'win-win' situation.

Clearly there's one big difference between the American and the Irish housing downturns, and that is the extent of the sub-prime crisis evident in the American market. Fortunately for Ireland, the sub-prime sector is only a fledgling market category, worth only about $1½ billion, and we haven't had the weaknesses and shortcomings in lending practices that they have had over the last three to five years. The bottom line is that this problem is certain to continue for the next year or two in the United States, especially when one considers that there were still another $400 billion worth of sub-prime mortgages with special low introductory interest rates likely to reset between now and the end of 2008. Borrowers were enticed into these products with low, usually two-year fixed-rate deals, which revert back to the standard variable rate at the end of the initial discount period. The Americans call these adjustable-reset mortgages. This is an additional problem unique to the American situation that we won't have to endure.

The one lesson that Ireland can draw from the American experience is that it is better to acknowledge the extent of the problems in the housing sector, deal with them by slashing prices of new homes by at least 40 per cent, and have a shorter, sharper shock. For this is precisely what is going to happen in the American housing market. Deep discounts in new home prices occur every time the 'inventory-to-sales' ratio of unsold new homes creeps up to the one-year mark. Meanwhile, Éire Teoranta remains in denial. Developers have chosen to rent out unsold new homes instead of selling them at a clearing price. Banks have let developers away with this by allowing capital deferral of interest payments. That is hurting the balance sheets and share prices of the banks, because of the deferral of this bad loan problem, but it also crowds out lending to real businesses in the economy that are desperately short of cash. Untold damage is being done to the economy by the failure to grasp this issue. The sooner that new home prices are cut to whatever the market will bear, the sooner the banks can lend again to non-builders and the sooner the economy can move forward again. This is where the similarity with the American market ends and a resemblance to Japan in the mid-1990s emerges.

Chapter 23

When have you heard an Irish estate agent tell the truth?

There exists a universal acceptance, particularly in contemporary democracies like Ireland's, that the collective view is usually superior to the viewpoint of the individual. The entire basis for democracy is the principle that the majority view ought to prevail. This accepted truism is indeed true when it comes to politics and to effecting legislation for the people. Bad politicians and unpopular pieces of legislation have toppled governments in the past. In everyday life, citizens can generally see what is going on around them, even if what is reported in the media is different. This is the reason why snapshot surveys of consumers are so popular with economists and market analysts, because they reflect the here and now, the opinions of prospective buyers. As the old saying goes, 'you can fool all the people some of the time . . .'

However, there's one grey area where everybody can be led down the wrong path: the future, and specifically predicting the future. Forecasting where the economy or markets will be just a couple of years ahead is notoriously difficult. This difficulty is compounded by the typical herd mentality, where forecasters are more afraid of being different from the rest of the pack than they are of getting it wrong.

This sheepish approach when predicting growth in house prices is very much in evidence. Year after year the estate agents' view of the prospects for growth in house prices are so uniform that each one could almost claim to have the 'consensus' view. The corollary of this is that if a few voices dissent, are different from those of the vips, the politicians and the media, they're vilified, ridiculed as 'doom-mongers'. Often, in the not-so-distant past, they have even been portrayed as social pariahs, guilty of talking the economy down. In short, their opinions, which may be quite valid, are debased and are portrayed as being wrong, whether they are or not.

Firstly, let's examine the notion that the collective view is the preferred one. If you go to a fairground you'll often find a stall where you can pay to predict the quantity of something in a jar: it could be marbles, or it could be small sweets, like jelly beans. If a jar containing 750 jelly beans was placed on a table and people were asked to guess how many there were there would be some very divergent guesses. Some would be wildly optimistic, while others would be too conservative and therefore too low. This wouldn't really matter, though, because the average guess would be reasonably close to the truth. Imagine, for example, that the first four people guessed 280, 1,200, 450 and 970. All would be far off the correct figure of 750, but their average of 725 would be very close. This is an extremely simplistic yet honest representation of how the collective view is better than one person's guess.

But this example is contingent on surmising what is happening at the present time. You get to see the jar of jelly beans, touch it, hold it up and measure the weight in your hand. A similar pattern exists with the property market today. You can drive down your street, see the 'For sale' signs, compare prices with last year's, talk to people who are having difficulties achieving their asking price, and view properties for yourself, put in low bids and gauge the response. All of this is what is known collectively as 'anecdotal evidence'. You can't deny the facts—though many commentators attempt to distort them or explain them away, using factors that have nothing to do with the original problems.

Estate agents are quick to point out that sentiment is poor, or interest rates are too high; but when have you ever heard one say that prices are too high? (You do in other countries, but not in Ireland.) When have you ever heard an estate agent say there was little value to be had at prevailing price levels? When have you ever heard an estate agent tell the truth?

The biggest part of the problem with forecasts is that all the forecasters use history to predict the future. They take all the historical data, put it into a spreadsheet or whatever, make further assumptions about which factors influence other factors, then extrapolate into the near future, possibly up to the end of the present year or possibly the end of the subsequent year. That's it.

But in order for them to properly encapsulate the business or property cycles over a reasonable period they really need to use quite a lot of historical data, which may not be available to them in the first place. For instance, to properly analyse the property market the data would need to be provided for at least thirty or maybe fifty years. But in Ireland the only mix-weighted house-price index, the PTSB-ESRI one, began only in March 1996. So there's a very limited time-series history. Furthermore, it represents today merely a fifth of the mortgage market and historically, at most, a quarter of the Irish home-loan experience. Consequently, it has serious shortcomings. To make matters worse, almost the entire history of this house-price index is dominated by a single 'boom' cycle. In effect, there's not much of a cycle, rather a straight 45° line.

Lastly, there's the problem of the lazy person's approach, or the stick-your-finger-in-the-air method. This is also where one market analyst simply copies another. It happens a lot with estate agents: they take economic growth predictions from banks, brokers or the Economic and Social Research Institute and regurgitate them.

How many estate agents' economists do you think attempt to model inflation, or build macro-economic models for the supply or demand of new homes? They don't, because if they did they would certainly have published them by now. Instead they pretend they do and pull numbers out of the air, just as a magician pulls a rabbit out of a hat. There's very little scientific basis for their predictions. Their figures don't stand up to even the simplest scrutiny.

The universality concerning the natural demand for new homes is a perfect example. So many commentators have fixated on the requirement of 60,000 new homes per year that it has become gospel now. It's almost as if they're hoping that if they say it often enough it will become true—a self-fulfilling prophecy. The fact that it's predicated on massive population growth is a flaw in itself.

The entire demographic presumption—that the population of the Republic will be at least 5 million by 2020—is nothing short of propaganda, initiated inadvertently by brokers such as NCB with their report 20:20 *Vision: The Irish Demographic Dividend,* published in early 2006, as well as the Government's own population projections, which have been hijacked by estate agents and journalists, holding up these estimates as fact.

The truth about these growth projections is that they're based on huge constant inflows of immigrants of between 55,000 and 70,000 for the next fifteen years. These are unrealistic flat-line assumptions. The NCB report erroneously emphasises rising fertility rates, in direct opposition to the most recent work carried out by Dr John FitzGerald at the Economic and Social Research Institute, who has correctly shown the Irish fertility rate falling to 1.9 (i.e. an average of 1.9 children per woman of child-bearing age), a rate that's well below the natural replacement rate of 2.1 required to keep the population static. Not to mention the fact that immigrants are not big buyers of new homes. Many of them rent instead, saving money either to send home or to return home with to buy a property there. Many of the assumptions made by NCB (and stated as assumptions in that report) were explicitly based on the pace of growth between 1996 and 2002–04 being maintained until 2015. Again this was a classic example of the asymptotic fallacy.

The best way to show how flat these forecasts really are is, as always, by way of example.

We begin with forecasts for the principal economic indicators, using those provided by AIB, the country's largest bank. AIB is chosen because it produces these forecasts in its published monthly economic bulletins; and it has an archive available on its web site, so you can go back and verify the numbers if you feel so inclined.

Arbitrarily, five indicators were selected, namely growth, unemployment, inflation, housing output and average earnings growth. The following table illustrates AIB's predictions for 2007. The column on the left gives the date of publication.

Table 25: AIB macro-economic forecasts for 2007, by publication date

2007 estimates	GDP	Unemployment	Inflation	Earnings	New homes
16 Nov. 2005	5.5	4	3	5	77,000
16 Dec. 2005	5.5	4.1	3	5	77,000
31 Jan. 2006	5.5	4.1	2.8	5	77,000
17 Feb. 2006	5.5	4.1	2.8	5	77,000
23 Mar. 2006	5.5	4.2	2.8	5	77,000
21 Apr. 2006	5.7	4.2	2.8	5	85,000
23 May 2006	5.7	4.2	3	5	85,000
27 Jun. 2006	5.7	4.2	3	5	85,000
20 Jul. 2006	5.8	4.2	3.6	5	85,000
22 Aug. 2006	5.5	4.2	3.6	5	85,000
26 Sep. 2006	5.5	4.4	3.6	5	85,000
26 Oct. 2006	5.5	4.4	3.5	5	85,000
23 Nov. 2006	5.5	4.4	3.9	5	85,000
21 Dec. 2006	5.5	4.4	4.2	5	85,000
26 Jan. 2007	5.5	4.4	4.1	5	85,000
27 Feb. 2007	5.5	4.4	4.3	5	85,000
29 Mar. 2007	5.5	4.4	4.5	5	85,000
27 Apr. 2007	5	4.4	4.7	5	82,500
30 May 2007	5	4.5	4.7	5	82,500
28 Jun. 2007	5	4.5	5	5	82,500
15 Aug. 2007	5.2	4.5	5	5	80,000
15 Nov. 2007	4.8	4.5	4.9	5.2	77,000
14 Dec. 2007	4.8	4.5	4.9	5.2	77,000
6 Feb. 2008	5.5	4.5	4.9	5.2	78,000
8 Apr. 2008	5.3	4.5	4.9	5	78,000

What is most obvious is that the numbers don't change very much, or very often. The forecasts generally extend one full year ahead and sometimes up to two years.

If we begin with the estimate of 5½ per cent growth in GDP, this was pretty close to the eventual outcome of 6 per cent for 2007 as a whole. Actually two years ago John Beggs and his team were expecting growth closer to 6 per cent. As 2007 drew to a close, and with the beginning of the global financial crisis, they revised this growth estimate downwards to below 5 per cent. Clearly they were becoming more negative in their view of the economy, and we can see the culprit in the downward revision of their forecast of new homes built. But in February 2008 they ratcheted it back up again when interest rate expectations altered and it seemed there might have been some light at the end of the global liquidity tunnel.

Take a look at their predictions of new-homes completion for 2007. Over the period January 2006 to December 2007 it averaged 82,500—a good 4,500 above the eventual outcome of 78,000 that year. Again their initial prediction was bang on but they revised it upwards in the spring of 2006, when the housing market was on fire.

Table 26: AIB macro-economic forecasts for 2008, by prior publication date

	GDP	Unemployment	Inflation	Earnings	New homes
26 Oct. 2006	4.5	4.4	2.4	5	78,000
23 Nov. 2006	4.5	4.4	2.4	5	78,000
21 Dec. 2006	4.5	4.4	2.4	5	78,000
26 Jan. 2007	4.5	4.4	2.7	5	78,000
27 Feb. 2007	4.5	4.4	2.7	5	78,000
29 Mar. 2007	4.5	4.4	2.7	5	78,000
27 Apr. 2007	3.7	5	2.6	5	75,000
30 May 2007	3.7	5	2.6	5	75,000
28 Jun. 2007	3.7	5	3.3	5	75,000
15 Aug. 2007	3.3	5	3.4	5	62,500
15 Nov. 2007	3.3	5.2	3.2	4.5	57,000
14 Dec. 2007	3.3	5.2	3.5	4.5	57,000
6 Feb. 2008	2.5	5.2	3.5	4.5	45,000
8 Apr. 2008	2.2	5.7	3.9	4.5	50,000

Their unemployment estimates appear to just lag the market in relation to what actually happened. Their prediction for average earnings growth appears to centre around 5 per cent. Likewise, their guess at unemployment rates seems to be pretty much anchored at 4.4 per cent, and the second table shows that they ratcheted this up for 2008. In other words, we had already hit an unemployment rate of 5.2 per cent by the end of February. It seems that more ratcheting up of forecasts will be on the cards. Their best guess on inflation didn't hit the button until the middle of that year, in June 2007 to be precise.

The 2008 forecasts show a stark contrast with the previous year. Inflation, which had been expected to fall, remained stubbornly high. Growth and housing projections have been cut dramatically. Average earnings growth has been trimmed a little, but that may depend on the unemployment rate, and, as I mentioned before, it looks like more upward revisions were needed for the calendar year 2008.

What is interesting is that their prediction for construction activity in 2008 remained high, at a constant 75,000 units right up to August 2007, despite the fact that new-home guarantee registrations had peaked as far back as September 2006 at an annual rate of almost 69,000 but had fallen to a rolling twelve-month rate of 49,000 by August 2007—a drop of nearly 30 per cent! Did the AIB economists not believe the figures, which Davy's were regularly commenting on and predicting, would drop to 55,000 for 2008 a year previously? Was it a coincidence that the AIB forecast for 2008 was now identical to the Construction Industry Federation's prediction that came out at the beginning of the year?

We don't mean to single out AIB's economists here. They're merely a reflection of the consensus view of that time. There's an economic forecasts publication called *Consensus Economics,* which polls all the economists making predictions for each country and then publishes the mean prediction along with the upper and lower-range forecasts. It's dominated by banks and investment-bank economists. For example, for the United States or Britain there may be anything from sixty to eighty forecasters making predictions on the principal economic indicators, such as those listed in the previous tables. The conclusions one can draw from these published consensus forecasts is that they're invariably similar and almost invariably wrong.

The consensus forecast for most of the indicators, perhaps with the exception of GDP growth, have a horrible record in predicting interest rates, inflation, unemployment, stock markets and especially exchange rates. Why do they exist, then? And why do so many people rely on them? Well, because of the jelly-bean example at the beginning of this chapter. There's an implicit assumption that the average or consensus forecast is better than the individual one, because this is the market average or collective view.

The asymptotic-fallacy trap is not confined to macro-economic indicators. For a great example look at the share price targets that brokers placed on banks and construction companies as late as the end of 2007.

I've chosen the period from the end of September 2007—a full month after the financial turmoil began in the United States—to be fair to them and to choose the bad period that we're still in. This was also seven months after the Irish stock market had peaked, so it was well into the correction phase.

On 26 September 2007 NCB had an 'add' recommendation on Kingspan at €15.75 a share. At the time of writing, Kingspan is trading at around the €2.75 level, or 82 per cent less per share. NCB also had a 'buy' recommendation on Grafton Group at €8 per share; by the winter of 2008 it was trading close to €2.

Davy's had a 'buy' on Bank of Ireland with a price target of €16.50 when the shares were actually trading at €13; they're now below €1. Davy's also had a very high price target of €3.50 on McInerney Homes, the house-builders, even though the share price then was about €1.40, having been €2 higher at the end of February 2007. (Davy's are brokers to this company and were constrained by a conflict of interest in maintaining this unrealistic price target, so they reduced their 'short-term' price target to €1.60. What's their definition of 'short-term'? How long is a piece of string? Perhaps it's as short or as long as they want it to be.)

Meanwhile over at Dolmen Securities, on 28 September they lowered their (May) price target on McInerney's from €2.30 to €1.86, still significantly above the €1.40 price then. This was still implying a +25 per cent potential. Now the McInerney price is languishing at €0.19, not far from the recent lows of about €0.17.

Over at Goodbody's at the same time there was a 'buy' recommendation on Cement-Roadstone Holdings at €27.52 a share. Now CRH are changing hands at €17, having traded at €11 lower nine months after their call on the stock. Potentially this could have meant losing investors a third of their money in less than a year. Goodbody's also had a 'buy' on Grafton Group at €7.95 a share at the end of September. As previously mentioned, it's quoted at a quarter of that price now.

You get the picture. We could go on but it would only be repetitive and boring. There's an inherent upward bias in brokers' estimates for share prices, just as there exists an estate agents' bias for predicting positive price growth. Part of their bias can be explained by their desire to please larger clients who already have a serious existing financial investment (or vested interest) in the market. They have to predict it one way, therefore, and that way is always up. They're not independent and so are not objective. Many of them don't deny this.

The other major part of the problem is that they're taught that their markets enjoy a natural positive growth rate over time. This is true to an extent. The stock market is not a zero-sum game, because new money is flowing into the equation (most of the time). Companies have an inherent growth rate closely linked to the real economy, and a good example is that they retain part of their earnings, which are reinvested in their businesses. So share prices ought to reflect this positive growth rate over time. Generally they do, over extended periods.

Similarly, the housing market has an inherent upward bias, because of general price inflation, increasing population and rising home equity, as well as the transfer of property wealth from generation to generation.

Both stock markets and property prices are what mathematicians call 'non-stationary' time series, which is a fancy way of saying they have a rising average level over time (a 'secular change in mean' is how a statistician would put it) or trend growth. But this doesn't move in a straight line: it follows the 'S curve' or the path of a typical cycle.

Often these market cycles may be as long as fifteen years, and often too they have smaller cycles within them lasting for seven or eight years. This is common; therefore it's also normal. It's not abnormal for the price of a house, or a company, that has increased tenfold over a decade to give back a third or even a half of those gains; for it still shows incredible price appreciation over the long run. We're in that downward part of the curve now, so it's a cyclical downturn. Historically, these 'bear' phases last three to five years, depending on how quickly people react to them. But they can go on for considerably longer. It just depends on the rapidity of price adjustment.

It's important, I believe, to finish this section on the asymptotic or flat-line approach to forecasting by looking at one estate agent's predictions over an extended period. We shall use Sherry FitzGerald, not only because they're the largest residential agent in the country but also because their chief economist and forecaster, Marian Finnegan, has been there for more than a decade. This eliminates forecaster bias. Traditionally, Marian Finnegan has produced the Sherry FitzGerald market price forecasts in their quarterly outlook publications. Fortunately, once again, these are available on their web site, so physical verification is possible.

The following table summarises Sherry FitzGerald's annual average house-price predictions for the last four years, together with their prediction for 2008.

You don't have to be a potential 'Mastermind' contestant to realise that Marian likes the numbers 8–10 per cent, 10 per cent and 15 per cent. Furthermore, any forecast below 8 per cent is too low to merit a numerical forecast, and a description is the preferred alternative. You can also deduce that numerical revisions, where they occur, are always upwards. The best Sherry FitzGerald could do for 2007 (or should I say the lowest they were prepared to go) was to say 'static,' in a year in which prices dropped by 10 to 15 per cent on average around the country (not reflected in the PTSB-ESRI index because of time lags and the small section of the total market that this index represents). There's a massive credibility gap here.

Table 27: Sherry FitzGerald's predictions of annual average growth in house prices

	2004 (e)	2005 (e)	2006 (e)	2007 (e)	2008 (e)
Outlook 2004	8–10%				
Spring 2004	10–12%	'single digits'			
Summer 2004	15%	10%			
Autumn 2004		10%			
Outlook 2005		10%			
Autumn 2005		15%	<2005		
Outlook 2006			10%		
Spring 2006			15%		
Autumn 2006				8–10%	
Outlook 2007				'single digits'	
Spring 2007				'positive'	
Summer 2007				'static'	
Outlook 2008					'robust'

Source: Sherry FitzGerald Outlooks

Once more we can see that forecasters typically produce very flat forecasts, based on their most recent experiences. This linear interpretation of future growth is due to human nature, specifically psychology. It's very difficult for the human psyche to discount more recent events in the way we naturally do for events that occurred a long time ago, even though there may be an increased likelihood of occurrence. Our brain tells us that recent history is a guide to what is likely to happen in the near future.

To make matters worse, we have in Ireland today a generation born since 1980, sometimes called 'Generation Y', most of whom are now in their mid to late twenties today, the typical first-time buyer age, who have only known one market. They have watched their older siblings and friends grow rich by doing absolutely nothing—nothing, that is, other than purchasing a home and getting onto the property ladder. They have no frame of reference in their psyche that tells them that house prices do fall as well as rise.

How do you convince these people that the market could be negative for several years to come? The short answer is you can't. They have to learn it for themselves; they have to watch their peers jump in at the 'suckers' rally' stage, or perhaps they themselves have already bought, and they see people they know experiencing the unpleasantness of negative equity and the serious social consequences it has for people's lives. Only then will they come to fully understand it.

But that lesson may prove to be short-lived, because once home prices begin to rise again, which they eventually will, these people may revert to type and believe in the flat-line fallacy that home prices move only one way: up.

What happens if estate agents decide to tell the truth and come clean? Well, the only circumstances that could provoke such an event would be if fear turned to panic. Panic results in capitulation. That leads to large price falls, often overshooting below where normal market fundamentals dictate where value should be. This phenomenon always precipitates the market bottom, signalling the best opportunity to buy. In short, you should always treat the VIPs as contrarians: do the opposite of what they say, and you'll be fine.

Chapter 24

Tall tales; but where's the density?

Despite the massive cutback in new home-building during 2008, the most contentious property topic is not the question of how many new homes we need per year but rather the hot debate on whether or not Éire Teoranta needs skyscrapers. Not only have the big developers got it wrong in market timing for new properties but they have become so mired in their own greed and so lost in the euphoria of outdoing one another that they seem to have lost touch with reality. The question whether or not Ireland needs tall buildings right now is irrelevant, oversupply being the dominant theme of the property market and possibly still so in 2012. So the real question should be . . . Next question, please.

Nonetheless we devote this chapter to this property issue that has apparently divided the nation. We begin with the well-known television programme 'Questions and Answers', which features a panel of prominent politicians, journalists and special-interest groups as well as a studio audience (often containing vested-interest parties).

28 February 2008.

About half way through the programme John Bowman, the presenter, asked for the next question from a member of the audience.

Rory Byrne: 'Are high-rise buildings in Dublin the way of the future?'

Bowman repeats the question and then opens the debate up to the panel members, beginning with Joan O'Connor, an architect and managing director of Interactive Project Managers.

Joan O'Connor: 'Not necessarily. They will be and should be if we have a decent transport infrastructure on which we can found high-rise buildings, but there's no commercial or economic necessity for them in the absence of a decent transport infrastructure.'

Perhaps at this juncture I should inform you that Joan O'Connor was at that time engaged as a consultant by Seán Dunne, managing director of Mountbrook Homes, which had sought planning permission for a 37-storey tower block in Ballsbridge, Dublin 4, on the Berkeley Court

Hotel and Jury's Hotel sites. Dunne's vision is to make Ballsbridge a mini-Manhattan.

You may be surprised to hear Joan O'Connor utter such words: those tall buildings are not really necessary at all, except with the proviso of being accompanied by a good transport infrastructure. This is the salesperson's first rule of psychological reciprocity: agree with the tone of the question, and then qualify the response with a favourable caveat. Of course Ballsbridge already has a good transport infrastructure: it's the last stop on the train before Dublin city centre.

Joan O'Connor: '. . . By the same token I do hope that we get a number, a select number of really excellent high-rise buildings in certain locations in Dublin, because I think the city needs it. The skyline is a—urban design is like a skyline written of full stops, commas and exclamation marks, and our tall buildings are the exclamation marks in the skyline of urban design.'

What she is cleverly doing here is persuading the audience that in fact we do need high-rise, but only a select few in certain areas. Presumably, then, she is referring to Ballsbridge and to the site that her company has been employed to promote. She then went on to promote the proposed Seán Dunne tower as an 'exclamation mark' in the skyline of urban design. She repeated certain words several times to reinforce them for the listener—another sales technique. There's no point mentioning three different things: it's far better to say the same thing three times; that way it sinks in.

Interestingly, within the opening two minutes of the discussion on density Joan O'Connor firstly says that high-rise buildings are conditional and not necessary, then within a few sentences is saying that Dublin needs it ('it' being the Mountbrook proposal). 'We don't have enough of them to reflect where we are today. The churches were high-rise all those years ago; they were expressions of the church's power. The Custom House was a relatively high-rise building of its time. We don't have any contemporary high-rise buildings that say what society is about now.'

The television camera pans across the studio audience. Everyone is sitting with head tilted attentively. Rarely have I seen a television audience so glued to every syllable being uttered by one speaker. She's in full swing and is in control. No interruptions from the adjudicator or any of the other panel members. This is an architect, an *expert* (the most-misused word in Ireland), telling a grateful public what they need to be told. High-rise buildings are like the Mercedes-Benz S500: they're a sign of success, of power, a metaphor for the New Hibernia. We need them as an expression of 'who we are today.' Three minutes earlier they were unnecessary; now we dare not be without them.

The Custom House, by the way, is low-rise, at only four storeys. Most churches I've ever visited are single-storey buildings, some with a mezzanine level. Yes, they have a high ceiling, because lots of people are crammed in once a week and people need air to breathe and space to move around in; but I've yet to see even a picture of a 37-storey church. Many have steeples or bell-towers, but they're like chimneys, tall and narrow, and don't cast a large shadow, or block any views; and nobody lives in them. I have yet to see a church steeple with a concrete lift shaft.

But who are we to argue with an expert?

Bowman finally interjects. 'The banks' buildings are pretty self-important, aren't they?'

To which the response from Joan O'Connor caused me to fall off the sitting-room sofa. 'Banks' buildings in Baggot Street?'

For the uninitiated, Baggot Street is adjacent to the Mountbrook development in Ballsbridge. O'Connor swiftly brings the subject back to her client's proposed new tower block. Just as Baggot Street leads directly down to the existing hotel site of the proposed new tower, she leads Bowman and the audience back to her promotional topic. Her focus and dedication to duty are unparalleled. If she wasn't an architect she could easily have been a bond salesperson. She certainly has the smarts to be one. She outsmarted Bowman et al. very swiftly on that one.

Next Bowman hesitantly interjects, and without much success: 'Well, everywhere—and if you go into town they're usually higher-rise than everywhere—but that's a small matter.'

What is he talking about? Just look at AIB's Bank Centre in Ballsbridge. It's two-storey with a little bit of three-storey thrown in for good measure. Hardly high-rise. As for Bank of Ireland's head office, which is in Baggot Street, it's less than five storeys.

There's no high-rise in Dublin, that's the whole point, with the obvious exception of the seventeen-storey Liberty Hall, the SIPTU building, which sticks out like a sore thumb, just as Centre Point in New Oxford Street, London, does. The two buildings are similarly ugly—in fact they're the best argument against high-rise in any city centre.

The conversation heats up, and begins to become more informative.

Joan O'Connor: 'That's the power of money. Buildings are built tall as an expression of power.'

Good on you, Joan! Once again she reinforces that notion of 'expression of power' so as to let everyone know that tall buildings are status symbols, and much-needed ones too. Keep mentioning the same point: eventually it will sink in. Everyone will leave the studios that evening with a sense of lacking: we need tall buildings.

John Bowman: 'You're a consultant to the Seán Dunne consortium in Ballsbridge, which is the highest offer in Dublin.' For the first time he informs the audience, both in the studio and at home, that O'Connor is a VIP and has a major vested interest in one particular tall building. She responds very quickly, her voice overlapping his. This is a lady who doesn't take prisoners. 'No, it's not the highest offer in Dublin. The highest offering in Dublin is the U2 Tower, which is running at around 180 metres. The Mountbrook scheme contains one signature iconic building right on the apex of Pembroke Road which is 132 metres.'

She has made two quick points. Firstly, it's not the tallest proposal. (So what?) Secondly, she moves into marketing speak: 'one signature iconic building . . .' When have you ever heard another human being speaking naturally in such terms? This sounds rehearsed. Nobody off their own bat would come out with a phrase like that on television—so concise, so contrived.

John Bowman: 'This is on the Jury's and Berkeley Court site, eight-acre site there, yeah?'

Joan O'Connor: 'Yeah, eight-acre site, and the building is thirty-seven storeys tall. It's 132 metres tall, so it's a long way from being the highest one on the drawing-boards at the moment. It's—in urban design terms I think correct, because it's a punctuation mark that marks Ballsbridge. It also happens to be a very beautiful building, which fulfils two of the three criteria.'

Beauty is in the eye of the beholder. This building is purely aspirational: it doesn't exist yet, if it ever will. In O'Connor's personal opinion it's correct in 'urban design' terms—again opinion, and not fact. (She also agreed with Bowman that it was an 8-acre site though it's only 6.82 acres. Well, she was only out by 14¾ per cent.)

Also, it 'fulfils two of the three criteria.' What criteria? She is answering her own questions though they have yet to be asked.

Meanwhile the camera again pans across the studio audience. The audience still attentive, not even a murmur, which is very unusual.

'The third one is that a developer for a high-rise building must commit the necessary financial resources. The worst thing that could happen to us is that we build poor-quality, badly built high-rise buildings. And that's what has given a lot of tall buildings a bad name.'

Seán Dunne earlier that week announced that he had the financial backing to build his dream skyscraper should he eventually get the requisite planning permission. By inference, Joan O'Connor too implied that their proposal (still on the drawing-board) would be high-quality and well built. (Have you ever met a property developer who set out to build a poor-quality skyscraper on the cheap?)

At this juncture Bowman opens the discussion up to the rest of the panel. First Noel Whelan: 'Why not?' But he went on to acknowledge that mistakes had been made before in high-rise living in Ballymun, and they were only sixteen storeys high. Next Aonghas Ó Snodaigh TD began with the point that Dublin has had a history of bad planning, and he thought the proposed tall buildings ought to be clustered together in the Docklands. This last point makes a lot of sense; it's the pattern followed by many other European cities that are built around a major river. There's a strong case for placing the skyscrapers adjacent to the water, so not blocking many other properties and casting a shadow on the water instead. Also, as you move outwards from the city centre along the estuary you can gradually increase the height. The discussion digressed to wooden cladding on buildings in Dublin.

Joan O'Connor: 'To get back to the whole thing about high-rise buildings, I wonder do we have the type of companies who will occupy a high-rise building in Dublin. And I'm looking forward to seeing that happening for the first time. The highest building we have in Dublin at the moment is number 1 George's Plaza, which is about three metres more than Liberty Hall. We have no high-rise buildings.'

Clearly, then, by her last comments the Mountbrook scheme is specu-lative. They're not building to requirements, and they have not pre-let any office space. This was a slip from O'Connor, but she finished on a high note: Ireland is deficient in high-rise buildings; ergo, they're needed straight away.

Bowman referred the discussion back to the original questioner, Rory Byrne. 'Yeah, I think it's definitely the way of the future. I think possibly it's debased a little bit by the media Dublin 4 attitude of "We don't want it in our own back yard," which is understandable, but you know also there's the issue of hundreds of thousands of people coming in and out of Dublin every day, spending hours on the train commuting. I think we're missing that side of things. I think it's the way of the future, but it has to be part of a comprehensive plan, where the services are going to be; it won't be stand-alone. It won't just be about private companies with a lot of money and not putting in the extra things that are needed as well.'

This response could very well be described as typical of many young Irish people. His point about commuters benefiting was really a rhetorical one, because they wouldn't benefit at all from the Mountbrook proposal, unless they have a couple of million euros or more to splash out on a new pad in the 37-storey tower. If they have, what are they doing commuting on a train? In fact he answered this with his final comment about the pro-posed tower in Ballsbridge being for the rich or for companies with a lot of money. At a cost of €1 billion or more (land plus construction costs), this development is not for the masses, it's for the elite few, the plutocrats who can afford it.

John Bowman: 'Where does An Taisce stand on this, Kevin Duff?'

Kevin Duff: 'I think we need to distinguish between high-rise and high-density. Some of the recent press releases put out by Dublin City Council would have you believe that high buildings are needed to solve urban sprawl; but just now we have examples now in Dublin—Adamstown and Pelletstown in Dublin 15—of high-density which is not high-rise. So just—we should be wary of that: communities should be wary of high buildings being put over to them as "this is needed to solve sprawl". Finally someone makes the most important point of the entire debate: that high-density doesn't equal high-rise.

John Bowman: 'What is your view of the Berkeley Court, Jury's Hotel site?'

Kevin Duff: '. . . Possibly—I mean, as it is there will be a few, a couple of high buildings in the Docklands and one or two in the Heuston [Station] area. Some would say that's fine, that's enough, we should leave it at that. Obviously not everybody in Ballsbridge is happy about the proposed high building.'

John Bowman: 'Well, €380 million was spent by the developer in buying the site. Do you think then that there's a moral leverage then against the corporation or An Bord Pleanála then, that something better happen here?' This is the perceived wisdom in the fantasy world of Irish estate agents. If a big client spent a lot of money then it was inevitable that they would ultimately get planning permission.

Kevin Duff: 'Proper planning and sustainable development is the ultimate criteria which An Bord Pleanála will judge proposals, so I mean the figure he paid for the site shouldn't be a major influence or factor.'

Bowman then calls on a specialist from the audience, Seán O'Leary, president of the Royal Institute of the Architects of Ireland. 'I think that Joan O'Connor would reflect the views of many of my colleagues, and indeed other respondents to the question. I think the solution is not high-rise clearly. I think we're also talking about Dublin, which is probably just a little bit parochial. The real debate facing this country is one which possibly was summarised by, I think, a colleague of George Soros on the radio talking this morning about where to put your money in the future. He advocated that you put it in commodities and oil, which is another way of saying that in the next five or ten years the costs of essentials, like transport, are going to become so intolerably high. That's not an architectural background to my answer. I think that systematically—and maybe the earlier discussion shows how much we're distracting from it—if we don't actually as a society look at joining the dots, high-rise is very much a part of that debate, as is intensification. But clearly at a national level I really just wonder what is wrong with our systems in a small country that we can't actually look at making it work.'

Striking stuff! What he says is that the answer is not high-rise, but many people assume that it is, including lots of architects. They obviously want to build their crowning achievements. He goes on to say that higher energy and transport costs will make higher density a must, a definite priority. He was right to say so, but he also criticises the entire national planning system by asking why it is that such a small island like Ireland can't get it right.

The real answer is that corrupt local politicians are to blame for the country's planning system. Payments and bribes to county councillors are a way of life. Crony capitalism is alive and well in Ireland. A big builder and property developer that I know well used to moan about An Bord Pleanála that they rotated the fellas in there for two or three-year stints and that he couldn't get at them. The problem is endemic in Irish society. It's not seen as a bad thing by the general populace, as evidenced by the re-election of Bertie Ahern as Taoiseach in 2007, despite the Mahon Tribunals investigating planning irregularities and other unanswered questions, which subsequently led to his early resignation. The Irish culture of turning a blind eye to what is perceived as a 'clever stroke' rather than the criminal act of bribing elected public officials is what is to blame for the urban sprawl of Dublin today.

CONCLUDING REMARKS

This television debate was useful because it crystallised a few important issues. High-rise is not the same as high-density. Higher density was favoured by all participants in the debate, and the remaining panel members were all in favour of clustering any high-rise buildings together. As Ger Colleran, editor of the *Irish Daily Star* put it, why should residents of the local villages of Sandymount and Ballsbridge suffer the intrusion of high-rise, especially if there were less pricey, more attractive and more appropriate sites elsewhere?

And indeed there are, even within the environs of Dublin 4. Less than a mile as the crow flies from the proposed Ballsbridge site, in Ringsend on the Poolbeg peninsula, is the former Irish Glass Bottle site, which was sold a year after the Ballsbridge site in question for even more money, €412 million. That site cost €17 million an acre, or a quarter of the Ballsbridge hotels site, and is adjacent to the Irish Sea at the estuary of the River Liffey, and it will be the terminus for the Luas tram extension at some point in the future. So it will have the necessary purpose-built transport infrastructure; it could also be built with specific regard for larger family apartment living.

The 'sheer weight of money' argument doesn't hold water. You don't build the tallest building in the country on the most expensive land in the country, just because it's the most expensive, and call that 'density'. It's driven solely by the profit motive.

What Dublin really needs with regard to density is taller buildings, possibly capped at eight floors, but built in concentric circles outwards from the centre of the city. *Consistency* of density through radial development is what is required, like such compact European cities as Munich. If you travel on the DART suburban rail line into Dublin, as you enter the inner city you see a smattering of one to four-storey nineteenth-century buildings (1850s and 60s) and Georgian buildings (even earlier) interspersed with sporadic twelve-storey glass office buildings. This is not adequate density.

Every day while commuting to work, on leaving Lansdowne Road station—a stone's throw from the proposed Mountbrook skyscraper proposal—I would see lots of single-storey terraced nineteenth-century cottages running parallel to the railway. I used to muse to myself, if Dublin City Council wants real density, all they have to do is set the maximum building height at eight storeys in the local area plans, then let capitalism and free markets do the rest. Developers wouldn't be long in buying up those old cottages and knocking them down, one by one, engaging in site accumulation, and then building new eight-storey blocks of three and four-bedroom family apartments. That's what Dublin now needs. (Why only eight floors, you may ask? Well, ask any firefighter how long their longest ladder is.)

There's no need for tall tales about true density. Fifty or a hundred years from now, when Dublin is completely composed of buildings of eight floors, then and only then should the city planners resort to eyesores on the landscape.

Anyway, who says Dublin is not already as dense as other big cities around the world, at least in population?

The Republic is about 70,000 square kilometres in total land area, with a population estimate of 4.4 million in mid-2008. That tells us that it has a very low population density: a national average of only sixty-three people per square kilometre. Among European countries Ireland ranks just above Lithuania, Latvia, Estonia, Finland and Sweden. The other twenty-one EU countries all rank above Ireland in population density, with Belgium and the Netherlands having six to seven times the density, while Malta's is twenty times that of Ireland. Even Ireland's nearest neighbour has four times the population per area. So we're not exactly short of space, especially when you realise that urban areas account for only 4 per cent of the total land of the country.

The city of Dublin, at 44 square miles or 115 square kilometres, is not that big really, even with an urban population of 1,045,000 according to the most recent census (2006) and a city population of about half that. The following table puts the city's population density into some perspective, comparing it with some of its international peers.

Table 28: Comparative area, population and population density of twenty-seven cities

Rank	City	Size (km²)	Population	Density
1	Paris	87	2,167,994	24,919
2	Mumbai	603	13,662,885	22,658
3	Seoul	605	10,452,000	17,276
4	Tokyo	620	8,535,792	13,767
5	Istanbul	831	11,372,613	13,685
6	Jakarta	664	8,576,788	12,916
7	New York	789	8,250,567	10,456
8	Tehran	760	7,797,520	10,259
9	Moscow	1,081	10,452,000	9,668
10	Lima	804	6,954,517	8,649
11	Yokohama	440	3,602,758	8,188
12	Delhi	1,483	11,325,124	7,636
13	São Paulo	1,523	10,886,518	7,148
14	Singapore	699	4,436,000	6,346
15	Beijing	1,370	8,495,000	6,200
16	Riyadh	800	4,465,000	5,581
17	Mexico	1,550	8,609,347	5,554
18	Shanghai	2,050	10,231,000	4,990
19	Rio de Janeiro	1,260	6,093,500	4,836
20	London	1,577	7,581,052	4,807
21	Bogotá	1,590	7,137,849	4,489
22	Dublin	115	506,211	4,401
23	Bangkok	1,569	6,704,000	4,272
24	Lahore	1,772	6,577,000	3,711
25	Karachi	3,530	12,130,000	3,436
26	Cork	37	119,143	3,220
27	Los Angeles	1,290	3,849,378	2,984
n.r.	Dún Laoghaire and Rathdown	127	193,688	1,525
n.r.	South Dublin	223	246,919	1,107
n.r.	Fingal	448	239,813	535

Source: various

The Irish media and the VIPs are fixated on the whole notion of urban sprawl and almost always seem to compare Dublin with Los Angeles. Our table shows that this is factually incorrect, but you can see why they would seek to misinform the public. According to one Progressive Democrat senator's web site and several other reports, by 2010 Dublin, in terms of urban sprawl, will equal the land mass of Los Angeles.

They couldn't be further from the truth. Dublin and Cork are denser in population than Los Angeles. Only the outer suburbs have a lower population density. Dublin as a city fares well when compared with the likes of London, a truly large metropolitan city with very few tall buildings (with the exception of a cluster in Canary Wharf in the Docklands and a sprinkling throughout the financial 'Square Mile').

Having lived myself for twelve years in central London (my last home was in Islington, half a mile from Shoreditch and less than three minutes by car from Liverpool Street station, in the heart of the financial district), I can tell you that there are very few residential buildings higher than four storeys. All the tower blocks of twelve storeys and more in Hackney, not far from Islington, have been blown up and demolished, just as the seven towers in Ballymun, north Dublin, were.

Top of the table is Paris, a comparatively small city, about half the size of Dublin but with four times the population. They have achieved enormous density, with almost 25,000 people crammed into each square kilometre; yet how many 37-storey residential tower blocks are there? Paris is a compact city, not a high-rise one. Big buildings and not tall buildings were the solution there, as well as a fantastically efficient underground railway system.

The entire county of Dublin, including Dún Laoghaire-Rathdown, Fingal, South Dublin and the city of Dublin itself, is a little over 900 square kilometres or 70 per cent of the size of Los Angeles, with a population below 1.2 million people, or less than a third of Los Angeles. There's absolutely no danger of 'urban sprawl' resulting in Dublin consuming as large an area as Los Angeles by 2010, 2020 or even 2050. It's nonsense to even suggest it.

Dublin is half-urban and half-suburban and won't probably change that much over the next century in people's preference for either urban or suburban living. What does need to change is the transport system. In 2008 it's not even possible to travel by bus, train (DART) or tram (Luas) with the same ticket, as it was in London thirty years ago. Dublin doesn't have an underground like the London Tube or the Paris Metro.

'Transport 21' is the Government's strategy for creating a 21st-century transport system, and it entails spending at least €34 billion. What it will deliver, though, is a transport infrastructure similar to what Ireland's European neighbours enjoyed in the 1970s and 80s, but it will only be there in the 2020s. Now there's density for you!

Just because the transport system is seriously wanting is no justification for tall buildings for the wealthy minority.

Chapter 25

Rising rumours, falling rents

SPRING 2008

This may come as a shock to many people, but Dublin residential rents were not rising then, contrary to what was being reported regularly in the mass media. The media reports were biased. The media provide a forum for those with an agenda, the VIPs or vested-interest parties. I have being tracking rents in Dublin for almost two years now. I've kept records, by property type and by area or postal district. It's not difficult with today's technology: all you need is a computer, broadband, and spreadsheets; and of course property web portals like www.daft.ie and myhome.ie are invaluable.

Rents in many areas were actually falling; and the number of rental properties that had come onto the market had soared. No surprise, really; I expected as much. What do you do if you're a professional property investor and can't offload your investment in a buyer's market where activity has come to a standstill? You do the next most obvious thing: you rent it out as soon as possible. This is precisely what had happened during the latter part of 2007. It reminds us of the 'fire in the cinema' analogy: everyone heads for the door at the same time, and no-one gets out.

The following are samples of media reports on the so-called rising rents phenomenon at that time.

Dermot O'Leary, economist, Goodbody Stockbrokers, 17 September 2007:

Rents and yields in Irish residential property—Not as bad as we thought . . . Rents are ahead by 12 per cent year-on-year. Private rents continue to grow at a stellar pace. According to the latest CPI [consumer price index] data, rents grew at an annual pace of 12.1 per cent in August, the fastest pace of growth since October 2001, but rental yields remain low. Despite this increase, private rents, according to the CPI private rents series, are only 10 per cent ahead of the level pertaining at the beginning of 2002. However, new data released by the CSO as part of Census 2006 reveal that rents may in fact be higher than we originally thought. The Housing Volume from Census 2006 reveals that rental values actually increased quite significantly over the inter-censal period. While the CPI series reveals that rents declined at an average annual pace of 1.4 per cent over the period from April 2002 to April 2006, the Census data show that rents (in private furnished or partly furnished accommodation) grew by 13 per cent, or by 3.1 per cent per annum.

Dermot O'Leary again:

We now estimate that the rental yield nationally currently stands at 3.8 per cent (from a previous estimate of 3.3 per cent), up from a trough of 3.3 per cent in the third quarter of 2006. Nevertheless, given that average mortgage rates are currently estimated at approximately 4.8 per cent, investors still face a significant funding gap. With rents growing at an annual pace of 12 per cent and house price inflation now in negative territory, rental yields are expected to continue their ascent over the coming quarters (to 3.9 per cent by the end of 2007).

Ronan Lyons, economist, 'Daft' Rental Report, 27 November 2007:

Rents are rising, house prices are falling . . . The average increase in rents across Ireland over the past 12 months is 6.6 per cent. In Dublin rents have increased between 8 per cent and 13 per cent compared with the same period last year, while Dublin's commuter towns have been experiencing a slight fall-off in rents—down 3 per cent on this time last year. However this trend of increasing rents may not continue, as the rate of growth in rent has slowed to single digits and the supply of rental property has never been higher.

Geoff Tucker, economist, Hooke and MacDonald, *Sunday Business Post*, 13 January 2008:

Housing turnabout . . . Rents have been rising significantly, and there will be a gradual realisation among first-time buyers that in many cases they would be better off buying than continuing to rent . . . We're not expecting the market to suddenly snap back to how it was in 2006, but we do believe that confidence will start to return.

Dominic Coyle, *Irish Times*, 21 January 2008:

Dublin house prices fell by 10 per cent last year . . . The annual price survey of the Irish Auctioneers and Valuers Institute (IAVI) finds that as many as 40,000 apartments in Dublin lay vacant, causing concern that prices have some way to correct before activity is restored and prices are stabilised. Rents, however, continued to rise, according to the IAVI data, increasing by between 3.3 and 4.2 per cent across the State.

Austin Hughes, chief economist, KBC Ireland (formerly IIB Bank), on 'Prime Time', RTE television, 22 January 2008:

The reality is rents are rising. I think the national average is 12 per cent, in some instances 20 and 25 per cent.

Niall O'Grady, head of marketing, Permanent TSB, reported by Laura Slattery, *Irish Times*, 2 February 2008:

Property prices fall back more than 7 per cent to 2006 level . . . Property prices plunged 7.3 per cent in 2007, but soaring rents will bring buyers back to the housing market and stabilise prices later this year, according to one of the Republic's biggest mortgage lenders . . . Rents are now growing at their fastest rate since October 2001, climbing at an annual rate of 12.3 per cent, Central Statistics Office (CSO) data shows. The buoyant rents, combined with possible interest rate cuts, will also boost yields for buy-to-let investors, who will flock back to the market, thus halting the downturn in prices and giving first-time buyers the confidence to buy.

Hubert Fitzpatrick, director of the Irish Home Builders' Association, *Sunday Independent*, 3 February 2008:

A good year really does lie ahead . . . During 2007, rents rose by 12pc nationally and by in excess of 20pc in some parts of Dublin. This is a direct consequence of the fall off in rental properties coming to the market and the fact that people who would previously have bought have opted to rent.

None of these comments in the media bore any resemblance to the reality at that time. (Dublin rents had already begun falling in the early spring of 2008.) The commentators were basing their opinions (not facts) on a theoretical rental index used by the Central Statistics Office when calculating the monthly consumer price index. The CSO imputes some notional rent as paid by all individuals, whether or not they pay rent or own their own house or even have a mortgage. You see, the CSO assumes that each person in effect pays rent to themselves. To anyone but economists this will seem like a silly notion, and to a degree it is. Why do they do it? Well, they need to estimate the 'price' costs of housing, as housing is a big component of the consumer price index. Although housing is lumped in that portion of the cpi that includes gas, water and electricity, there are also three sub-components to 'housing' itself: maintenance and repairs, mortgage interest payments, and rent. The first two can quite easily be estimated, but the third is tricky, as most people in Ireland own their own home and don't rent. However, the cso needs to calculate the costs associated with home ownership, as well as the costs of putting a roof over one's head.

On a simplistic level, let's assume you know someone who owns their home without a mortgage, perhaps an elderly relative. The cso has a price index of the cost of housing and within that index a sub-index for rent. In effect they say that the 'imputed' rent is rent that the owner-occupiers, as tenants, notionally pay to themselves as occupiers. Another way of looking at it is to say it's the same amount they would have to pay if they were to go and rent a property similar to the one they already live in.

For argument's sake, let's say today that this imputed rent is x and last year it was y; then the annual percentage change or growth rate is the difference between x and y. This fictitious rent is what the bankers, brokers, estate agents and construction industry representatives were talking about. It doesn't actually exist: it's notional.

In fact if you look at this so-called rental growth over time it merely tracks European Central Bank base rates—with a bit of a time lag. Indeed we will show in the following pages that there are only two factors that drive rental levels, and interest rates are the usual driver.

The other dominant factor is the total supply of properties for rent.

REALITY IS NOT WHAT YOU MAY THINK

Based on my own empirical research (that's hard slog in plain language) conducted at the beginning and end of each month, I discovered that there were some surprises when you examined what had happened to rents, especially over the previous year.

But before we take a look at the numbers we need to set the scene, and we need to anchor my results with a proper paper trail. Turn the clock back to 15 March 2007, to an article in the *Irish Times* that day headed 'Research shows rising rents pushing up rental yields,' reported by Fiona Tyrell, concerning a report prepared by myself when I was engaged in a different capacity, namely as head of research at Savills HOK.

That article provoked quite a bit of interest, especially among professional property investors—so much so that I received numerous phone calls that day from individuals, all complaining that their specific properties were not achieving the average monthly rents quoted for their area.

One man in particular had two properties let in an upmarket development in Dublin 4. He complained that both his two-bedroom apartments were valued at about €800,000 but were not fetching the €2,000 per month average rent I had listed in my article. He was actually getting about €1,800 per month each or a yield equivalent of roughly 2.7 per cent—about 1 per cent less than European Central Bank rates back then and 1½ to 2 per cent below the typical mortgage interest rate.

I asked the obvious questions, such as how long were the sitting tenants there? When was the last time the rent was reviewed? And of course the most important question, how much finance was outstanding on the properties? The answers were completely as I had expected. Both had tenants that had been in situ for several years, the rent had not changed from year to year and, as he'd bought them several years back, the loan-to-value ratio on the apartments was actually quite small (he had accumulated a lot of equity in the properties).

He also articulated most landlords' most common complaint: If I raise the rent the tenants might move; it could be empty for a month or two, and then I'd have to paint the place. Those readers who rent property out are probably nodding in agreement right now.

The March 2007 *Irish Times* article:

Rent yields in Dublin have been rising steadily in the last six months and more increases are on the way, according to new research. The average rental yield in Dublin is 4.4 per cent, representing a 0.5 per cent increase in the last six months, according to a rental yield survey conducted by Savills Hamilton Osborne King. The survey was based on the average monthly rents of almost 600 Dublin two-bedroom apartments.

Yields are at their highest in the city centre where landlords are currently enjoying a 4.9 per cent yield on their investment properties, up 0.75 per cent from the same time last year, according to the Savills HOK research. The most dramatic growth has been in the south of the county where rental yields are now at 4.39 per cent, up over 1 per cent, from 3.07 per cent at the start of 2006. Yields in the north of the city have increased by just over 0.5 per cent and are now at 4.49 per cent. On the south of the city, landlords are now getting a 4.28 per cent yield; this is up from 3.87 per cent at the start of last year. In the north of the county, landlords are enjoying yields of 4.45 per cent—up from 4.17 per cent in the first quarter of last year—while in west Dublin yields are now at 4.49 per cent, a marginal increase from 4.26 per cent.

The survey indicates that rents have been rising since the middle of last year, but especially since the start of 2007, explains Derek Brawn, head of research at Savills HOK. Following seven successive interest rate hikes there has been "a fundamental re-appraisal of property valu-ations and thus rental values" in recent months, he explains. Prior to this investors accepted lower yields based on an expectation of returns from future capital appreciation, according to Brawn.

Now as capital values are no longer expected to rise as they did in the past, rental income will become more important and rents are likely to edge up further, he says. Yields are at their highest in the Dublin 18 area of Sandyford, Foxrock and Carrickmines, where average house prices are €440,423 and average rents are €1,934, result-ing in a 5.3 per cent yield.

In Dublin 5 rental yields are at 5.1 per cent, an average two-bedroom apartment costs €365,000 and average monthly rents are €1,505. In Dublin 2 landlords are enjoying yields of 5 per cent. Rents in this area are €2,005 and the average apartment prices are €481,250. Surprisingly, yields are at the lowest, according to the research, in Dublin 14, where average apartment prices are €527,500 but monthly rental is just €1,538 giving a yield of 3.5 per cent. Areas such as Dundrum and Churchtown in Dublin 14 have experienced significant price increases thanks to the arrival of the Luas but rents have yet to follow suit, explains Brawn.

The gradual disappearance of the first-time buyer means that investors will play a more dominant role in the new homes market, says Brawn. He advises residential investors to look at areas where there is good supply and where yields are above the average of 4.5 per cent, like Dublin 11 and 15. If you can afford it, go for prime areas such as Dublin 1, 2 and 18 where yields are high, he says. One reason why professional investors are always targeting Dublin 2 and 4 is because they are more "recession-proof", he adds.

I have a confession to make. I knew that rents would rise as interest rates had. It's like predicting that night will follow day.

Irrespective of property prices, anyone who was letting out a property financed with a mortgage had experienced half a dozen rate increases, while their tenant was paying the same monthly payment. Obviously, at the end of the rental period they would attempt to jack up the rent. They would be mad not to.

I still stand over everything I said in that report. It still holds true today, even the last line regarding city centre locations. Property prices may fall in Dublin 2 or Dublin 4, but people will always want to live there, so rents should stay reasonably firm, thus keeping yields relatively high compared with the rest of Dublin. Put it another way. If you had two people renting a two-bedroom in Dublin 6 or 6W for €1,800 a month in 2007, they would probably move to Dublin 4 if they only had to pay the same rent or less in 2008 (as the following table with actual monthly average rents sorted by Dublin postal district shows). After all, who wouldn't want to live closer to town, and move into the embassy belt?

THE SPRING 2007 TO WINTER 2008 RENTAL SURVEY

The following table is an updated version of the one I used in 2007 for my research article on asking rents for two-bedroom apartments in Dublin. I chose two-beds originally for a very good reason. You might think that a three-bedroom semi-detached house in the commuter belt or the greater Dublin area might have been more representative of the average family home. However, as most people are aware, the big growth in new homes in recent years was in what the Americans call 'multiple-dwelling units' or the estate agents refer to as apartments (flats to you and me).

In fact a quarter of all new properties built in Ireland since 2003 were flats, and most of these were in Dublin. Between January 2003 and November 2008, 97,180 new homes were constructed in the Co. Dublin area (Fingal, Dún Laoghaire-Rathdown, South Dublin and the city of Dublin), but these included 52,626 apartments, or 54 per cent of the total build. So you see, the glut of new homes consisted of apartments in the Dublin area.

Furthermore, investors are more likely to buy apartments as investments (easier to let), rather than houses, though obviously they do both. The other reason for focusing on two-bedroom properties is that first-time buyers typically buy new two-bedroom apartments (originally because of the stamp duty incentive on 'new' properties, which no longer exists) and because if necessary they could rent out one room to help pay the mortgage, especially if they're a single person.

Usually nowadays it takes two incomes to finance the mortgage multiple for a new home anyway, so it seemed like a good idea to pick two-bedroom units, as this is what first-time buyers can only afford in the city. If they want a bigger property they're forced to look outside Dublin. When surveying the asking rents for two-bedroom apartments I carefully excluded penthouses, town houses, cottages, mews and duplex properties, as these types of property may command a premium. I also wanted to ensure a like-for-like comparison. The results, shown below, were startling.

Table 29: Average asking rents for two-bedroom apartments (per calendar month), Dublin region, 2007–08

	Mar. 2007	Number for rent	Feb. 2008	Number for rent	Nov. 2008	Number for rent	Rental growth	Numbers
Dublin 1	€1,688	16	€1,829	91	€1,445	134	−14.4%	8.4×
Dublin 2	€2,005	38	€1,998	64	€1,690	109	−15.7%	2.9×
Dublin 3	€1,34?	19	€1,47?	36	€1,276	69	17.?%	3.6×
Dublin 4	€2,192	72	€2,138	160	€1,756	215	−19.9%	3.0×
Dublin 5	€1,505	11	€1,462	13	€1,316	25	−12.5%	2.3×
Dublin 6	€1,785	20	€1,627	69	€1,357	93	−24.0%	4.7×
Dublin 7	€1,345	23	€1,442	33	€1,294	103	−3.7%	4.5×
Dublin 8	€1,463	30	€1,510	76	€1,345	172	−8.1%	5.7×
Dublin 9	€1,289	23	€1,332	61	€1,192	133	−7.5%	5.8×
Dublin 10	n.a.	0	€1,250	1	€1,138	13	−9.0%	n.a.
Dublin 11	€1,304	14	€1,228	39	€1,126	78	−13.6%	5.6×
Dublin 12	€1,150	5	€1,287	10	€1,169	40	+1.7%	8.0×
Dublin 13	€1,752	28	€1,502	54	€1,418	63	−19.1%	2.3×
Dublin 14	€1,538	24	€1,593	41	€1,441	60	−6.3%	2.5×
Dublin 15	€1,298	44	€1,311	137	€1,155	208	−11.0%	4.7×
Dublin 16	€1,392	6	€1,456	17	€1,325	48	−4.8%	8.0×
Dublin 17	€1,310	5	€1,207	7	€1,195	5	−8.8%	1.0×
Dublin 18	€1,934	41	€1,659	131	€1,430	138	−26.1%	3.4×
Dublin 20	€1,157	7	€1,329	8	€1,184	24	+2.3%	3.4×
Dublin 22	€1,178	18	€1,234	29	€1,103	54	−6.3%	3.0×
Dublin 24	€1,213	15	€1,303	36	€1,157	67	−4.7%	4.5×
South County	€1,640	49	€1,649	161	€1,407	175	−14.2%	3.6×
North County	€1,214	73	€1,341	182	€1,185	268	−2.4%	3.7×
Total	€1,592	581	€1,584	1,456	€1,346	2,294	−15.5%	3.9×

Source: Daft web site (not rental survey)

The negative growth in monthly rents over the previous year was no surprise to me. The jump in the number of properties available for rent this time around was not exactly a surprise either: it was more of a shock. A big jump was expected but not four times the number on the market or, in proportion terms, an additional 300 per cent. Even by early February to mid-March the number of Dublin rental flats trebled and the total Dublin average monthly rent was slightly down on the same month the previous year. Hang on a minute, though. I watched Tom Parlon of the Construction Industry Federation on RTE in February telling the viewers that rents were rising by as much as 20 per cent! Just a few weeks earlier his colleague Hubert Fitzpatrick of the Irish Home Builders' Association had been quoted in the *Sunday Independent* as saying that rents were rising by a similar amount, and that the supply of rental properties was *'falling'*, as more and more people had opted to rent instead of buying. Both men were engaging in propaganda. Rents had turned in February and in absolute money terms were falling month on month. With regard to increased excess supply of rental properties, well, that goes without saying. The dogs in the street knew that this was happening.

This increased supply had been driven in part by the sheer number of brand-new apartments that have flooded the rental market. The survey shows an increase from 600 two-bedroom apartments for rent to about 2,300 over eighteen months. That's quite a big increase, wouldn't you say? My instinct told me this was just the tip of the iceberg, especially when you consider that I had to exclude a lot of what you'd call generic advertisements for properties in new development schemes.

Another complication caused by the onslaught of all these new unsold properties, now available for rent, was that the asking rents tended to be considerably higher than second-hand properties of a similar size in the same area. In other words, they really distort the averages quite a bit—upwards. Consequently, if these newer apartments are excluded, rental growth would be even more negative than a year ago.

The best way to show this is with specific examples. The biggest jumps in the numbers available are in Co. Dublin, both north and south of the Liffey. If we take north Dublin first, the most noticeable change between then and a year before is the huge number of new properties for rent in Malahide. There was a plethora of properties for rent at Marina Village—approximately eighteen on my count—and they were not cheap either, averaging about €1,750 a month. At the Strand and the Green a few were available in each development, all reasonably priced (not!) at an even €2,000 per calendar month for two-beds. However, none of the aforementioned was as pricey as the Casino, where prices ranged from €1,800 to €2,500, or Clearwater, ranging in asking rents from €2,000 to €3,800 a month.

Without a shadow of doubt the north Co. Dublin average was massively distorted by the Malahide effect. In fact if you stripped out all the central and seafront Malahide properties the average for north Co. Dublin in February 2008 dropped below €1,150 per month, well down on the previous year. The lower asking rents in Swords, Balbriggan and Lusk and the surrounding Malahide area not close to the sea were closer to €1,300 to €1,400 per month or below.

Turning to the other side of the river, South Dublin is where the largest increase in the supply of rental properties has occurred.

Stillorgan features very prominently now for those seeking a two-bedroom flat for rent on the south side. The culprits are primarily the

Grange and Beechwood Court developments. There are so many advertisements for these two complexes that it took me a lot of extra time just to weed out the duplicates.

It makes me wonder if they have sold any apartments in those two schemes, or who is actually letting them. Is it the developers, doing what Liam Carroll has been forced to do with the Gasworks in Barrow Street, Dublin 4 (letting them out, as none are selling), or have they been bought by unwitting property speculators — sorry, investors — who had intended to set them from the outset?

Does it really matter? There was a huge number for rent then, all hitting the market at the same time. Interestingly, over at Dublin 18 a lot of new schemes have hit the market at the same time too, it would appear. A year ago there were not that many apartments to let in Sandyford (believe it or not), as most were still in the pipeline, as they say. However, that's no longer so, and the excess supply has taken its toll on rental values, with the average monthly asking rent now considerably below (about 26 per cent below) what it was one year and a half earlier.

There was an abundance of new two-beds available at the Edges or at the Cubes at Beacon South Quarter, or at Aiken's Village, where the average asking rent was about €1,650 a month at that time but had fallen to €1,350 a month by September.

What is really scary is that these newly built developments are just part of a total of 4,800 new apartments to be built there, in the industrial estate—the same total amount as all the new homes built in Co. Kildare during 2006. That was a record year for new home-building in Ireland, and in the same year that more homes were built in Co. Kildare than any other county, with the exception of Dublin.

To think that a similar number will be constructed in one square mile of Dublin suburbs, in buildings up to twenty-four storeys tall, is simply frightening. Traffic is already brutal there; what is it going to be like in a couple of years' time on a Saturday morning when all the new residents take their cars out from the underground car parks and hit the streets at the same time, heading for Dundrum Shopping Centre?

If you look just beyond Sandyford Industrial Estate to sunny Stepaside, the more discerning renter can save three to four hundred a month, but then they won't have the tram on their doorstep. A big price, it seems, just to be close to public transport. I mean €3,000 per year additional cost just to be a hop, skip and jump from the overcrowded Luas—standing room only, if you're lucky.

Elsewhere in prestigious Dublin 18 there were expensive pads for hire where the asking rents were no different from the previous year's levels. For instance in Hollybrook, in Brighton Road, there were truly large apartments (greater than 125 square metres) for lease at a mere €3,000 per month. They ranged from €2,800 to €3,500 per month, though most were either €3,000 or €3,300—a snip at the price! Who said rent was dead money? On www.daft.ie there were fifteen listed for rent in this one development; but further inspection reveals that some were duplicates. The previous year there were far fewer at Hollybrook for rent, and back then €3,500 to €4,000 per month was the going rate. Not exactly a ringing endorsement for salubrious Brighton Road, then, as monthly rents were down more than €500 per month. By November 2008 those same Hollybrook apartments could be rented out for €1,950 to €2,300 per month, a drop of about €1,500 per month.

While we're on the subject of expensive South Dublin apartments for rent it would be unfair not to mention the most expensive development for two-bedroom rentals: Killiney Court. This was the former Court Hotel, which was demolished, apart from one old section in the middle that has been redeveloped into three apartments and sold on in a joint venture between the previous owners and Ellen Construction of Wexford. The joint agents, Kelly-Walsh (along with Hooke and MacDonald) told me that all the top floor 'penthouses' were sold for €3 million a pop back in 2006.

You may be glad to hear that some of these are available to rent. One was competitively priced at €4,500 a month, while another landlord was seeking a paltry €6,000 a month (for penthouse with roof garden). Do I jest? Well, let's think about it in terms of rental yield. €4,500 per month is only €54,000 per year on a €3 million gaff, which is less than a 2 per cent yield (1.8 per cent, to be precise), whereas €6,000 is equivalent to a paltry 2.4 per cent gross yield—gross yield being before costs, because the service charges at Killiney Court are €5,000 per year per apartment. Penthouse or ground floor, it doesn't matter: they're all the same. So after you've knocked off service charges, added in insurance, painting and decorating every couple of years and so on, a 1½ to 2 per cent net yield doesn't really cut it when the cost of money was 5½ per cent at that time. By early October 2008 two-bedroom apartments at Killiney Court were from €2,600 per month, while the most expensive one in the example above dropped by half to €3,000 per month.

Footnote: Rents generally move in the same direction as prices. Sometimes there is a bit of a time lag, because leases tend to be for twelve months. However, property yields tend to move in the opposite direction to price, so as price falls, yields typically rise. This is because yield is a quotient or fraction (annual rent ÷ price). What consumers need to know, though, is that during 2008 the Irish experience is that rents have fallen just as much as prices in percentage terms. Overall Irish property yields remain little changed and are still stuck at 2007 low levels. This tells us that we're a long way off the bottom.

THE DAFT RENTAL SURVEY: SOME SHORTCOMINGS

Some of you might say, well, doesn't Daft produce a rental survey? Why not use that published survey instead of doing your own? Two reasons why. Firstly, their most recent rental report at the time of writing was May 2008, citing data for January to March, so that was already several months out of date. Secondly, to be frank, I don't trust their data collection and analysis.

Every month last year I collected Daft data, and it never tallied with their own published results. My own experience of dealing with large data-bases (and I was one of the principal advisers on the MSCI bond indices when I worked at Morgan Stanley) is that you need data-base specialists with market knowledge. Also, before that I'd cut my teeth in 1995 at SBC Warburg (now UBS) by producing their sterling bond indices. I created a massive 64-gigabyte data-base with 110,000 fixed-income securities; and—trust me—these were infinitely more complex than property listings, as each one had several hundred data fields, and the unique identifiers or primary keys could change over time.

No disrespect to the Fallon brothers, but www.daft.ie is a web portal. What experience do they have in data-base design? Their web site is riddled with duplicates, and they provide tools to allow estate agents to 'refresh' data whenever they feel like it. Added to this is the fact that their data-base obviously has no referential integrity (the same properties and same addresses are listed multiple times, often with different features or descriptions, and with multiple agents, sometimes even with different prices!).

Back in the mid-1990s I had a team of seven IT professionals at my beck and call, and two of these (Martin Radcliffe and Susan Nightingale) were Sybase data-base engineers with fifty-five years' experience between them. Both had been with the bank when it was called Mullen and Company in the 1970s; Martin had built data-bases when punched cards were the method used to input the raw data.

At UBS Warburg we had to produce daily A3 printed sheets, crammed with data and calculated values from the data-base. We then duly sent them on to the major sterling bond investors, such as Legal and General, Prudential, Scottish Widows and Scottish Amicable, to name but a few. Many of these large institutional funds were benchmarked or measured against the Warburg sterling indices. There was no room for error: they had to be perfect every time. The daily deadline was akin to that of a newspaper, but with a big difference: 100 per cent accuracy.

Let me cite one specific example of difficulties with Daft data. On the day that my article appeared in the *Irish Times,* 15 March 2007, Daft released its report called 'Rental Market Is in Rude Health,' with commentary from Geoff Tucker as their guest blogger. If you look at that report and check the average rents throughout Ireland in March, specifically the table entitled 'Daft snapshot of rents nationwide,' under two-bedroom for the Dublin 2 area the average given is €1,679, as opposed to my own findings (using Daft as one source, incidentally) of €2,005 per month. Now on the very same day I printed a list of all the two-bedroom properties for rent in Dublin 2, and virtually all of them—all bar two— were far above their average figure. How can you have an *average* for an area where more than 90 per cent on your system are €200 to €400 per month above that average?

I distinctly recall querying this at the time. I not only raised it with my colleague who helped me with the report but I felt so strongly about it that I raised it with a journalist at the *Irish Independent*, Donal Buckley. Indeed I sent him a spreadsheet, via e-mail, containing all the Dublin 2 properties and asked him to ask Daft why everything available for rent on a Dublin 2 search was far above their quoted average. Averages, as we discover time and time again, are a great way of distorting the truth.

Well, if you look more closely at their report you will see a footnote in very small type:

*Warning: This snapshot provides a highly generalised view of the rental market and is based on many thousands of properties advertised on Daft.ie between December 06 and February 07. These figures should be used as a guide only and should not be used to set rental levels as many qualitative factors affect rental prices besides area.

The old small print aptly prefaced with 'Warning: do not rely on these figures.' Nice.

The official average figures for March 2007 were actually three-month averages between December 2006 and February 2007. Why call it a 'snapshot' then? This beats me. There's nothing worse than an average that has been averaged over time. Averages are awful: they disguise the real truth; they hide and distort the like-for-like comparisons. We still need them for examining trends over time, but to do this we need discrete snapshots at definite points in time.

The Permanent TSB works with the Economic and Social Research Institute in collating and producing the data for monthly house prices, as does KBC Ireland when drafting the monthly consumer sentiment index. Even Ulster Bank collaborates with NTC Economics Ltd on its monthly construction purchasing managers index. Daft, please note. Perhaps credibility and, hopefully, quality would be improved if you teamed up with, say, Trinity College or another academic institution, such as Dublin Institute of Technology, that has a property bent and some expertise in data collection and analysis.

Anyway, another gripe I had with their data was that Dublin 2 rents appeared higher than Dublin 4 in their survey. Again using their web site, Dublin 4 was more expensive, property for property, than Dublin 2. As one would naturally expect, Dublin 4 rents are the most expensive in Dublin, full stop. Ballsbridge beats Hanover Quay every day. Indeed the Roads—Shelbourne, Merrion, Raglan, Anglesey and Pembroke—are clearly a lot pricier than the Streets—Leeson, Merrion, Grattan, Baggot and Townsend for properties of similar sizes. Not so in that particular Daft rental survey.

Even today you can expect to pay €3,000 to €4,000 per month for a ground-floor two-bedroom apartment in a period residence in Raglan Road, whereas €2,750 to €3,000 per month will get you an enormous penthouse anywhere in Dublin 2 overlooking O'Connell Street or Kevin Street, or even one with views over St Stephen's Green.

This is the litmus test: the most expensive area ought to show up as the most expensive area in the survey results. It doesn't always with Daft.

One final point on the Daft rental survey that worried me was the admission at the end of every report that they use econometric and regression analysis.

About the Daft Rental Report
The Daft Rental Report is based on an analysis of the 350,000 rental properties advertised on Daft.ie since January 2002, including 70,000 posted since February 2007. This figure represents the bulk of the available properties to let in the country and therefore gives the most accurate and timely reflection of what is happening in the Irish rental market. Figures are calculated from econometric regressions using standard methods.

Far be it from me to take offence at econometric regressions, as I began my career in the City of London working for the chief economist of Barclay's investment bank as an econometrician. I spent two years working under Michael Hughes, building and maintaining the bank's global equity and bond econometric models. Econometrics, for those not in the know, is the science of the mathematical modelling of time-series data. It's a very esoteric field—about as specialised a job as one can get. However, the one thing I learnt back then, which still holds true today, is that it's far more art than science. Two people with the same monthly data could quite easily come up with varying results and arrive at different conclusions. Such factors as start dates and end dates are critical, as are the techniques used to 'difference' or smooth the data that has a serial component (today based on yesterday, and so on), as well as rules of thumb for coping with 'outliers' (numbers far below or far above the average figures that could skew them), not to mention the choice of model specification. In other words, econometric regressions are prone to subjective influences. Model choice rather than data usually prevails. Lastly, there's nothing as vague as quoting 'standard methods' or standard practices. It reminds me of a former colleague who I worked with briefly in New York at Morgan Stanley. His preferred remark when asked a difficult question concerning data integrity issues (especially filling in gaps in the data) was always 'I'm in the business of business.' It meant absolutely nothing, and neither does the term 'standard methods'.

Often the media will refer to econometric models at banks as 'black-box' techniques. This term is often used in relation to the stock market. The bottom line with black-box regressions is that the only people who know how the models are run are the modellers themselves. If you ever wonder where the Taoiseach or the Minister for Finance get their forecasts for growth projections for the economy—that's right, you guessed it: econometricians working at the Department of Finance, the Economic and Social Research Institute or the Central Bank.

Most of you probably don't really care about econometrics or regressions, and that's fine. But just remember this: these Daft figures may not stand up to close scrutiny or bear accurate resemblance to reality, which is why they add the warning note. So consider yourself warned.

Rents were declining in Dublin from the beginning of February 2008. The supply of new homes to the rental market had resulted in more availability (and therefore choice) and this additional supply will keep the lid on rents. So for potential home-buyers, then, this is good news, really. Don't believe the propagandists when they exaggerate the facts and use scaremongering tactics to instil fear into young potential first-time buyers.

Fear does exist, but this time it's on the other side of the fence—with the speculators and developers—for a change!

POSTSCRIPT

Daft produced their rental survey for the third quarter of 2008 several months after I had written this chapter. However, I noticed that their average rents by postal district were below what I found on their web site for each area. Now, I've already explained the time lags with their data, but the biggest problem appears to be duplicates. For example, if you have two apartments for rent, one at €1,000 per month, the other at €1,600, the average is €1,300. If the first apartment is included twice, then the total is €3,600 and the average is €1,200 or €100 less than observed. It's easier to spot the more expensive duplicates. I found this to be so when I had to remove them.

Aside from this oversimplified example, I have selected specific areas and tested my hypothesis and it seems to be true. The conclusion, therefore, is that Daft data in their survey doesn't stand up to scrutiny and should be accompanied by a serious health warning.

Secondly, in their rental survey for the fourth quarter of 2007—the one with commentary from Dan Boyle—they re-base the rental index so that 2007 = 100. Re-basing is never a problem: the cso does it all the time with such items as inflation. However, when you plot the annual percentage change on the old series against the new series, the indices are the same for each year except for 2006. The growth rate in rents in 2006 is now perceptibly higher from April of that year until May of the following year—so much so that more than a year ago, in March 2007, when they published a growth rate of 12½ per cent, it now appears above 14 per cent.

This is index revision, and it breaks the cardinal rule of index methodology: never go back and rewrite the numbers without telling anyone. If you got it wrong in the past, say so; then print the amended version. Do likewise if you change your data methodology. There's nothing in the latest report on this topic.

Finally, if one examines the rental differences for two-beds in Dublin between the Daft surveys for the third quarter of 2007 and the third quarter of 2008—to arrive at annual, year-on-year changes—some spurious results are uncovered. For example, they show a slight increase for Dublin 1, whereas my own monthly analysis shows a drop of nearly a fifth! They also show a 10 per cent rise in Dublin 13 rents for two-bed properties (up €140); again, my list of two-bed flats for that area shows a drop of a fifth. Perhaps they've included houses, cottages and bungalows—in which case their published analysis is of very limited use to investors anyway.

Daft also showed a €48 increase on average in Dublin 14 two-bed rents. This is an area with a lot of new apartment-scheme developments. Rents have not gone up in this area, let me tell you. Their average figure is most probably being distorted by the sheer scale of new unsold apartments that flooded the rental market during 2008. Examples include Rockfield, Altamont Hall, Dundrum Gate, Dundrum Point, Hazelbrook, Millmount Court, Southmeade and Wyckham Point, to name but a few. All of these appear regularly on Daft with asking rental prices from €1,500 to €1,600 per month for two-bedroom flats. And all of them have witnessed falls in asking monthly rent of at least €100 to €200 over the course of the year (some by almost double that).

Essentially what we are witnessing here with the Daft rental survey is a problem similar to the one encountered with the house price index of the Department of the Environment, Heritage and Local Government, that is, a property mix problem within specific regions. In the case of Daft it is 'new' versus 'old', as opposed to 'big' versus 'small'. However, the principle is identical.

Better rental indices are needed, just as more reflective house price indices are required.

I use the Daft web portal to retrieve raw data, just as irishproperty watch.com and others do, but I also look at the PRTB rent registrations, which are very telling indeed. Singling out Dublin city and county from the rest of the country, the number of registered rented properties for Dublin as a whole increased from 41,845 in 2005 to 63,551 by the end of 2006, and to 81,677 by 31 December 2007. However, by 30 June 2008 that figure had passed the hundred thousand mark, at 100,166 rented properties. This means that during the first half of 2008 a record number of people—some 18,500 of them—decided to rent a home in Dublin. Despite this record demand, rental prices fell. What is more telling, though, is that, irrespective of this huge new take-up of rental homes, the supply of properties for rent has trebled over the same period. Therefore, it's not a case that rents are falling and supply is rising because enough people are not renting. They are, in their droves! Massive oversupply of new homes has been killing the rental market too, just as it prompted the decline in house prices.

Chapter 26

Rates v. rents, and the importance of yield

In the last chapter we examined the level of rents for apartments in Dublin and showed how they were no longer rising, thus exposing the contradictory media reports claiming the opposite. In this chapter we'll endeavour to be more forward-looking. This may be truly difficult for many who are conditioned to be backward-looking and accustomed also to the daily diet of newspaper rhetoric proclaiming the virtues of post-'Celtic Tiger' Ireland, which is persistently performing better than our international peers. When all this back-slapping is over and Homo Properticus Celticus is brought down to earth by the grim reality of house-price gaps and falling rents, the debate may eventually turn to the real question of where rents are likely to head.

Also, what do rents (expressed as property yields) tell us about current property valuations? Over a decade and a half of rising prices (the analogy of the fifteen-year bet on the one-horse race) the importance of 'yield' as a true measure of valuation has been lost, because so much attention was given to future capital appreciation, and anyway credit was cheap and bountiful. Since banks have begun to rein in their credit exposure, and credit availability becomes more important than the cost of credit (interest rates) itself, the emphasis should and will shift back to rental income rather than blind optimism regarding future property price growth.

RATES ARE A MAIN DRIVER OF RENTS
We know already that historically the biggest driver of property rents was the level of interest rates. Please take a glance at the next graph. It shows the Daft rental index alongside short-term interest rates; in this instance three-month Euribor, a reference interest rate that is published daily. Even though the Daft rental survey has many shortcomings, like the PTSB-ESRI house-price index, it's the only published series available.

Fig. 20: Daft rental index and short-term interest rates

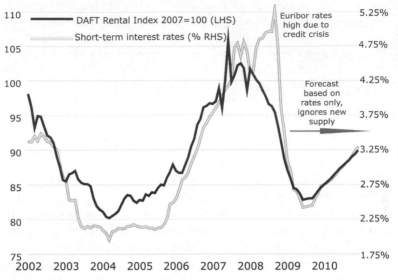

Source: DAFT Rental Report, EuroNEXT Financial Futures, Euribor.org

Conversely, lower interest rates may provide a short fillip to the market in the form of an upswing in sales, but it's a double-edged sword for savers (with negative equity) and investors, especially as the 'buy versus rent' argument once again may take centre stage.

As affordability improves, rents will typically fall. Just because affordability is better doesn't necessarily mean there will be higher prices—for two reasons. Firstly, credit availability after 2008 will be nothing like the loose credit of 2005 or 2006. Secondly, the 'trend is your friend' argument will still hold sway, and house-price declines may face a temporary reprieve, as some bottom-feeders are tempted back into the market; but most sidelined buyers may be forced to wait while others will claim that the wait-and-see stance has been so successful for the last year, why not wait for one more? The lure of potential big savings may be too strong.

Falling rates, other things being equal, suggest that there ought to be some negative rental growth in 2009, with the Daft rental index once again remaining well below the 90 level and possibly dipping below an index reading of 83 by mid-2009. That corresponds to annual rental growth being −15 per cent between March and June 2009. The problem is further compounded, though, by the massive supply of new rental properties that flooded the market in early 2008. This additional supply of mainly new homes should depress rental growth further, and this (not interest rates) will probably become the dominant factor for the foreseeable future. (See appendix D for further explanation.)

THE IMPORTANCE OF YIELD

Not enough attention is given to property yields. Yield is actually a better measure of property valuation than income multiples. Yield is an often-misunderstood metric. Typically, prices and rents both move in the same direction; but as yield is a fraction—namely, annual rent as the numerator and property value as the denominator—there's an inverse relationship between price and yield. As prices rise, yields fall (because rents are typically static for extended periods), and as prices fall, yields normally rise. Therefore, falling yields is considered 'bullish' and rising yields is 'bearish', for property markets.

This may seem counter-intuitive, but it makes perfect sense when you think of it this way: low yields mean that buyers are willing to pay more for the income stream, whereas high yields equate to a greater demand for more cash return.

The best analogy I can suggest for this opposite relationship between price and yield is that of a see-saw. When yields are rising, it means either that rents are increasing and prices are the same or that rents are the same and prices are falling, or that rents and prices are both falling. Yields decline only when prices are rising faster than rents. So when yields are falling, that's a sign of a stronger market, and vice versa for rising yields (namely weakness).

Those property investors who are interested in examining an actual case study of just how important initial purchase price yield is can read appendix E—a realistic worked example based on the latest market data in various likely scenarios. The results are scary. As residential rental yields are still low, an investor would make more money over a ten-year period by simply putting their money on term deposit and paying the DIRT. Cash is definitely king.

Using Daft data—as the only published independent source of rental yields—we would find that the average Dublin rental yield in early 2008 was slightly above 4 per cent, whereas the cost of money was almost 6 per cent.

The harsh reality, though, is that all residential property yields in all postal districts in Dublin are substantially below the current standard variable mortgage rate by quite some margin—some by 2 per cent or more. Essentially, what occurred throughout the land was that landlords were subsidising their tenants, by quite a margin.

Alternatively, if their rents were at the right level their properties would not be worth what they thought they were. Which is it? It can't be both.

A quick illustration will explain. In July 2008 you could have bought a two-bedroom flat in the Onyx (number 5) at the Grange in Stillorgan for €575,000. Wyse, the estate agents, had one for rent in the same block for

€1,600 per month, which amounts to €19,200 per calendar year less, say, €2,000 for service charges, leaving €17,200 minus another month's commission, a balance of €15,600 or the yield equivalent of 2.7 per cent net—at a time when the average Irish mortgage rate was double that, at 5.8 per cent.

Using this recent real-life illustration, for the net rental yield to cover the mortgage costs the property would have to cost €270,000. That's still a long way off €575,000.

Yield, or annual return, is everything in property investment. It's the best standardised comparative measurement tool when you're comparing two properties, whether they're alike or not, or even if they're in completely different places.

MONEY HAS TIME VALUE

Money has a value that is time-dependent. (This will be explored in chapter 28.) Money also has a cost: that's how banks make a profit, putting their spread or margin on that cost. Why would an investor buy a residential investment property and rent it out for less than their monthly repayment? There's only one reason: they expected large positive growth in capital value (price appreciation) over the subsequent years. The biggest factor affecting every investment decision by every investor in any market is timing.

Timing, like yield, is vital. Yields today tell us that the timing is still wrong.

In a couple of years' time, as prices continue their downward trend, the timing will eventually be right. Some of you may be able to seek out bargains from distressed sellers; but ask yourself this: Will the rent cover the mortgage and other associated costs? Is the property self-financing? Until that point is reached—when rental flows exceed the borrowing costs—prices will continue their downward trend.

Chapter 27

The art of spin

Earlier we covered the topic of new-home supply extensively, and we also mentioned the ability of estate agents to confuse the issue and bombard the unsuspecting public with a plethora of meaningless and useless statistics. Deliberately putting out misinformation at a time of great uncertainty is a clever ploy, especially when it's done on the back of new reports and economic data from independent sources to which it can be attributed so as to add credibility, and particularly if those sources are the Central Statistics Office and the new reports are based on census data.

Another long-timer of the Irish property market, Dr John McCartney, then head of research at Lisney, had the same article quoted or printed in three different national newspapers in the second week of June 2007. On 10 June in the property section of the *Sunday Business Post* an advertorial appeared, this time under the heading 'Sustainable growth is key to the strength of the Irish market.' Notice the use of the words 'sustainable', 'growth' and 'strength'. Each one on its own is a positive description, but when they're used together they may allay the fears of potential buyers.

He began the article with an assertion that 'if 1967 was the summer of love, then 2007 should be the summer of sustainability.' What on earth is he referring to? He proceeds with some observations about China, pollution, George W. Bush and planning and development being a central issue in Ireland. It would be no wonder if many readers flicked straight to the motoring section by then, or back one page to 'Beautifully refurbished home in Clontarf,' or back a further page to 'Period house in Dalkey tastefully upgraded.' At least those stories had better photographs.

Anyway, he cuts to the chase, citing recent figures from the 2006 census to give some idea of the challenges ahead. Then we get a glimpse of what the article is really about.

Between 1995 and 2005 Ireland experienced the second fastest population growth in Europe, and our numbers continue to expand by more than two percent per annum. This presents many planning challenges and raises at least three fundamental questions. Firstly, are we building enough dwellings to accommodate our expanding population? Secondly, are we building the right type of dwellings? And thirdly, are we building these properties in the right locations?

All of these are pretty innocuous but, I suppose, important issues. But the way they're phrased would lead one to suppose that we have some shortfall. After all, are we building enough? Are they big enough and, of course, are they in the right places?

When was a property ever in the right place? We'd all love to live in Aylesbury Road, or Shrewsbury Road, Dublin 4. We'd all prefer larger homes. But the tone of these questions would suggest that most of the huge building boom that occurred over the last decade was somehow erroneous. We have the wrong homes in the wrong places. Perhaps we've had a cock-up of gargantuan proportions.

Then he makes the same mistake as the Sherry FitzGerald guru: he points out that we have had five times the growth in home-building that we experienced in population growth.

The first question can be dealt with quite easily. Census figures show that the population has grown by 8.2 percent since 2002. However, due to the continued building boom, our housing stock has increased by 38 percent in that period.

In this way he shoots himself in the foot. He tells us that supply exceeded demand—a contravention of the most basic economic principle, which we all understand; even those who never studied economics know this one. When supply is five times demand, prices do tend to tumble eventually.

As a result, we have gone from having one dwelling for every 3.1 persons to having one for every 2.4 persons. On this evidence, it seems that Ireland's housing stock is expanding sufficiently to accommodate our rapid population growth.

Why doesn't he just put us all out of our misery and tell us straight that there are now 1.9 million homes in the country but only 1.47 million households—more homes than families, in fact up to 400,000 additional homes. (The agents will contradict this figure by telling us that they're all holiday homes in Cos. Kerry, Leitrim and Cavan.)

Of course, this does not imply that further house building is unnecessary. The population will continue to grow and building will have to keep pace with this. Furthermore, new construction will be needed to replace our obsolete housing stock and to meet the growing demand for second homes (15 percent of properties are currently second homes).

Who believes that 15 per cent of the 1.9 million homes in the Republic are second homes? This equates to almost a quarter of a million second homes. There are 1½ million households in total; do one in six of these own a second home? And these are not investor homes, because they're covered in the occupied-households category (whether owned or rented) by the census—which, incidentally, showed that a sixth of all homes in the Republic were vacant on census night in April 2006. I would dearly love to know where he got that 15 per cent from—the one in six of us who has at least two properties. There are a lot of people who would be happy owning one single home!

The sums don't compute, especially when you consider that home ownership has slipped to 73 per cent.

Finally, additional dwellings will be required because people are dispersing into smaller family units—average household sizes have fallen from 2.94 to 2.8 persons since 2002.

Why don't they just move into their second homes? But hang on a second: he just established that we have already built one dwelling for every 2.4 persons. So we have more than we need, isn't that right? We must all be stupid, because if you multiply 2.4 by 1.15 it comes to 2.8. Therefore Ireland was spot-on in terms of housing: the construction industry got it absolutely right. So you see where the 15 per cent came from. Supply always equals demand for estate agents. 'Oversupply' or 'supply overhang' or 'supply backlog' are terms that don't exist in their vocabulary. If the numbers don't add up, just scale them and multiply those by a factor; and you can always work out that factor in a spreadsheet, or even with a pocket calculator.

It's true that there are a few thousand holiday homes or second homes around the country, particularly in the west and south-west. Vacancy in Co. Cavan is 27 per cent and in Co. Kerry is 24 per cent. So this makes sense. Wait a minute, though: the vacancy in Dublin is 14 per cent. These must be the holiday homes of the rural population: *their* expensive second homes are in the capital.

We move on to the next revelation.

The shrinking of the family units brings us to our next question—are we building the right type of properties? Again, the Census sheds light on this. It shows that almost three quarters of Irish households live in relatively big properties, equivalent to three bedroom houses or larger.

It all depends on your definition of 'large'. The average Irish property is 124 square metres, or 1,333 square feet—one of the lowest in Europe, by the way. According to the Central Statistics Office and to planning permissions granted since 1975, the average floor area of Irish houses is 135 square metres and of flats is 76 square metres. (Flats make up less than a fifth of the total.) But anyway, most of us supposedly live in bigger properties, so I suppose that's a good thing.

As more than half of the Irish households are small (they have just one or two persons) current dwelling sizes appear to be more than adequate. This conclusion is reinforced by recent Lisney research, which showed that less than 1 percent of large families were being squeezed into small properties.

But hasn't Ireland a much higher average household size than our European counterparts? Therefore, if half our households are less than the European average (1 to 2 persons), then the other half must be bigger, and no-one is shoehorning them into tiny cottages. Okay, so far so good.

In fact, there is significant under-crowding, with 63 percent of one and two person families living in 3 bedroom properties or larger.

If there's massive 'under-crowding' and a large proportion of these people own second homes, why then do we need to keep building more?

If anything, this suggests that we should be building smaller housing units. But why, then is Dublin City Council proposing substantial increases to minimum apartment sizes?

Because Éire Teoranta doesn't need smaller units (we already have more than enough); and because Dublin City Council realises this, and also knows that people are fed up with commuting up to thirty miles each way to work every day and don't get to spend time with their children. So if fewer, bigger city apartments were built we could accommodate the larger Irish household closer to where the breadwinners work.

The other problem I have with this writer's statistics is that more and more professional people are choosing a career over having a family and can thus afford to spend that bit more on a property. Also, the increase in the number of divorces means that these people need to live somewhere too. They're not going to be squeezed into one-bedroom flats, not if they want their children to visit them on weekends and over the school holidays. If people choose to live alone, or if some people can afford to live by themselves in a house with three to five bedrooms, then good luck to them.

In a discussion document which is currently out to public consultation, the council is proposing that one-bedroom apartments should be increased in size from 45 to 55 square metres, that two bed units should be increased from 65 to 80 or 90 square metres and that three-beds should be raised from 80 to 100 square metres.

And so they should. Having lived in Spain for five years, I can say that the smallest property I lived in there was a 110-square-metre two-bedroom apartment. Another two-bedroom apartment I rented for a year had 130 square metres of interior space, plus another 20 square metres of terrace, on the second floor. For the first three years I lived in a 230-square-metre three-bedroom town house.

Young Irish people are crippled with mortgage debt and are forced to live in rabbit hutches. In early 2007 I looked at a 42-square-metre 'studio apartment' (one-bedroom unit) in Cabinteely in south Co. Dublin priced at €360,000! This is bananas, at almost €9,000 a square metre. Before I looked at that one I had looked at the Grange in Stillorgan, because I grew up around the corner. Here 80-square-metre two-bedroom units were from €750,000 (at that time, not now, of course), or then from €660,000 in July 2007; the last price quoted on the Savills HOK web site was in the spring of 2008, from €635,000. However, by the summer even that figure was replaced with the dreaded 'Price on application'. (By October 2008 the same units were from €525,000.)

But even €525,000 for a two-bedroom flat on the Stillorgan dual carriageway, one of the busiest roads in the country, is very pricey. Recent owners of these properties will probably be the first to enter the negative equity trap, if they haven't already. Well, they would be if they had paid those mad prices. It's a nice Dublin suburb, but for that price you could buy a bigger house overseas and still have money for a similar-sized apartment elsewhere in Dublin.

Anyway, back to Dr McCartney, complaining about Dublin City Council.

It also proposes an average floor area of 85 square metres across all apartments in a scheme and suggests that one bed units would comprise no more than 20 percent of apartments in the scheme—they are currently 45 percent.

So the local authorities and planners are suggesting average sizes that are still smaller than the national average home size. This makes good sense to me, but they should be bigger. Additionally, they recommend reducing the number of smaller one-bedroom units to a fifth of the total. Who wouldn't agree with that?

There were too many small one-bedroom apartments built in recent years, especially in Dublin, as three-quarters of all new dwellings built in the city were apartments, and two-fifths of these were single-bedroom ones. Does Joe Public realise that 40 per cent of all the newer multiple-dwelling units built a few short years ago were just one-bedroom flats? That's an appalling statistic and probably had more to do with exorbitant prices than with actual demand for smaller and smaller accommodation. So much for market forces when first-time buyers are forced to buy tiny single-bedroom properties, as that's all they could afford.

To understand the thinking behind this we have to address our third question—are we building our properties in the right locations? Overall Ireland is building enough housing units. Furthermore the units appear to be big enough.

So what's the problem then? And who builds properties for sale in the wrong places? I'm sure the public would like to know which builders are guilty of this crime.

Critically, however, there does not seem to be enough big properties available in our major cities, and this is driving families further and further into the suburbs. As a result, we are experiencing urban depopulation. Census figures show that the population is falling in some inner suburbs of Dublin, while the numbers living in Cork city and Limerick city are also declining. Conversely, as families are forced into the suburbs, urban sprawl has led to a sharp rise in the population of our commuter counties.

Perhaps this is why Dublin City Council wants larger-footprint, family-type apartments in the city centre. We all know that high city prices and smaller properties have forced families out into the surrounding counties. This was obvious to all at the time. That's merely history.

The article goes on to say that greater access to family-sized properties in these city areas, close to public transport, would ease the commuter burden. So he essentially agrees with the city council.

The good news is that public policy is on course to improve matters . . . stamp duty changes will make it easier for smaller families to trade down, freeing up existing large properties in our cities for growing families.

Am I the only one missing something here? People living in big properties don't make way for larger groups living in smaller ones. What about the small matter of price? Smaller properties outside the cities tend to be a lot cheaper than bigger ones in the city. Or at least that's what I and others always thought. And there's more:

> Furthermore, if the principle of Dublin City Council's proposals is accepted, the supply of larger properties in the city could increase sharply, making apartment living a realistic alternative for many families that, until now, have had no alternative to the daily commute.

Who sold all those commuter-belt homes in the first place? Perhaps Lisney are exonerated from that one, now that they're advocates of the new, cheaper, larger city-living principle. Notwithstanding this, even talking about sharply rising supply, as if we really need that in this weaker market, does nothing to improve market sentiment.

And it's not like Lisney to jump on the bandwagon, especially now that property prices are falling more rapidly in the commuter counties than in the cities. Heaven forbid that they should succumb to the follow-the-money principle too!

FOOTNOTE

In case you're wondering whether I enjoy debunking other people's research, the short answer is yes. It's fair game when somebody publishes an article or something in the media for public consumption. I always stood over everything I wrote, whether it was right or wrong. (If I was wrong I said so afterwards.) It was always based upon what I believed to be true at the time.

If Dr McCartney believes his own research, then good for him, but you're free to make up your own mind. Please don't take my word for it: treat all this like a debate, and choose what you wish to believe. But do think about it, because it's worth thinking about.

FOOTNOTE 2

Dr John McCartney was the guest writer on the Daft Rental Report for the third quarter of 2007. His tag line back then was 'Rent or buy, decision swings towards home ownership.' History has proved him totally wrong. One year later, rental growth is negative. Just as affordability has improved because of declining home prices, so too have rents fallen. It is still considerably cheaper to rent than to buy in the same location. This situation will probably continue until property rents exceed mortgage repayments (for similar properties), and that may not occur until early 2010.

Chapter 28

The global credit crisis: Ramifications for Irish home prices

The first week in August 2007 was when the global credit crisis came to town and hit Europe. Although the seeds of the liquidity crunch lay in the American sub-prime mortgage crisis, which were sown several years earlier, this was the time when the symptoms bubbled to the surface. Everyone knows that the European Central Bank had doubled its base rate since December 2005, from 2 to 4 per cent by June 2007; but what some people may not be aware of is that short-term interest rates, like the three-month Euribor rate, had only been hovering just above the European Central Bank rate, at 4.1 to 4.2 per cent, at that particular time.

On 9 August 2007 all this changed. Short-term rates began to rise, even though the European Central Bank rate remained unchanged. On that particular date Euribor jumped to 4.4 per cent, and then it rose daily so that within a month it was at 4.8 per cent, and with only a few shopping days to Christmas it had reached a new peak close to 5 per cent—a full percentage point above the European Central Bank rate.

These rates are critically important, because they determine two things. Firstly, they determine the rates at which banks can borrow; thus in turn they affect the rates at which businesses and individuals may borrow. Secondly, and perhaps more importantly, higher short-term interest rates are a sign of reduced liquidity, especially when longer-term rates remain low, particularly in the face of rising inflation.

DEVELOPERS KEEP ONE EYE ON SWAP RATES

It wasn't just the Euribor rates that went up but bank swap rates began to climb too. Don't be put off by the jargon. Swap rates are bank rates that signify where banks fund themselves. Banks have assets (loans) and liabilities (deposits), and they always account in floating (think 'variable') rates. That's their lowest common denominator. Banks are in the business of lending money and taking a 'spread' or margin. They're not in the business of taking unnecessary interest-rate risks, because rates, like currencies, do move sharply from time to time.

Enter the swaps market. A common-or-garden swap is when a bank swaps fixed-rate borrowing (after it issues a new bond to investors such as insurance companies and pension funds) in return for paying floating rate. Banks don't want a mismatch between their assets and their liabilities. They may fund a lot of their borrowing by issuing debt with a fixed-interest coupon, say 6 per cent, which is what investors want, but they always swap it back immediately to floating rate. This is facilitated by investment banks in what is known as the swaps market. The bank in question has committed itself to paying regular fixed payments to the holders of its debt, but it wants to lend variable, so it enters into a swaps agreement, whereby it agrees to receive fixed (to pay to its bondholders) and pay variable (what its customers are paying them). It really is that simple.

The fixed-income markets, or bond and swaps markets (including other interest-rate derivatives and instruments), are the largest market in the world. The Bank for International Settlements estimated in 2007 that the size of this market was $1,715 trillion. The bond market (including swaps as well as credit and interest rate derivatives) is bigger than the global property market and global stock markets put together.

Think about it for a moment. Every company uses debt and equity on its balance sheet. The equity, if a company is listed or quoted, is traded on the stock market. The debt, on the other hand, is traded in the lesser-known bond market, as is government debt or the national debt of many OECD countries (including Ireland's €50 billion). The bond market is also the source of much funding for both the residential and the commercial property markets, often where development sites, homes, offices and shopping centres etc. are funded with 75 to 100 per cent debt.

During the Clinton administration an adviser told the president that you couldn't do this or that because the 'bond market' wouldn't like it. A close adviser to Clinton who was present that day retorted at one point that when they died they would like to come back as the bond market, so that they could intimidate everybody!

Another way to think about it is that the bond market is similar to a vast reservoir that services all these rivers and tributaries (bank and property lending, to name but two). This reservoir is fed daily by rainfall (older bond redemptions, or repaid debt) as well as the steady trickle of mountain streams (coupon or interest payments from existing bonds), not to mention the underground streams or wells of new money (pension payments, annuities, savers contributing monthly to regular savings schemes, otherwise known as positive institutional cash flow).

So why do the big property developers care about this market? Well, just as you and I borrow at the European Central Bank rate or Euribor plus a certain amount when we borrow to purchase a house, the big developers typically borrow at the five-year swap rate plus a margin. Usually it's the five-year rate, as that's the essential benchmark, as opposed to, say, the three or four or seven-year: it's just accepted practice by the banks. You need an anchor rate, so why not use the five-year rate? It also ties in nicely with buying a site: two years of preparation and planning and then one to two years' building, followed by a year or so to sell all the newly built units.

Not every developer or builder borrows at the same fixed spread or margin: it depends on their creditworthiness and the size of their loan. But it's fair to say that during the last few years most borrowed at the five-year euro swap rate plus a margin between 0.75 and 1.25 per cent. Often they fixed at this interest rate.

When Seán Dunne bought the 6.82-acre Berkeley Court Hotel and Jury's Hotel sites in Dublin for €379 million in 2005—then a record sum per acre—he borrowed about €270 million of the funds required from Ulster Bank. He would probably have been offered a rate of between 4 and 4½ per cent at the time, fixed for a number of years and with no interest payable for the first two years or until the hotels were vacated. You see, he bought the two hotels as separate transactions. The first to be bought was the 4.82-acre Jury's site for €260 million, or slightly above guide price, at the equivalent of €53.96 million per acre, in early September. Two months later he bought the adjacent 2-acre Berkeley Court site for €119 million, or €59.45 million per acre, which was a 19 per cent premium over the €100 million guide price. Five-year euro swap rates began to move upwards at that time, from 2.7 to 3.2 per cent by the time the second site was acquired. Assuming that Dunne had to pay 1¼ per cent above this, you arrive at the probable loan rate of 4½ per cent, though it could have been lower.

But it doesn't really matter, because by now you should get the gist of it. Purely as a matter of interest, at the time of going to press (November 2008) the five-year euro swap rate was 3.5 per cent (but had been 4.8 per cent as recently as August); so if Dunne was to sell the site today to someone else their funding costs would still be higher than his were, at the very minimum. Indeed, because of the liquidity crunch and the scarcity of bank finance, particularly for large mixed-use property developments, they might have to pay 5½ per cent or more. What does this mean for the value of those Dublin 4 sites? If they don't get planning permission for high-density, then the answer is obvious.

When I worked at Savills HOK, I sat directly opposite the investment division, where the staff also kept one eye on the five-year swap rates in euros as well as British pounds. These rates are widely available from any of the major banks' web sites and are published daily in the financial sections of the newspapers.

Another way to look at the additional interest payments required after August 2007 is to examine the spread or difference between swap rates and government bond yields of the same maturity. For instance, the difference between the five-year swap rate and the benchmark (read 'German') five-year bond yield is a credit spread, a bank credit spread.

Governments, unlike banks, are not considered to be a credit risk; they're classified as risk-free when they issue debt in their own national currency, because, unlike private corporations, they can raise taxes to repay any outstanding national debt.

In March 2007 the five-year *bond-swap spread* (as the difference between bank swaps and government bond yields is called) was about +0.15 per cent. In November 2008 the spread had increased sixfold to +0.90 per cent. Essentially what this reveals to us is that 'real-money' or cash investors didn't want bank debt: they preferred the safe haven of risk-free debt, and in addition they were prepared to forgo the extra three-quarters to one percentage point in yield each year to do so. That's a lot of additional return for bond investors to turn their noses up at, when they normally aim to secure a mid-single-digit annual return.

THE LIQUIDITY CRUNCH IS THE REAL ISSUE
The global credit crisis is actually a 'liquidity' crunch; it's not a simple credit crisis in the old sense of the word. Credit is less widely available; but it's not just that you have to pay a lot more for it. There have been many localised credit crises in the past, including those afflicting one sector of an economy, regional ones, short, sharp shocks caused by a currency crisis (Mexico in 1994, Asia in 1997) and failures of hedge funds in the United States (LTCM in 1998 following the Russian government debt default that summer). All of these were short-lived, and financial contagion was limited.

This time things are very different. The world has entered a new era, a global de-leveraging phase. The root cause of the liquidity crunch was not that too many Americans with a poor credit history were given loans and now one in five of them are not in a position to pay them back. If that was so, ask yourself why a German *Landesbank* (state bank) had to be bailed out. Why did the British government take over the Northern Rock bank? And why did the US government have to bail out two of its biggest wholesale mortgage providers, the Federal National Mortgage Association (FNMA, commonly called 'Fannie Mae') and the Federal Home Loan Mortgage Corporation (FHLMC, commonly called 'Freddie Mac'), which never lent directly to the public? The real answer is 'leverage'.

LEVERAGE CAUSED BY THE INCREASED SECURITISATION OF SECURITIES (MORTGAGES INCLUDED)

When banks repackaged debt such as mortgages into pools and sold them on to other investors, they were in effect reducing their total credit risk while simultaneously increasing their liquidity risk through over-reliance on securitisation as a cheap form of capital. It also meant that the original bank lenders were not as focused on the creditworthiness of the borrower, because it didn't matter as much any more. They also became fixated on writing more and more new business and earning fees from transactions, rather than on the quality of the individual lending business.

LEVERAGE CAUSED BY INCREASED GLOBALISATION

—which really means increased Americanisation, as the American consumer purchased goods insatiably, goods produced by such countries as Japan and China. The governments of those countries lent the United States money by purchasing its treasury bonds, and it in turn printed more money, further stoking the fires of inflation and allowing Americans to consume even more. The entire planet has been aware that American consumers were living beyond their means for years, as evidenced by the ballooning trade deficit and the balance-of-payments deficit in recent times. The worst case of this was the Bush administration's rebate cheques to millions of citizens during 2008, enabling them to immediately spend more and delay the inevitable correction that will require them to save more and consume less.

LEVERAGE CAUSED BY EXCESS GLOBAL LIQUIDITY

This was brought about by the prolonged lowering of interest rates between 2002 and 2005. The new economic paradigm that became universally accepted was that inflation was dead and that the worldwide web, coupled with globalisation, meant that consumers ruled while producers no longer had any pricing power. Competition and price transparency were the new demigods, which would ensure price stability in the future. They forgot about the emerging east, the rapid development of the new 'tiger' economies and their attendant jumps in real living standards, with all the western-style accoutrements that come with new wealth. Conveniently, the world seemed to forget that we live on a planet where all natural resources are scarce, especially food and energy, and population growth was perceived to be a positive feature and not a time bomb.

DE-LEVERAGING WILL BE A CONTINUING THEME

The entire de-leveraging process will be a continuing one that will probably last several years. All the excess liquidity that manifested itself as lower longer-term interest rates and therefore an increased appetite for risk (yield) was spread evenly around the globe. Cheap money, like a spilt liquid, seeped into every nook and cranny, in every corner of the world. When there's too much money chasing too few assets, price rationale and rational thinking become second fiddle. Caution is thrown to the winds. When returns are small, leverage is used like a simple lever to amplify returns. Great in a rising market, but devastating when the tide turns. And it has.

In February 2007 while commuting on the train to work I was reading an article about an esoteric product called constant proportional debt obligations or cpdos—essentially pools of securitised bonds that are then leveraged up around fifteen times to produce a better overall return. I thought to myself, what a late bull-market phenomenon! It was a story about a structure whereby aaa-rated securities—such as those issued by the European Investment Bank, or the International Bank for Reconstruction and Development (commonly called the World Bank), or a well-known Dutch agricultural bank, Rabobank, which typically yielded only nine or ten basis points (0.1 per cent) above risk-free government bonds—were geared up fifteen times to produce a spread of +1½ per cent. I mean, using fifteen times gearing just to achieve 1½ per cent extra yield! Then the game is well and truly over. My previous job as European credit strategist at large investment banks taught me that this was madness. Leverage is just another form of outright risk.

About the same time there were articles in the newspapers about Tiernan O'Mahony (formerly of Anglo-Irish Bank) and his company, istc, which provided liquidity to banks by trading in their less-liquid junior 'subordinated' bonds, which were issued as a form of bank capital. At that time O'Mahony was hailed as a guru for setting up istc in May 2005 with €165 million, raised largely from private investors whose names read like the who's who of Irish society. A little over two years later his company, with a staff of eighteen people, managed to go under with a deficit totalling €860 million. One article in particular in the *Irish Times* described his business model and how his firm was trading in deeply subordinated bank debt (which just means that as a creditor in the case of default they rank last) that was yielding an additional 50bps (or 0.5 per cent) over senior debt issued by the same borrowers. It reminded me of an article I jointly wrote on bank capital securities ten years earlier, in 1997, when I worked for Morgan Stanley. Then similar securities were offering between +225bps and +275bps incremental yield, or five times more extra spread than similar securities were in 2007.

Any time there's any sort of financial crisis, such as the global credit crunch, these riskier ones are the first to fall in terms of price. Lo and behold, that's precisely what occurred in the autumn of 2007. Many warnings had been issued by financial market commentators, especially in Britain, at least a year before the credit blow-out, just as there were many warnings that went unheeded about the Irish property market.

Returning to the theme of de-leveraging, it's necessary to relate all this to the value of money and in particular to what is known as the 'time value of money'. First we shall examine the evolution of money.

A CONDENSED HISTORY OF MONEY

Before money existed in its modern form, traders were forced to use barter if they needed to pay for goods. This form of exchange was incredibly cumbersome and extremely inefficient. If you needed clothes and had a goat, you needed to find a tailor who had clothes to trade and who was also in the market at that particular time for a goat. In the distant past people worked not for money but for food or goods. (The English word 'salary' is derived from the Latin word for salt, because Roman legionnaires were paid in salt. Hence also the expression 'He's not worth his salt'.)

Wealthy merchants and landowners realised that a precious metal—gold—was largely indestructible. It enjoyed scarcity value, and it could be smelted easily into bars, nuggets or even coins by goldsmiths. Those same wealthy goldsmiths built strong rooms and vaults to protect their valuable new commodity. So secure were these new repositories that other wealthy people were prepared to pay the goldsmiths for guarding their gold too. It wasn't long before they realised that most of the gold stayed in the vaults and only about a tenth of it was ever withdrawn. This meant that the goldsmiths could issue certificates backed by this gold and lend up to ten times the amount they held in their vaults. Accordingly, money and credit were invented, and these goldsmiths were the early bankers. Thus the fractional reserve system was born. The other owners of the gold saw this and demanded a share in the interest earned on their deposits, and so the deposit account came into being.

What's the point of this story? There are two really important points. The first is that in ancient times a wealthy merchant with an ounce of pure gold could easily have purchased fine robes, a cape, sandals and a hat, just as a business person today could buy a tailored suit, leather shoes and a coat and scarf today for the price of an ounce of gold. At nearly $900 a troy ounce, gold has retained its purchasing power throughout the centuries. It's an excellent hedge against inflation. In fact it's the best hedge.

The second point is that all money used to be backed by gold deposits, until 1944 and the Bretton Woods agreement; following which only the us dollar retained this backing. With all the American gold held in Fort Knox backing the greenback, it was no wonder it became the global reserve currency of choice. That arrangement ended in 1971, and since then virtually all major currencies have become 'fiat' money, or money backed by faith. When we speak of faith we're talking about the belief that governments would manage the monetary system and regulate the lenders and financial institutions with rules that ensured that reserves were adequate to prevent a 'run on the bank'.

It's this latter point that's so poignant now in the light of recent events. Regulation was lax. It was too loose in the American system, which allowed lenders to lend money to those without the ability to repay, especially as many of those loans had periods of cheaper rates or initial discounts. Regulation in Europe too was lenient. The capital treatment of securitised debt products that were repackaged and sold on was flawed because of the way that arrangers could get triple A ratings secured on large pools of debt. Regulation was absent too for the bond insurers, who lent their ratings to such issues for a fee, especially when they were doing this more and more (huge leverage). The thinking of the major credit-rating agencies was also flawed; in not realising there was a massive concentration of credit risk among a few market participants.

There had already been a similar occurrence in the world of insurance in the late 1980s and early 90s at the global insurance giant Lloyd's of London. Underwriters insured themselves with specialist 're-insurers', who in turn insured themselves with a smaller group of specialist re-insurance syndicates known as 'Retrocessionaires'. The latter group ended up carrying the entire can when the *Piper Alpha* oil rig disaster happened, or paying for the aftermath of Hurricane Hugo, or even the massive costs of the asbestosis litigation in the United States. To return to the betting analogy, this would be the equivalent of all the Irish bookmakers laying off bets with Dublin bookies, who in turn lay off all bets with one or two single firms. Then when a particular team won a game or an individual long-shot horse won a race, that bookie would have to make good on all the winning bets and would end up technically insolvent as a result.

Part of the problem of globalisation (i.e. Americanisation) was that increased financial innovation left regulators behind. They couldn't keep up with the rapid pace of development of financial products, especially those new financial products created by 'rocket scientists' earning phone-number salaries at the big bulge bracket investment banks. How can civil servants earning €70,000 to €80,000 per year at central banks or regulatory authorities compete with young financial wizards earning ten or twenty times that amount? The result is that the regulators are inevitably playing catch-up. Eventually, a credit or financial event occurs, and then it's too late.

MONEY HAS TIME VALUE!
The most important principle that underpins all financial markets is that money has time value. This same principle is what drives the property

market, especially the commercial sector, when debt finance is used and prospective rental yields are calculated.

A euro today is worth more than a euro in one year's time. This sounds obvious, but you would be amazed to know how many people fail to understand this cardinal financial rule. For instance, if a group of individuals were told they had won the national lottery and could each receive €800,000 today or, alternatively, could have €1 million in a year's time, how many would take the €800,000? The correct answer is none, because with the million guaranteed twelve months down the road you could borrow €800,000 today from a bank, which might charge you 5 per cent interest. One year later you could repay the loan at a cost of €40,000; however, you would be €160,000 better off just by waiting, and you could have earned interest in the interim or put the money to good use by investing it. The irrational person would take the money today, because they wanted to buy things *now!*

That has been part of the global leverage problem. Consumer ideology was 'buy now, pay later,' using credit and loans as the tools with which to do so. Eventually repayment has to be made.

There's one exception to the wisdom of taking the €800,000 now instead of waiting, and that's when inflation is rampant, or hyper-inflation exists. If you had Zimbabwe-type inflation, running into the millions per cent, you should take the money now and buy real assets with it. Inflation is like negative interest rates: it devalues the value of your money. The smart-alecs will say there's another exception, and that's to take the lower amount now when you can invest it today to generate 25 per cent interest or more in the short run. This was the kind of thinking behind much of the amateur property speculation that caused so many to be sucked into this property fantasy world. The notion that you could buy a site, submit a planning application, sit on it for nine months or so and then double your money by flipping it was pure fantasy. Sure, it worked briefly for some; but the same people should try doing it now. That was the exception and not the norm, an extremely high-risk strategy that worked only during the bull-market times.

Back to the time value of money. Everyone should be aware of compounding—how money left on deposit should grow more and more quickly, as interest is soon earned not just on the capital but on previously earned interest as well. The opposite of compounding is discounting, or how much something is worth today according to future cash flows (known or otherwise) and based on today's rates of interest. There's no universal rate of interest or a one-size-fits-all rate for everyone. Obviously there are different rates for different levels of credit standing— we all know that; but there are also different rates for different tenures of loan. In other words, there's one rate for borrowing for a year, a different rate for a loan over five years, and so on.

INTEREST RATES NORMALLY RISE WITH THE LENGTH OF THE LOAN

These varying rates for each specific time interval are collectively known as the 'term structure of interest rates'; the short name is the 'yield curve'. Generally speaking, the longer you borrow money for, the higher the rate of interest. This is to compensate the lender for the increased risk. Economists and bankers spend hours each day poring over the shape of this yield curve. Bets are made by the treasury departments of these banks, as well as by the large institutional funds and investors. Billions are bet each day on whether the two-year or the five-year yields will rise more or less than the ten-year benchmark yields. At this point there's no need to get hung up on all of this, just to understand that it exists.

Earlier we mentioned that short-term overnight or 'base' rates had been cut to ridiculously low levels after 2001. We also mentioned later on that inflation was perceived as having been consigned to the history books, though recent events tell us that this may no longer be so.

Putting expectations of short-term interest rates together with expected inflation, putting them into the same mixing bowl, you should arrive at longer-term interest rates or bond yields. This is what these longer-term rates of interest are supposed to be about. These longer-term rates are commonly called 'bond yields', because they're represented by yields on risk-free government bonds issued by the governments of Germany, Sweden, France, Ireland and so on.

When this curve or collection of rates is flat, when longer-term rates move down closer to short rates or base rates, it affects liquidity for one thing but it also dramatically alters the risk profile of investors. Take, for example, the pension and life insurance companies that wrote policies on the back of higher yields or sold annuities to retired people at higher rates of interest. They then have to buy bonds with a similar yield (or buy more at a similar yield when the first ones they bought mature), or they have to increase their risk appetite and buy riskier assets with a higher yield. Often they do this just to maintain a certain amount of yield or return.

This increase in risk appetite due to lower rates throughout the maturity spectrum, coupled with low absolute rates of inflation, resulted in many so-called 'blue-chip' investors having to reappraise their investment criteria to allow them to buy new and different types of securities. A good example would have been Latin American debt, where, according to the J. P. Morgan emerging market bond index (EMBI), some South American countries' bonds offered an additional yield pick-up of 14½ per cent on top of US treasuries less than a decade ago yet quite recently were offering only an extra 4 per cent. Globally this phenomenon resulted in more and more 'hot money' filtering into new places, buying new, riskier assets, causing their yields to drop, which in turn exacerbated the entire demand-for-yield dilemma. It became a virtuous circle, which has since begun to unwind. (Today those emerging sovereign yields have returned to double-digit levels.)

So you see how too much liquidity can shift the goalposts for investors and force them into areas where formerly they would never have dreamt of going. The liquidity cycle, as measured by the lower, flatter yield curve, was self-fulfilling.

IRISH COMMERCIAL PROPERTY YIELDS

Nowhere was this global phenomenon of declining yields more prevalent than in the Irish commercial property markets. In the twelve-year period 1995–2007 Irish retail yields fell from 6¼ per cent to 2½ per cent and Dublin office yields compressed from 7¼ to 3¾ per cent, whereas average industrial or warehousing yields dropped from 9½ to a mere 4¾ per cent—all below the cost of money.

In fact a startling revelation is that 80 per cent of total Irish commercial property returns arose from this 'yield compression' phenomenon. It was not superior management, better rental growth, improved quality of building or any other factor that was the main driving force behind commercial property returns during this twelve-year period: the principal factor was the secular downward trend in declining global yields (thus rising prices as they move in opposite directions) in total annual returns from investment in commercial property. The only time that yields failed to compress continually was the period 2000–02, because of the technology stock correction and the slowdown in 2001. Notwithstanding these two events, most of the money made in increased capital values was from the increased global demand for yield.

THE 'MORAL HAZARD' BELIEF HAS BEEN VINDICATED

The us government's bailing out of the Federal National Mortgage Association ('Fannie Mae') and Federal Home Loan Mortgage Corporation ('Freddie Mac') proves beyond a shadow of doubt what many of us already knew: that big banks and large strategic financial institutions were 'too big to fail', for if they did it could cause systemic risk and the entire financial system could grind to a halt. Between them, Freddie Mac and Fannie Mae provide funding for about €5.3 trillion of the total €12.1 trillion American mortgage market. Though they don't lend directly to home-owners, they bought the mortgages off the banks, which in turn allowed them to lend more money to more people. Evidently, when you're nearly half the total home-loan market you're deemed too big to fail.

The same is true today in Ireland: the Government could never let AIB or Bank of Ireland fail; to do so would devastate the economy. For this reason it creates a financial moral dilemma or what has come to be known as 'moral hazard'. Why? Because the banks themselves know they're too big to fail; so Eugene Sheehy and Brian Goggin can play the 'win-win' game. Bet heavily on the property market; if prices go up they win and can pay themselves huge bonuses; if, on the other hand, the market tanks and property prices fall heavily for several years in a row and the banks' bad debts rise, the Government will always bail them out should it ever come to that. Then they could resign, with massive sever ance packages. Either way they come out on top, with a bundle of money in cash, stock options and of course shares.

The last time there was a credit crisis based on excessive leverage was the credit mini-crisis in September 1998 caused by the collapse of the American hedge fund Long Term Capital Management. I remember it well, because back then the prices of anything with a 'credit' label dropped quite sharply, including AAA-rated Fannie Mae dollar-denominated bonds. I was working on the bond-trading floor of Morgan Stanley in London, and we were 'long' these bonds (we owned them). The yields or spreads on Fannie Mae rose as the prices came off, but other AAA-rated paper, such as the World Bank and European Investment Bank, stayed relatively expensive and their yields were largely unchanged. We were 'short' some of these, so we needed to buy them and sell the Fannie Mae ones. A colleague of mine, an American bond salesman who spoke Spanish, was having difficulty persuading a large bank in Madrid to do the trade with us, so he asked me to join the call with him, which I did. Within five minutes we had 'crossed' $200 million of benchmark ten-year EIB bonds that they sold us with another $200 million of the Fannie Mae ten-year bonds that we had, to sell to them. The net result was they kept the same rating on their investment but picked up an additional 25 basis points (+¼ per cent) of spread or yield. The big Spanish bank trusted me, because they read my weekly research reports and were convinced by my argument that, although the US agency was *not* explicitly guaranteed by the government, there was an implicit guarantee through funding arrangements and the 'too big to fail' case. Everyone got what they wanted out of the trade, so we were all happy.

This anecdote serves a valuable purpose, because a decade later the US authorities did indeed step in and support both agencies by buying shares in them and extending credit facilities to them that were normally reserved for the big commercial banks. Later, in early September 2008, they bailed them out completely by taking them over.

A strong precedent already exists in Ireland for Government support of a major retail bank. In 1985, AIB managed to persuade the Government, then headed by Dr Garret FitzGerald, to take over an insurance sub-sidiary, Insurance Corporation of Ireland, which had become technically insolvent. The Government wrote off the debts of ICI but was able to sell on the profitable life assurance part of the business to the Prudential Assurance Company, which later sold the life business to the Irish Permanent Building Society. AIB's directors at that time relayed a story (whether true or not) to the Government of the day that ICI's losses were becoming insurmountable and that this could cause AIB to fail, and if that happened the whole banking system would be in jeopardy. Whether or not it happened just like that is largely irrelevant: what is historical fact is that the Government bought ICI for the princely sum of £1, and AIB walked away from its investment in ICI without incurring any further liabilities. A precedent had been set. Anyone who believes that the Government wouldn't step in at the mere whiff of a collapse is delusional.

CONCLUSION

The global liquidity crunch has begun to unwind. Some $918 billion of write-downs by banks around the world has already taken place (October 2008), according to Bloomberg, a financial media company, with most of the pain being felt in the United States. A new potential ceiling for the total cost of the American sub-prime problem has been estimated at $2 trillion. Bill Gross, a well-known bond investor, said that banks there may end up writing off $1.3 trillion of bad debts, based solely on the housing slump there, which is now into its third year. On that basis, in mid-2008 we're half way through this crisis.

Don't be put off by the apparent complexity of the issue. Much of the information surrounding the global liquidity crunch is clouded by jargon. Once this jargon has been explained, it's merely a case of peeling back the layers of complexity. Each on their own is easily explainable. In this way, despite the convoluted nature of the issue, I have attempted to give you the big picture. This is what strategists who are employed by big banks do: they attempt to piece together the smaller pieces of the jigsaw puzzle and in doing so they reveal the bigger picture. Most of it is just common sense.

Already Irish commercial property yields have begun to gap more widely. In essence, the commercial sectors are about one year behind the residential property market. Stupidly low rental yields may have become a thing of the past, such as the 2 per cent average gross yields witnessed in Henry Street and Grafton Street in 2007. In July 2008 a large commercial property agent, CB Richard Ellis, came out with a report that, because of the credit crisis and liquidity crunch, it may be difficult to get financing; there's a dearth of buyers anyway at these lower yields. The net result is that values may be 50 per cent lower even in Grafton Street, Ireland's premier shopping district, as new investors typically demand yields of 4 per cent or more.

The onset of the global liquidity crunch has been the death knell of the trophy asset era. De-leveraging by financial institutions around the world will raise the price of credit for all, despite falling rates. Property as an investment asset is no different from any other asset: it all revolves around cash flows, money out and money in and the value of those cash flows.

What does all this mean for the average Irish property-buyer?

Global de-leveraging means that banks everywhere, including Irish banks, will be lending less money to fewer people, not only for mortgages but on credit cards, overdrafts, car loans etc. This process will last for a couple of years at least.

Put it another way: tighter credit standards at the lenders will result in reduced credit availability, which will result inevitably in lower house prices.

The estate agents and the other VIPs erroneously see reduced credit availability as the problem. It's not: in fact it's part of the solution. Many property market commentators view the lower availability of credit as a problem when they really ought to view it as a symptom of the underlying fundamental problem of too much household debt. The banks have lent too much of other people's money (leverage) in the past, now they need to rein in this excess. After all, it was the creation of excessive credit that caused the property bubble in the first place.

Think of it like an illness. The property market is plagued by the cancer of oversupply at exorbitant prices. The loss of credit availability is analogous to hair loss following chemotherapy and radiation treatment. Hair loss is not the problem: cancer is. In the same way, a lack of funding is not the problem: too many new homes with unattainable price tags are. Ultimately, prices will fall to an appropriate level, a level from which the market can heal itself. We're a long way off that point still—just as a patient for whom cancer has been correctly diagnosed knows that it takes a year of treatment before they can even dream of getting the all-clear. But, just as it's important to diagnose the problem early and to begin treatment straight away, the property market pundits have been living in denial for two years—from October 2006 to the end of 2008. The sooner the inevitable is accepted, the sooner sales will accelerate and house prices will bottom.

Chapter 29

Ireland's next top
MODEL

In America there's a popular reality television show called
'America's Next Top Model', where young women compete to win
a contract with a modelling agency and ultimately to pursue a
career in the fashion industry. In Britain, as with so many of the reality
shows, the format has been copied and they have 'Britain's Next Top
Model', now in its fifth year. Normally I don't watch reality shows
and remain bemused by the number of young people who become
obsessed with shows like 'Big Brother' and 'Celebrity Big Brother'. But
the 'top model' shows are a little different: the contestants are ordinary
people looking for a job in a particular industry that could elevate
them to fame and fortune.

I thought it would be a good idea if one of Ireland's television chan-
nels were to replicate the format, but with a bit of a twist. Instead of using
hopeful young models they could use Marketers who Openly Defy
Economic Logic, or MODELS. There are plenty of these in the banking,
broking and construction industries. In fact if such a show was put on,
the producers would be spoiled for choice, as there are so many potential
candidates.

The usual format is that there are three or four judges, each with
experience of the industry or some related field. Without a doubt our
panel would have to include, firstly, Dr Alan Ahearne, lecturer in economics at the J. E. Cairnes Graduate School of Business and Public Policy
at NUI, Galway, who consistently warned about the impending property
slump in his weekly column in the *Sunday Independent*. The second panel
member would have to be Professor Morgan Kelly of NUI, Dublin, for his
sheer brazenness in going against the establishment and especially for
getting right up the nose of the former Taoiseach, Bertie Ahern, whose
party engineered the second phase of the property boom (after 2002)
with pro-cyclical budgets at a time of plenty, the extension of the section
23 tax incentive at a time when the property market was already on fire,
and so on. (The list is endless.)

As the host is normally a former model, it makes the chairperson a difficult choice. The most suitable candidate by far, though, is somebody who has already had television experience, namely David McWilliams. Although technically David didn't defy economic logic, he did defy market logic by calling the market overvalued as far back as 2000, a time when demographic change and a rapidly rising economy, coupled with greater demand driven by cheap money, combined to propel the market spiral upwards. He has been proved to be correct, with the sole exception that he was a little premature, but he can be forgiven for that. The final reason, though, is that it would be nice to hear the man most vilified by the property pundits (yes, even more than Shane Ross) proclaiming his verdict on each of the contestants, just as the host in the reality show does.

Now all that's left to do is to find the most suitable candidates. We begin with the most obvious group, the estate agents.

GEOFF TUCKER (ECONOMIST, HOOKE AND MACDONALD)

Geoff is frequently heard on the air waves, both RTE Radio 1 and FM104, glorying in how affordable new-home ownership has become. Hooke and MacDonald are a specialist new-homes agency, so to be fair to him it is his business to talk up the market at every opportunity.

Geoff merits inclusion also because in early 2007, just before the stamp duty reform (a U-turn by Brian Cowen when he was Minister for Finance) he said that first-time buyers had to be quick and get back into the market before prices rose 3 per cent. Prices, of course, continued to fall, but this didn't stop him remaining upbeat on the market. Before that, in March 2007, he was the guest writer on the Daft Rental Report, and his outlook for the property market finished with this sentence:

> To sum up, the residential property market is performing well, particularly when compared to spring 2004 and 2005 rather than the overheated market environment dominated by spiralling prices in spring 2006. Bricks and mortar have consistently proved to be a reliable long-term investment—nothing has changed in this respect.

One thing *has* changed in this respect: property prices have fallen every single month since that comment was made. Sure, on a 100-year view Irish property may turn out to be a fantastic investment, but in economists' jargon 'long-term' equals ten years. On a ten-year view it has been shown that three or four years of price weakness—double what we've already experienced—followed by twice that period of sustainable positive price growth (say 5 per cent per year) would still leave 2016 property prices lower than they were in 2006.

By the end of 2007 Geoff was quoted in the *Irish Times,* in an article written by Edel Morgan, as saying that he foresaw that high rents would prompt more tenants to try to buy property in the New Year.

> I expect some increase in rents in 2008, albeit at a more moderate pace. It's fair to say the supply is going to be a bit tighter and we are not going to see as much new investor property becoming available.

Rents have been *falling* since the beginning of 2008. Just go and look at the weekly rental reports from www.irishpropertywatch.com, where you'll see that supply is anything but tight. He did say 'tighter'; tighter than what? Perhaps he meant tighter than the oversupply of the last two years. As regards new investor property becoming available, there are hundreds of new-home schemes around the country with thousands of unsold homes that developers and agents are desperate to offload on unsuspecting investors.

David: 'Geoff, you're in the running for Ireland's next top MODEL!'

KEN MACDONALD (MANAGING DIRECTOR, HOOKE AND MACDONALD)

One of the best-known cheerleaders for the Irish new-homes market is the managing director of Hooke and MacDonald.

Writing in the *Sunday Independent* in late March 2007, Ken defied economic logic with an article headed 'Property market's no house of cards.' But the most extraordinary part of his opinion piece was the paragraph in which he laid the foundation-stone of his own mis-perceptions.

> As one who has been involved in the Irish property market for 40 years and has experienced every type of market scenario, I am totally convinced that the market is currently in good shape and that anyone buying now will do extremely well in the years ahead. There is no better investment than Irish property at present, and I believe that I will be proved right in this conviction.

History has a cruel way of showing up foolish comments. So far he has been proved totally wrong in this conviction: ask anyone with negative equity who bought into the new-homes market in 2007 on the strength of his advice.

In the same article he heavily criticised those commentators who warned of the coming slump by saying:

> Why do we allow scaremongers and doomsayers with unfounded pessimism and unbridled negativity dictate our thinking and blunt consumer confidence?

The short answer is that Ireland is still a parliamentary democracy: it's not a police state. And by the way, people who talk up a declining market do more damage and cause more financial hardship than those who talk down a falling one. The latter group provide a useful economic function in speeding up the correction process.

To use Ken's own words, he has seriously misjudged the market and his predictions were totally irresponsible. But my favourite quotation, which not only defies economic logic but seeks also to reinvent economics, was his outlook for 2007 in the *Irish Times* on 7 December 2006, where he was quoted as saying:

> The price stability that entered the market in autumn 2006 will follow through for the next year. Price moderation will take the impact off any interest rate increases. Still, I feel that the spring market will be good. There is a pent-up demand out there; going on the level of enquiries we get on each development.

Property prices are stagnating, but rejoice, for viewings and enquiries are up. Best of all, though, is the new economic concept of 'pent-up demand'. This notion doesn't exist in the field of economics. Demand is always there at the right price, and people will buy anything if it's cheap enough. Just look at the German retailers Lidl. Once a week they print a sales brochure of items that will be for sale the following week. By lunchtime on Monday they're always sold out. The same is true when developers slash prices on unsold new homes by €100,000. They then sell what is needed to be sold in a single weekend; but they also devalue all the other properties in the same development and the surrounding area in the process. Right now there's enormous 'pent-up demand' for the new V-10 Ferrari F430 F1-Spyder at a price of €20,000. Unfortunately for all the petrol heads and Ferrari aficionados, the manufacturer insists on charging ten times that price. This 'pent-up demand', therefore, remains unsatisfied.

David: 'Congratulations, Ken! You have not only proved your worth as someone who repeatedly defies economic logic and has misinterpreted the principles of demand and supply but have managed to go one step further and invent a new economic oxymoron. You're definitely in the running for Ireland's next top MODEL!'

MARIE HUNT (DIRECTOR OF RESEARCH, CB RICHARD ELLIS)

In the middle of February 2008 it was reported that Marie Hunt was predicting a 0 per cent outcome for home prices by December 2008. She forecast that prices would fall until the summer, then level off and rise at the end of the year. As we shall learn in chapter 31, the leading bookmaker

Paddy Power quoted the odds of that happening at 12 to 1. It was unusual for Hunt to suddenly become a contrarian and go out on a limb like that. In CBRE's 2008 outlook, published on 8 January, she said:

> Forecasting property market performance in the current climate is extremely difficult. While we can monitor supply and demand with a reasonable degree of accuracy, influencing factors such as the performance of the Irish economy and the availability and cost of bank funding are largely dependent on what transpires in global economies and financial markets. While we believe that 2008 will be a challenging year for some sectors of the property market, we are confident that while the first half of the year will be slow, strong underlying fundamentals should ensure that momentum picks up as the year progresses.

How can you monitor 'demand' accurately when it's impossible to predict the Irish economy and the availability of credit? Then the dreaded 'strong underlying fundamentals' appear again. One of the three most-quoted phrases by the VIPs: the 'strong economy' (now actually in recession), 'demographics' (applications for PPS numbers falling and the ESRI predicting net emigration of 50,000 next year), and of course the perennial 'strong fundamentals' (the fundamentals in both the residential and the commercial property market couldn't be worse: excess supply and a growing backlog at a time of reduced sales activity).

> Many investors and developers will see 2008 as a year of good buying opportunities. However, the key ingredient that will drive transactional activity is confidence and this to a large extent will be determined by wider global factors, which at this point are difficult to predict.

I don't get that last statement. Buying is dependent on confidence, and this is another factor that is difficult to predict. So why mention it?

David: 'Marie, you've just about scraped through this last round, thanks to your perpetual optimism at a time when all the economic indicators have turned south. You nearly let the side down on 2 July 2008 when your firm reported that Grafton Street prices may be worth 50 per cent less because of the higher investor demand for yield. However, you're still in the running for Ireland's next top MODEL!'

MARIAN FINNEGAN (CHIEF ECONOMIST, SHERRY FITZGERALD)

Marian has been around longer than most but has become very quiet of late. Previously you could expect to see her quoted weekly or certainly monthly, but no more. At the beginning of the year in her 2008 outlook Marian was quoted as saying:

> 2007 was undoubtedly a challenging year for the property market but the outlook for 2008 is somewhat brighter. The combination of the ending of speculation in relation to stamp duty, greater certainty in terms of the interest rate environment and a reduction in the supply of new product on the market will facilitate a more robust year in 2008. That said we do not anticipate an immediate revival in price performance, rather a gradual improvement in market sentiment and demand trends. Overall, the fundamentals underpinning this market remain sound. We have a sound economic base with a young dynamic population operating in a strong European economy, factors which will underwrite the performance of the property market in the medium term.

Again the three 'reliable factors' are mentioned: the 'sound economy' (used to be 'strong'), sound fundamentals (used to be 'strong' too), and young population. She has perfected the art of saying nothing at all while using lots of words. One could be forgiven for attributing the same quotation to a politician like Mícheál Martin TD, a master of speaking endlessly without saying anything concrete. No longer do we have the outlook for this year: as we saw in an earlier chapter, Marian doesn't deign to use fixed terminology like 'this year' or '2008' or 'next year' but rather 'the medium term'. And what is the definition of the medium term? Whatever she chooses it to be.

Marian has undergone a 'road to Damascus' conversion in recent months. She was quoted in the *Sunday Business Post* on 6 July 2008 as saying:

> If one takes in consideration CPI [consumer price index] inflation, the real price deflation is closer to 25 per cent, a factor which suggests that the current phase of price correction is much more advanced than many commentators or other indices suggest. This bodes well for price realignment in the short to medium term.

When estate agents began talking about inflation-adjusted house prices in 'real' terms and then compound this by making a virtue out of price falls, it's not just patronising, it's hypocritical, especially for someone who repeatedly underestimated the capital value appreciation in the boom years and has repeatedly underestimated the subsequent falls during the slump years.

David: 'Marian, you're still in contention, not so much for defying economic logic as for failing to use any at all. Your general vagueness and non-committal response to market events ensures that you're definitely in the running for Ireland's next top MODEL!'

DR JOHN MCCARTNEY (FORMER HEAD OF RESEARCH, LISNEY)

John McCartney is an economist and former head of research at Lisney, the large estate agents. Unlike Marian Finnegan, he still featured regularly in the papers in 2008 and was a frequent commentator on the state of the market. He was also quoted in the same *Sunday Business Post* article as saying:

> Getting credit is one of the main issues facing buyers in this market. It's hitting first-time buyers the most. But those first-time buyers who are able to get assistance from their parents are not in a bad position to buy in a more affordable climate.

Perhaps I'm wrong, but was it not the fact that prices became too expensive in the first place that forced parental assistance to become such a prominent feature of the market? This only exacerbated affordability for the majority who don't have a wealthy mammy or daddy. If the only people in a position to buy are those first-time buyers with rich parents, maybe the parents would prefer that their children wait and see and not catch a falling knife. After all, if they're rich enough to donate the deposit—10 to 20 per cent of the purchase price—they're surely more market-savvy about investing at the wrong time.

Recall that McCartney was the economist who wrote in 2007 that the wrong people were occupying the wrong homes and that supply imbalances were localised. On 16 March 2008 he wrote an article for the *Sunday Independent* criticising Alan Ahearne's view on the reduced demand requirement. We've covered this already, but there's one aspect of that article that deserves additional comment. Firstly, let's refresh our memories.

> Writing in the *Sunday Independent* two weeks ago, [the] Galway economist Alan Ahearne suggested a continuing need for 22,000 housing units per annum. In arriving at this figure, his methodology was simple. He assumed 1½ per cent population growth, which equates to an increase of about 65,000 persons per annum. He then simply divided by three, as this approximates the average number of persons per household. Allowing for replacement houses and second homes, Dr Ahearne concedes that this figure could go a little higher than 22,000, but insists that our long-term housing requirement is less than 30,000. While the methodology underpinning these calculations is appealingly simple, it may also be seriously flawed. Surely, our additional housing requirement depends not on average household size, but rather on the

size of newly formed households? This makes a critical difference to our sums.

John then went on to talk about his demand figure, which was based on a population growth of smaller households—singletons and couples—as well as a requirement for building 7,000 new replacement homes (to replace derelict ones)—an absurdly high figure for a country where half the homes are now less than twenty years old. He also assumed that the annual requirement for second homes was 15 per cent (equal to the vacancy rate on census night—convenient, that), even though the Economic and Social Research Institute published a figure for holiday homes of less than 3 per cent in 2006. He arrived at an annual demand of 50,000, which was completely flawed, for the reasons mentioned. He certainly defied economic logic on that score.

But he does make an interesting point about future demand being based on 'household formation'. This is true. Now, without getting into a raft of statistics about average household sizes and international comparisons and all that, why not step back, use proper economic theory and ask ourselves what is the number 1 determinant of new-household formation.

The answer is of course—'jobs!' A 27-year-old with no job and no income doesn't rush out and buy a new home. But a 25-year-old graduate with a good job, earning €50,000 a year after three years working for a big company, no longer wishes to live at home with their parents. This over-simplistic example is true on a macro-economic basis. Young people with new jobs earning good salaries buy new homes. The key to household formation is more young people with jobs, and not just more young people, full stop. Any economist worth their salt will tell you that during an economic slowdown the first thing people worry about is their job, then their pay, the cost of living, and so on down the line. With the unemployment rate jumping by half in one year alone, that's going to be a bigger determinant of new-household formation.

David: 'For openly defying a panel member, using wacky sums that still don't even come close to the number of new homes being built, for telling us that it was better to buy than to rent a year ago, for telling us that supply imbalances have occurred in the wrong places and for repeatedly using biased and completely unbalanced assumptions, John, you remain a leading contender to be Ireland's next top MODEL!'

PAUL MURGATROYD (ECONOMIST, DOUGLAS NEWMAN GOOD)

Paul Murgatroyd said in the *Sunday Business Post* in mid-February 2008 that there had been evidence of a pick-up since Christmas.

That wouldn't have been too difficult seeing as activity was nonexistent in the last quarter of 2007, but we are now seeing first-time buyers out viewing properties. Most of these buyers are already loan-approved and have been for several months—many were in the market last summer but they decided to rent until the market steadied. We are now seeing price reductions in play and first-time buyers are semiseriously starting to buy and make bids, albeit under the asking prices.

What does 'semiserious' mean? If first-time buyers are bidding below the asking price, that means they're expecting further price falls or are not happy with present price levels. He also admits that sales activity in the period October to December 2007 was nil.

Two years ago, in July 2006, Paul was cited in a British newspaper with the heading 'First time buyers to gain from gradual slowdown of house prices in Ireland.' He was quoted as saying:

We do seem to be moving into a period of soft landing. The downturn, everything will be fine scenario we have been hearing about, it looks like it is coming to fruition. We are moving into a soft landing and stabilising of house price growth, but certainly there is no crash or big dip. The balances of power are shifting back to the buyer from the vendor slightly but the downside is that there is the double-edged sword of raising increased sums to fund the buying and paying back loans.

The article went on to say:

Mr Murgatroyd also warned that first time buyers sat on their hands in 2001 expecting prices to keep on falling but in the first quarter of 2002 prices saw a 6.5% rise, making up all the ground that was lost in the previous year.

This was the classic fear tactic used by the estate agents. If you wait too long when prices head south you may miss the boat after the much-vaunted turnaround. Earlier he mentioned the 'soft landing' scenario, which is no longer mentioned by estate agents, for some strange reason.

David: 'Paul, you definitely remain in the race to become Ireland's next top MODEL!'

WADE WISE AND RONAN O'HARA (SAVILLS HOK RESIDENTIAL)
This double act of Wade Wise, director of Savills HOK Residential, and Ronan O'Hara, manager of the Dún Laoghaire branch (who appeared earlier in the chapter on Top of the Drops), were involved with a large period house in Killiney, Co. Dublin, called 'Eirene'.

First off, in the Savills HOK property outlook for spring 2008, a snazzy colour supplement in the *Irish Times,* Wade Wise used a large photograph of the property as a backdrop to his outlook with the heading: 'Buyer confidence returns to the market.' The caption under the photograph was 'With more people out viewing, and less available properties, we believe that the market has found equilibrium.'

So the property slump is officially over. Hurray! But why then did they slash the price of the property that takes up a third of the page from €6 million to €4.15 million in a matter of months following this publication if the market had found equilibrium?

We're back to the dreaded 'viewings are up' nonsense. And we're told there are fewer available properties. Has Wade not been looking at the Daft reports, showing that the supply has increased to sixteen months' normal market sales? Does he not realise that fewer properties are coming onto the market because even fewer are selling? To predict the bottom in any market is downright dangerous; you're going to be wrong 99 per cent of the time.

We have already discussed Ronan O'Hara's appearance on the 'Capital D' programme that featured this house in Killiney, but before that he was quoted in the *Sunday Business Post* on 17 February 2008 in an article by Michelle Devane headed 'Buyers reclaim the market' as saying:

> There is a shortage now of new build first-time buyer properties because the developers have halted all their schemes, so first-time purchasers are looking towards the second-hand market.

What shortage is he talking about? Not in Ireland, surely! He should jump into a car with one of his colleagues and visit a development by one of Savills HOK's bigger clients, like the Carrickmines Park development, or the Grange in Stillorgan, or Levmoss Park at the Gallops. There's definitely no shortage of first-time buyer properties: there are thousands of them for sale, many not a million miles from the Dún Laoghaire branch of Savills HOK.

David: 'Wade and Ronan, you make a great double act; but why employ two economists if you're not prepared to use them? It was a bold move to call the bottom of the market—a little premature, though. You're both through to the next round of Ireland's next top MODEL!'

TOM PARLON (DIRECTOR-GENERAL, CONSTRUCTION INDUSTRY FEDERATION)

What happens when the electorate fails to re-elect a former Government junior minister? He gets a plum job at the Construction Industry Federation and as a lobbyist for the building industry.

The biggest problem I have with Tom Parlon is not that he went on 'Questions and Answers' in early 2008 to talk about rents being up at an annual pace of 12 or 20 per cent in some cases—a figure that was based on data for October 2007 and when rents were actually falling in money terms at the time he appeared—but the incessant chanting that the economy needs 60,000 new homes per year. Indeed up to July 2008 the Construction Industry Federation's web site used the words 'The Irish central bank estimates demand in excess of 60,000 units.' The most recent CIF Construction Activity Report for 2007 contains a section on the residential market. It states:

> There is widely acknowledged to be a demand for some 60,000 houses per annum over the medium term. A question which is currently occupying the minds of commentators is the point at which that level will be reached. It is likely that while 2008 will see further significant reductions in the production of housing to perhaps 45,000, a plateau of supply and demand will be achieved in 2009. From that point, ensuring a stable supply of new homes in the right location will be the main priority for the industry.

Now, this topic has already been discussed at length in this book, but it's the number 1 mistake made by the VIPS, the estate agents and their pundits. An estimate made by the Economic and Social Research Institute a decade ago, probably drawn from the Bacon Reports, said that 60,000 new homes per year would be needed because of the explosion in population growth at that time. It didn't necessarily equate to a demand for 60,000 new dwellings per year *ad infinitum*.

Usually estimates are made for a particular period. Demand figures change as the market dynamics change. A quick example in 2008 was the response of airlines to higher oil prices, with both Aer Lingus and Ryanair curtailing routes and Europe's lowest-cost airline mothballing eighteen planes and reducing its staff by five hundred. As the chief executive of Ryanair, Michael O'Leary, said, if there were going to be 500,000 fewer passengers flying out of Dublin on Ryanair flights in the later part of that year, there would be less demand for staff.

When will this penny drop with the estate agents? Too many homes were built between 2004 and 2007. Many of the homes built in recent years remain unsold. There's a supply overhang, just as there is in the United States. The annual demand estimate needs to be revised in the light of all this.

David: 'Tom, for repeatedly defying the most basic principle of economics, that of supply and demand, assuming always that supply *equals* demand, you remain in contention to be Ireland's next top MODEL!'

HUBERT FITZPATRICK (DIRECTOR, IRISH HOME BUILDERS' ASSOCIATION)

The Irish Home Builders' Association is a sister-organisation of the Construction Industry Federation. Its director, Hubert Fitzpatrick, said in November 2007 in an interview with Barry O'Halloran, under the heading 'CIF warns [that] house building may fall sharply in 2008':

> Its director of housing, Hubert Fitzpatrick, warned yesterday that if completions slipped below this figure it would take time for the industry to get back up to the point where it would be able to meet this demand. We're going to end up with an imbalance in supply and demand, he said.

Em, we already have a massive imbalance between too much supply and too little demand. The old 'supply tap' fear tactic won't work any more. The fundamentals have been reversed.

David: 'Hubert, for telling us all what we already knew a year ago, because of the sharp drop in new housing starts and for consistently failing to scare up enough demand to make any dent in the supply overhang, you can join Tom and the others back at the MODEL house!'

ALAN COOKE (CHIEF EXECUTIVE, IRISH AUCTIONEERS' AND VALUERS' INSTITUTE)

At the end of October 2007 Alan Cooke published an attack on David McWilliams in the *Sunday Business Post* with the tag line 'Have we discovered the limit of David McWilliams's enormous talents?' He went on to criticise an article David had written in the same paper a week earlier.

> McWilliams's unique insight into the nature of property valuations (21/10/07) suggested that, because the residential property market has softened marginally, every property valuation carried out previously was 'wrong' and every valuation overvalued the asset. Property values fluctuate and, while the pace will vary and may even reverse in the short term, the long-term graph is going inexorably upwards. A valuation is a snapshot of value on a particular day—it is not a moving picture. Lenders want to know what the property will fetch on the date of valuation, and that is what a qualified valuer will provide.
>
> McWilliams seems to imply that a valuation, once given, should hold true in all future circumstances or fall short of his own perception of correctness. DIT, LIT and GMIT had best provide a new piece of equipment for their graduate Valuers: a crystal ball. Perhaps McWilliams will lend them his.

Now, there's nothing wrong with sarcasm as long as it's intelligent. So let's analyse Cooke's comments objectively and constructively. Property values fluctuate. This is true, and they also trend over time. However, Alan should note that when I worked for Savills HOK in 2007 property prices were only allowed to go up. One small article in the *Independent* that said they might end the year below where they began and I was left no choice but to resign, and that was the end of my short career at a member-firm of the Irish Auctioneers' and Valuers' Institute.

Nobody has a problem with a valuation being a point figure in time and therefore having a short shelf life. Perhaps the IAVI should ask its members to put a time limit on all valuations, say ninety days, and after that a new valuation is required. But I don't recall David McWilliams being summoned to the National Consumer Agency's office because of sharp practice and hugely misreporting property results. (One example used by the NCA was a home that sold for €620,000 being reported by an IAVI member in the press with a price 'in the region of €950,000.')

Alan's comments were that property prices may reverse in the short term; and in the financial markets as well as the world of economics the 'short term' is a period of one year or less.

During the latter part of 2001 there was a five-month period when residential property prices did fall, up to January 2002. That was then; this is now. Prices have been falling continuously now for almost two years, month after month. And as for the long-term graph, again 'long term' is usually taken to mean a period of ten years or more. I've shown throughout this book that three to four years of famine followed by six to seven years of feast could well leave home prices in 2016 back where they were in 2006. Alan no doubt would disagree. But that's fine, because we'll all see in due course who is right and who is wrong.

David McWilliams was right about the speculative property bubble, he was right about the ensuing bear market correction, he was wrong merely about the timing, whereas many of Cooke's IAVI members were wrong on all these fronts.

In December 2006, when the *Irish Times* asked a group of market pundits to express their views on the outlook for 2007, this is what Alan Cooke had to say:

The market went ape in the first quarter—you had 25 per cent increases in some areas and as a result vendors' expectations went wild. Those who went to sell in the autumn got a rude awakening. The correction was justified. Money had lost its value. Now that we have all had a wake-up call we can move on. Next year, prices won't go down, but there won't be major growth, though there will be pockets of strength. The truth about interest rates is that money is still cheap.

I totally agree with the first and last points: that the euphoric increase in early 2006 was too good to last, and that interest rates were still low and money still cheap by historical standards. But I totally disagree with his comment that 'prices won't go down' in 2007. What happened to the IAVI's crystal ball back then? And where are the 'pockets of strength'? The entire market fell in 2007, and it was only a question of which areas saw prices fall the most. That's a historical fact. Many prospective buyers look to the IAVI for guidance during times of market uncertainty. Alan's advice was poor advice. If anyone had bought on the strength of this implicit price guarantee they could certainly be facing financial hardship. Has Alan Cooke ever suffered 35 per cent negative equity for up to six years? I know I have, and it's not very pleasant.

David: 'Alan, you're through to the next round!'

KEVIN O'CONNOR (JOURNALIST, *IRISH TIMES*)

Many horrendously bad articles have been written about the property market, but on Thursday 22 November 2007 possibly the worst piece of tendentious claptrap ever written by an Irish person appeared in the *Irish Times* under the headline 'Why the baby-in-the-buggy factor makes property best bet long-term,' with the tag line 'What do you get when you cross 150,000 baby buggies with 150,000 impending immigrants? A leap in property values starting around 2009.'

But the article was so badly written that it would be unfair to the other contestants to even mention it any further.

David: 'Kevin who? Next contestant, please!'

ANNETTE HUGHES (DIRECTOR, DKM ECONOMIC CONSULTANTS)

Anyone who has ever bought the *Irish Property Buyer* or who has heard of the EBS-DKM affordability index will know who Annette Hughes is. She is a director of DKM and a former lecturer in economics at the University of Limerick. She has been working at DKM Economic Consultants since 1993 and is well versed in the construction industry and the housing market. So imagine my surprise when I read in the April 2008 edition of *Irish Property Buyer* that, taking a medium-term view, it was cheaper to buy than to rent after only three years. She began by outlining her model.

The model is based on a set of assumptions for the key variables which impact on the decision to buy or rent. We begin with the assumption that the first-time buyer couple has the initial deposit (10 per cent of purchase price) and is faced with either using it to purchase a starter home, or investing it and renting a property instead. This is important to ensure that both options are consistent and comparable. We also assume that the first-time buyer couple typically stays in their first home for seven years, based on information received from EBS. Seven years is also the term for the state's maximum mortgage interest relief for first-time buyers.

So far so good—all commonsense stuff; but then the logic gets thrown out the window. A whole range of assumptions was made about a 35-year mortgage, interest rates falling back so that mortgage rates fall to 4½ per cent within two years, and so on. However, an assumption for growth in property prices was made for 2008 of −10 per cent! So as long as rental yields were less than 10 per cent it's cheaper to rent for the first year, and therefore the buyer should wait one year and then buy. Under this model the profit-and-loss profile for the buyer as opposed to the renter would be hugely superior if they did nothing for a year or rented—notwithstanding that most of the model assumptions were barmy: rents rising while property prices fell (the opposite is happening), mortgage rates falling and not rising (as they did in July, three months later), that the buyer must buy today, etc.

Another assumption on the renter side of the equation was that they invest their savings (deposit) at an interest rate 2 per cent below the current mortgage rate. You don't have to be a genius to work out that there's a continuing liquidity crunch and global credit crisis and that banks are offering savers special rates that are a lot more than the average mortgage rate.

David: 'Annette, you'll never live it down, even using your own flawed assumptions. Your own model suggested that it was more profitable to wait a year before purchase than to buy in 2008. You defied your own logic as well as economic logic. You're through to the next round and are still in contention to be Ireland's next top MODEL!'

Side note: A week after the publication of this piece a guest on the Marian Finucane programme on RTE Radio 1 (presented by Rachael English that day), when discussing the newspaper stories for that weekend, said she was surprised that none of the papers picked up on this story that it was 'now cheaper to buy than to rent—fact!'

This kind of ignorance knows no bounds, but it's a constant reminder to me of Pat Moynihan, a former Speaker of the US House of Representatives, when he said, 'Everyone is entitled to their own opinions, but they are not entitled to their own facts.' I know I've probably used this quotation already, but it's so apt that it's worth reiterating. Unfortunately, many ordinary folk in Ireland treat all opinions as facts, especially when they see them in print.

DR DAN MCLAUGHLIN (CHIEF ECONOMIST, BANK OF

IRELAND) AND AUSTIN HUGHES (ECONOMIST, KBC IRELAND)

Dan McLaughlin is chief economist at Bank of Ireland, and Austin Hughes is an economist at KBC Ireland (known previously as IIB Homeloans). There's so much to say about these two Über-bulls on the economy and of course the residential property market; but there's one area where they both got it catastrophically wrong during 2008 and subsequently had to make much undignified U-turns. (Not a pleasant thing when you're a well-known face in almost every home in the land, thanks to regular appearances on the television news.) Without labouring the point, both predicted that interest rates would be cut substantially by mid-2008. Dan said in January 2008 that the European Central Bank would cut by 0.5 to 3.5 per cent, but Austin went one step further in February by forecasting three rate cuts to 3.25 per cent. Both had forecast euro zone rates to peak at 3.5 per cent a full year earlier. Needless to say, Jean-Claude Trichet and the European Central Bank moved in the opposite direction.

Following the European Central Bank rate rise in July 2008 to 4¼ per cent, both recanted and changed their interest-rate tunes. Obviously ECB rates did start to fall in October, especially after the spectacular collapse of an American investment bank, Lehman Brothers, on 19 September. However, like the oncologist who informs their terminally ill patient that they have but six months left to live, they cannot claim foresight when a week later the same patient gets run over by a bus!

The moral of this tale is simple. When there is a large, well-developed market for interest rate futures, where huge investors place enormous money bets on where interest rates are likely to be, then you should adopt the follow-the-money rule and not go out on a limb. If you do go out on a limb for a specific reason and you believe in that reason, then stay there if you really believe that you're correct.

In his July outlook piece Dan McLaughlin said: 'A fall in oil prices and lower interest rates would lead to stronger growth than forecast, but neither is guaranteed.' Both rates and oil prices did actually fall, and by a lot! So why then did Dr McLaughlin shave 1.6 per cent off his 2008 growth forecast later in the year and 2.5 per cent off the 2009 prediction? Between July and November, Austin Hughes revised downwards his 2008 economic forecast by 2 per cent, and he trimmed the 2009 one by 0.8 per cent.

There's no need to say any more on the subject, as Michael Hennigan, founder and editor of *Finfacts*, does a pretty good job of keeping these two in check when their outlandish forecasts cut against the grain from time to time.

David: 'Dan and Austin, for defying the laws of monetary policy in the face of rising inflation and for doubting the "price stability" credentials of Jean-Claude Trichet last spring, you're both still in contention to be

Ireland's next top MODEL!'

EUNAN KING (SENIOR ECONOMIST, NCB STOCKBROKERS)

On the television programme 'Prime Time' on 7 June 2007 Eunan King made some remarkable claims. Firstly, when Mark Little spoke about the notion of a perfect storm and competitiveness being eroded, Eunan jumped in and said:

> Competitiveness has not been eroded. There is only talk of crisis. What's the evidence? The data we have for the first quarter are very strong.

He went on to talk about backward-looking factors, such as historical retail sales, historical car sales (both aided by the SSIA effect) and unemployment remaining static. Then the other panel member, Marc Coleman, complained that Ireland was over-dependent on the construction industry, just as Germany had been in the early nineties, when construction accounted for 12 per cent of economic output.

Mark Little rephrased this point as a question, whether Ireland was abnormally dependent on property and construction.

> We're not, because we're a very young population, we're growing employment at a tremendous rate. We need a lot of office space for that. We need a lot of accommodation for our young population, and that's an influence that's going to continue for most of the next ten years. The fundamental thing that has been driving this economy is not suddenly going to dry up, simply because there is some kind of issue about stamp duty and we start talking about an economic crisis. There isn't a crisis.

Oh, yes, there is. It's here, and young people don't buy homes, rather the problem is of young people with jobs earning real money that's not being gobbled up by inflation. You see, NCB were one of the biggest proponents of the residential property boom. They also produced '20:20 Vision', which essentially explained the property boom solely using demographic data.

Actually Marc Coleman responded to his remarks by saying, yes, we do have a young population, but we have more people employed in construction than we have in manufacturing, and Ireland has double the European average in the number of workers engaged in the building industry. That was economic logic.

David: 'Eunan, for suggesting that the demographic explosion will last for another ten years, fuelling the speculative fires of property-price growth in the face of a real looming crisis, you've certainly earned a place in the running for Ireland's next top MODEL!'

EUGENE SHEEHY (CHIEF EXECUTIVE OFFICER, AIB)
The chief executive officer of AIB lashed out at the negative commentary on the economy at a lunch organised by the Small Firms Association in early November 2007.

> Almost all of the negative comment comes from within Ireland. We are dealing very consistently now with a negative perception of the country, and all familiar with clichés know that perception can become reality.

All of this is indeed true, for who knows better what is going on in the economy than commentators who live in the country? He went on to list what he believed to be economic positives, quoting from the most recent Central Bank quarterly report.

> Economic fundamentals—a good budgetary position, strong employment growth, an adaptable economy—continue to be sound . . . Domestically, the housing sector is adjusting from its very strong performance in recent years towards a more sustainable level of activity.

All right, then, one by one. Firstly, the budgetary position had deteriorated in late 2007 and even more rapidly in early 2008. Secondly, unemployment had risen from 3.9 to 4.7 per cent at the time of his comments (and thereafter to 7.1 per cent)—the fastest jump in the unemployment rate for decades. Thirdly, with regard to an adaptable economy, Irish growth has slowed by more than the rest of the European Union, the euro zone and the rest of the world, while the Irish share of foreign direct investment was falling and there was a continuation of the secular decline in exports and the trade surplus. Finally, with regard to the point about the property market—well, falling prices and recessionary output levels don't smack of 'sustainable activity' in economists' jargon.

David: 'Eugene, for attempting to talk up a declining economy when all the indicators are against you, you can go forward to the next round!'

BRIAN GOGGIN (CHIEF EXECUTIVE OFFICER, BANK OF IRELAND)
You can't include the chief executive of one of Ireland's two main banks without the other.

> We have a growing population, full employment, strong job creation, rising household income, a high savings ratio, together with strong retail sales and industrial production. This economy is in great shape,

and the outlook remains positive.

Those comments were made by Brian Goggin at a press conference to discuss the bank's results in 2007. The population bit is correct. The full employment comment is economically incorrect, as the rule of thumb for 'full employment' is an unemployment rate of 4 per cent or less. As far as rising household income is concerned, well, yes, it's rising, just not as fast as inflation or the price of goods in the shops (so in real terms it fell during 2007—by about a fifth of 1 per cent, but a fall nonetheless). Retail sales have fallen off a cliff, the economy is flabby and not in great shape, with a bloated public sector and declining productivity, while the outlook is decidedly uncertain.

David: 'Brian, what can we say that hasn't already been said? Go and sit with Eugene and compare salaries. You're still a contender for Ireland's next top MODEL!'

There were many more candidates who made it to the qualifying rounds, but in the interests of time, space and sanity we have to draw a line here.

Many of the aforementioned candidates had been openly critical of any commentator who previously dared to question the Irish economic miracle or the perceived wisdom that the property boom would last for ever.

(To discover who eventually won the title of Ireland's next top MODEL you'll have to wait for *Ireland's House Party, 2: Residential Contagion: A Global Phenomenon*.)

Chapter 30
The Gazunderer's apprentice

27 JANUARY 2008

It was a Sunday morning, and a friend of mine phoned and asked me what I was up to. Was I free to go and look at property with him that afternoon? It was midday and I had just finished going through the Sunday papers, so I said, 'Sure; where do you want to go?' He said, 'Don't worry; I'll pick you up in fifteen minutes.'

My friend—for the purpose of this story let's call him Andy—already owned several properties, and he owned a property-related business in Cork. Sure enough, within a few minutes he was in the car outside the apartment in Dalkey where I was living at the time. Despite owning several properties in Cork and abroad, Andy didn't own any in Dublin, even though he was living there, but was renting a town house in Sandycove, just down the road.

We headed off towards Blackrock. 'I bought an apartment,' he said.

I replied, 'That was quick, seeing you were only talking about buying one in Dublin last week.'

He said, 'Yeah, I know. I'm thirty-two years old, I own several properties but I'm living in rented accommodation myself. I want to get my own place that I can live in for a few years before I settle down.'

'But you know my opinion regarding the Irish property market,' I replied. 'There's another two to three years of falling prices yet before the market stabilises and before you'll see a real recovery . . . Where have you bought?'

'Near Mount Merrion Avenue.'

'Yes,' I said. 'I'm from Blackrock, so I know that area really well.'

'Well, I put a deposit down on one of the apartments there. It's a two-bedroom 900-square-foot apartment with a balcony. It's nice, it's in a gated community, with no designated car spaces and a night watchman. I went and had a look at it on Friday and stuck a €20,000 booking deposit down. The asking price was €590,000, but I put in a low offer of €520,000, and they accepted it.'

'So it's a two-bed apartment,' I replied. 'But you know my opinion on two-bed apartments. There's a glut of them on the market at the moment. It'll take years to clear the backlog. Sure, just go up to the top of the avenue, turn left, and five minutes further up the Stillorgan dual carriageway you'll find a ton of new apartments that the developers can't shift, like Beechwood, or the Grange. Or just go across to Sandyford Industrial Estate, where they've begun building 4,800 new apartments in blocks up to twenty-four storeys high. The market is going to be saturated with two-bedroom apartments in that area. If you really need to buy a place why don't you buy a three-bedroom semi-detached house? You're far better off getting a starter-family home that you can shift on again in two to three years' time, plus the price difference isn't that much greater. What's your budget? How far can you go up to?'

'€700,000 to €750,000,' he said.

'Look,' I said, 'you're mad. You're not short of a few bob. For your budget you can get a much bigger property than that. Do you want me to give you a hand to look for a place? It'll be good research for my book, because I'm already doing a load of research as it is. I've got spreadsheets up the Wazoo, with all the property prices around the country, month by month, including all the price drops over the last year. I can tell you which properties have been on the market for a year or more. And I can even tell you which properties are the ones where the asking price has been dropped by the seller several times already.'

We arrived shortly before lunchtime and pulled into the car park. 'It's the first block on the right,' he said. We drove to the end of the car park and pulled up directly underneath the apartment.

'Do you have the keys? Can we go inside?' I said.

'No . . . What do you think?' he asked.

'It's a good location and a nice area, but it's a hell of a lot of money for a two-bed. Okay, you'll have no problem letting this in the future, and you could probably get about €1,400 per month quite easily, as it's so close to Blackrock, only ten minutes' walk to the DART station and a short stroll to Frascati Centre. Great if you need to go to Marks and Spencer to get your food shopping etc. But it's a lot of bread. I mean, half a million for an apartment—you'd be better off buying a house, especially if you were only thinking about living in the place for a couple of years.' I didn't want him to buy a flat for more than half a million euros, even if it had been substantially reduced in price.

We jumped back into the car and headed down to Blackrock. After brunch we headed across the road to the new Starbuck's, built on the site of the old post office. We grabbed a couple of large lattes and headed out to the back, facing out to the sea. I was determined that I was going to change his mind on this. There was a lot for sale at that time. It was a buyer's market, and he should take full advantage of this.

GAZUNDERING

'Do you know what gazundering is?' I asked. He had never heard that expression before. 'Have you heard of gazumping?' Of course he knew what gazumping was. The word 'gazump' is believed to come from the Yiddish word *gezumph*, which means to cheat or steal. In property transactions, being gazumped is where someone else takes your property by tempting the seller with a better offer, even after they've agreed the sale with you. It happens when there's a fast market with lots of euphoria, and people bid against each other until it becomes ridiculous. This was a common phenomenon in the British property market back in the late 1980s.

Well, I explained, gazundering is the exact opposite of gazumping. Instead of one seller and many buyers, all vying to get their hands on the same property, there's a dearth of buyers and lots of properties on the market. ('Cash is king,' as they say, or 'The golden rule is that he who has the gold makes the rules.') In those circumstances the buyer is in total control, and they're certainly in the driving seat when it comes to price. What happens is that they first agree a sale price with the seller. Next they start the paperwork and pay a booking deposit. Then, just before the conveyancing takes place, often on the steps of the solicitor's office, they threaten to pull out of the deal completely unless the seller accepts a new, lower price. When this happens, the seller has been gazundered!

This is a phenomenon that everybody will see more of in 2008 and 2009. Often it may be completely unintentional on the part of the potential buyer, simply because they panic at the time of signing the contract—a sort of pre-purchase dissonance, if you will. They get cold feet because they think if they wait a bit longer they'll probably get a much better price. After all, they've already waited a year or so, and that paid off, so why not wait a bit longer? The seller then panics and comes back with a counter-offer that's just too good to refuse. They're so desperate to sell that they'll take any price, no matter how low it is, especially if they're in a chain; and anyway, they've already negotiated a good discount on the property they're purchasing. As the expression goes, 'net-net': they're still better off, despite the annoyance of being financially blackmailed by the buyer.

THE SHORTLIST

I persuaded Andy to let me help in his endeavour to find a new place to live. 'Why don't we take only one day this week? You set aside the time,' I said, 'and we'll go and look at half a dozen or more properties.' So it was all set.

Looking solely at the South Dublin area, I went about picking out several properties, ranging in price from €560,000 to €950,000. It didn't really matter if any of the asking prices were above his budget, as we had agreed that he would be low-bidding them all anyway, to see what gives. When we say 'low-bidding' we mean that he would be making offers that were at least 15 per cent below the asking price. We had agreed that Sunday that if he did buy it would be at 2009 or 2010 prices, if you catch my drift. This was at my behest. I insisted that if he was going to bite the bullet and buy in this weak market then he should at least immunise himself from further price declines by getting a good bargain today. I mean, I have no problem with people proceeding in a buyer's market, as long as they know the facts and negotiate a substantial discount. That's only a form of insurance against further falls in the market this year or next. It's only common sense. This appears to be happening now in the market anyway and possibly explains some of the big price drops.

So, on the morning of 31 January, Andy collected me in Dalkey and we headed off to our first port of call: Blackrock. I'd spoken to an agent the day before and he told me about a new listing in Barclay Court, opposite Maxwell Motors, the BMW garage. It was a four-bedroom semi-detached 1980s-style, quite bland, even ugly. This was a small housing estate that was like a mini concrete jungle. The location was good, but this 1,200-square-foot property was coming on the market looking for €750,000, so it was definitely not cheap. Marks out of ten? It would be a push to go past four. We didn't hang around long and decided we would go directly to our second stop, which was only a few minutes away in Stradbrook.

It didn't take us long to get to Rowanbyrn, opposite Stradbrook Road, just before Dean's Grange. We were early, so we decided to park the car and go for a coffee, then walk around and get a feel for the area. There were two properties we had to view here. The first one was a three-bedroom semi-detached 1,250-square-foot property, and the acting agents were the Blackrock office of Savills HOK. While we were strolling around we received a call from one of the women at the office to tell us that we couldn't view the property that day, because the owner was sick.

Don't worry, I said, we're not really that interested in this one, as it's priced at €755,000; but there was one around the corner, a four-bedroom detached house that was on the market at €790,000 and appeared to be better value. It had been on the market for more than a year and originally had an asking price of €895,000. It was at the end of the street, next to the green space and facing the main road. It had plenty of potential for expansion.

However, it was getting close to 1 p.m., so we decided we would take a trip up to Carysfort Avenue, as there was a modern semi-detached three-bed in Carysfort Park, just under 1,200 square feet, that had recently come on the market with an asking price of €775,000. It was the same agent, and they had informed us that a quick, urgent sale was necessary, as the seller had already bought another house. It sounded interesting.

We got there a little early, and we decided to park outside and go in. The agent was there, with another viewing. (Funny that, how they like to have them all viewing at the same time.) The house was nice, great location, but a little on the small side. It was probably too small, in fact; at least so Andy thought. The agent told us there was already an offer of €750,000 on the table. We decided to cut and run, as there were no bargains going there that day.

Properties in this area had been making just under the million euros mark a year earlier. At the peak, in 2006, this particular house might have sold for €900,000 or possibly as much as €925,000. The owners didn't want to get caught in a chain: it was priced to sell—though, come to think of it, it wasn't really a bargain when you consider the size of the property. We gave it seven out of ten.

We went back to Rowanbyrn and got there bang on time. The agent arrived a few minutes later. We asked all the usual questions, such as how long had the house been on the market? Why was the seller selling? Were they stuck in the chain? And, more importantly, how long had they lived at this address? It turned out that the owners had been there quite some time but wanted to move closer to their grandchildren. The house was okay but had been extended several times over the years, and it showed. There were lots of small rooms and a staircase that went up at an angle of 45 degrees. The staircase was also bang in the centre of the house, thereby seriously impinging on the size of all the rooms. The architect should be shot, I thought to myself.

Both price and location were good, and with the property on the market for so long, and the existing owners having been there a long time, which meant there was probably little if any mortgage secured on it, the seller would surely be amenable to a low offer.

The appeal of the bigger, detached house was growing on Andy, but he knew he would have to throw another €100,000 into remodelling it to get it to the way he would like to have it. We knew this because as we walked around, both upstairs and downstairs, we could feel a severe slope in the floor. The staircase was far too steep: you'd break your neck after a couple of pints. This house got only six out of ten from yours truly.

We didn't have far to go to the next viewing, a couple of hundred yards up the road at Stradbrook Close. This was one of those properties that look great in the advertisement—the joys of using a wide-angle lens. It was a small, three-bedroom terraced house and had been on the market for some time, now at €595,000, but I'd seen it before at €655,000, back in September 2007. It was not to our taste. The interior was very dated—

a serious let-down compared with the exterior—and in dire need of redecoration. It was a rental. The agent told us it was owned by a brother and sister who had bought it off their mother after their father died. First off, it needed a whole new kitchen. A lick of paint wouldn't have gone amiss either. I gave it only three out of ten. Andy wasn't happy either: he felt the photograph had more than flattered the property, especially in respect of the driveway and parking space.

Andy was chatting to the agent outside, about the general state of the property market and why new homes and in particular new apartments were not selling. I told them it was nearly half past two and time to go to the next viewing or we'd be late.

A little later we arrived at Merrion Park, off Sion Hill Avenue, which in turn is just off Mount Merrion Avenue. This was a three-bedroom town house that had been reduced from €780,000, now quoting €750,000. We got there just before the agent. He brought us inside; and it was one of those occasions when in the first five seconds you just know it's not right. I mean, fantastic location, not a million miles from where Andy was originally going to buy. But this was a house, not an apartment. It actually felt a whole lot smaller. Even worse, it had no central heating, only electric storage heaters, which everyone knows take about a day and a half to come on and are nowhere near as efficient as oil-fired or gas central heating. Houses without radiators—forget it! Another four out of ten and that was being generous. The agent told us it was a probate sale, and the family would take €700,000. Andy shook his head. 'I can't stand houses without central heating, and I can never get those storage heaters to work anyway.' This was a definite no.

So far that day we were very unimpressed with all the properties we'd seen, with the possible exception of the one in Carysfort Park, and that was going to go near the asking price because the location was so sought after.

Our next stop was going to be very interesting indeed: we were off to Killiney to see the most expensive property on our list that day. It was, of course, Killiney Court, the salubrious up-market apartment complex built on the site of the old Court Hotel. This development was completed at the beginning of 2006, so these properties had been on the market for a full two years. According to the pleasant salesperson from Kelly Walsh, there were eighteen apartments still for sale. They had been advertised on line from €950,000, but I knew they had previously been advertised from €1.15 million not long before. So the prices had already been dropped by €200,000. We had already decided before we went inside that Andy was going to offer no more than €750,000, or, to put it another way, he wanted another €200,000 discount.

The agent showed us into the show flat, which just happened to be on the second floor, but we were told that all the apartments were of a similar size. The only discernible difference, therefore, was that the view depended on which floor you were on.

A shock was awaiting us. We went into the reasonably large open-plan apartments, ranging in size from about 129 to 139 square metres, and we began to have a sniff around. Presumably, I said to the agent, the upper-floor apartments are a bit more expensive than the ground-floor ones. We were certainly not expecting what she said next. This particular apartment, she said, as seen, is on offer at €2.84 million. I could hear the expletives from Andy in the next room. We thought she was joking but soon realised she had a straight face. Good God, I thought to myself. Who's going to pay nearly 3 million for a two-bedroom apartment, even if it does have plasma televisions in the bedroom?

We quickly explained to the young woman that this wasn't in Andy's budget and that we were interested in the 'entry level' prices. So we headed off downstairs and to the next building, ending up in the middle of the complex at the back of the old building that still stands. No sea views, then, from this glass-walled property. The apartment we were now in was finished, though it had no flooring, just bare concrete. I think we were both still in shock. I proceeded to ask, 'If this is nearly a million quid, how much are the ones on the top floor?' These were the ones that have a roof garden as well, namely the penthouses.

'Oh,' she said, 'they all sold two years ago—quite quickly, really: shortly after the apartment scheme was launched. They all sold for €3 million each.'

'So how many are left?' I asked a second time—just to make sure.

'There are eighteen apartments still for sale,' she said, 'ranging from €950,000 for the ground floor with no view up to €2.84 million for the first apartment we've seen on the second floor.'

I thought to myself, that's a long time to be still on the market: two whole years! But then again when you think about it, the property market was on fire in the first three or four months of 2006, though by May the euphoria had begun to fizzle out. Then, unbeknownst to many people back then, new-homes activity dried up that summer, and the market never regained its strength in the autumn, as increases in interest rates began to bite and of course the big issue of stamp duty reared its ugly head.

In short, had this development been completed earlier, say by about six months, they would probably all have been sold by the middle of 2006. I suppose you could just call it a case of bad timing. Anyway, we realised quite quickly that we were wasting our time here. Andy told the sales-person he wouldn't be paying more than €750,000; he might be interested, all the same, in this particular property if the developers were prepared to let it go at that price, because he thought it might make a good corporate rental.

To be brutally honest, I couldn't rate these properties at more than six out of ten; and I'll tell you why. Essentially they're all single-aspect rectangular concrete boxes and therefore are quite dark inside when you move from the living-room/kitchen through the hallway into the bedrooms at the rear. There were small balconies at the back, but they were facing the cliff wall, or really the retaining wall a couple of metres from the rear of the building. This made the bedroom dark all the time. The only way you can rationalise these prices is if you assume that the potential buyers are all older people trading down from properties that they could sell for considerably more money. Only a multi-millionaire could possibly buy these properties: no mere mortal could afford the mortgage if finance was an issue. Anyway, the agent said she would pass the information back to the developer, and she would be in touch with Andy in due course.

It was four o'clock, and we had one more property to see. We were off to Foxrock—'Mount Foxrock', to be precise, just past Foxrock Church as you head down towards Dean's Grange. This three-bedroom semi had been on the market at €715,000 but had been reduced to €699,000. The agent had told us that the seller bought the property four years earlier for €415,000 and had spent a bit of money doing it up. It was definitely the best one we had seen all day. It wasn't that big but it was laid out nicely: open plan with nice decor—a little chintzy, perhaps, but this had been a female-only household. The seller had prepared the house very well. There were scented candles burning in the living-room, and the place was spotless.

Once again we were in another very small property—probably the reason why the seller was attempting to trade up. According to the agent, the seller was realistic about price, knowing they would get a good deal or a 'value trade' in their trade-up. It was another case of the agent telling us a little bit more than you really needed to know, but it helped anyway. She made strenuous efforts to remind us that it was a Sorohan home, and they commanded a premium price. We gave seven out of ten to this Foxrock home. This last property we viewed that day definitely had a nicer feel to it than the one we'd seen earlier in Carysfort Park, and it was considerably cheaper. And it was Foxrock, Dublin 18, so there was nothing wrong with the address: if anything, for pure snob value it was probably better.

After an afternoon of traipsing around looking at different properties we were both hungry and decided that we would go and get something to eat and discuss all the properties we had seen that day and come up with a plan for bidding. First we eliminated several properties that Andy just wasn't interested in. He had already put in the offer of €750,000 on the Killiney property. On the Rowanbyrn property that was quoting

€790,000 he phoned the agent and said he would be prepared to pay no more than €630,000. The agent didn't think the seller would be tempted at that lower price, and he also came clean about how long the property had been on the market and that it had already been reduced considerably in price. With regard to the property in Foxrock, Andy liked it and also saw some potential there, but he felt it was just too expensive.

The next day he phoned me. He had put in an offer of €600,000 on the Foxrock house, and it had been accepted almost immediately. I told him I thought it was still too much, because I felt that in a year's time the same property would be trading in the €550,000–575,000 price range. Even at this lower price of €600,000 he would still be exposed a couple of years down the road.

Later the same day the agent from Kelly Walsh phoned Andy and told him the developer wouldn't accept his low offer and that they would proceed on the basis of their existing price. Likewise, the agent representing the seller of the detached house at Rowanbyrn, in Blackrock, phoned and said the seller would negotiate down a little bit but not much further from the asking price, as it had already been dropped substantially at the end of the previous year.

A few days went by.

Andy instructed his solicitor to seek the return of his €20,000 booking deposit from the apartment at Mount Merrion Avenue. But then a strange thing happened. He learnt that the sellers were desperate to sell. The agent informed him that the owners had bought it originally for their son, that there was an outstanding mortgage on the property, which now was in arrears. Andy discovered that they had bought the property only in 2005 and that the outstanding mortgage balance was about €285,000.

He now had two vital pieces of information that every potential buyer would love to have. He knew precisely when the property was bought, and he knew how much finance was involved. This was manna from heaven, because he knew he could bid a lot lower. I suppose you could call this a Gazunderer's dream, especially as time was also of the essence and he was a cash buyer with no chain. Serious negotiations were to ensue.

The agent opened with the first offer. Would he be prepared to pay €480,000, and could he move quickly? He replied with a counter-offer of €420,000. His logic was that he had seen quite a few properties that week and he realised how quick sellers were to drop their asking prices. So he told the agent that he was offering a hundred thousand less because he had seen much better value elsewhere on the market. Well, that was how he justified it.

A few minutes later the agent phoned back and said the seller might take €460,000 if they were to complete within thirty days. Andy said the most he would pay would be €430,000, and he could move quickly and complete within their time limit. A deal was then struck at that price.

16 June 2008. The conveyancing had gone through, after much delay with signing the paperwork. This delay rested with the seller. Perhaps they thought that after accepting such a low price they could gain some time in the hope that a better offer would come along. They wanted to have Andy gazumped, after he had already gazundered them!

Andy had all his contracts signed and submitted lickety-split. The final purchase price, including fixtures and fittings, came to €434,500. However, during the conveyancing process Andy's solicitors had informed him that the previous purchase price paid by the seller was €650,000 or 50 per cent more than the recent sale price. What's more, digging a little deeper we discovered that they had originally listed the flat for sale at €625,000 in late 2007. Then they reduced the price in early 2008 by about €35,000. The sellers were obviously desperate to sell. Both are businesspeople; they were also the owners of multiple properties. We subsequently learnt that they had another apartment for sale nearby. What a turn-up for the books!

That was astonishing. This apartment had been on the market with an asking price of €625,000 a few months earlier, and now the seller was prepared to take €430,000 for a quick sale. That's a whopping 30 per cent discount! And to think that a mere one week beforehand Andy was prepared to proceed at the considerably higher price of €520,000, until he had been persuaded otherwise.

About the same time that this took place two other estate agents had listed similar but smaller two-bedroom apartments in the same development. Savills HOK in Blackrock had another two-bed for sale at €525,000 in January 2008, but it was considerably smaller, at 646 square feet, and was on the ground floor. This price was dropped to €505,000, then to €495,000 in the middle of April. By mid-June it had been reduced by a further fifty thousand to €445,000, representing a discount in the asking price of 15 per cent but still more expensive than the larger apartment that Andy had bought for less money. Incidentally, Wyse had listed another two-bed, this time on the first floor and smaller again, at 750 square feet, for €550,000. At the end of June 2008 that price was unchanged, and the property had been on the market at that point for at least six months.

The moral of this story is that 'Buyer, beware' applies when you're purchasing a property. You have to shop around, negotiate a good deal and, most importantly of all in a buyer's market, bid low. Pick a figure you would actually be embarrassed to offer; then take off a further €20,000, and that's what your offer should be.

As a friend, my loyalty was obviously to Andy and not to the seller of the property. This was a classic case of gazundering, and my involvement could result in me being referred to as the Gazunderer's apprentice.

The 2008 Paddy Power Hibernian Bear House-Price Championship Hurdle

H ow could you have profited from further property price falls in 2008? The answer was simple, really. All you had to do was have a flutter on the market indirectly by placing a bet with Paddy Power. The odds on offer at the beginning of 2008 suggest that punters believed that significant falls were likely for residential property prices that year. If betting indications were anything to go by, the punters saw −5 per cent as the clear favourite.

In fact Paddy Power had given the likelihood of a national average price fall of between 5 and 7 per cent as the most likely outcome for the year, with the shortest odds at 9 to 4. The odds for every possible scenario are summarised in the following table.

Table 30: The 2008 Paddy Power Hibernian Bear House-Price Championship Hurdle

Outcome	Odds quoted	Odds as a probability	Adjusted (A)	Outcome (B)	Expected (A × B)	Fair odds	Bookie's take
Increase	6 to 1	14%	10%	2.0%	0.2%	9 to 1	3 points
No change	12 to 1	8%	5%	0.00%	0.00%	19 to 1	7 points
−0.01 to −3%	4 to 1	20%	14%	−1.5%	−0.2%	6 to 1	2 points
−3 to −5%	3 to 1	25%	18%	−4.0%	−0.7%	11 to 2	2½ points
−5 to −7%	9 to 4	31%	22%	−6.0%	−1.3%	9 to 2	2¼ points
−7 to −9%	10 to 3	23%	16%	−8.0%	−1.3%	7 to 1	3½ points
−9% or more	4 to 1	20%	14%	−10.0%	−1.4%	6 to 1	2 points
Total		141%	100%		−4.8%		

Source: Paddy Power PLC

The first column shows all the possible outcomes, ranging from an increase in house prices in the calendar year 2008, with quoted odds at 6 to 1, which is a one-in-seven chance or 14 per cent probability. The next possibility quoted was for static prices, or no change whatever. The odds here were the highest, at 12 to 1, so representing a likelihood of only 8 per cent. The next four rows represent falls of up to 3 per cent, between 3 and 5 per cent, between 5 and 7 per cent, and between 7 and 9 per cent. This is the part of the field where most of the betting was focused, with the shortest odds going to a drop of at least 5 per cent but no more than 7 per cent, at 9 to 4. Finally, the worst possible outcome, bear-market falls of 9 per cent or more, receive a one-in-five or 20 per cent probability.

The third column is the simple mathematical probability, based on Paddy Power's quoted odds. As the quoted odds are shorter than the realistically fair odds—the bookie has to make a crust too—the next column normalises the probabilities so that they add up to 1, or 100 per cent. After all, there can only be one outcome on 31 December 2008. The next column, headed *Outcome*, lists the typical return for each given scenario.

In this instance, for the price-increase scenario a low single-digit figure of 2 per cent was arbitrarily chosen. This makes sense, because when these odds were first published, in early 2008, the banks and estate agents were predicting a weak first half to the year, followed by modest price appreciation in the later half. It doesn't really matter what figure you put in there, within reason, as the probability is so low anyway.

Next we multiply each possible scenario by its probability; this gives us the overall expected average outcome of almost −5 per cent. Therefore, we can view this as a consensus figure back then. It's a good consensus view, because it's based on real money wagers made by ordinary Irish punters.

The last two columns show what the 'fair odds' would be if Paddy Power was a registered charity or philanthropic organisation and not in it for the money. The final column then represents their 'spread' or take.

LONG AND SHORT ODDS EXPLAINED

Some people may be a little confused by betting odds, especially the maths. So let's begin with a really simple and well-known example, say a Premiership football game between Arsenal and Manchester United. There are only three possible outcomes in a soccer game: win, lose or draw.

Now here's the tricky bit. Three possible outcomes means there's a 1-in-3 probability of each occurrence; but this equates to odds of 2 to 1, and not 3 to 1. Quoted odds of 3 to 1 means three outcomes versus one other outcome, so a total of four outcomes, which is a 25 per cent probability.

Therefore, in a football game between two evenly matched teams, such as those mentioned, the bookies should quote the odds at 2 to 1 for either a win, lose or draw. The reality is that, using the two teams selected, the bookie would probably offer shorter odds of about 6 to 4 for the win and possibly 11 to 5 or longer odds for a draw. (6 to 4 is actually 1½ to 1, but bookies never use fractions, so they scale it up to avoid decimal points.) This is instead of the normal 2-to-1 probability odds. In effect, therefore, the bookies are taking half a point (2 to 1 minus 1½ to 1) for themselves. This is to cover their expenses and to make a profit. These are called 'short odds'—short because they're less than the normal odds based on probability.

Bookies may offer long odds on outcomes that don't happen very frequently. In this analogy this would suggest that football draws are less frequent than wins, either at home or away. One other reason that they may offer better or long odds for a draw is that most punters would typically be supporters of one or other team and therefore would almost always be natural betters on a win; so to entice more people to place a bet on the least favourable outcome the bookies offer better or longer odds.

Remember, it's in the bookies' interests to have an equal number of bets on each potential result, because there are three possible outcomes. (They profit from the difference between normal and short odds.) If there are only two punters with different bets, the bookie gets to keep the third bet. (For example, two football supporters each bet on their own team and the result is a draw; then the bookie wins, irrespective of the odds!)

Please note: The odds are *always* stacked in the bookies' favour.

Remember, if the bookies need to lay off too many negative property bets they can always short the banks. Paddy Power's biggest take is on the static price or 'no change' scenario, where fair odds suggest that there's a one-in-twenty (i.e. 19-to-1) chance of this event, based on the odds on all other likely scenarios. It's not a great surprise, therefore, to see them taking a bigger slice of the action on the offer with the longest odds.

It seems that Irish punters have been betting their hard-earned cash on further falls, while a few were tempted to plump for a property price increase in 2008 (hence the shorter odds, at 6 to 1 or half the no-change odds). Most football supporters would generally bet on the win for their team. Few bet on the draw, even though it has equal probability. The same phenomenon has happened here. Punters are polarised into two camps: those who see further price falls (the majority) and those who believe the estate agents (the minority). Unfortunately, these seven scenarios would be a bit of a tongue-twister in a real hurdle race, so the next table is an attempt to overcome this.

Table 31: The 2008 Paddy Power House-Price Championship Hurdle entries

Bookie's scenario	Appropriate field name
Increase	Wishful Thinking
No change	The Pundits' Promise
−0.01 to −3%	Fractions Don't Count
−3 to −5%	Already There
−5 to −7%	Necessary Slowdown
−7 to −9%	Slippery Slope
−9% or more	Doom-Monger Glory

With only seven runners it's a small field, so no each-way bets were allowed, as it was definitely a non-handicap race. In fact there could easily have been as many non-runners as there were runners. Examples could have included Celtic Tortoise, Fundamentals Are Sound, Sustainable Decline, Stamp-Duty Boy, Da Demographics Ya Know, First-Time Buyer's Dilemma and the real long shot, MacDonald's Ruby Slippers (alias 'There's No Place Like a New Home').

Epilogue
The party's over

Ireland's house party was in full swing between 2002 and 2007. The estate agents were the DJs, banging out the beat and getting the crowds moving. The banks were behind the bar, plying everyone with cheap alcohol and awarding interest-only 'bar tabs' to anyone who wanted one. *Drink now, pay later* signs were everywhere.

Outside the party, the mortgage brokers were acting as doormen, shepherding all the punters in. They had been given strict instructions that all first-time buyers were to be given free and priority entrance.

Up the street the property journalists were doing PR, handing out leaflets as well as chanting 'Take five at five hundred thousand.' They were also approaching bewildered potential punters and encouraging them to take the leap, join the party and get onto the property ladder. If they still seemed reluctant they were told to offer them special promotions, like 'Buy one, get one more at the same price,' as well as silly ones, such as 'Buy two, pay for three.' They didn't really understand them either, but hey, they had been plied with cheap booze too, so who cared.

Back inside, the party organisers—the builders and developers—were upstairs looking down at the party in full swing, directing their minions to keep the bar staff busy and shouting orders. 'Make sure there's plenty of drink. We don't want to run out!'

Sitting on the stairs were the police—the Government and politicians—who wanted to be upstairs with the developers but there wasn't enough room. Still, they were happy just to be there. 'It's a great party!' they congratulated themselves, as they were getting a big slice of the action off the top. 'Hope it lasts for ever!'

Bang! The lights went out. The music stopped.

The estate-agent DJs were still shouting at the tops of their voices, *'Let's paarteee!'* telling all the confused partygoers that it was just a power cut, a temporary blip, and the power would be coming back on shortly.

Unfortunately, the sound system had short-circuited. When the lights came back on, the bankers behind the bar revealed that there was no more drink to be had. Only a few bottles of beer, and those had all increased in price. They told the poor punters that happy hour was over and not to ask for any more credit, as 'a refusal often offends.'

The mortgage-brokers on the door were still handing out tickets, but no-one was willing to pay for them any longer.

The property journalists, having seen the lights go out and hearing the cries of dismay from the unhappy crowds, began walking further and further up the street until their fast walking became a jog, then a canter, and finally a sprint. They couldn't wait to get away from the place. They'd be back tomorrow, to frown on the hedonism that had occurred the night before, feigning ignorance and pretending they had had nothing whatever to do with the party in the first place.

The organisers upstairs said, 'No worries! We'll have an even bigger party next week.' They had been reliably informed by the bankers behind the bar that the 'demographics' suggested that Ireland was brimming with young partygoers wanting to own their own property and join the house party.

Meanwhile the Government politicians were bewildered. Should they stay or should they go? They didn't know! They said to themselves, 'We better keep the organisers and the bar staff happy, or we won't be getting any more invitations to the next house party.'

None of the vested-interest people knew what to do either.

Finally, a rogue solicitor entered the premises and gave them all an 'undertaking' that there would be no more parties here any more. The building had been sold, and he was the new owner. It was going to be a 'mixed-use' development: office, retail and apartments. He needed vacant possession, as he had to begin the redevelopment immediately. After all, he had four mortgages secured on this property; the repayments were going to kill him otherwise.

THE MORAL OF THE STORY

The moral of this story is: Don't be concerned if the party organisers, bar staff and DJs call you a party-pooper. Do your own research and educate yourself. You may be pleasantly surprised to learn that there will be much cheaper parties again in the future.

Ireland's House Party finally ended in March 2007. It had raged incessantly for more than a decade. The hangover will probably last at least five years, or half as long as the party itself. Just like an alcohol-induced hangover, when millions of brain cells are destroyed, billions will have been wiped off the value of all homes in the land.

Unofficially, Irish residential property prices are already in bear-market territory, having declined in value by 20 per cent or more from their peak valuations. However, the official PTSB-ESRI house-price index may not indicate a technical bear market until the start of 2009 or later—especially as, viewing the index, you're looking at a picture of the property world four or five months past. The magic number that signifies a bear market in Irish property is when the PTSB-ESRI national average house price hits €248,862 or less. The figure at the time of publication is only €15,200 shy of that, or a little less than the average price drop of 2007.

The plain truth is that too many new homes were constructed during the boom period, 2002–07. That supply overhang or backlog will take a couple of years to clear—even more so now that turnover or sales activity for both new and second-hand homes has fallen to new lows, thus compounding the problem.

The economy is reeling from the over-reliance on the construction industry. At one point during the boom it constituted 13 per cent of national income, whereas in other contemporary economies it typically made up about 5 per cent. Unfortunately, as with all market corrections, there's a tendency to overshoot the mark, especially now because of the inherent weakness in the market caused by the global credit crisis and domestic economic slowdown. The ending of the party couldn't have come at a worse time. But that, after all, is the nature of things.

One of the most important lessons to be learnt from Ireland's House Party is that sums really are important, whether they be the quantum of many years of price gains required to restore prices to their original values or valuation multiples, affordability or even rental yields. The last-named is a moot point, because Irish property yields are still far too low.

The market has entered a prolonged downturn—a property slump, to use the correct term. No surprise, then, that the VIPs—the vested-interest parties—especially the estate agents, were totally wrong in 2007 when they told us it would be a 'soft landing'. They got it wrong in 2008 as well when they predicted that in the second half of the year things would improve. So don't hold your breath in 2009; they'll probably say the same thing again: a weak start to the first half, with a pick-up expected in the latter part of the year! Ironically, it doesn't really matter to them. They would be better off if the market crashed quickly: that way the recovery could begin sooner. A 'V-shaped' property bear market would have been their ideal 'back to the races' scenario.

Now is not the time for recrimination, but a cautionary note is warranted nonetheless. There will eventually be some recovery, but along the way there may be one or more false dawns. The best that home-owners can hope for is a U-shaped slump: a slow downturn followed by a gradual recovery. But it may well turn out to be a W-shaped one. That's a bear market rally in the interim period. As the old saying goes, 'one month's data doesn't make a trend'; but neither does two or three months' data of rising prices in this example. Inevitably there will be 'bottom-feeders' who will attempt in vain to pick up the best bargains, but they may fire prematurely and end up shooting themselves in the foot.

As we said at the beginning of this book, it's a four-stage correction process. By the time you're reading this, hopefully we shall have moved on to stage 2 (recovery in sales) or even closer to stage 3 (reduction and elimination of the supply overhang). Both are necessary before a stage 4 recovery in prices can occur. Interest rate reductions may improve the likelihood of a transition to the next phase in the great Irish property bear market.

So the best advice is: listen to the *objective* academics and independent property commentators (they're not biased), take what the property editors and journalists say with a pinch of salt (they get paid to write stories) and under no circumstances believe the estate agents' propaganda. Just one caveat on that last point: when the estate agents and other VIPs capitulate and throw in the towel that will be a clear indication that the market is close to a bottom. In other words, treat them as 'contrarians at the gate'!

Finally, if you do need a place or need to move home, please remember the new property mantra: it's no longer 'location, location, location' but rather 'negotiation, negotiation, negotiation.' Negotiate aggressively, and get yourself a better deal.

Appendix A

The interest-rate crystal ball explained

In fact we don't need an interest-rate crystal ball, because all we have to do is follow the money trail.

The money trail we refer to here is the wagers made by investors on interest-rate futures in the financial markets. Who are these investors? They're the banks, insurance companies, pension and life funds, as well as professional investors and hedge funds. They're the same financial institutions that you have your mortgage with, your pension, endowment or life policy, or even your car insurance. All these financial companies have to hedge themselves from time to time for their interest-rate exposures or to hedge against declines in their investment portfolios. They do this by betting on the direction of short-term interest rates.

The most commonly traded short-term rate is the three-month interest rate. It's regarded by financial professionals as a crucial benchmark, and many financial products are directly linked to this number (just as tracker mortgages are linked to European Central Bank base rates, some are linked directly to Euribor). Moreover, there exist futures contracts on the three-month rate, which is very helpful indeed. These future short-term rates give us a strong clue to where investors think bank base rates are going to be.

Since the introduction of the euro in 1999, the three-month interest rate has tracked the European Central Bank base rate very closely; in fact the correlation daily has been 97 per cent. This means that they move together. So hang on, then. If we know, with some degree of certainty, where these short-term interest rates are going to be in three, six or nine months' time we will have a pretty good idea of the European Central Bank rate, correct? Correct.

Euribor—the three-month European inter-bank offered rate—is the interest rate that banks in Europe lend to the 'prime' banks, for example a AAA-rated institution such as Rabobank or a high-AA-rated bank like, say, Royal Bank of Scotland, which owns and operates Ulster Bank in Ireland, and not just to any other banks (as some erroneous descriptions of this prime rate sometimes suggest). Not all banks are created equal. For example, at the beginning of June 2008 three-month Euribor was 4.86 per cent, whereas the prime rates at Bank of Ireland and AIB were 4.95 and 5 per cent, respectively. Some banks fund themselves above Euribor, while others, generally the better-rated ones, can usually 'fund' themselves below. But this key rate is set collectively (almost fifty banks submit their rates every morning; the outliers are discarded, then a simple average is computed of the rest) and is used by all as a benchmark rate. And the futures contracts traded on this rate are simply known as Euribor futures.

To some people this might seem too technical, but it's just jargon. The formula for the pricing of these contracts is so simple that any primary-school pupil would understand it. It's simply this: *futures* = 100 − *R*, where *R* is what you think rates will be.

For instance, if an investor believed that the European Central Bank wouldn't change rates in 2008, they would expect rates to stay unchanged at 4 per cent and they would be willing to pay close to 96 for, say, the December futures contract. Another investor may believe there will be several more rate cuts, to 2 per cent, by the middle of 2009. In that instance they would be assuming that the June 2009 futures price would rise to about 97.50, assuming that Euribor remained half a point above the ECB rate. This is basic sums, and anyone should be able to work out the expected rates. You don't need to be good at maths to do this: you don't even need a calculator! The sums involved are less complicated than walking into a bar, ordering two pints of beer at €4.25 each, handing the barman a €10 note and working out that your change is €1.50.

Having established that a strong relationship exists between short-term interest rates and the European Central Bank base rate, we can now determine the effective future borrowing rate, as long as we know the direction of one of them.

There's more than one futures contract; in fact there are serial contracts for different periods. These provide a series of clues about where the big money has bet on where these short rates will be in a month, three or six months, a year or even several years from now. The market bets on where rates will be, up to five years from now.

EUROPEAN RATE BETS AT END OF DECEMBER 2008

The following table contains a summary of the bets made on 2008 interest rates on Wednesday 31 December 2008. This table of wagers tells us several things. Firstly, we can quickly ascertain that rates are expected to remain low or lower until September 2009. Secondly, the volume of investors' bets every day is large, at close to 300,000 contracts. (Now, each contract has a notional value of €1 million.) Thirdly, the outstanding number of open bets is also enormous, and their corresponding notional values run into the billions (*price* ÷ 100 × €1 million × *bets*).

Table 32: Short-term interest rate bets summary (as of 31 Dec. 2008)

Contract	Price	Implied rate	Bets that day	Number of open bets	Value (€ billion)
Jan. 2009	97.37	2.64%	22,900	64,894	63
Feb. 2009	97.55	2.46%	0	10	0
Mar. 2009	97.77	2.23%	76,097	734,482	718
Apr. 2009	97.79	2.22%	0	0	0
May 2009	97.90	2.11%	0	0	0
Jun. 2009	98.03	1.97%	50,615	526,627	516
Sep. 2009	98.00	2.01%	44,098	439,894	431
Dec. 2009	97.76	2.25%	34,755	356,203	348
Mar. 2010	97.57	2.44%	20,101	301,107	294
Jun. 2010	97.33	2.68%	17,531	210,628	205
Sep. 2010	97.14	2.86%	11,580	151,689	147
Dec. 2010	96.93	3.07%	6,837	88,998	86
Mar. 2011	96.83	3.18%	3,819	52,629	51
Jun. 2011	96.71	3.30%	2,157	30,051	29
Sep. 2011	96.62	3.39%	771	34,981	34
Dec. 2011	96.52	3.49%	143	13,655	13
Mar. 2012	96.48	3.52%	0	2,675	3
Jun. 2012	96.41	3.60%	0	434	0
Sep. 2012	96.35	3.66%	0	912	1
Dec. 2012	96.30	3.71%	0	110	0
Mar. 2013	96.25	3.75%	275	175	0
Jun. 2013	96.29	3.71%	1,050	950	1
Sep. 2013	96.24	3.76%	100	800	1
Dec. 2013	96.29	3.71%	0	0	0
Mar. 2014	96.35	3.65%	0	0	0
Jun. 2014	96.37	3.63%	0	0	0
Sep. 2014	96.39	3.61%	0	0	0
Dec. 2014	96.39	3.61%	0	0	0
Total			292,829	3,011,904	2,942

Source: EuroNEXT

These open bets or 'open interest', as the professionals call them, don't tell us who is betting for or against, nor do they tell us what proportion of these are which way. It just informs us how many bets are still running. Anyone who has ever bet on football, horse or dog racing on 'Betfair' will know how bets with varying odds meet in the middle, or the market rate. It's the very same for interest-rate bets. There's one subtle difference, however. Although the paper values of these bets are massive, the range of possible interest-rate outcomes is actually very small and limited. Rates aren't going to nil, nor are they going to 20 per cent! Realistically, the most an investor can lose is determined by the number of bets they place and at what price. They may be out by half a point or so. It's not like a football match, where your team loses and your bet is finished. Still, they can lose millions, or even billions, if they get it wrong.

The table above shows that the total number of outstanding Euribor bets at the end of November was a shade over €2.9 trillion of notional amount. But what if the market pros have got it wrong? Let's suppose that interest rates do not go down as far as they thought back in December 2008. We can work it out by adjusting the price of each Euribor futures contract. In this instance, based on the current prices and the total number of bets placed, €7.5 billion would be added to or subtracted from the combined value of all these Euribor bets for every quarter point increase or decrease in rates. For example, if ECB rates do not go to 2 per cent or below, Euribor rates will not fall much below 2.5 per cent, so anyone paying 98 for the June 2009 contract would lose money, as that contract price fell back to 97.5 to reflect a 2.5 per cent level (100 − 97.5 = 2.5). There were half a million June bets at 98 (notional value of €516 billion), and if the price of the bet fell half a point to 97.5 (notional value of €514 billion), €2 billion would be lost by those investors betting on lower rates in this example.

You see, large sums of money may be won or lost by betting on the future direction of interest rates. The market is always right at any given point in time. Sure, the market view changes, but you see from the numbers above that it is always better to side with the market and follow the money.

Empirical research on the demand for housing

An article entitled 'A descriptive analysis of the Irish housing market' appeared in the summer edition of the Economic and Social Research Institute's quarterly bulletin, July 2002. It was written by a long-time ESRI economist, David Duffy, a regular commentator on the residential property market. There were two notable points in that report. The first related to the demand for owner-occupied housing; the second area of interest was the ESRI 'Hermes' model for modelling Irish house prices.

Taking the first subject, Duffy referred to the Bacon, MacCabe and Murphy Report (1998) on the economic assessment of developments in house prices, where they found the four main drivers to be economic growth, demography, the cost of finance and supply (specifically the speed at which supply responds to changes in demand). But their method of estimating the cost of housing was a broad measurement that included not just the mortgage interest rate but the benefits of capital appreciation. They calculated this by taking the mortgage interest rate and subtracting the change in house prices. But when economists talk about changes in rates and house prices they invariably mean 'real' changes, those deflated by inflation. When they found that from 1992 to 1998 this user cost of housing had fallen dramatically, despite higher home prices, it explained to them that the low level of real interest rates, combined with the high levels of expected capital gains, boosted demand.

Ten years later, in 2008, real interest rates were still very low—less than 1 per cent, taking the average SVR (standard variable rate) mortgage of 5.8 per cent and annual inflation running at about 5 per cent (likewise when lower rates plus lower inflation existed towards year end). However, demand has now effactually been lowered, because of expected capital losses. Consumers still see future price falls. Even back in the latter part of 2006, just after the tremendous increase in home prices that occurred, consumers began to lose faith in further capital gains. They stopped believing in the boom. House prices were just too expensive.

As the age-old stock market adage goes 'buy low, sell high,' and not the other way around. Prospective home-buyers began to realise they were getting in at inflated, high or speculative prices.

Turning to the second topic, the ESRI model for estimating 'fair value' house prices, this was based on similar factors to the one listed in the Bacon Report (because the work was carried out by the same person, Anthony Murphy). It stated that home prices were a function of real disposable income, housing stock per capita (supply), the user cost of housing (discussed above) and the population aged between twenty-five and thirty-four (as this represents the typical household-formation age, or 'time to buy your own home' age). This model showed that house prices had begun to outpace the growth in incomes and that the model was unstable during the later years, particularly as population growth had created an imbalance and thus a scarcity of homes.

The same ESRI model results showed that short-term changes in house prices had a dramatic impact in boosting new-home completions. But in the long run the supply of new homes was influenced by real changes in house prices plus the mark-up of house prices over building costs (developers' profitability, in other words). They concluded then that, based on the big price increases of 30 per cent per year at the end of 1998 and early 1999, 60,000 new dwellings per year were needed. This is where the magic number of 60,000 first appeared. It was still being used by the Construction Industry Federation and the Irish Home Builders' Association a decade later, even though it's no longer applicable.

The average interest rate used by the Economic and Social Research Institute in its new house-price model is 'the user cost of housing based on the mortgage rate less the average change in house prices over the previous three time periods.' If we examine this equation for predicting new-home prices in detail it is further revealing. The interest-rate proxy, the *user cost of housing*, has the smallest coefficient: in other words, it's a minor variable. It's half the size of the change in the real disposable income factor. The two biggest factors in this new model are the population aged between twenty-five and thirty-four as a proportion of the population of working age and, secondly, the stock of houses divided by the population.

In May 2003 the *Economist* published a series of articles on property prices and in particular a report that identified Ireland as one of the countries where property was overvalued by 40 per cent. A few months later, in August, the International Monetary Fund came out with the comment that Irish property prices were 15 to 20 per cent above the values suggested by economic fundamentals. In response to these articles,

Professor Maurice Roche of NUI, Maynooth, published an article in the
ESRI's *Quarterly Economic Commentary* at the end of that year with the
heading 'Will there be a crash in Irish house prices?' His conclusion was
that at that time there was no evidence of a bubble and that actual home
prices were fairly close to theoretical or 'fair' value. His findings were that
at worst, Irish home prices were 5 per cent overvalued, based on the fundamentals in the market. This view is consistent with my own view that
the housing bubble began after 2002. The data Professor Roche used was
up to the first quarter of 2003. He dismissed the findings of the *Economist*
as being based solely on the ratio of house prices to income and having no
regard to other demand factors. He also dismissed the findings of the IMF,
because he believed they ignored 'supply-side' factors in determining what
the fair price of a home should be. He went on to state that 'the fundamental or long run equilibrium value of a house depends on factors that
affect both demand and supply.'

Professor Roche also identified another much-overlooked factor in
determining the value of new-home prices: that of land costs. According
to his results, 'real land costs caused real new house prices but not vice-
versa. This also suggests that land costs could be treated as exogenous in
a model explaining new house prices.' (In this econo-speak, 'exogenous'
means independent; in other words, the cost of development land is
totally independent of new-home prices and so may be used as an
explanatory variable or predictor of future prices.) This is a critical point,
and it contradicts the estate agents' rhetoric that 'high home prices drag
up land values,' a point my former boss Paul McNieve repeatedly tried to
impress upon me, without success.

Roche's 'demand-side' factors in his model included new-house prices,
net migration, disposable income, loans and finally mortgage rates. The
'supply-side' model had only four factors: new-house prices, building
costs, land costs and the number of home completions. Without labouring the point further, and without going into the boring detail of the
results, when Roche modelled new-home prices for the period from the
first quarter of 1979 to the first quarter of 2003, based on several different
variables (both demand and supply), the least important factor was again
'user costs', or the factor that included mortgage interest rates.

In fact in one of the model variations the t-statistic was *not* significant.
This is the number that tells us if that particular variable has statistical
reliability and is therefore a reliable predictor. Given this, together with
the fact that the interest-rate variable was tiny in terms of its number—it
explained only a couple of per cent of the total change in the prices of
new homes—it's safe to say that mortgage rates play only a small part in
determining house prices.

In Roche's model the two biggest factors were disposable income per capita and land costs (excluding building costs). Both make perfect sense, especially when one considers that back in 1991 land costs represented 13 per cent of the price of a new house; this had risen to 23 per cent by 2003 (when Roche published his article) but continued to increase, reaching almost 50 per cent by the first quarter of 2007.

CONCLUSION

Interest rates do play a part in the demand for housing—a small part—and we have shown that. There are two things to remember about housing finance. Firstly, the availability of credit is more important than the actual rate of interest paid on a mortgage loan. Even big property developers are not rate-sensitive when it comes to getting finance. One such developer told me in March 2006 that he didn't care if Anglo-Irish Bank charged him an extra half per cent in interest rates, because they brought him deals (read 'sites'), and if a deal was agreed on a Friday evening the money would be available—or at least the deposit component—by the following Monday morning.

Secondly, real interest rates, those deflated by consumer price inflation, are more important than nominal or money rates. It's true that Joe Public thinks in absolute terms, like what do I have to pay each month? But nominal rates are relevant only when it comes to determining house prices, and then they play only a minor role. When real interest rates are low it pays to borrow money, because you're repaying the bank money that will purchase less. Take, for instance, a couple whose mortgage payments increased by half from the end of 2005 to June 2007. Obviously they're not happy about that. But think about the value of those payments from June 2007 to June 2008 (the period when ECB rates remained unchanged), eaten away by 5 per cent inflation. The money that came out of their bank account to pay the mortgage may have remained the same over the course of that year, but it bought a lot less in the shops. By inference, it was worth a lot less too to their mortgage lender.

Appendix C

Historical first-time buyer experience

PRE-2005 METHODOLOGY OF IBF QUARTERLY MORTGAGE SURVEY

To produce average first-time buyer loan data for pre-2005 commences I used the Central Bank's quarterly mortgage statistics. The data published by the Irish Banking Federation clearly shows that first-time buyers, as a proportion of total loans, excluding 'remortgages' and 'residential investment lets', are always between 32 and 35 per cent and average 33 per cent. So this figure of roughly a third of all new home-owner mortgages as first-time buyer ones was used.

Secondly, the Central Bank data for new property-owner mortgages was adjusted for retiring mortgages (those loans that were taken out twenty to twenty-five years earlier and were now finished). Next we multiplied the incremental increase in total outstanding home-owner mortgages by the one-third estimate for first-time buyers. Finally, seeing that we already had the average purchase price for a first-time buyer home from the PTSB-ESRI, and we now had a total money amount attributable each quarter to first-time buyers, assuming that the typical first-time buyer borrowed 85 per cent on average, we could divide that total money amount by 85 per cent of the first-time buyer index price. This gives us a rough guide to the number of first-time buyers in 2003 and 2004, which was estimated at approximately 37,000 and 39,000, respectively.

This may sound convoluted, but really it's not. It's known as the *principle of extending*. For example, you know A and B but not C, but you also know D and have a reliable estimate of E, and C is related to E, so then you can work out the value of C. In our illustration above, the scenario matrix, C was the number of first-time buyers for the two-year period up to 2005. By putting all these pieces of the puzzle together we can estimate with reasonable accuracy the total number of first-time buyers who may end up with negative equity.

The Department of the Environment, Heritage and Local Government produces a quarterly summary of aggregate home-loan data as well as its own house-price indices, going back to 1994, and an annual summary going back to 1970. These figures corroborate the Irish Banking Federation and PTSB-ESRI first-time buyer index data, as well as the CBFSAI (Central Bank and Financial Services Authority of Ireland) numbers.

A separate analysis using the data of the Department of the Environment, Heritage and Local Government for all 'loan approvals' (including those of local authorities, banks and building societies) confirms the conclusion that a 30 per cent drop in property values from the peak would result in at least €3.8 billion of negative equity among first-time buyers and a further €2 billion in the second-hand homes market.

Appendix D

Making sense of rents and yields, as well as Daft indices

The left axis shows the index level; the latest figure was a reading of 93.4 for October 2008. The right axis is for short-term interest rates, which serve as a proxy for mortgage rates, especially as most mortgage-holders have variable-rate loans, often based on the European Central Bank rate plus some fixed spread, such as tracker mortgages, or even Euribor plus a fixed percentage.

The reason we use three-month Euribor rates is that there exists a well-established futures market for this particular benchmark interest rate—the Euribor futures contracts. Essentially this allows us to look at where investors believe short-term interest rates will probably be in the coming months and years. This is great, because it's not just one person's opinion or judgement but the collective bets of many banks and professional money managers, such as pension funds. So we're using a 'follow-the-money' route once more for where we think interest rates will be at the end of this year and the next. (This relationship between current interest rates and where the pros believe rates will be in due course was covered in more detail in chapter 19 and appendix A.)

What matters is that we can anchor our view on rates, and then extrapolate from that where the rental index level is likely to be. We've done this for the next two years—to the end of 2010. If we were to base our view of rents solely on interest rates and ignore new supply you would still expect the Daft rental index to decrease alongside the expectation of a reduction in the level of short-term interest rates.

Based solely on interest-rate expectations, this simple one-factor model suggests that rental growth ought to be negative, in the region of −15 per cent in early 2009. The reality, though, is that it could potentially be worse, as rents move in tandem with property prices, and the oversupply factor is dominant here. In an ideal world we would use a two-factor model: interest rates plus supply (expressed as a ratio or number of months' worth). Unfortunately, we don't have a reliable enough indicator of rental supply, because of the sheer number of duplicate letting advertisements on the popular web portals.

The peak in annual rents was in June 2007, when the index reached 105.8, which was nearly 17 per cent above the level of rents captured by the rental index in June 2006, with a reading of 90.5. Anyone can verify these numbers by looking at the archive of Daft rental surveys on their web site. Perhaps this is the 'near 20 per cent' growth rate in rents that many commentators were referring to on television and radio (such as Tom Parlon of the Construction Industry Federation on 'Questions and Answers' in early 2008). If it was, then it was nine months out of date—par for the course in Ireland: always use last year's figures, especially if they support your argument, and provide a good sound-bite on television.

That peak on the Daft index above 105 occurred when three-month Euribor was only 4¼ per cent but had jumped up from 3 per cent a year earlier. By September 2008 three-month Euribor was back above 5 per cent! However, that rental peak was an aberration, caused by the doubling of European Central Bank rates to 4 per cent that occurred up to June 2007. It prompted landlords to hike up rents, and it occurred at a time when annual growth in property prices was still positive (+0.9 per cent) on the PTSB-ESRI national house-price index. In effect it was a one-off increase in rents to compensate landlords for higher mortgage rates.

What everyone needs to remember is that all the so-called statistics are constantly changing. By the time you hear the latest statistics reported in the media they're already out of date. And when you hear comments referring to annual rates of change, they almost always vary dramatically from month to month. Imagine, for instance, that commentators are talking about house prices, and say the price remains unchanged for several months. Naturally the annual percentage change will begin to drop very rapidly each successive month as the base month in the previous year rolls forward. Ultimately, after twelve months under this flat scenario, annual growth becomes nil.

Even this basic model, based solely on interest rates back then, accurately predicted that annual rental growth would be negative by the summer of 2008. This is because it was a full year after the European Central Bank raised rates in June 2007. Rates were then left on hold or unchanged since then. So the catch-up increases in rents because of rising rates the previous year had already occurred.

Think of it another way. You're a landlord, you own twelve properties, and each lease begins on a different month of the year. So after your mortgage costs had risen you hiked up the rent for each tenant. After one year, you were finished.

YIELD AS A MEASURE OF TRUE RETURN

What is 'yield', and what does it really mean? The best definition of 'yield' is that it's an internal rate of return (IRR), which is the discount rate that discounts all future cash flows back to today's price. Now, that may sound complicated, but it really isn't, once it's explained by way of a worked real-life example.

Let's take an example of buying a flat for €300,000. The initial cash flow is −€300,000. So far so good; we all understand a negative cash flow as an outgoing or expense. Let's further assume that this purchased flat is let out to a tenant for €1,500 per calendar month. This equates to €18,000 per year in positive cash flows (12 × €1,500). Therefore the initial (flat) simple yield is 6 per cent, or 18,000 divided by 300,000.

But what it is in fact is the rate used to discount future money received, including, at some point, the sale of the property. Assume that we rent out this property for ten years and then sell it for the same price that we bought it for, namely €300,000; then the discount rate is 6 per cent. But there are lots of embedded assumptions in this calculation: that the rent remains unchanged for ten whole years—highly unlikely; that the sale price at the end of the period is the same as today—again, not likely; that cash flow (rent) is reinvested at the same discount rate used (implicit in the IRR calculation), in this example 6 per cent. So rent money received being reinvested at a constant rate, and not spent or used to pay down a mortgage etc., uncovers this rather obvious flaw, a constant discount rate. It doesn't change from year to year, as rates and yields do. Finally, the calculation doesn't take any taxes into account.

Every investment banker worth their salt knows that yield is a fundamentally flawed metric. But we all use it anyway as a standardised comparative, especially to compare rents on properties. For instance, you may often have seen or read in the papers about office buildings being rented out for a 3¾ per cent yield, or shops in Grafton Street or Henry Street let for an equivalent yield of 2 per cent, or even former branches of Bank of Ireland sold off *en masse* to investors for an initial 4 per cent yield. We see yields in use every day in the commercial property sector.

People who invest in residential properties also talk about yields, typically as an expression of the annual rental value as a proportion of purchase price. Yield is a good valuation measure in this context, as long as you understand the drawbacks inherent in yield calculations.

Finally, the best way to really understand yield is to assume that it represents your annual return. Forget about hoped-for future capital appreciation for a moment—for that's what got the property market into this overvalued mess in the first place! Future capital gains ought to be perceived as a bonus, an extra or additional return.

Every investment—and property investment is no exception—should stand or fall on the merits of the *known* cash flows, not the wishful-thinking ones. Property yields represent your known annual return. They should cover your known annual costs (at least most of the time). No exceptions! Yield is everything when it comes to property valuation.

Appendix E

A real-life worked rent v. cash example

The best way to prove a point is to use real-life examples that exist today. One of the most popular areas in which to both buy and rent in Dublin during the property boom was Dundrum, Dublin 14. Why? Because there has been much new development there, including Ireland's biggest shopping centre. It's close to the city centre—fifteen minutes by tram. And, of course, it's an established middle-income suburb that has had a recent influx of younger, professional types.

We could have used Sandyford, also in Dublin 18, as a good rental example, but the construction activity there is still continuing. Dundrum is similar in price, closer to town, and development is largely finished. According to the Daft rental survey for the third quarter of 2008, rents in Dublin 14, at €1,516 per calendar month, are a little higher than in Dublin 18, at €1,433 for a two-bedroom apartment. More importantly, though, rents have risen according to Daft in Dublin 14 but in Dublin 18 they've been falling. That's probably to do with the greater supply there.

Anyway, the example selected is a two-bedroom first-floor flat in Wyckham Point. Number 168 was for sale at €535,000. Similar apartments on the upper floor were going for more than €600,000 at the time, and €699,000 was being asked for the two-bedroom penthouses. Apartments for rent in this development seemed to average €1,550 per month at that time. This was extremely close to the latest Daft rental survey, and it's also very close to the Dublin 14 average that I discovered while conducting my own research in February last year. Seeing that it has not changed that much, it's perfect for our illustration. (Nobody can accuse me of choosing a bad location with falling rents.)

So let's establish the assumptions, as they say. The purchase price is €535,000 for a two-bed apartment in Wyckham Point, Dundrum. We use a ten-year investment period. The first illustration contains no taxes whatsoever (including no stamp duty). The bank deposit situation is Halifax, then offering 5.6 per cent gross on deposits up to €1 million.

(We also assume that deposit rates fall in 2009 and remain low until 2012.)

The second and third tables take out DIRT from cash at bank but include initial stamp duty payable, as well as capital gains tax on any sale where there's price appreciation.

Scenario A: The property is rented out for ten years at €1,550 per month, then sold for the same price that the purchaser paid (quite realistic if you think that two or three years like 2007 followed by +5 per cent per annum in price growth for six or seven years would only take us back to today in terms of price).

Scenario B: The rent goes up €50 per month at the end of each year, so that eventually it rises to €2,000 per month. The apartment is still sold for the same price that it was bought for.

Scenario C: The rent goes up each year, as in scenario B; put the property is eventually sold for €650,000, so there is a capital gain of €115,000 (+21½ per cent). This is the extremely optimistic scenario of rising rents plus rising prices.

Scenario D: The rent is static at €18,600 per year, but the value of the property declines by approximately 15 per cent, and the apartment is sold after the ten-year period for €450,000. (Already home prices have fallen 15 per cent from peak, so this is the scenario that prices fall no further, or if they do then they recover somewhat.)

Scenario E: Similar to scenario D, but this time the rent is raised each year by €600 (€50 × 12 months), so that the property in year 10 is let at €2,000 per month, while the value drops to €450,000. Therefore, the yield rises to approximately 5.3 per cent, or roughly the cost of money at that time. The mortgage illustrations assume a 75 per cent loan-to-value ratio, so the investor puts up a 25 per cent cash deposit (and borrows €400,000). The term of the loan is twenty years, and the mortgage rate is 5.8 per cent, dropping to 4 per cent in 2009 (consistent with 2 per cent base rates plus higher bank charges), then gradually back to 5 per cent by 2012, remaining at that level thereafter. Stamp duty, where payable, is €28,700, i.e. 7 per cent of the purchase price minus the initial €125,000. Legal fees are assumed to be only €1,300—a very low figure but purely for illustration purposes and to help with rounding. No letting agents' fees are included, nor are there any 'voids' or periods of vacancy, and service charges are nil.

The last assumption is an extremely generous one for the buy-to-let investor, because it assumes that there are no annual fees to be paid on the upkeep of the property, or commission to agents. It also assumes, unrealistically, that the flat is occupied and rented at all times. You couldn't be fairer than that—to investors, that is.

Our first illustration shows a cash-rich buyer who doesn't need to pay stamp duty. This person has two choices: either put the money in the bank (HBOS were offering 5.6 per cent; Anglo-Irish were offering 5.5 per cent on 'demand' accounts up to €100,000 gross then for deposits in excess of €20,000) or buy the apartment in Wyckham Point and let it out for the going rate of €1,550 per month (€18,600 per year).

Table 33: The cash-rich investor's dilemma: put the money in the bank or buy a two-bedroom flat and rent it out

5.8% Bank deposit	IRR	3.5% Scenario A	3.9% Scenario B	5.6% Scenario C	2.0% Scenario D	2.5% Scenario E
−€535,000	Cash	−€535,000	−€535,000	−€535,000	−€535,000	−€535,000
€29,960	Year 1	€18,600	€18,600	€18,600	€18,600	€18,600
€20,339	Year 2	€18,600	€19,200	€19,200	€18,600	€19,200
€23,412	Year 3	€18,600	€19,800	€19,800	€18,600	€19,800
€27,392	Year 4	€18,600	€20,400	€20,400	€18,600	€20,400
€31,805	Year 5	€18,600	€21,000	€21,000	€18,600	€21,000
€33,395	Year 6	€18,600	€21,600	€21,600	€18,600	€21,600
€35,065	Year 7	€18,600	€22,200	€22,200	€18,600	€22,200
€36,818	Year 8	€18,600	€22,800	€22,800	€18,600	€22,800
€38,659	Year 9	€18,600	€23,400	€23,400	€18,600	€23,400
€575,592	Year 10	€553,600	€559,000	€674,000	€468,600	€474,000
	Sale price	535,000	535,000	650,000	450,000	450,000
€852,438	Total	€721,000	€748,000	€863,000	€636,000	€663,000

Note: Bank deposit is cash at bank at 5.6 per cent gross interest per annum.

The table gives a good illustration of a rental example under different sale-price and rental-growth scenarios. The column on the left is just the €535,000 deposited in a high-interest bank account, at 5.6 per cent gross interest for year 1 (2008), with interest paid falling to 3.6 per cent in 2009, 4 per cent in 2010, 4.5 per cent in 2011 and 5 per cent thereafter (in line with rate expectations). After ten years this sum grows to almost €853,000. That's compound interest for you; and the top row shows that this is an equivalent internal rate of return (IRR) of 5.8 per cent.

So buying a flat for the same amount of money and getting an excellent rent of €1,500 a month, then selling the property for €535,000 in ten years' time, produces a much lower return than depositing a similar sum in the bank. (Cash in the bank generates interest on the interest!)

Anyone with that kind of money will immediately point out that DIRT (deposit interest retention tax) has to be paid on interest received on bank deposits, and this whittles away almost a quarter of the interest received. This is true, of course, and we account for this in the second table.

Likewise, rental income received from a let property is also subject to personal tax. All income is taxable, after all. Let's just leave income tax out of the equation for now, as it will only complicate things too much. And, with rents now lower than the monthly mortgage interest repayment schedule, it's not likely to be an issue really—well, not immediately. But for the sake of simplicity we'll ignore personal taxes and include only the obvious ones, such as DIRT and stamp duty.

Scenarios B and C will be of more interest to professional property investors, for two reasons. They assume that every year the rent increases by an extra fifty a month. Example C also factors in a 20 per cent capital gain on the property when sold: that is, it eventually sells for €650,000. The annual yield or return rises by 1.7 per cent more, to 5.6 per cent. For those property 'bulls' who think a recovery is just around the corner, if you assume a 50 per cent price increase to €800,000 by year 10, the annual return rises to 7.4 per cent. That would be an extremely rosy scenario, and yet you wouldn't even make double digits. And it assumes no capital gains tax (of 20 per cent), which would bring this back to a mere 5½ per cent. Really makes you think, doesn't it?

Examples D and E show what would happen if the property price fell by €85,000, to €450,000. This is the so-called 'worst case' following a property correction (could be worse than this, though, with the property slump, but I'm being generous). Both scenarios produce a return significantly below that of cash deposit at a bank.

The first example, scenario D, still assumes that rents stay high and fixed, resulting in a 2 per cent annual return (despite the capital loss). Scenario E, on the other hand, is based on a higher rental of up to €2,000 per month eventually on a €450,000 property. This is a more realistic rental yield scenario in bringing the income return back closer to where the cost of borrowing money is. It also assumes that rents rise by a third in money terms over the next decade. This is realistic only if general inflation returns, but it's predicated on the fact that after three or four years of weak prices there would be a five to six-year period of rising prices.

According to Daft, their rental index was 98.2 in January 2002 and virtually unchanged at 98.6 in December 2007. That's nil rental growth over six calendar years!

The first illustration didn't include any transaction costs, such as stamp duty payable by professional investors, nor does it realistically take into account service charges, building insurance, and of course letting agents' commission (typically between 5 and 10 per cent, or at least one month's rent). Factoring in these extra costs will obviously reduce the annual return quite considerably. However, we won't be petty and begin totting up loads of incidentals and costs, but we should factor in the major ones, such as stamp duty, which is payable by all.

The obvious big factor not accounted for in this example is mortgage debt. We assumed that the investor is a cash buyer and doesn't need to borrow. The Irish Banking Federation's quarterly mortgage survey tells us that buy-to-let property investors usually borrow about 75 per cent of the value of the property. So if we stick with the same property example, the €535,000 rental flat, that would imply a mortgage of about €400,000. Using the latest mortgage rates from the latest Central Bank quarterly bulletin, your average investor could borrow this at about 5.8 per cent APR (annualised percentage rate) in mid-2008, when the example began. Assuming a twenty-year loan term, this mortgage would cost €2,820 per month in year 1, but dropping to €2,340 in year 2 (2009) and returning to €2,640 by 2012. But after ten years there would still be an outstanding balance of approximately €250,000. An interest-only loan, however, would cost only €1,933 in year 1 (collapsing to €1,200 per month in year 2 etc.) a month in repayments but would still leave the outstanding balance of €400,000 unpaid at the end of the ten-year period in our example.

We account for all of these in the second, more realistic illustration (table 32). As the purchase cost is €535,000, plus €28,700 stamp duty and conveyance costs of €1,300, this adds up to a grand total of €565,000, less the €400,000 mortgage loan, which results in a net investment requirement of €165,000. So, assuming then that our cash-rich investor is not that rich—perhaps a couple wishing to buy a property for their child— they wish to use leverage to finance the property. They have the money to pay for the deposit plus stamp duty but need to borrow the rest.

Again, in keeping with our realistic example, we assume they have two choices: either move ahead and buy the apartment to let out for ten years (as their child is only eight or nine years old today) or leave their cash in the bank but be prepared to pay 23 per cent DIRT tax.

This time we assume an initial investment of €165,000, with additional borrowings of €400,000 at various rates over a twenty-year term. The corresponding monthly payments are €2,820 (falling by the middle of the following year to €2,340 per month), and these have been taken away from the monthly rent flows. We assume some change in interest rates. If rates fall, generally rents will decline too. In this instance we're very optimistic and further assume that rents never decline. This is called giving the amateur landlords and property speculators the 'benefit of the doubt'!

Table 34: Example of a borrower using a 75 per cent loan-to-value mortgage

4.3% Bank deposit	IRR	-0.2% Scenario A	1.0% Scenario B	5.2% Scenario C	-5.0% Scenario D	-3.4% Scenario E
-€165,000	Cash	-€165,000	-€165,000	-€165,000	-€165,000	-€165,000
€7,115	Year 1	-€15,240	-€15,240	-€15,240	-€15,240	-€15,240
€4,771	Year 2	-€9,480	-€8,880	-€8,880	€9,480	€8,880
€5,448	Year 3	-€10,488	-€9,288	-€9,288	-€10,488	-€9,288
€6,318	Year 4	-€11,760	-€9,960	-€9,960	-€11,760	-€9,960
€7,263	Year 5	-€13,068	-€10,668	-€10,668	-€13,068	-€10,668
€7,543	Year 6	-€13,068	-€10,068	-€10,068	-€13,068	-€10,068
€7,833	Year 7	-€13,068	-€9,468	-€9,468	-€13,068	€9,468
€8,135	Year 8	-€13,068	-€8,868	-€8,868	-€13,068	-€8,868
€8,448	Year 9	-€13,068	-€8,268	-€8,268	-€13,068	-€8,268
€173,773	Year 10	€271,932	€277,332	€392,332	€186,932	€192,332
	Sale price	535,000	535,000	650,000	450,000	450,000
€71,646	Cash return	-€5,376	€21,624	€136,624	-€90,376	-€63,376

The returns appear mediocre when the final sale price is the same as the purchase price, at €535,000 or above after ten years, and the outstanding balance of €250,000 is reduced in year 10 in all examples. If the final selling price (after purchase costs) is lower than this, as in examples D and E, the returns drop sharply and become horribly negative. The reason for this is that rental yields are significantly below borrowing rates (the mortgage costs are more than the rent received); landlords are subsidising tenants.

For those investors who like to fund interest-only, the projected returns are disastrous. (See the final table in our illustration.) I've always believed that Irish people are addicted to credit. They'll finance anything as long as credit is available.

Well, assuming that the availability of credit remains good (highly unlikely though it is, given the global financial turmoil in all credit markets) and that our plucky investors don't opt for a repayment mortgage (because they believe that property prices are going to go to the moon, and anyway they can always refinance in a few years' time), they get instead an interest-only mortgage—you know, to bring down that monthly repayment, closer to the rental income. There will still be a shortfall, but not much, and sure they can carry that anyway.

Table 35: Interest-only borrower with 75 per cent loan-to-value mortgage on a property initially valued at €535,000

4.3%	IRR	−2.4%	−0.6%	4.3%	−12.2%	−8.7%
Bank deposit		Scenario A	Scenario B	Scenario C	Scenario D	Scenario E
−€165,000	Cash	−€165,000	−€165,000	−€165,000	−€165,000	−€165,000
€7,115	Year 1	−€4,596	−€4,596	−€4,596	−€4,596	−€4,596
€4,771	Year 2	€4,200	€4,800	€4,800	€4,200	€4,800
€5,448	Year 3	€2,604	€3,804	€3,804	€2,604	€3,804
€6,318	Year 4	€600	€2,400	€2,400	€600	€2,400
€7,263	Year 5	−€1,404	€996	€996	−€1,404	€996
€7,543	Year 6	−€1,404	€1,596	€1,596	−€1,404	€1,596
€7,833	Year 7	−€1,404	€2,196	€2,196	−€1,404	€2,196
€8,135	Year 8	−€1,404	€2,796	€2,796	−€1,404	€2,796
€8,448	Year 9	−€1,404	€3,396	€3,396	−€1,404	€3,396
€173,773	Year 10	€133,596	€138,996	€230,996	€48,596	€53,996
	Sale price	535,000	535,000	650,000	450,000	450,000
€71,646	Cash return	−€35,616	−€8,616	€83,384	−€120,616	−€93,616

Ergo, table 35, same as the last example but this time with an interest-only mortgage. What a difference! Why? Because the debt is not being paid down, so they still owe €400,000 to the bank at the end of year 10. Banks are funny like that: they like the principal to be repaid. In fact they usually insist on it.

This knocks the socks off the annual returns, and nearly all are negative.

The only positive return was the scenario that assumed a 21½ per cent capital gain in property price. And that's a totally unrealistic scenario; and it only manages to match cash on deposit with DIRT removed! The total DIRT paid over the ten years works out at €26,500 and reduces the total interest earned on the initial €165,000 to €71,650.

Once more we didn't include other property costs in the annual calculations. We didn't even knock off the 20 per cent capital gains tax on the €115,000 price gain under scenario C. This lops off another €23,000 to the tax man and brings the annual expected yield down from 3½ per cent to below 3 per cent. This is still a positive number but nowhere near as good as simply putting the money on deposit in the bank and forgetting about it.

Cash is always king! Unless you start with a high initial property yield (low price) or you can count on seriously high capital appreciation. Nobody at the end of 2008 was forecasting any significant property price rises for 2009 or 2010 for that matter. And no-one was predicting rent rises (or even static rents) in a falling property price market that would equate to average residential yields significantly above average mortgage rates. That, ladies and gentlemen, may occur in early 2010 and would be seen to be the start of the bottoming process, the inflection point where it becomes cheaper to buy rather than rent.